THE ROUGH GUIDE TO

DUBLIN

by Geoff Wallis, Margaret
Greenwood and Mark Connolly

with additional contributions by
Paul Gray

ROUGH
GUIDES

We set out to do something different when the first Rough Guide was published in 1982. Mark Ellingham, just out of university, was travelling in Greece. He brought along the popular guides of the day, but found they were all lacking in some way. They were either strong on ruins and museums but went on for pages without mentioning a beach or taverna. Or they were so conscious of the need to save money that they lost sight of Greece's cultural and historical significance. Also, none of the books told him anything about Greece's contemporary life – its politics, its culture, its people, and how they lived.

So with no job in prospect, Mark decided to write his own guidebook, one which aimed to provide practical information that was second to none, detailing the best beaches and the hottest clubs and restaurants, while also giving hard-hitting accounts of every sight, both famous and obscure, and providing up-to-the-minute information on contemporary culture. It was a guide that encouraged independent travellers to find the best of Greece, and was a great success, getting shortlisted for the Thomas Cook travel guide award, and encouraging Mark, along with three friends, to expand the series.

The Rough Guide list grew rapidly and the letters flooded in, indicating a much broader readership than had been anticipated, but one which uniformly appreciated the Rough Guide mix of practical detail and humour, irreverence and enthusiasm. Things haven't changed. The same four friends who began the series are still the caretakers of the Rough Guide mission today: to provide the most reliable, up-to-date and entertaining information to independent-minded travellers of all ages, on all budgets.

We now publish more than 300 titles and have offices in London and New York. The travel guides are written and researched by a dedicated team of more than 200 authors, based in Britain, Europe, the USA and Australia. We have also created a unique series of phrasebooks to accompany the travel series, along with an acclaimed series of music guides, and a best-selling pocket guide to the Internet and World Wide Web. We also publish comprehensive travel information on our website: **www.roughguides.com**

Help us update

We've gone to a lot of trouble to ensure that this Rough Guide is as up to date and accurate as possible. However, things do change. All suggestions, comments and corrections are much appreciated, and we'll send a copy of the next edition (or any other Rough Guide if you prefer) for the best letters.

Please mark letters **"Rough Guide Dublin Update"** and send to:

Rough Guides, 80 Strand, London, WC2R ORL, or
Rough Guides, 4th Floor, 345 Hudson St, New York NY 10014.

Or send an email to mail@roughguides.com
Have your questions answered and tell others about your trip at
www.roughguides.atinfopop.com

Acknowledgements

The authors would like to thank Polly for all her hard work and good humour. Thanks also to Sam Kirby for the maps, Rachel Holmes for typesetting and Melissa Graham for proofreading.
Paul Gray: Julia, Delphine, Nick, Niamh, Andy, Alexia and all the Gurkleys.
Geoff Wallis: Finbar Boyle, Dublin Tourism, Laura Duffy, Noel Hill, Henry King, John Lahiffe and Tourism Ireland, Joanie McDermott, Barry Ward.

Readers' letters

Apologies to those inadvertently slipped through the net, and to those whose signatures couldn't be deciphered.
Bu, Jeff Alterman, F. Dewar, Tamsyn East, Gavin Garth, E. Hadley, Lee Martin, J. Price, Jane Price, John Roberts, Bryan Robinson, Nigel Stewart.

Cover credits

Main front picture Christ Church Cathedral & Synod House
© Imagefile
Small front picture Seahorses on lamp-post, Grattan
Bridge © Robert Harding
Back top picture Fitzwilliam Square © Neil Setchfield
Back lower picture The Four Courts © Imagefile

CONTENTS

MAP LIST

Introduction

Avibrant and compact city, **Dublin** has a pace and energy quite at odds with the relaxed image of Ireland as a whole. Prosperity generated by the Republic's economic boom has brought fundamental changes to the life of its capital, reversing the tide of emigration and creating a dynamic cultural centre. The ongoing rapidity of transformation is constantly apparent; new exhibitions, chic bars and restaurants and fashionable shops all signify a major shift in Dublin's identity, no longer dominated by the insularity of the past, but increasingly adopting a more global outlook.

The city's emergence from provincialism is, however, only part of the picture. Increases in population have left Dublin bulging at the seams which, of course, brings its problems, not least in terms of the high cost of housing and rents: spend just a couple of days here and you'll come upon inner-city deprivation as bad as any in Europe. Furthermore, the arrival of numbers of refugees and asylum-seekers has challenged perceived notions about Ireland's homogeneity – and not all Dubliners have embraced the concept of multiculturalism.

Dublin's collective spirit has its contradictions, too, with youthful enterprise set against a deeply embedded traditionalism. However, the collision of the old order and the forward-looking younger generations is an essential part of the appeal of this extrovert capital, and, despite their differences, its inhabitants' famous wit and garrulous sociability are a constant feature of Dublin life. In the legendary – and plentiful – bars, the buskers of Grafton Street and the patter of the tour guides who ply the streets with visitors in tow, there's an unmistakable love of banter. The city's considerable **literary heritage** owes much to this trait, and on either side of the Liffey you'll find reminders of literary personalities who are as intrinsic to Dublin's character as the river itself – from the bronze pavement plaques following the route of Leopold Bloom, hero of James Joyce's *Ulysses*, to the Oscar Wilde statue striking an insouciant pose in Merrion Square.

Ireland's economic growth during the 1990s has lent new impetus to just about every facet of the capital's cultural life. **Historic treasures** are being innovatively promoted and displayed, from the new Millennium Wing of the National Gallery to the wealth of decorative arts on show at the Collins Barracks, while the city's social and political history is evoked with flair, both in the abundance of theme-based tours and in the fabric of the city itself. Everywhere in Dublin you'll find evidence of a rich past well worth exploring: exceptional **Viking** finds excavated at Wood Quay (and now on show in the National Museum); impressive reminders of **Anglo-Norman** and **British** imperial power; elegant Georgian streets and squares; and monuments to Ireland's violent struggle for **independence** from the British. The **visual arts** are enjoying a higher public profile too, with mouthwatering exhibitions in the city's numerous galleries supplemented by the development of a unique design scene that's characterized by subtlety, experimentation and exploration of Ireland's Celtic past. Throughout the city there's a palpable sense that Dublin's cultural heritage is coming into its own – with striking confidence.

Dublin is, of course, known for its **pubs**, and for many, sampling the myriad bars and buzzing nightlife is an integral part of visiting the city. There's also plenty of **music** on offer and, while the capital has nothing to match rural Ireland, there are plenty of traditional music bars as well as an abundance of rock and jazz venues, and a vital and ever-changing **club scene**. **Theatre**, too, has long played a part in the city's cultural life – you can catch plays by O'Casey, Synge and Shaw all year round at venues such as the Abbey Theatre, as well as experiencing the vitality of Dublin's continuing dramatic tradition during the annual theatre and fringe **festivals**.

Where to visit

Central Dublin is easy enough to navigate – it's fairly compact, and you're likely to make most of your explorations either on foot or via short bus hops. One obvious axis is formed by the **River Liffey**, running from west to east and dividing the city into two regions of very distinct character (the **northside**, poorer and less developed than its **southside** neighbour), each of which has a strong allegiance among its inhabitants. The other main axis is the north–south one formed by **Grafton Street** and **Westmoreland Street** south of the river, running into **O'Connell Street** to the north. The centre as a whole is bordered by two waterways: the **Royal Canal** to the north, and the **Grand Canal** to the south.

The majority of the better-known attractions are south of the river, and for many visitors, the city's heart lies around the best of what is left of Georgian Dublin: the elegant set pieces of **Fitzwilliam** and **Merrion squares**, where the graceful red-brick houses boast ornate, fan-lighted doors and immaculately kept central gardens, and the wide, decorous open space of **St Stephen's Green**. The southside is also the setting for the compelling displays of the **National Gallery** and the **National Museum**, as well as **Trinity College**, Dublin's august seat of learning and home of a famous library; **Grafton Street**, the city's upmarket shopping area; and the **Temple Bar** area, the in-place for the arts, alternative shopping and socializing. Parallel to the river, **Dame Street** strings together a handful of historic monuments: the **Bank of Ireland**, **City Hall**, **Dublin Castle** (new home to the glorious collections of the **Chester Beatty Library**) and **Christ Church Cathedral**. The tangle of lanes between here and Wood Quay are remnants of the medieval city, though these too are now undergoing renovation in a new development aimed at complementing Temple Bar. South of Christ Church lies the majestic **St Patrick's Cathedral**, while to the west a drab urban scene unfurls, worth exploring nonetheless for the **Guinness Brewery** and, slightly further out, the **Irish Museum of Modern Art** and **Kilmainham Gaol**.

North of the Liffey, the key monument along O'Connell Street is the **General Post Office** building, which still bears the scars of incursions during the Easter Rising of 1916. Elsewhere, the northside is noted for its strong literary and artistic connections; at the north end of O'Connell Street lies **Parnell Square**, around which you'll find the **Dublin Writers Museum** and **Hugh Lane Municipal Art Gallery**. A little way to the east is the **James Joyce Cultural Centre**, dedicated to the memory of one of Dublin's most renowned literary scions. The inner-city area northeast of O'Connell Street (specifically, east of Gardiner Street) is run-down and should be explored with caution, especially at night. However, regeneration is taking place around the river, and to the east of O'Connell Street, lodged amidst all the new buildings beside the quays, stands the impressively elaborate **Custom House**. The streets running west of O'Connell are busy with a mix of workaday shops and markets, but beyond here are the elegant **Four Courts**; **St Michan's Church**, its crypts containing mummified remains; and **Smithfield**, famous for its monthly horse fair. Further west is the National Museum's prestigious decorative arts collection at the **Collins Barracks**, as well as **Phoenix Park**, one of Europe's largest urban open spaces.

Travel beyond the centre is fairly straightforward. The DART line allows easy access to the outskirts along the curve of Dublin Bay such as **Sandycove**, which boasts another fascinating James Joyce museum, as well as the scenic headlands of **Dalkey** and **Killiney** to the south and **Howth** to the north. Regular buses serve all the other suburbs: in the north, **Glasnevin** – home to botanic gardens and a historic cemetery – and **Marino** – site of the exquisite Georgian folly of the Casino – and to the southeast of the centre, **Ballsbridge** and **Donnybrook**, which are fruitful areas for accommodation.

There are also plenty of options if you plan on heading out into the surrounding countryside. Dublin is within easy reach of the wild, open heights of the **Wicklow Mountains**, which shelter the secluded monastic settlement of **Glendalough**; a sprinkling of choice **stately homes**; and some of Europe's most important prehistoric sites, including **Knowth** and **Newgrange**.

When to visit

Dublin's warmest months are usually July and August, which are also often the wettest. However, no month is especially hot or cold, and though the climate of Ireland is often damp, the weather shouldn't be the main determining factor in deciding when to travel. Obviously, the **summer** is the most popular time and, consequently, the most expensive for both flights and accommodation. If you're planning to visit then, make sure you've got your travel arrangements and accommodation sorted out well before you go – and if your stay is going to straddle a **weekend**, book your room in advance whatever time of year you visit. Before making your decision, you should take a look at the city's **calendar of festivals and special events**, which range from the parades of St Patrick's Day in March and the meanderings of Bloomsday on June 16 to rock music in and around Temple Bar in early May and the All-Ireland hurling and football finals in September.

Dublin's climate

	F°		C°		RAINFALL	
	AVERAGE DAILY		AVERAGE DAILY		AVERAGE MONTHLY	
	MAX	MIN	MAX	MIN	IN	MM
Jan	46	34	8	1	2.6	67
Feb	47	35	8	2	2.2	55
March	51	37	10	3	2.0	51
April	55	39	13	4	1.8	45
May	60	43	15	6	2.4	60
June	65	48	18	9	2.2	57
July	67	52	20	11	2.8	70
Aug	67	51	19	11	2.9	74
Sept	63	48	17	9	2.8	72
Oct	57	43	14	6	2.8	70
Nov	51	39	10	4	2.6	67
Dec	47	37	8	3	2.9	74

BASICS

Arrival

Dublin's main **points of arrival** are all within easy reach of the city centre, with the bulk of tourist traffic entering either via the airport, seven miles to the north, or the ferry terminals at Dublin Port, two miles east, and Dún Laoghaire, nine miles south.

BY AIR

Dublin Airport arrivals hall has a **tourist office** (daily: July & Aug 8am–10.30pm; Sept–June 8am–10pm), a *bureau de change* (open for arrivals and departures), various car rental desks and an ATM. For airport information call ☏704 4222.

Buses into town leave from outside the arrivals exit. The cheapest choice (€1.65 single) is to catch a regular #16A bus to O'Connell Street or a #41, #41A, #41B or #41C bus to Eden Quay, near O'Connell Bridge. Airlink buses #747 and #748 (Mon–Sat 5.45am–11.30pm, Sun 7.15am–11.30pm; €4.50 single, €7.50 return) run every ten minutes (or every fifteen to twenty minutes on Sundays) directly to Busáras, the central bus station, via Connolly Station, with some continuing on to Heuston Station, twenty minutes further along. Tickets can either be purchased at the CIÉ travel information desk in the arrivals hall or on board the bus, though you'll need the exact fare for the latter. Alternatively, the privately run Aircoach serves the main shopping areas and hotels (Mon–Sat 5.30am–11.30pm, Sun 6.30am–11.30pm; €5 single) every fifteen minutes. If you're heading straight to accommodation that's near a DART (see p.13) station, a further option is to take Aerdart bus #A1 (Mon–Fri 5.45am–11.45pm, Sat & Sun 6.30am–11.45pm; €4.50 single), which connect with the DART rail service at Howth Junction and leave the airport every fifteen minutes. A taxi into the centre from the rank outside the arrivals exit should cost about €25, but can be much dearer during rush hour; cars are there to meet all incoming flights, but be prepared to queue at peak times.

BY BUS

Busáras on Store Street (Map 4, G3), Dublin's main bus station, is within ten minutes' walk of O'Connell Street. Buses from all parts of the Republic and Northern Ireland arrive here, along with Airlink buses and coaches from Britain. City buses into the town centre pass along Talbot Street (Map 4, G2), a block to the north, and taxis can usually be hailed on Beresford Place (Map 4, F3), just to the south of the bus station. Busáras has a *bureau de change* (daily 8.45am–2.30pm and 3.30–7pm) and a left-luggage facility (Mon–Sat 8am–7.45pm, Sun 10am–5.45pm; €3.40).

BY FERRY

Arriving by ferry from Britain, you'll dock at either **Dublin Port** (Map 1, E5), two miles east of the centre (for Irish Ferries, slower Stena Line services, the Isle of Man Steam Packet Company and Norse Merchant Ferries) or **Dún Laoghaire** (Map 1, E5), nine miles to the south (for

ARRIVAL

Stena Line high speed ferries). The former is served by bus #53, which is timetabled to meet ferry services and heads directly to Beresford Place, next to the bus station (€1.30). Dún Laoghaire is twenty minutes from the centre by DART (€1.45) train, and its station is handily placed opposite the ferry terminal. There's a tourist office at the ferry terminal (Mon–Sat 10am–6pm), plus a *bureau de change* (daily 9am–4.30pm, also open earlier/later to meet ferries arriving or departing outside these times) and an ATM. There's also an interactive video unit available for booking accommodation when the tourist office is closed. Note that some coach passengers from Britain will be driven directly to the city centre.

BY TRAIN

Connolly Station (Map 4, H2), a couple of hundred yards northeast of Busáras, is the terminus for trains from Belfast to the north, Sligo to the northwest and Wexford and Rosslare to the south; it's also on the DART line (see p.13). There is a left-luggage office (Mon–Sat 7.40am–9.20pm, Sun 9.10am–9.45pm; €3.20) in the concourse. **Heuston Station** (Map 3, C4), its counterpart on the south bank of the Liffey, two miles west of the city centre, is the terminus for trains from Cork, Killarney, Tralee, Waterford, Limerick, Galway, Westport and Ballina. There are left-luggage lockers here (€1.50–€5 depending upon luggage size) accessible during station opening hours (daily 6.30am–10.30pm). Bus #90 runs between the two termini. **Tara Street** (Map 3, H4) and **Pearse Street** (Map 3, H5) stations are on the south side of the Liffey and serve DART and suburban train services. For all train information and times call ☎836 6222.

ARRIVAL

Information, tourist passes and maps

The main **Dublin Tourism Office** (Map 4, D6; July & Aug Mon–Sat 9am–6.30pm, Sun 10.30am–3pm; Sept–June Mon–Sat 9am–5.30pm; Ⓦ www.visit dublin.com) is a walk-in centre in a converted church near the western end of Suffolk Street, just off College Green. There are separate desks for information, accommodation (for more on this, see p.235), coach trips, bus and rail tickets, theatre bookings, money exchange and car rental. The first two can be incredibly busy and a numbered ticket queuing system operates, so head directly for the ticket-dispenser when you enter. There's also a smaller and less busy tourist office on the northside at 14 O'Connell Street Upper (Map 4, D2; Mon–Sat 9am–5pm). The offices at the

---

The Dublin Tourism Office doesn't have a direct telephone number for information. For general tourist information on the whole of Ireland ring ☏1850/230330 from within Ireland; ☏0800/039 7000 in the UK; ☏1-800/223 6400 in the US or Canada; and ☏00 353 669/792083 from other countries.

---

airport and the **Dún Laoghaire** ferry terminal (see p.3 and p.5) provide similar facilities, though they stock a less comprehensive range of printed information.

A good way to get up-to-the-minute local **information** is to pick up a copy of *The Event Guide* (ⓦwww.event guide.ie), a freesheet which provides concise **listings** of gigs, clubs, exhibitions and tourist sites; it's available from tourism offices and various bars, cafés and shops around the city. The other major listings guides are *In Dublin* (€2.48), available at most newsagents, with lots on clubs and style and a listings section that also covers exhibitions and theatre, and *Hot Press* (€3.17), Ireland's recently revamped rock, politics and style magazine, which is the best place to find music listings. All three are published fortnightly. Daily cinema and theatre listings appear in the *Irish Times* and the *Evening Herald* (see p.211).

The telephone code for the Dublin area is ☎01.
Calling Dublin from abroad (or Northern Ireland), dial
☎00-353-1, followed by the subscriber's number.

TOURIST PASSES

If you're planning to visit a lot of attractions in Dublin it may be worth getting a copy of Dublin Tourism's *The Guide to Dublin* (free from tourism centres) which includes two-for-one **discount vouchers** covering the James Joyce Museum, Dublin Writers Museum, the Shaw Birthplace and Malahide Castle.

Dúchas Heritage Service (☎647 2453; ⓦwww .heritageireland.ie) takes care of Dublin's national parks, monuments and gardens, of which seven have admission charges: the Casino at Marino, Kilmainham Gaol, Phoenix Park Visitors' Centre, Rathfarnham Castle, St Audoen's

USEFUL WEBSITES

ⓦ **www.browseireland.com** The Dublin section of this enormous directory of Irish sites includes links to accommodation providers, businesses and shops, the arts, events and places of interest.

ⓦ **http://dublin.local.ie** Thoroughly impressive and useful site with copious information on Dublin's history, both social and cultural, as well as plenty of detail on current events, activities and affairs, and lively discussion boards.

ⓦ **www.dublinfinder.com** Portal to a host of local links, handily organised into sections covering visiting the city, getting around, events, venues and services, as well as discussion forums.

ⓦ **www.dublinpubs.net** If you can stomach the "scoring women" section, this otherwise fine site reviews a host of Dublin's pubs for atmosphere, decor, the quality of the pint and even the cleanliness of the toilets; also includes a map of all the pubs reviewed.

ⓦ **www.entertainmentireland.ie** Up-to-the minute info on virtually every aspect of entertainment, including films, exhibitions, festivals, plays and clubbing.

ⓦ **www.houseofireland.com/dubguide/dubguide.htm** General Dublin information, including attractions, shopping, accommodation, getting around, car rental, entertainment listings and a pictorial "virtual walk" around the city in springtime.

Church, St Mary's Abbey and the Waterways Visitors' Centre. A **Heritage Card** (€19) covers entry to all, and is particularly good if you're planning to travel elsewhere in Ireland. It's valid for one year (you may visit each site as many times as you like) and available at most of the sites mentioned or, if you've a credit card, by calling ☎647 2461.

@ **www.indigo.ie** One of Ireland's major ISPs, this massive site has the lowdown on Irish news, sports, entertainment, lifestyles and jobs, with a distinct Dublin focus; also has an efficient search engine.

@ **www.ireland.com** Massive portal for information about every tourist essential, as well as hosting the *Irish Times* site.

@ **www.irish-architecture.com/archdublin** Everything you need to know about virtually every building of note in Dublin, from medieval times to the reconstruction of Temple Bar, plus information on the derivation of street names.

@ **www.setanta.com** Ireland's specialist sports site, covering up-to-date news and results and forthcoming fixtures for association football, Gaelic football, hurling and horse-racing; also includes features and competitions.

@ **www.softguides.com/dublin** As near to the horse's mouth as you can get, this comprehensive information site is compiled by locals and covers such things as weather, shopping, entertainment listings and exhibitions; city maps, too.

@ **www.temple-bar.ie** Day-by-day listings of one-off and ongoing events and activities in and around the Temple Bar area; as well as reviews from some of Ireland's leading critics, and features on new ventures in the area.

@ **www.travelinsights.org/guide/dublin.html** Locals' insights on the best places to eat, drink, hear music and see comedy with brief reviews of each entry.

MAPS

The **maps** in this book should suffice for your visit, but you might also want to pick up the *Rough Guide Dublin Map* (£4.99/€7.76), designed to be used in conjunction with this guide. Full-colour, non-tearable, weatherproof and pocket-sized, it details attractions, places to shop, eat, drink and sleep as well as the city streets, and includes transport routes and a "time map" of opening hours; it's available in bookshops. Alternatively, small freebie maps of the centre can also be picked up in tourist offices, the Dublin Bus office and in most hotels and guesthouses.

Money

On January 1, 2002, Ireland was one of twelve European Union countries which changed over to a single currency, the euro (€). One euro consists of 100 cents. There are seven euro **notes** – in denominations of 500, 200, 100, 50, 20, 10, and 5 euro, each a different colour and size – and eight different **coin** denominations,

---
Prices quoted throughout this Guide are in euro, €1 being worth approximately 60p sterling or 95¢ in US currency.
---

including 2 and 1 euro, then 50, 20, 10, 5, 2, and 1 cent(s). Euro coins feature a common EU design on one face, but different country-specific designs on the other. Note that all euro coins and notes can be used in any of the twelve member states (Austria, Belgium, Finland, France, Germany, Greece, Ireland, Italy, Luxembourg, Portugal, Spain and The Netherlands).

BANKS

You're never far away from a **bank** in Dublin, and the vast majority have an automatic teller machine (ATM). The two major Irish banks are Allied Irish (AIB) and the Bank of Ireland, and there are also plenty of branches of Northern Bank and Ulster Bank, both Northern Irish banks. Standard banking **hours** are Monday to Friday 10am to 4pm; most also open until 5pm on Thursdays. Most will change travellers' cheques, and ATMs will accept non-Irish cash, credit and debit cards which bear the Cirrus or Maestro symbol and dispense funds from your account in euro.

EXCHANGE

There are **foreign exchange** desks at both the airport and the Dún Laoghaire ferry terminal, while central Dublin locations include the American Express desk in the Dublin Tourism Centre on Suffolk Street (Map 4, D6; Mon–Sat 9am–5pm); Thomas Cook at 118 Grafton Street (Map 4, E5; Mon–Sat 9am–5.30pm, Thurs until 8pm) and the General Post Office on O'Connell Street (Map 4, D3; Mon–Sat 8am–8pm). However, while these are useful outside banking hours, the best exchange rates and lowest commission charges are usually offered by the banks.

Travellers' cheques and major credit cards are almost universally accepted in Dublin.

MONEY

Getting around

The only real way to get to know central Dublin is to **walk**, but to visit the farther-flung sights you'll probably want to use the city's **public transport**.

BUSES

Buses are the mainstay of public transport, reaching most parts of Dublin as well as places beyond the city limits. Regular services operate from 6am; last buses leave the city centre at 11.30pm. Special **Nitelink** buses run out to the suburbs from Monday to Saturday, departing from D'Olier Street (Map 4, E4), Westmoreland Street (Map 4, E4) and College Street (Map 4, E5) at 12.30am and 2am on Mondays to Wednesdays and every twenty minutes from 12.30am until 4.30am on Thursdays and Fridays. On Saturdays, there are buses every twenty minutes from 11.30pm to 12.30am. Most journeys cost €4, but for longer distances, such as Maynooth or Ashbourne, the fare is €6; travel passes are not valid. The price of **tickets** on regular buses ranges from €75 to €1.65; it's prudent to

---

For Dublin Bus information call ☏ 873 4222; for bus travel beyond the city contact Bus Éireann (☏ 836 6111).

GETTING AROUND

12

TRAVEL PASSES

Travel passes come in many forms, and are obtainable from Dublin Bus at 59 O'Connell Street Upper, from newsagents displaying the Dublin Bus sign, and from DART and suburban railway stations. Dublin Bus produces a variety of Rambler passes, which are accepted on all buses except Nitelink and Airlink, and cover one (€4.50) to seven days (€16.50). If you don't intend to use public transport every day, you might want to get a Rambler Handy Pack (€14), which includes five one-day passes. A family one-day Rambler (€7.20) covers two adults and up to four children, and there are student seven-day bus passes too (€13.30). One-day passes are also available: for the rail short-hop zone which covers the DART between Balbriggan and Kilcoole and suburban services to Maynooth and Celbridge (adult €6, family €10.15); and for all buses (except Nitelink and Airlink) and rail travel in the short hop zone (adult €6, family €10.15). Weekly rail-only tickets (€18.40, students €13.95) for the inner zone, covering the Dart between Rush and Bray and suburban services to Maynooth and Celbridge, or rail/bus tickets (€24) for buses (except Nitelink and Airlink) and rail travel in the short-hop zone, are also available.

hoard coins as most routes are exact fare only. If you have to pay more than the actual fare, you will be given a receipt which can be refunded at the Dublin Bus office, from where you can also pick up free **timetables**.

DART, SUBURBAN TRAINS AND LUAS

The other vital public transport service is the Dublin Area Rapid Transport system, or **DART** (Mon–Sat 6.30am–11.20pm, Sun 9.20am–11.30pm; ☎703 3523), whose trains link Howth and Malahide to the north of the city with Bray to the south, via such places as Dún Laoghaire and Dalkey, and connect with suburban services to even further afield. The maximum single fare is €2.95, but if you're considering taking more than one or two trips a day, it may be worth buying a travel pass (see box on p.13). This advice also applies to some of the **suburban trains** operated by Iarnród Éireann, which use the same tracks as the DART but make far fewer stops en route (Connolly, Tara and Pearse Street stations in the centre, Howth Junction to the north and Dún Laoghaire and Bray to the south). The Northern Suburban service from Pearse Station to Dundalk is the speediest way to make day excursions to Malahide (see p.210) and Newgrange (see p.230) while the Arrow service from Heuston Station includes Celbridge, for Castletown (see p.226).

Walking around Dublin you'll become rapidly aware of the work being undertaken to build the new **Luas** underground railway system which is expected to come into operation around 2006.

TAXIS

Dublin's **taxis** come in a variety of forms, from old London-style black cabs to family saloons or people-carriers; all are identifiable by an illuminated box on the roof bearing the driver's taxi licence number. It is possible to hail taxis on the street, though you're sometimes better off heading for one of their centrally located **ranks**, such as opposite the St Stephen's Green Shopping Centre (Map 4, D8), in front of the Bank of Ireland on College Green (Map 4, D5) and opposite the *Gresham Hotel* on O'Connell Street (Map 4, D2); bear in mind, though, that after 11pm on busy nights you'll probably have to wait at least an hour. If you want to order a taxi by phone, try Satellite Taxis

(☏677 2222, or southside ☏454 3333, northside ☏836 5555) or City Cabs (☏872 7272). It's generally better to ask for a metered taxi, as unmetered, fixed-fare hackney cabs tend to cost more and, unlike their metered counterparts, can't use the city's bus lanes. **Wheelchair-accessible** cabs are available if ordered one hour in advance from Eurocabs (☏872 2222). Finding a taxi after midnight on weekends is difficult, so if you know you'll need one, book it. Conversely, if you're heading back to the centre from the suburbs, it can often be easy to hail a cab returning the same way. In terms of **fares**, expect to pay €5–€6 for a short-hop journey and around €9 for a trip from the centre to a suburb such as Ballsbridge, Clontarf or Donnybrook. The financial pressures on taxi-drivers have increased markedly over the past few years, so keep half an eye out for any sharp practice – and be prepared to put up with an occasional whinge from the fellah behind the wheel.

CARS

The streets of central Dublin can be phenomenally **congested**, especially along the quays and around St Stephen's Green, a situation exacerbated by numerous roadworks (particularly in connection with the Luas rail development). **Parking** can represent a serious challenge, although large indicator boards on the main roads provide details of the number of spaces available in various car parks, of which one of the most central and useful is the Royal College of Surgeons multi-storey on the St Stephen's Green West (Map 4, D8). On-street parking spaces fill very quickly and can be exceptionally hard to find in the city centre, though Merrion and Fitzwilliam squares are often good bets. Many city centre parking spaces have coin-operated meters, but increasingly, and especially in the closer suburbs such as Ballsbridge and Donnybrook, a disc display system may

GETTING AROUND

CAR RENTAL COMPANIES

Argus Airport arrivals hall and Dublin Tourism Centre ☎490 4444, ⊛www.argusrentals.com.

Atlas Airport arrivals hall ☎844 4859, ⊛www.atlascarhire.com.

County Car Rentals Airport arrivals hall and Dublin Tourism Centre ☎235 2030, ⊛www.countycar.com.

Dan Dooley 42 Westland Row ☎677 2723, ⊛wwwdan-dooley.ie.

SixT Airport arrivals hall ☎1-850/206088, ⊛wwwirishcarrentals .com.

operate, with discs available either from machines or from nearby shops.

There's no real need to **rent a car** during your stay in Dublin, unless you intend to spend a significant time visiting outlying attractions. The cost of a week's rental ranges between €140 and €210, depending upon the company, though you may often have to pay additional insurance cover. Local firms are often a cheaper option and significant reductions can be gained by booking in advance through a company such as Go Ireland (⊛www.goireland.com). Whether driving your own or a rented vehicle, take heed that theft from cars is very common in Dublin and make sure to remove all valuables and stow any belongings in the boot.

BIKES

If the weather is fine, **cycling** can be an excellent way to tour the city and is probably the best means of exploring the expanses of Phoenix Park. However, riding a bike around Dublin is not an activity for the nervous or inexperienced cyclist. Road surfaces can be appalling, and some motorists seem, at best, oblivious of the presence of cyclists or, at worst, regard them as a legitimate target; it's also essential to be on the lookout for errant pedestrians. It's advisable to take especial care cycling along the hectic quays or when dealing with any traffic lights. However, despite all these perils, many people do cycle in Dublin and it's relatively easy (and free) to take your bike with you on a DART train and enjoy some of the outlying sites. The cost of insurance has cut down the number of companies **renting a bike**, but one that still does is Cycle Ways, 185 Parnell Street (☎837 4748) which charges €20 per day and €80 for a week's rental. A few hostels also rent bikes and also have bike storage facilities.

BUS AND WALKING TOURS

If you're only in Dublin for a short time or just want a quick feel for the city's landmarks, you could take one of the many **city tours** on offer, most of which include commentary on local sights from an on-board guide. We've quoted adult prices below, but most of the operators give discounts to children, senior citizens or students.

For details of out-of-town tours, see p.216.

OPEN-TOP BUS TOURS

Dublin Bus (☎873 4222, ⓦwww.dublinbus.ie) offer a daily guided "Dublin City Tour" which commences outside the company office on O'Connell Street, and allows you to hop on and off at any of the sixteen different stops, including Parnell Square, Trinity College, St Stephen's Green, Dublin Castle, the cathedrals, the Guinness Storehouse, the Irish Museum of Modern Art, Phoenix Park and Collins Barracks. Tours run every fifteen minutes from 9.30am until 4.30pm, then half-hourly until 6.30pm. Tickets (€10) can be purchased on the bus, are valid all day and include discounts to attractions.

GETTING AROUND

Guide Friday (☏ 676 5377, ⓦ www.guidefriday.com) have a "Discover Dublin" guided tour, which runs from outside the Dublin Tourism Centre on O'Connell Street Upper every ten minutes from 9.30am until 5.30pm between May and September, with reduced frequency and earlier finishing times during the rest of the year. The route is similar to that of Dublin Bus, but doesn't include the Irish Museum of Modern Art. Again, it's a hop-on, hop-off service and tickets are valid all day (€12). Tickets can be purchased on the bus or at the tourism centre and include discounts to attractions on the company's tours to sites outside of Dublin.

Irish City Tours (☏ 872 9010, ⓦ www.irishcitytours .com) also operate a similarly routed open-top tour of the city, starting from outside 12 O'Connell Street Upper. Again, you can hop on and off, but this time at nineteen different stops. Between mid-July to the end of September, tours run every ten minutes from 9.30am to 5.30pm. From April until mid-July and in October, frequency is every fifteen minutes between 9.30am and 5pm; between November and March, services stop at 4pm. Tickets (adults €12) can be purchased on the bus, at tourist offices or online. They're valid for twenty-four hours and again give discounts to certain attractions.

LAND AND WATER TOURS

If you're travelling with children, **Viking Splash Tours** (☏ 855 3000, ⓦ www.vikingsplashtours.com) offer the most innovative and enjoyable tour option, aboard reconditioned World War Two amphibious vehicles known as "Ducks", which take you on a road-tour around the city's major sites before splashing into the water at the Grand Canal Harbour and heading for home; the complete tour lasts 1hr 15min. Ten tours depart daily (Feb–Nov) from Bull Alley, next to

St Patrick's Cathedral; call the number opposite for timings. Tickets (€13.50) are available at the Dublin Tourist Centre or adjacent to the departure point at 64–65 Patrick Street; you can also reserve over the phone with a credit card.

WALKING TOURS

Conducted by graduates from Trinity College, the two-hour excursions on offer from **Historical Walking Tours** (☎ 878 0227, ⓦ www.historicalinsights.ie) bring history alive, with well-chosen locations and witty insights into the history of Dublin and Ireland. Tours start at the college's front gate (May–Sept daily 11am & 3pm, plus Sat & Sun noon; Oct–April Fri–Sun noon); tickets cost €10 and can be purchased at the start of the tour or in advance from the Dublin Tourism office on Suffolk Street (see p.6).

The **Literary Pub Crawl** (☎ 670 5602, ⓦ www.dublin pubcrawl.com), tours Dublin boozers that have literary connections, using professional actors to perform extracts from some of Ireland's greatest works. It's a great way to spend an evening, elevated by poetry and pints, and there's a literary quiz to test your memory. Starts upstairs at *The Duke* on Duke Street (April–Oct Mon–Sat 7.30pm, Sun noon & 7.30pm; Nov–March Thurs–Sat 7.30pm, Sun noon & 7.30pm). Tickets (€10) can be purchased at the start of the tour or booked at the Dublin Tourism office. Tours last two and a quarter hours.

Another evening roam – or stagger – through Dublin's pubs, the **Musical Pub Crawl** (☎ 478 0193, ⓦ www.music alpubcrawl.com) features two musicians recounting the story of traditional Irish music by performing songs and tunes while visiting half a dozen pubs in Temple Bar. It's fun and informative, though as the musicians move with the party you are left in doubt as to the point of changing pubs at all. Tours last 2.5 hours and start upstairs at *Oliver St*

GETTING AROUND

John Gogarty's in Temple Bar (May–Oct daily 7.30pm; Nov & Feb–April Fri & Sat 7.30pm); arrive early to be sure of a ticket (€9), or book ahead through the Tourist Centre.

The **1916 Rebellion Walking Tour** (☎676 2493, ⓦwww.1916rising.com) offers an expert and insightful two-hour stroll around some of the sites associated with the uprising, with guides recounting the events of the week which led up to the fateful Easter Sunday. Tours (mid-April to mid-Oct Mon–Sat 11.30am & 2pm, Sun 1pm) commence at the *International Bar* on Wicklow Street, and last approximately two hours. Tickets (€10) may be purchased at the beginning of the tour or in advance from tourist offices.

The media

ubliners are a news-hungry lot and you'll find a wide range of **newspapers** and **magazines** available in the newsagents around Grafton Street and O'Connell Street. There's also a broad range of **TV channels** and **radio stations** on offer.

TELEVISION AND RADIO

Radio Telefis Éireann (RTÉ) is the national state broadcasting company and provides two **television** channels, the mainstream, news-focused RTÉ 1, and the more downbeat Network 2. Additionally, there's the decidedly lowbrow independent TV3 and the Irish language channel, Telefis na Ghaeilge (known as TG4), which often features excellent traditional music. As well as a plethora of cable and satellite channels, Dublin's geographical position means that it's usually also possible to receive British channels, such as BBC 1 and 2, ITV and Channels 4 and 5. RTÉ also runs three **radio** stations: Radio 1 (88–94FM), devoted to middle/highbrow music and cultural and political programmes; 2FM (90.2–92.4FM), a popular music and entertainment channel; and the Irish-language station Radió na Gaeltachta (RnaG; 92.9–94.4 & 102.7FM). Additionally, there's the national commercial station, Today FM (100–102FM), while local Dublin independents include 98FM, 104FM, Anna Livia (103.2FM) and the Irish-language Raidió na Lífe (106.4FM).

NEWSPAPERS AND MAGAZINES

Two of Ireland's three national daily broadsheet **newspapers**, the heavyweight *Irish Times* and the lighter *Irish Independent*, are produced in Dublin, while the third, the *Irish Examiner*, emanates from Cork and, consequently, has a more southwestern focus. The *Star* is Ireland's own salacious tabloid, while both the UK's *Daily Mirror* and *Sun* produce special Irish editions. Sundays see the production of five newspapers – the liberal *Sunday Tribune*, the right-leaning *Sunday Times*, the downmarket *Ireland on Sunday*, the *Sunday Business Post* (which has a broader coverage than its name might suggest), and the more sensational *Sunday*

THE MEDIA

World. Dublin's own evening newspaper is the *Evening Herald*, packed with both local and national stories. British newspapers are readily available as well, and most good newsagents also stock a range of newspapers from Europe and further afield.

The most extensive range of magazines, including many British and European publications, can be found at the O'Connell Street branch of Eason's bookshop (see p.323). Dublin-produced magazines to look out for include *MacGill*, for astute political and economic analysis, the satirical *Phoenix*, the music- and style-focused *Hot Press*, and champion of the homeless, *The Big Issue*.

THE GUIDE

The Georgian southside

The richest and most attractive part of the city centre, the **Georgian southside** is the focal point for much of Dublin's cultural life. While replete with institutions like Trinity College, the Irish Parliament and the National Gallery, it also fizzes with restaurants and watering-holes, the latest fashions and music, and a confidence that impresses visitors and Dubliners alike. Ireland's economic boom is reflected in the windows of Grafton Street's stores and the shiny new cars parked around Merrion Square, whose elegant terraces are redolent of a previous era of pride and prosperity.

Most visitors gravitate towards **College Green**, where the world-famous *Book of Kells* can be seen at **Trinity College**; from here it's a short walk to **Grafton Street**, effectively Dublin's high street, busy with buskers, shoppers and tourists. Alleyways off to the west lead to the classy shopping centre of **Powerscourt Townhouse**, a former Georgian mansion; east across Dawson Street and along Molesworth Street brings you to the splendidly ornate entrance to **Leinster House**, home of the Irish Parliament, on Kildare Street.

Grafton, Dawson and Kildare streets all run out onto **St Stephen's Green**, once the centrepiece of Georgian Dublin and a place infused with literary and historical associations. The finest examples of Georgian architecture may be found to the east of here, their level of refinement peaking around **Merrion** and **Fitzwilliam** squares. The Wide Streets Commission's aim (see History, p.360) to create a European-style capital is most successfully realized in these squares and in the grand thoroughfares of Leeson and Baggot streets, the elegant canal-side Herbert Place, and above all in **Fitzwilliam Street**, whose position affords an expansive vista leading out to the Wicklow Mountains. Examination of the detail of Georgian interiors is particularly rewarding at **Newman House** (where Joyce studied), on St Stephen's Green, and the nearby **No. 29 Fitzwilliam Street Lower**.

Ireland's cultural treasure-houses are here too – the outstanding prehistoric gold and medieval metalwork on display in the **National Museum** are prime attractions, while the **National Gallery of Art**'s fine collection of European art is similarly worthwhile, and the **RHA Gallagher Gallery** in Ely Place is an important space for contemporary art.

TRINITY COLLEGE

Map 4, E5. Grounds: daily 8am–midnight (Sat & Sun, main gate locked at 6.30pm; use Nassau St gate); free. Old Library: June–Sept Mon–Sat 9.30am–5pm, Sun 9.30am–4.30pm; Oct–May Mon–Sat 9.30am–5pm, Sun noon–4.30pm (closed for ten days over Christmas and New Year); €7. Dublin Experience: late May–Sept daily 10am–5pm (hourly shows); €4.20. Combined ticket for both €10. ⓦwww.tcd.ie.

Dublin's most famous institution and Ireland's oldest university, **Trinity College** was founded in 1592 by Queen Elizabeth I to rectify "the barbarism" of the Irish and prevent them from being "infected with Popery" at foreign universities. Admission was restricted to Protestants, but Catholics could get free education by rejecting their faith. Trinity had a formative influence on the Anglo-Irish tradition, as Protestant families sent their sons to be educated here rather than in England, and its alumni made their mark in politics (Edmund Burke, Wolfe Tone, Robert Emmet, Edward Carson, Douglas Hyde), literature (Jonathan Swift, Oliver Goldsmith, Oscar Wilde, Bram Stoker, J.M. Synge, Samuel Beckett) and other fields.

Although religious restrictions were abolished in 1873, its Protestant character survived after Irish independence, since as late as the 1970s Catholic archbishops forbade their flocks to study at Trinity without first obtaining special permission, on pain of excommunication. Today, seventy percent of its students are Catholic and Trinity is one of three universities in the city: Dublin University (of which Trinity is the sole college); University College Dublin, based near Donnybrook; and Dublin City University, out in Glasnevin. However, neither of the others can match Trinity as an architectural set piece, which dominates the heart of the city.

College Green and the university grounds

College Green is something of a misnomer for what is today a heavily trafficked junction outside the College, where a tiny lawn is about as green as it gets. The name commemorates the fact that when Trinity was founded it stood on open common land outside the walled city, including a flat-topped mound, 39ft high and 207ft in circumference, that had once been the Viking *Thingmount*, or

TRINITY COLLEGE

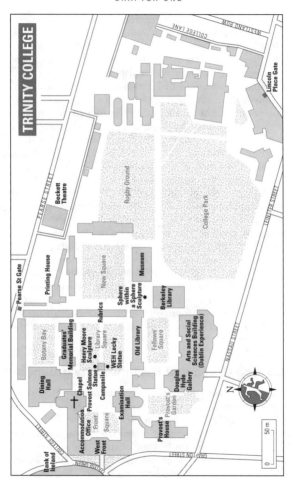

TRINITY COLLEGE

parliament (otherwise known as the *Haugen*, hence College Green's old name, Hoggen Green). In Georgian times the ground was levelled to provide the foundations of Nassau Street, and College Green became the centre of political life, as power briefly diverted from the viceregal seat in Dublin Castle to the Protestant Irish parliament, established here in 1782.

The **West Front**, facing College Green, is flanked by statues of two eighteenth-century graduates, the Tory philosopher and statesman Edmund Burke, and the wit and poet Oliver Goldsmith. Both were sculpted by John Foley, who also did Grattan's statue outside the Bank of Ireland, leading to jokes that he cast the legs of all three from the same mould to save money. At all times of year, Dubliners lounge against the railings by the main gate here, the city's most popular meeting place. In the summer, the steady traffic of visitors is steered towards the **Dublin Experience** in the Arts and Social Sciences Building, an audio-visual show that takes you through over one thousand years of Dublin history in 45 minutes – a useful introduction if you are unfamiliar with it all and need an overview.

Trinity graduates lead 30min walking tours of the college, starting from the blue kiosk just inside the main gate, which are good value as they include admission to the Old Library (5 daily; €8).

Trinity's main quad is a harmonious composition of eighteenth- and nineteenth-century buildings centred on a 39ft high **Campanile** that's thought to mark the site of the All Hallow's Priory, on whose confiscated land Trinity was built using materials pillaged from other Catholic orders. To the left of the Campanile is a statue of Provost Salmon, who fiercely opposed letting women into Trinity and made good his threat "Over my dead body!" by expiring when they

TRINITY COLLEGE

did in 1903. On the lawn behind the Campanile is the Henry Moore sculpture *Reclining Connected Forms*. The sports pitches of College Park stretch beyond the main University buildings, providing a quiet green space in the heart of the city centre, open to students and the public alike.

The buildings

If you can get inside (the doors are often locked), it's worth visiting the Examination Hall and the Chapel on either side of Front Square. Both were designed in the 1790s by Sir William Chambers, a Scottish architect who never visited Ireland but executed many commissions in Dublin. The **Examination Hall** (or Theatre) contains a chandelier from the old Irish Parliament and an organ reputedly salvaged from a Spanish ship in 1702. Trinity's **Chapel** is the only one in the Republic shared by all denominations. Its main window is dedicated to Archbishop Ussher, one of the first students at Trinity (which he entered at thirteen), who went on to lecture there, devoting years of study to establishing that God created the world on October 23, 4004 BC.

Beyond the Chapel is a grand **Dining Hall** hung with vast portraits of college dignitaries; it has been much altered since it was built by the German architect Richard Cassels in 1742, and was totally restored after a fire in 1989. The oldest surviving building – dating from 1700 – is the red-brick student dormitory called the **Rubrics**, overlooking Library Square. Behind the Graduates' Memorial Building is an open area known as **Botany Bay**, so-called because the unruly students living in the vicinity were considered worthy of transportation to Britain's penal colony.

Most tourists make a beeline for the **Book of Kells** (see box, opposite) in the **Old Library**, entered from Fellows' Square. On the ground floor is a superb exhibition called

THE BOOK OF KELLS

Created around 800 AD, the Book of Kells probably originated at the monastery on Iona off the west coast of Scotland, which had been founded around 561 by the great Irish scholar, bard and ruler St Colum Cille (St Columba in English). In 806, a Viking raid on Iona left 86 monks dead, prompting the Columbines to move to the monastery of Kells in County Meath – after which the book is named. In Ireland, life didn't get much easier for the hallowed book: first it was stolen, in 1007, to be later found buried in the ground, then its metal shrine or *cumdach* was looted by the Vikings (who wouldn't have valued the book itself) and some thirty folios (double-page spreads) disappeared. To prevent a worse fate during the Cromwellian wars, the *Book of Kells* was brought to Dublin and given to Trinity by the Bishop of Meath sometime after 1653. Since then it has been jealously guarded, despite the legend that Queen Victoria autographed it during her first visit to Dublin (she actually signed a parchment that was bound into the volume). In 1953 the folios were rebound in four calfskin volumes, of which two are on display, one showing an illuminated page, the other text. Both are turned to a new page on a regular basis.

The 340 lavishly decorated folios of the *Book of Kells* contain the four New Testament gospels with prefaces and summaries, all in Latin. The text is in rounded Celtic script, with human or animal forms at the margins. The real highlights, however, are the opening letters, which cover an entire page ornamented with arcane symbols and images, and geometric and floral patterns, probably influenced by metalwork such as the Ardagh Chalice and the Tara Brooch in the National Museum.

"Turning Darkness into Light", which sets the *Book of Kells* and other Irish illuminated manuscripts in context – ranging from Ogham (the earlier, Celtic writing system of lines

TRINITY COLLEGE

carved on standing stones) to Ethiopian books of devotions. Displayed beside the *Book of Kells* itself in the dimly lit final room are two of the following four books, rotated at regular intervals: the *Book of Armagh* (807), the *Book of Durrow* (675), the *Book of Mulling* (seventh century) and the *Book of Dimma* (eighth or ninth century).

Upstairs is Thomas Burgh's magnificent library of 1712–32, aptly known as the **Long Room**, to which a second tier of bookcases and a barrel-vaulted ceiling were added in 1860; today it houses 200,000 of the library's oldest books in wonderfully antiquated oak bookcases. As a copyright library, Trinity is entitled to a copy of every book published in Ireland and Britain, so its collection of three million titles grows by 100,000 per year – the bulk of them being kept in a repository in the suburb of Santry. Besides fascinating temporary exhibitions of books and prints from the library's collection, the Long Room also displays a gnarled fifteenth-century **harp**, the oldest to survive from Ireland, and an original printing of the 1916 Proclamation of the Irish Republic, made on Easter Sunday in Liberty Hall.

On other sides of Fellows' Square stand the 1960s Brutalist-style **Berkeley Library** and **Arts and Social Sciences Building**. The library is named after Kilkenny-born George Berkeley, who studied at Trinity when he was fifteen; a philosopher and educationalist whose influence spread to the American colonies, Berkeley contributed to the foundation of the University of Pennsylvania in 1740 (California's Berkeley University bears his name). In front of the library sits a suitably intriguing sculpture, *Sphere within a Sphere* by Arnaldo Pomodoro, though its magic is somewhat diminished by its local nickname, "the half-eaten Malteser". As well as the summer-only Dublin Experience (see above), the arts block contains a cheap sandwich and coffee bar and the **Douglas Hyde Gallery** (Mon–Wed &

Fri 11am–6pm, Thurs 11am–7pm, Sat 11am–4.45pm; free), an experimental art venue that's usually worth checking out.

Just beyond the Berkeley Library, the School of Engineering occupies a former **Museum** designed by Benjamin Woodward (who raised the height of the Old Library) and carved with monkeys, owls and parrots by the O'Shea brothers, whom Woodward invited to carve freely like medieval artists, but then fired after the College authorities expressed displeasure with their work. It's worth looking inside the entrance hall to view the skeletons of a pair of giant Irish deer that were found at Lough Gur, County Limerick (the species became extinct 11,000 years ago). To the north of New Square is Cassels' first building in Dublin, a **Printing House** resembling a Doric temple, which now houses the departments of microelectronics and electrical engineering.

THE BANK OF IRELAND

Map 4, D5. House of Lords Mon–Fri 10am–4pm (until 5pm Thurs), guided tours Tues 10.30am, 11.30am & 1.45pm; free. Story of Banking Tues–Fri 10am–4pm; €1.50.

Across the road from Trinity the massive **Bank of Ireland** flanks the curve into Dame Street. It was here that the Anglo–Irish Ascendancy's efforts towards self-government culminated in the **Grattan Parliament** of 1782, where Henry Grattan – whose statue stands outside – declared "Ireland is now a nation." Work on a suitable building began as early as 1729, when Sir Edward Lovett Pearce designed a bicameral house with a colonnaded forecourt facing College Green. The Corinthian portico on Westmoreland Street was added by James Gandon (see p.159–165) in 1785, as the Lords' entrance (they objected to sharing a door with MPs). Like the Ionic portico on

Foster Place, it's linked to Pearce's building by a curved screen wall.

Grattan's Parliament was short-lived: by patronage and bribery, Britain induced a majority to pass the Act of Union (1801), which subsumed their authority in Westminster. Bereft of a function, the building was sold to the Bank of Ireland for £40,000 sterling, after the House of Commons chamber had been demolished to prevent it from being used again as a parliament.

The real attraction is the old **House of Lords**, with its vaulted ceiling, 1233-piece crystal chandelier, and tapestries depicting the Protestant victories of the Siege of Londonderry (1689) and the Battle of the Boyne (1690). Though its long table seems authentic, the Lords actually sat back-to-back around the walls for debates, with the Lord Chancellor on a woolsack. The stuccoed **Cash Hall** looks like part of the House of Commons but is quite unlike the original, which had galleries for some seven hundred spectators; parliamentary debates were a fashionable entertainment at that time. Around the corner on Foster Place, an armoury added during the Napoleonic wars now serves as an **arts centre** where concerts are often held, and as the venue for the **Story of Banking**, a film "narrated" by David La Touche, the bank's founder, and an exhibition including the silver-gilt **mace** that belonged to the House of Commons. Sold by Speaker Foster's descendants, it was bought back from Christie's in London by the bank in 1937.

GRAFTON STREET AND AROUND

Running uphill from College Green to St Stephen's Green, pedestrianized **Grafton Street** (Map 4, D7) is the best place to catch street entertainers – and there are plenty to choose from, ranging from string quartets to groups of guitar-playing eight-year-olds with as many chords as years.

Here too, you may catch the peculiarly Irish phenomenon of street poetry, the performers of which are said to be descended from the Celtic bardic tradition. The famous **Molly Malone statue** (by Jean Rynhart) at the bottom of the street is nicknamed the "tart with the cart" due to its brazen décolletage and what Molly reputedly got up to while wheeling her barrow of cockles and mussels through streets broad and narrow. It is thought that she died in 1734 and was buried near St Werburgh's Church (see p.95). At that time, Grafton Street was a fairly rudimentary lane which led to the execution grounds and common that was then St Stephen's Green. Today it boasts malls and department stores, a handful of places to eat and some famous **pubs** on its side streets – there are none on Grafton Street itself – including **Davy Byrne's** on Duke Street, the "moral pub" of Joyce's *Ulysses*.

For more on *Davy Byrne's*, see p.287. *The Duke* across the way is the starting point for "Dublin's Literary Pub Crawl" – see p.19.

Detouring in the other direction off Grafton Street you'll find the **Powerscourt Townhouse** (Mon–Fri 10am–6pm, Thurs till 8pm, Sat 9am–6pm, Sun noon–6pm; see Shopping on p.331), an imaginative conversion of the eighteenth-century mansion of Viscount Powerscourt, built using granite from his estate in County Wicklow (see p.218). Its grand entrance on William Street South opens into a hall, with a staircase leading to the finest surviving reception room on the top floor; others have been converted into shops. Like the Georgian Room on the floor below, it was executed by Michael Stapleton, who was responsible for the plasterwork at Trinity. The café in the atrium is notable for its location, in what was once the mansion's inner courtyard – bathed in light on sunny days, and filled with live piano music on Saturdays.

While in the vicinity, check out the **Dublin Civic Museum** (Tues–Sat 10am–6pm, Sun 11am–2pm; free) at 58 William Street South. Though it's mainly devoted to temporary exhibitions on anything from barges to Count John McCormack, the great Irish tenor, you can be sure of seeing a number of permanent features, including historical views of the city, old shop signs and the 1877 bylaws of St Stephen's Green, denying entry to persons "in an intoxicated, unclean or verminous condition" and "any dog which may be reasonably suspected to be in a rabid state". Castle Market, the narrow street over the road, leads to the Market Arcade, which comes out on to South Great George's Street (see p.113).

For more on *Bewley's* see p.265.

Returning to Grafton Street, you can't miss the Egyptian mosaic facade of **Bewley's Oriental Café**, a Dublin institution where all classes mingle over tea, coffee, all-day fried breakfasts, cakes and sticky buns. Founded by the Quaker Bewley family in the 1840s as a (then) teetotal bulwark against the demon drink, it almost folded in 1986, provoking such a national outcry that the government had to step in until a buyer was found.

DAWSON STREET AND MOLESWORTH STREET

To the east of Grafton Street lie some quieter streets that are ripe for a wander. **Dawson Street** (Map 4, E7) is home to the city's major bookshops as well as the **Mansion House** (not open to the public). Originally built for the aristocrat Joshua Dawson (after whom the street is named), this august edifice has been the residence of Dublin's Lord Mayor since 1715 – its stucco facade and porte-cochère were added in Victorian times. It was here that Dáil

Éireann (the Irish parliament) adopted the Declaration of Independence in 1919 and where the truce that ended Anglo-Irish hostilities was signed in 1921. Beyond the Royal Irish Academy next door stands **St Ann's Church**, whose interior dates back to the early 1700s. The shelves behind the altar were used for storing bread to be distributed to the poor of the parish under the terms of a bequest. Past parishioners include Wolfe Tone (who was married here in 1765), Bram Stoker and Douglas Hyde, and the graveyard contains the tomb of the poet Felicia Hemans, who wrote "The boy stood on the burning deck . . ." and lived at no. 21.

It's worth checking out the lunchtime and evening concerts of classical music at St Ann's Church – call ☎676 7727 for details.

Molesworth Street, running towards the eighteenth-century grandeur of Leinster House, retains three Huguenot-style gabled houses from the mid-eighteenth century. At no. 17 is **Freemasons' Hall** (Map 4, F7), the headquarters of Ireland's Grand Lodge, which runs guided tours (June–Aug Mon–Fri 2.30pm; €1.50). Its interior combines every style of Victorian architecture from Egyptian to Roman and Gothic, all wildly over the top. The tour also includes a twenty-minute video show and a museum of Masonic regalia. Visitors are solemnly assured that what little influence the Freemasons have in Irish society is only for the good.

LEINSTER HOUSE

Map 4, F7.
Kildare Street, at the top of Molesworth Street, is the heartland of Dublin's establishment. Its centrepiece is **Leinster House**, which houses the Irish Parliament,

LEINSTER HOUSE

flanked to the north by the National Library, the Royal College of Physicians (closed to the public) and the former Kildare Street Club, and to the south by the National Museum. The area was developed by James Fitzgerald, Earl of Kildare, who in 1745 bought some cheap land on the edge of town and commissioned Richard Cassels to build a mansion on it. Asked if he regretted leaving the fashionable northside, the Earl replied, "they will follow me wherever I go" – and he was right, for Lord Fitzwilliam then laid out Merrion Square, starting a development boom on the southside. The Earl's mansion was designed so that the facade facing town resembles a townhouse, and the side on what is now Merrion Square looks like a country residence – it's thought to have been a model for the White House in Washington. Approached from Kildare Street, its imposing pedimented facade sits behind elaborate ornamental railings beyond a wide courtyard. Its present name, Leinster House, honours the elevation of the Earl to Duke of Leinster. One of his sons, Lord Edward Fitzgerald, escaped arrest here by the British after spies betrayed his preparations for the 1798 Rebellion.

The mansion was converted into the **Irish Parliament** in 1922 after the establishment of the Irish Free State. Despite calls to fulfill Daniel O'Connell's dream of restoring the former Grattan Parliament (see p.33), the provisional government at the time deemed Leinster House easier to defend. Beset by enemies at home and abroad, they felt, as Kevin O'Higgins confessed – like "eight young men standing amidst the ruins of one administration with the foundation of another not yet laid, and with wild men screaming through the keyhole".

Parliament generally sits from mid-January to July (breaking for Easter), and October until Christmas, on Tuesdays at 2.30pm, and Wednesdays and Thursdays at 10.30am.

THE IRISH PARLIAMENT

Few legislatures have been so hard won – and divisive – as the Irish Parliament (*Oireachtas na hÉireann*; @www.irlgov.ie). Its basic form was hammered out in the London negotiations that established the Irish Free State (a title reflecting Britain's objection to the term "Republic"). Under the Anglo-Irish Treaty it had to vow loyalty to the British monarch and accept Ireland's partition into a 26-county Free State and a 6-county Northern Ireland.

Both conditions split the Nationalists down the middle, with the anti-Treaty side initiating a bitter Civil War (1922–24) with the Free State forces. Both sides claimed to be the rightful heirs of *Dáil Éireann*, the Irish shadow parliament of 1919 to 1921, whose own legitimacy derived from the Proclamation of the Republic during the Easter Rising. Not until 1927 did de Valera and his Fianna Fáil party grudgingly recognize the Free State and enter parliamentary life "with guns under their coats". In 1937, citizens voted to accept a new constitution formulated by de Valera, which is the basis for the Republic of Ireland's present system of government.

While the president is the head of state, legislative and executive powers are vested in parliament, which has two chambers: *Dáil Éireann* (House of Representatives) and *Seanad Éireann* (Senate). The Dáil (pronounced "doil") has 166 representatives (*Teachtaí Dála* or TDs), elected by proportional representation, whereas the sixty senators are appointed by various authorities including the Prime Minister or *Taoiseach* (pronounced "Tea-shock") and the universities. Critics say that the system encourages cronyism and corruption – as evinced by a stream of scandals involving nearly every party and government since the 1970s.

LEINSTER HOUSE

Visitors wishing to visit Leinster House should telephone the Captain of the Guard or the PR office, preferably two weeks in advance (☎618 3000); free **tours** are then arranged subject to the political diary and the number of people wishing to visit at any given time. Irish citizens need to be sponsored by their TD to gain admittance. The sedate Senate meets in a semicircular blue salon in the north wing – the Dáil sits on the other side of the building and is more of a bear-pit. Visitors are guided from one chamber to the other by frock-coated ushers.

THE NATIONAL LIBRARY AND HERALDIC MUSEUM

The **National Library** (Map 4, F7; Mon–Wed 10am–9pm, Thurs & Fri 10am–5pm, Sat 10am–1pm; free; ⓦwww.nli.ie) was built in the late nineteenth century, along with the National Museum, to flank Leinster House. Less of a crowd-puller, it's chiefly worth visiting for its asso-ciations – almost every major Irish writer from Joyce onwards has used it at some time. On the ground floor, temporary **exhibitions** feature anything from old Irish maps to the diaries of Joseph Holiday, describing Dublin's theatrical life. Ask for a visitor's pass to enter the stately domed **Reading Room** on the first floor, scene of one of the great set pieces of *Ulysses* – Stephen's extravagant speech on Shakespeare. If you want to trace your ancestors, visit the **Genealogy Room** (Mon–Fri 10am–4.45pm, Sat 10am–12.30pm; free) where professional genealogists are on hand to give you advice about how to access the parish, land and state records held here and elsewhere in the city (and in Belfast).

At the bottom of Kildare Street stands the former **Kildare Street Club** (Map 4, F6), a Venetian-Gothic red-brick edifice with whimsical figures carved on its pillars – including monkeys playing billiards and a mole with a lute.

Once a bastion of Anglo-Irish conservatism, it was described in 1886 by novelist George Moore as "a sort of oyster-bed into which all the eldest sons of the landed gentry fall as a matter of course. There they remain spending their days drinking sherry and cursing Gladstone in a sort of dialect, a dead language which the larva-like stupidity of the club has preserved". It now houses the Alliance Française and the **Heraldic Museum** (Mon–Wed 10am–8.30pm, Thurs & Fri 10am–4.30pm, Sat 10am–1pm; free), which contains such items as Sir Roger Casement's Order of St Michael and George, the Lord Chancellor's purse, and the mantle and insignia of the Order of St Patrick.

If your mantelpiece just isn't complete without an Irish coat-of-arms, the Office of the Chief Herald (@www.nli.ie) in the former Kildare Street Club is the place to come – it'll cost you around €3000 and take up to a year to complete.

THE NATIONAL MUSEUM

Map 4, F7. Tues–Sat 10am–5pm, Sun 2–5pm; free.
@www.museum.ie.

With its prehistoric gold, medieval treasures and Viking finds, as well as material covering the period 1916–21 and a small but impressive Egyptian collection, the **National Museum** is one of the city's essential sights. Occupying part of a building raised in the late 1880s to accommodate both the museum and the National Library, the core of the collection was acquired in 1891 as a donation from the

----

Times for guided tours (40min; €1.50) of the National Museum vary – they're posted up at the entrance each day.

THE NATIONAL MUSEUM

Royal Irish Academy, a society founded in 1785 by the Earl of Charlemont. The collection has grown a great deal since then, and in 1994 the museum acquired the Collins Barracks (see p.135) which now houses artefacts covering social, political and military history, and the decorative arts.

Only the highlights are listed below, and by focusing on these you could see the best of the museum in an afternoon – the **numbers in the text** correspond to the floor plans opposite and on p.47. In addition, you might want to catch one of the museum's free lunchtime **lectures** (usually Wed at 1pm; ☎677 7744 ext.332 for details), while the shop in the beautiful entrance rotunda sells a range of high-quality crafts, from pottery to jewellery, inspired by works in the museum.

Ór – Ireland's gold

The museum's stunning collection of prehistoric gold (*ór*) occupies the sunken main hall; less glamorous artefacts from the same era are ranged around the raised perimeter – and all is made eminently accessible to the non-specialist. A central display section [1] explains how gold was extracted in ancient times and why peat bogs have yielded so many treasures during turf-cutting, when so few have been found at excavations of inhabited sites.

In the Earlier Bronze Age (c. 2500–1500 BC) goldsmiths created **lunulae** [2] – crescent-shaped collars made from thin sheets of beaten gold – and decorated them with delicate chevrons or stripes, incised on the front or hammered out from behind, by the technique known as repoussé. Basket-shaped ear- or hair-rings (it's not known which) and sun discs which were sewn onto clothes [3] show evidence of the same techniques.

A marked change occurred around 1200 BC – at the beginning of what's now termed the Later Bronze Age

THE NATIONAL MUSEUM

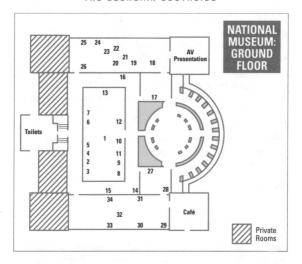

- with the introduction of new techniques such as twisting, which required greater quantities of gold, suggesting that new sources of the metal were found around this time. Sheet-gold was beaten into armlets, ear- or hair-rings and necklaces – as in the **Derrinboy Hoard** [4] – or twisted into **torcs**; one from County Antrim is as chunky as an industrial drill [5]. Note three that would probably have gone around the waist, with different kinds of fasteners [6]. Gold beads were also combined with chunks of amber, to form lustrous necklaces [7].

A further expansion in production, pointing to some sort of economic boom, seems to have happened around 800 BC. Cast or hammered-bar goldwork gave rise to bracelets and dress- or sleeve-fasteners with cupped terminals, which generations of Irish schoolkids know as the gold telephones [8]. Applying elaborately decorated gold foil to base metal objects produced *bullae* – purse-shaped artefacts that were probably used as charms or amulets – and so-called ring money [9]. The **Tumna Hoard** [10] of nine gold balls the size of doughnuts – they're perforated, suggesting an extravagant necklace – is flanked by two sunflower pins from the **Ballytegan Hoard** [11], as well as the **Meenwaun Hoard** [12] of an amber necklace, a gold bracelet and dress-fastener and two bronze rings – all dating from 800–700 BC.

From the same period come the magnificent **Gleninsheen Gorget** (one of several gold collars with roundel fastenings attached by gold wire) and the **Mooghaun Hoard** [13]. The latter, comprising around 150 gold objects, was found by navvies digging the West Clare Railway in 1854.

Prehistoric Ireland

Less dazzling prehistoric material around the walls of the main hall includes a partial reconstruction of a late Neolithic (3400–2800 BC) **passage tomb** [14], incorporating decorated stones from Newgrange; and the astonishing **Lurgan Logboat** [15], which was unearthed in a Galway bog in 1902 and is made of hollowed-out oak trunks, over fifteen yards long (c. 2500 BC). The **Dowris Hoard** [16] of over two hundred bronze finds from the final phase of the Irish Bronze Age (900–500 BC) includes horns, akin to didgeridoos, which were probably used as part of a fertility cult associated with bulls.

The Treasury

The Treasury holds most of the museum's better-known ecclesiastical objects. In the ante-room, which deals with the prehistoric Iron Age, enough remains of the fragmented **Petrie Crown** (second century AD) to recognize the sumptuous, fluid curves of La Tène-influenced metalwork, a Celtic style which came from continental Europe [17].

The main room kicks off in spectacular style with the **Broighter Hoard** (first century BC), a beautifully ornamented gold collar and a miniature gold boat, representing an ocean-going, hide-covered *curragh*, complete with tiny oars and mast [18]. Found in 1980 in County Tipperary, the **Derrynaflan Hoard** [19 and 20] contains a silver paten and chalice and a bronze church sieve dating from the eighth and ninth centuries, though they're somewhat overshadowed by the more elaborate chalice from the **Ardagh Hoard** [21], also from the eighth century. Perhaps the finest example of Irish metalwork is the **Tara Brooch** [22] found on the seashore near Bettystown in 1850, both sides of which bear intricate patterns that may have inspired those in manuscripts such as the *Book of Kells*. Such "knot" designs also appear on the shaft of a stone **cross** from County Offaly, depicting a horseman and a stag [23].

During the Middle Ages, elaborate reliquaries were made to hold holy relics or texts. **St Patrick's Bell Shrine** [24] contains a bell reputedly owned by the saint. Adorned with gold wire upon a silver backplate, it was created in the early twelfth century and handed down through generations of the Mulholland family until the late 1770s. In the same case is the disconcerting bronze **Shrine of St Lachtin's Arm**. Book-shrines decorated with repoussé saints include the intricate **Soiscél Molaise** [25], begun in the eighth century. (Similar, later reliquaries and shrines now form part of the Medieval Ireland exhibition upstairs.)

As you head back into the main hall, you'll find a couple of **Sheela-na-Gigs** [26] either side of the door, enigmatic female figures that appeared on many early Irish churches despite their pagan antecedents and their overt sexuality. Before you leave, it's worth catching the twenty-minute **AV presentation** at the other end of the Treasury, which takes

THE NATIONAL MUSEUM

you through the history of Celtic art at a swift pace and includes enticing shots of ancient sites around the country.

The Road to Independence

The final exhibition on the ground floor relates the struggle for Irish independence, but lacks the space to do justice to its subject and will eventually be moved to the Collins Barracks. Meanwhile, the first room covers events ranging from the abortive uprising of Robert Emmet (whose death mask [27] is displayed) to the activities of the Fenians in America, before returning to Ireland and the campaigns of O'Connell and Parnell. After both failed to achieve reform through Britain's parliament, a new generation sought to revive and promote Irish culture through the Gaelic League, founded by Douglas Hyde, whose bust shares a display case with the first Gaelic typewriter [28].

The **main section** is devoted to the Easter Rising and the War of Independence. You'll see the uniforms of the Irish Volunteers and the Citizen Army that fought in 1916 [29]; Sir Roger Casement's dress suit and a sword-stick and barrister's gown belonging to Pádraig Pearse [30]; the pistols fired by Countess Markievicz [31]; Michael Collins's death mask [32] next to a uniform of the hated British Black and Tans [33]; and one worn by Collins as Commander-in-Chief of the Irish Republican Army [34]. A video-wall at the far end displays various images from the Easter Rising including contemporary newsreel footage.

Viking-age Ireland

Upstairs, the exhibition on Viking-age Ireland (c. 800–1150) overlaps chronologically with the Treasury on the floor below and proves a worthwhile contrast. While the ecclesiastical treasures on the ground floor illustrate the

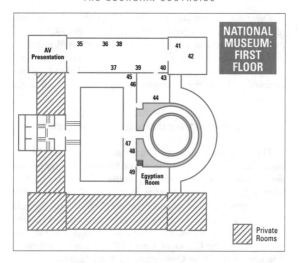

richness of life emanating from Irish religious foundations, the Viking exhibits and attached AV presentation tell the story of a very different culture, with artefacts of conquest, international trade and the beginnings of urban Dublin.

The early Viking invasions are represented by artefacts from burial grounds at Islandbridge and Kilmainham, including the **skeleton of a warrior** [**35**] with a long sword and a dagger. It was partly due to the Viking threat that the *crannog* or lake dwelling persisted for so long in Ireland; one from County Westmeath has yielded a wooden bucket and gaming board, and antler combs [**36**]. While the Vikings appreciated the skills of Irish jewellers – as evinced by penannular **rings** and "thistle" **brooches** [**37**] – others were liable to be enslaved or killed, like the man whose hacked-about **skull** was found with a gruesome iron slave-chain [**38**].

The next section covers **Viking Dublin**, with **models** of a house and the layout of Fishamble Street [39], accompanied by a host of finds from excavations on Winetavern Street and Wood Quay, ranging from loom weights to iron-workers' tools. Notice the finely carved **deer-antler combs** [40] that the Vikings used as money as well as for taming their hair.

For more on Viking Dublin, see pp.101 and 102.

The final room displays Christian artefacts from Viking times, including some of the museum's most famous possessions. The **Tau Crozier** [41] is the only surviving one with a T-shaped head, though they were often depicted in early manuscripts, while the exquisite **Crozier of St Tola** follows the familiar form of a shepherd's crook [41]. Iron and bronze bells (often hand-held rather than hung in belfries) presage the **Cross of Cong** [42], made to enshrine a fragment of the True Cross given by Pope Calixtus II to the King of Connacht in 1123 but which was later lost.

Medieval Ireland 1150–1550

The museum's most recent exhibit moves on in time from the Vikings, and the Treasury downstairs, to cover the period of the first English colonists, their withdrawal to the area around Dublin known as "the Pale" after 1300, and the hybrid culture that developed all the while. The confused nature of the cultural map becomes clear in the first room, devoted to **Power** (ie the ruling classes), where you can listen to recordings of poetry written in Ireland in Middle Irish, Middle English and Norman French. Nearby, you can't miss the house-shaped **Breac Maodhóg Shrine** [43], richly decorated with saints and apostles, and its accompanying satchel, with incised Celtic motifs. Containing the relics of St Maodhóg, it was carried into battle and at coronations to reaffirm the power of the O'Reilly kings. On a more secular note, the impressive **Kavanagh Charter Horn** [44], made of exotic ivory, was for centuries one of the symbols of the kings of Leinster. Other exhibits cover hunting, food, games – including an early form of backgammon – and, of course, warfare. A variety of gruesome weapons are wielded, to show how the lightly armed Irish horsemen were well-suited to raiding across the bogs at home, but were regarded as something of a joke, with their throwing spears and stirrup-less saddles, when they went to fight in foreign wars; the Irish lords' favourite mercenaries, however, axe-wielding Gallowglass soldiers of mixed Viking/Gaelic descent from the west of Scotland, were feared by all.

Exhibits in the next section, **Work**, are, as you'd expect, more run-of-the-mill. Countless bits of pottery, coins and seals from newly established market towns attest to the boom in trade in this period – where few towns had previously existed, the English, in just over a century from around 1170, founded the backbone of Ireland's present urban network. Set around a monumental **copper basin** [45], over 3ft in diameter and probably used for brewing, exhibits trace agricultural developments. Ploughshares and sickles were used on the English lords' new feudal manors, where cereals were farmed as cash crops until the Black Death led to a drastic recession in the fourteenth century. Meanwhile, with the English occupying the best arable land, traditional dependence on cattle increased among the Irish. Look out for the keg of **bog butter** [46]: on remote grazing lands, milk was churned into butter on the spot and preserved in the bogs for later use; to this day, such kegs are often turned over by peat-cutters, who'll swear the butter is still edible.

Prayer reveals the twelfth-century reorganization of the

THE NATIONAL MUSEUM

Church into dioceses with bishops and new monastic orders, bringing to bear some interesting contemporary quotations and a mass of finely decorated shrines and reliquaries. Ireland's three patron saints are all represented [47]: the **Shrine of St Patrick's Tooth** (the tooth is said to have fallen out at Killespugbrone, and was used in later centuries to cure sick animals); the even stranger **Shrine of St Brigid's Shoe**; and the **Shrine of the Cathach**, containing a manuscript written by St Columba of Iona, legendary bard, scholar, ruler and evangelizer of Scotland. Keep an eye out also for the adjacent **Mias Tighearnáin**, an unusual dish-shaped reliquary – it was probably made for a relic of St John the Baptist, whose head was presented to Salome on a plate. Opposite, a whole display case [48] is devoted to a fascinating explication of the **Domnach Airgid Shrine** – note especially the lower left panel, showing St Patrick presenting a book (the relic for which this shrine was made) to St Macartan. The exhibits beyond this are far less compelling, apart from the **souvenirs of pilgrimage** [49] brought back by medieval tourists: flasks of holy water from the shrine of Thomas Becket at Canterbury, scallop shells from Santiago de Compostela, and bits of marble and candle wax from St Peter's in Rome.

Finally, tucked away off the upper gallery you'll find the tiny, but very worthwhile, **Egyptian Room**, highlights of which include Egyptian hieroglyphic scripts and material on how to read them, some splendidly decorated mummies and a wonderfully detailed wooden model of a Nile boat, complete with rowers and armed guard.

ST STEPHEN'S GREEN

Map 4, E8. Mon–Sat 8am–dusk; Sun 10am–dusk.
While **St Stephen's Green** is the largest – and perhaps the most famous – of Georgian Dublin's squares, the Green

itself is the least Georgian in character. A central floral display, herbaceous borders and jubilee bandstand all mark its identity as essentially Victorian; **Lord Ardilaun** (Sir Arthur Guinness) funded the present layout in 1880, and a statue of him faces west out of the Green. Originally an open common in the vicinity of a lepers' hospital, the Green was surrounded by buildings by the late seventeenth century but nonetheless remained a dangerous spot, with footpads lurking on every corner. Public hangings occurred here until the eighteenth century, and as late as 1800 the Green was surrounded by a fetid ditch clogged with dead cats and dogs. To try and improve matters, railings and locked gates were installed in 1814 and an annual fee of one guinea was levied on users, but it was only when Lord Ardilaun bought the property, paid for its new layout and donated it to the people of Dublin that true bourgeois respectability was attained. Worried locals complain that drunks and ne'er-do-wells are returning the Green to its former unsavoury nature – making wildly exaggerated comparisons to New York's Central Park in the 1970s – but it's still a pleasant, popular spot to take a break from the rigours of the city centre.

St Stephen's Green is also worth visiting for its great range of **statues**, which bear testimony to the city's varied history and cultural life; maps pinpointing the location of each are situated at the Green's main entrances. "Crossing Stephen's that is my green" is inscribed beneath a keenly fashioned bust of **Joyce** towards the south side; an abstract bronze of **W.B. Yeats** by Henry Moore conveys something of the spirituality of the poet (take care here as this secluded spot can be dangerous) and the Green's more violent history is remembered in a bust of **Countess Markievicz** (see box, p.52) who, along with Commandant Mallin, led the insurgents occupying the Green during the Easter Rising. For further evidence of this take a look at the Royal

ST STEPHEN'S GREEN

COUNTESS MARKIEVICZ

A confirmed feminist and ardent socialist, Constance Gore-Booth was one of Ireland's most remarkable women, whose dynamic role during the upheavals in Dublin at the beginning of the century marks her as one of the great figures of twentieth-century Irish political history.

Born into the Anglo-Irish aristocracy in 1868, she spent much of her childhood in Lissadell, County Sligo, and, after studying art in London, moved to Paris in 1898, where she met and married Polish Count Casimir Markievicz. On her return to Ireland her nationalistic sentiments began to evolve and she joined Sinn Féin, where she quickly made her mark by founding na Fianna Éireann, the Sinn Féin youth movement, in 1909. Influenced by the socialism of Connolly and Larkin, she became involved in class politics, working with the poor and organizing soup kitchens during the 1913 lockout (see p.131).

Having joined the Irish Citizen Army, Countess Markievicz was second-in-command at St Stephen's Green in the 1916 Easter Rising (see p.136) – the death sentence she received for her involvement was commuted on the grounds of her sex (an inequality which disgusted her). She went on to become president of the Women's Volunteers and the first woman to be elected to Westminster, though as a member of Sinn Féin she boycotted parliament and instead became the Minister for Labour in the first Dáil Éireann in 1919. During the War of Independence the Countess was jailed twice and in 1922 was firmly on the anti-Treaty side, boycotting the post-treaty Dáil with other anti-Treaty republicans; however, when de Valera formed Fianna Fáil in 1926, she joined and was elected to the Dáil shortly before her death in 1927.

ST STEPHEN'S GREEN

College of Surgeons on the west side of the Green, whose pillars are still scarred with bullet-marks; the insurgents, having failed to seize the *Shelbourne Hotel*, were forced to retreat into the building when pinned down by snipers. At the northwest corner of the Green the **Fusiliers' Arch** honours the 212 Royal Dublin Fusiliers killed in the Boer War, and is still known to some as "Traitor's Gate" – enlistment or conscription into the British army being a long-standing *bête noire* of Nationalists. A **monument to Wolfe Tone** (see box, p.116), nicknamed "Tone-henge" for its granite slabs, is situated at the northeast corner; behind that lies one to commemorate the **Great Famine**; near the Leeson Street exit you'll find Joseph Wackerle's **Three Fates** fountain, presented by the German people in gratitude for help given by the Irish to World War II refugees; and finally a statue of **Robert Emmet** stands on the pavement opposite the Royal College of Surgeons, looking across to the site of his birthplace at nos. 124–5, now demolished.

St Stephen's Green North and West

Aside from its memorial role, the Green is an important point of orientation and its sides, designated as North, South, East and West, retain a number of important Georgian buildings. Once known as "Beaux Walk" after the dandies who promenaded there in the eighteenth century, **St Stephen's Green North** (Map 4, E7) still reeks of money, with pedestrians gabbling into their mobiles as they stride towards the **Shelbourne Hotel** (see pp.241 and 289). The *Shelbourne* boasts of having "the best address in Dublin" and has been a meeting place for the upper echelons of society since it was founded in 1824. Non-residents can wander in for a drink and something to eat in the lobby at any time of day. Afternoon tea (from 3pm) is popular, but the lobby and bars really come alive in the evening, when they're great for celebrity spotting. Just past the hotel, look out for the small **Huguenot Graveyard** (Map 4, F8) at the start of Merrion Row, established in 1693 for the French Protestant refugees who settled in Dublin's Liberties (see p.115). Only a few simple tombs are left, but this seems a fitting tribute to their quietly industrious way of life.

St Stephen's Green West (Map 4, D8) is dominated by the extravagantly decorative facade of the **St Stephen's Green Shopping Centre**, a 1980s extravaganza whose frothy white "Mississippi Steamboat" facade mimics the Georgian frontages overlooking the Green; and, midway down, **the Royal College of Surgeons**, an early nineteenth-century classical building topped by figures representing Medicine and Health.

NEWMAN HOUSE

Map 4, D9. Hourly guided tours only: June–Aug Tues–Fri noon–5pm, Sat 2–5pm; €4.

On **St Stephen's Green South**, nos. 85–86 are collectively known as **Newman House**, named after Cardinal Newman, the first rector of the Catholic University of Ireland. Founded in 1854 to provide a Catholic equivalent to Trinity College, the institution provided education for generations of Catholics who would otherwise have been obliged to study abroad or submit to the Protestant hegemony of Trinity; James Joyce, Pádraig Pearse and Éamon de Valera were among its alumni. The university later moved out to Belfield, changing its name to University College Dublin (UCD) along the way.

Newman House is fabulously decorative. **Number 85** was originally Clanwilliam House, a miniature Palladian mansion built by Cassels in 1738 for Captain Hugh

Montgomery to entertain while in town for the "Season". Inside, the **Apollo Room** on the ground floor is decorated with superb stucco work by the Swiss-Italian Lafranchini brothers, including the nine Muses on the walls, putti and rabbits over the doorway, and a fine figure of the god himself above the fireplace.

Upstairs is the **Saloon**, with its coffered ceiling and allegorical relief of good government and prudent economy. When the Jesuits acquired the building in 1883, they covered the naked female bodies on the ceiling with what look like furry bathing costumes, to protect the morals of their students; the garments were removed when the house was restored in the 1980s, but one was left *in situ* to show how bizarre they appeared. At the back of the house is an extension in the Gothic style, used as a **Physics Theatre**, where Joyce once lectured to the "L & H" (Literary and Historical Society).

Number 86 is a larger house built in 1765 for Richard "Burnchapel" Whaley, a virulent anti-Catholic who earned his sobriquet by torching chapels in County Wicklow. His son, Buck Whaley, was a founder of the Hellfire Club (see box, p.83). The saloon has flowing Rococo plasterwork by Robert West and is known as the **Bishop's Room**, having been used for meetings of the university's committee. On the top floor are the **classroom** where Joyce studied from 1899 to 1902, and the **bedroom** of the poet and Jesuit priest Gerard Manley Hopkins, who was Professor of Classics from 1884 until his death in 1889, a miserable period during which he wrote what are called the "Terrible Sonnets".

Beside Newman House stands the Byzantine-style **University Church**, whose opulent interior is adorned with marble quarried from five different sites in Ireland (definitely worth seeing) and regarded as a chic location for weddings. **Iveagh House**, further along, was the first

NEWMAN HOUSE

building that Cassels designed in Dublin, a stately pedimented building which now houses the Department of Foreign Affairs.

HARCOURT STREET AND THE IVEAGH GARDENS

Harcourt Street (Map 4, D9), leading off the southwest corner of the Green, is a well-preserved Georgian street, laid out in 1775, and one that has its fair share of noteworthy addresses – no. 6 was formerly the headquarters of Arthur Griffith's Sinn Féin; Sir Edward Carson, a staunch opponent of Home Rule who founded the Ulster Volunteers, was born next door; and George Bernard Shaw once resided at no. 61. Here, too, in the former Harcourt Street railway station, is **Findlater's** wine merchants, established in 1823; you can visit their small **museum** (Mon–Fri 9am–6pm, Sat 10.30am–5.30pm; free) in the vaults to peruse interesting memorabilia of assorted bottles, advertisements and news clippings related to the history of the wine trade.

Whilst in the vicinity, it's worth visiting the secluded **Iveagh Gardens** (Map 4, D9; Mon–Sat 8.15am–6pm, Sun 10am–6pm, closes at dusk in winter; free) off Clonmell Street. With its own grotto, cascade, maze and rosarium, it was the back garden to Clonmell House, the former home of a Lord Chief Justice whose jailing of the owner of the *Dublin Evening Post* resulted in a devious act of revenge. The *Post* advertised a "Grand Olympic Pig Hunt" near the judge's country estate in Blackrock, gave whiskey to everyone who turned up and invited them to catch soaped pigs, which fled into the estate pursued by thousands of tipsy Dubliners – causing the judge to rush off to Dublin Castle telling the viceroy that Blackrock was in a state of insurrection.

The garden's far exit brings you out on to Earlsfort Terrace near the **National Concert Hall** (Map 4, E10; see p.304), Dublin's premier classical music venue. An imposing building constructed for the Great Exhibition of 1865, it subsequently became the centrepiece of University College Dublin, before being inaugurated as the National Concert Hall in 1981.

EAST OF ST STEPHEN'S GREEN

The area to the **east of St Stephen's Green**, bound to the east by Wilton Terrace and to the south by Leeson Street, constitutes one of the finest areas of **Georgian Dublin**. A product of the immense prosperity generated during the eighteenth century, when the Wide Streets Commission gave speculators carte blanche to buy up greenfield sites on both sides of the Liffey, this whole district repays exploration on foot. Starting in **Leeson Street** (Map 4, F10), which was originally devised as a grand approach to St Stephen's Green from Donnybrook, turn into Pembroke Street, whose rows of ornamental balconies and elegant fanlights lead off to the private green lawns of **Fitzwilliam Square** (Map 4, G10). Occasional gaps between the mature beech, laurel and holly trees afford a glimpse of the well-tended privilege enjoyed by the Georgian gentry. Laid out between 1791 and 1825, the square was the last and smallest to be developed by the Fitzwilliams and is a fine example of Georgian Dublin at its most intimate. It retains, too, a sense of the vigorous cultural life long generated in this part of the city: W.B. Yeats resided at no. 42 between 1928 and 1932, his brother Jack, the painter, lived just around the corner at no. 18 Fitzwilliam Place, and the building adjacent to no. 19 on the square itself was the home of Robert Lloyd Praeger, eminent naturalist and author.

Either the north or the south side of the square will bring you to **Fitzwilliam Street Upper** (Map 4, H10) which, along with Merrion Square and Fitzwilliam Place, once formed the longest stretch of uninterrupted Georgian housing in Europe. Despite the demolition of 26 houses in the 1960s, it still affords a marvellous perspective on the planners' ambitions to bring the wild grandeur of the hinterland into the heart of the city. (It's also worth pausing here to admire the view south as the street opens out to a spectacular vista of the Wicklow Mountains.) Continuing north, Fitzwilliam Street crosses a number of fine Georgian streets, and at the top of Mount Street Upper you will see the delightfully poised pepperpot church of **St Stephen's** (Map 3, I6), a Neoclassical work dating from 1824.

NO. 29 FITZWILLIAM STREET LOWER

Map 4, H8. Tues–Sat 10am–5pm, Sun 2–5pm, closed last three weeks of Dec; €3.15.

Once the home of the Beatty family, this assiduous reconstruction of a Georgian townhouse at the southeast corner of Merrion Square is well worth visiting. An engaging and informative **guided tour** explains the kind of society developed by the political and merchant classes of late-eighteenth-century Dublin and the minutiae of bourgeois life, starting in the basement, where water was filtered for drinking and coal and wine were stored in the cellar. Next door to the pantry the housekeeper's room has a small window, through which she could keep a close eye on light-fingered servants (who slept in slums elsewhere). Gracious living began upstairs, where you'll see such contraptions as a lead-lined wine cooler and a belly-warmer for soothing gastric complaints. The nursery contains a doll's house and a bed for the governess, who was hired to instruct the daughters (boys went to boarding school) in such ladylike arts as embroidery; the governess's needlework samplers on the wall were the Georgian equivalent of a curriculum vitae.

Back outside, the building you can see at the bottom of Fitzwilliam Street Lower is the **National Maternity Hospital**, founded in 1894, the largest maternity hospital in Europe, but the real attraction here is Merrion Square.

MERRION SQUARE

Merrion Square (Map 4, H7) marks the zenith of Georgian town-planning and was laid out by Lord Fitzwilliam of Merrion in the 1770s. Its spacious terraced houses have belonged to diverse famous citizens, and a stroll past their commemorative plaques gives a marvellous sense of the cultural legacy of the place. Though most of the houses now serve as offices, enough people still live here for the square to retain a residential feel.

Like St Stephen's Green, **the north side** of the square was once the most fashionable. The childhood home of **Oscar Wilde** (see box overleaf) was at no. 1; it's been heavily restored as the base of the American College Dublin and several of the rooms are open to public visits (Mon, Wed & Thurs 10.15am & 11.15am; €2.54), but it's really only for Wilde freaks. However, **Merrion Square South** (Map 4, H8) has the greater concentration of eminent ex-residents. Daniel O'Connell bought no. 58 in 1809, to the dismay of his frugal wife Mary, who lamented, "Where on earth will you be able to get a thousand guineas?". The Austrian physicist Erwin Schrödinger, co-winner of the 1933 Nobel Prize, occupied no. 65; the poet, mystic and painter George Russell (A.E.) worked at no. 84, and in 1922 W.B. Yeats moved into no. 82, having previously lived at 52 Merrion Square East. There's nothing to recall the British Embassy at no. 39, burnt out in 1972 by a crowd protesting against the Bloody Sunday massacre in Derry. On weekends during the summer, the park railings offer a splendid array of paintings as artists gather to sell their work.

MERRION SQUARE

OSCAR WILDE

Oscar Fingal O'Flahertie Wills Wilde was born in 1854, his mother a literary hostess and sometime poet, his father an eye specialist. A star at Trinity College, Wilde won a scholarship to Oxford, where he immersed himself in aestheticism and gained his reputation as a brilliant conversationalist – making him the essential party guest. While his outlandish dress sense and incisive repartee made him many enemies, this didn't seem to bother him – his belief being that "there is only one thing in the world worse than being talked about and that is not being talked about" – and he went on to write dazzling satires such as *Lady Windermere's Fan* and *The Importance of Being Earnest*, ensuring his success as a dramatist.

Although he was heterosexual in his youth and married Constance Lloyd in 1884, Wilde began to have homosexual relationships from 1886, finally falling in love with Lord Alfred Douglas, the son of the Marquis of Queensbury. The Marquis' wrath over Wilde's involvement with his son resulted in the famous court case, when he was prosecuted by his erstwhile friend Edward Carson for indecent acts. He was jailed for two years' hard labour, and whilst in prison wrote his famous poem *The Ballad of Reading Gaol*, containing the line "each man kills the thing he loves". Imprisonment broke his spirit in many ways. His long-suffering wife died in 1898 and Wilde, living the life of a social pariah in Paris, was abandoned by his "beloved Bosie", Lord Douglas. He died alone in 1900, heartbroken and impoverished.

A trio of fine public buildings occupy **Merrion Square West** (Map 4, G7): the National Gallery of Ireland (see opposite), the Natural History Museum (see p.75) and Leinster House (see p.37), the entrance to which faces onto Kildare Street. The obelisk on Leinster Lawn is dedicated to Michael Collins, Arthur Griffith and Kevin O'Higgins, the architects of the Free State.

Merrion Square itself is a real pleasure to **walk** through (daily, daylight hours), with its thickets of low-flowering shrubs, tulip-filled borders and bluebells. At the centre are perfectly manicured lawns from which the upper storeys of fine Georgian houses are visible above the treetops. It was from here in 1785 that Richard Crosbie from County Wicklow, attired in a fur-lined silk robe and a leopard-skin cap, made Ireland's first balloon ascent. Flamboyance, however, was not confined to the eighteenth century, and a remarkable statue of Oscar Wilde languishes against a rock near the northwest corner of the square opposite his childhood home (see above), in a pose of outrageous insouciance that has earned the figure the nickname "the fag on the crag". Before him stand the figures of a pregnant woman, representing his wife Constance expecting their second child, and a male torso; the columns on which they rest are inscribed with Wildean epithets, from the witty "Only dull people are brilliant at breakfast", to the poignant "Who, being loved, is poor?" Before leaving the park look out too for the bust of Michael Collins and that of Bernardo O'Higgins, liberator of Chile.

THE NATIONAL GALLERY

Map 4, G7. Mon–Sat 9.30am–5.30pm, Thurs until 8.30pm, Sun noon–5.30pm; free (€3 donation suggested). ⊛www.nationalgallery.ie.
the **National Gallery** houses a fine collection of European art dating from the fifteenth century to the present day. **Level 1** is chiefly given over to the development of **Irish painting** from the seventeenth century onwards, including a marvellous **Yeats Museum**, as well as seventeenth- and eighteenth-century British painting. **Highlights of Level 2** include a small but choice selection

of works from the Early Renaissance, superb paintings by Caravaggio, Velázquez, Rubens and Vermeer, a fascinating room devoted to art in eighteenth-century Rome, and an excellent survey of French art from Poussin to the Cubists.

The collection grew out of an enthusiastic public response to the Fine Art Hall of the Irish Industrial Exhibition of 1853, organized and funded by the railway magnate William Dargan. To pay tribute to Dargan's munificence, a committee was formed with a view to setting up a permanent public art collection, and with surprising speed an Act of Parliament was passed in 1854 establishing the National Gallery of Ireland. Dargan was so impressed that he donated his profits to fund the National Gallery. Since its inauguration in 1864, the gallery's collection has grown from 125 paintings to more than 12,000 pictures and sculptures, partly thanks to bequests by the likes of the Countess of Milltown (who gave almost 200 paintings from Russborough House) and George Bernard Shaw (who left one third of his residual estate to the "cherished asylum" of his youth).

The old building, divided into **Beit**, **Milltown** and **Dargan** wings with an entrance on Merrion Square West, has now been joined by the **Millennium Wing**, which gives access to the gallery from Clare Street, opposite the back corner of Trinity College. Opened rather belatedly in 2002, the new wing makes the most of its narrow frontage with a lofty atrium bathed in natural light, around which are arrayed galleries dedicated to major international temporary exhibitions, as well as the collection of twentieth-century Irish art. The resulting **layout** of the gallery, however, can be confusing: various mezzanines intrude, including the Millennium Wing entrance which is set below the rooms of the main collection, while the gallery's **room-numbering**, which we've followed in the account below, runs across the building taking little account of the chronology of the collections. In addition, some further reorganization is planned, including a new National Portrait Gallery on the Dargan Wing's mezzanine.

The first thing to do when you go in is to pick up one of the free leaflets containing an invaluable **floor plan**, but if it all gets too much for you, head for the Shaw Room (Dargan Wing Level 1) to hook up with one of the free **guided tours** on Saturdays (3pm) and Sundays (2pm, 3pm & 4pm). As well as **concerts**, the gallery also offers a range of **lectures** and **workshops**, some of them intended for children and for people with disabilities (as detailed in the monthly *Gallery News*, available in the foyer). In the **Print Gallery** (Beit Wing mezzanine) various temporary exhibitions are held throughout the year, and watercolours by **Turner**, including views of Rhineland castles and the Doge's Palace in Venice, are exhibited every January (when the light is low enough for these delicate works).

In a prime location under the Millennium Wing's glass roof, *Fitzer's* run a restaurant and a cheaper café – see p.276.

Level 1: The Milltown Wing

The ground floor of the Milltown Wing (Rooms 14–19) covers **Irish art 1700–1900**, beginning with the eighteenth century, a period when many Irish painters found employment in England. Notable among the exiles was **Nathaniel Hone the Elder**, who spent most of his life there and became a founder member of the Royal Academy. His most famous painting, *The Conjurer* (Room 16), is a vicious satire of the RA's president, Sir Joshua Reynolds, whose practice of borrowing from Old Master paintings is characterized by Hone as plagiarism; not surprisingly, it was requested that the painting be removed from the Academy, prompting

THE NATIONAL GALLERY

Hone to furiously throw in his membership and organize for himself the first one-man show ever held in Britain – you can size up Hone for yourself in his striking self-portrait in Room 15.

In the late eighteenth and early nineteenth centuries the emotionally charged extravagances of Romanticism emerged in pictures such as **James Arthur O'Connor**'s *A Thunderstorm: The Frightened Waggoner*, with its wind-tossed trees and dramatic lighting, and in the pyrotechnic excesses of *The Opening of the Sixth Seal* by **Francis Danby** (both Room 17), an apocalyptic vision based on the Book of Revelations, which carries a then-topical abolitionist message – only the slave whose chains are broken rejoices at the cataclysm. An interest in individuality becomes increasingly apparent later in the nineteenth century as painters began to take people from all social strata for their subjects: in **William Mulready**'s *The Toy Seller* (Room 17), the artist's interest clearly lies in the racial interaction between a black toyseller and a wealthy white woman; while *An Ejected Family* (Room 18) is one of remarkably few depictions of the horrific events surrounding the Famine, albeit a rather tame, romanticized treatment, by a Scottish artist, **Erskine Nichols**, who spent many years in Ireland.

Many artists of the second half of the nineteenth century drew their inspiration from France, Impressionism and post-Impressionism – a development exemplified by **Walter Osborne** and **Roderic O'Conor** in paintings (all Room 19) such as Osborne's *Apple Gathering at Quimperlé*, which demonstrates his preoccupation with atmospheric light and colour and his love of simple rustic settings; and his *In a Dublin Park*, where he seems far more interested in experimenting with the light's dappling effects than in telling the stories of his working-class Dublin characters. O'Conor's wonderful *La Jeune Bretonne*, a warm study of a Breton girl, and vibrant *Farm at Lezaven, Finistère* date from his

1890–1904 stay in Brittany, where his willingness to experiment with bold colours and compositions put him in the vanguard of a Gauguin-influenced, post-Impressionist school.

For more on Roderic O'Conor, visit
the Hugh Lane Gallery – see p.145.

Level 1: The Millennium Wing

From Room 19, the best plan is to press on with **modern Irish art** via a short detour into the new building, before backtracking to the Dargan Wing. In Room 5, the landscapes of the west of Ireland are memorably realized in the much-loved paintings of **Paul Henry**, notably *A Connemara Village* and *Launching the Currach*; the latter is likely to have been painted from memory, as the Achill islanders at the time felt that by sketching their likeness, Henry was removing part of their souls. In the same room, you can't miss *The Artist's Studio*, a striking painting of controversial society lady, Hazel Lavery, by her husband **Sir John Lavery**; the composition will be familiar to anyone who's been to the Prado in Madrid, as it's based on Velázquez' intriguing portrait of the girls of the Spanish court, *Las Meninas*, even down to the portrayal of the artist himself, who is seen here reflected in the mirror clutching his brush and palette. An even more famous portrait of Lady Lavery by her husband hangs nearby: showing her as a country girl symbolizing Eire, it was used on Irish banknotes from 1928 on and was recently given to the gallery by the Bank of Ireland on the introduction of the euro.

Garish and confrontational, **William Orpen**'s satirical *The Holy Well* dominates Room 4, depicting villagers of the west tearing off their clothes to seek succour at the well; a

THE NATIONAL GALLERY

lone figure derides their faith, bestriding the well in a posture of defiance. Under the influence of Orpen, many Irish artists largely ignored modernism but continued to produce vigorous work in the academic tradition, as evidenced in Room 3. **Sean Keating**'s *Allegory* is a particularly affecting piece, produced in 1922 when civil war was tearing Ireland apart. Two men, one a regular soldier, the other an Irregular, dig a grave for the tricolour, while the artist himself, sprawled in front of them, scowls his disillusionment at the viewer; none of the figures in the painting acknowledge the presence of any of the others. **Albert Power**'s sculpture of a *Connemara Trout* also deals with the struggle for life, cleverly exploiting the inconsistencies in the green Connemara marble to suggest grasses, weeds and even bubbles of foam on the water.

**Room 2 displays three representative paintings
by Jack B. Yeats, but the bulk of his work is on
show in the Dargan Wing – see below.**

In Room 2, modernism – championed largely by women artists – makes its entrance with the unconventional arrangement and colouring of *Still Life with Marble Torso* by **Grace Henry**, wife of Paul; and proves that it was here to stay with **Mainie Jellett**'s *Decoration*. Though strongly recalling icon painting, this was the first abstract work to be exhibited in Dublin, in 1923, and didn't go down too well – one reviewer called it "subhuman art". The more confident, individualistic responses of Irish artists between 1930 and 1959 are displayed in Room 1. Notable here is *The Family* by **Louis le Brocquy**, conveying the sense of alienation in the years after World War II; the work, which was recently bought by an Irish businessman for nearly €3 million – a record for a living Irish artist – and donated to the gallery in exchange for tax breaks, was flatly rejected by

Dublin's Municipal Gallery of Modern Art when offered free of charge in the 1950s.

Level 1: The Dargan Wing

The grandiose **Shaw Room** is lined with images of the seventeenth- and eighteenth-century aristocracy – the most interesting of which is the portrait by **Charles Jervas**, principal painter to George I and George II, of the travel writer, satirist and pioneer of smallpox inoculation, Lady Mary Wortley Montagu. On the back wall, the gigantic *Marriage of Princess Aoife of Leinster and Richard de Clare* by **Daniel Maclise** depicts the consummation of the alliance between the King of Leinster and the Norman warlord Strongbow, which took place on the battlefield after the capture of Waterford in 1170 (hence the corpses in the foreground). Opposite, a splendid statue of Shaw by **Paul Troubetzkoy** stands taut with intellectual rigour as he casts a critical eye down the length of the gallery.

The **Yeats Museum** is dedicated to **Jack B. Yeats**, but also covers the work of the talented family from which he came, including portraits of family members and Irish notables such as playwright J.M. Synge and poet Douglas Hyde by his father, **John Butler Yeats**, and pieces by his sisters **Lily** and **Elizabeth Corbet**, founder members of the Irish Arts and Crafts Movement. However, it's the paintings by Jack B. Yeats, arranged on a loosely thematic basis, that really steal the show. The early work on view here shows his preoccupation with everyday scenes, yet *Before the Start* (1915) gives a tantalizing glimmer of the raw energy that was to characterize his later, more abstract paintings. The Dublin pictures of the 1920s display Yeats's passionate interest in the life of Ireland; *The Liffey Swim* generates all the gritty excitement of the Dublin crowd as they watch the contestants surge along the river. As the paintings progress,

JACK B. YEATS

The art and politics of Jack B. Yeats (1871–1957) were profoundly affected by the happy years he spent living with his
grandparents in County Sligo, from the age of eight to sixteen.
During this time he developed a deep love of the country and
its people and acquired a pool of memories that were to sustain him throughout his adult life in England and Dublin – the
immediacy of his paintings is often deceptive since many were
produced retrospectively rather than by direct observation.
Yeats spent his first eight years in England, and lived there
again from 1887 to 1910, first studying art in London and then
settling in Devon, supporting himself and his wife through
painting and black-and-white illustrations for magazines such
as *Punch*. In 1905 he made a tour of the west of Ireland with
J.M. Synge to produce illustrations for the *Manchester
Guardian*. The trip renewed his connection with the landscapes
of the west and this, along with his subsequent association
with Synge, fuelled a desire to return.

On his relocation to Ireland in 1910, where he was to live
until his death in 1957, he learnt Irish and attended Sinn Féin
meetings. War, however, appalled him, and he was greatly dis-
tressed by the events surrounding the 1916 Rising. While elder
brother W.B. Yeats became a senator in the Irish Free State,
Jack remained a more idealistic patriot, whose belief in the
dignity of ordinary Irish people is evident in his numerous
paintings of farm workers, jockeys, tinkers and sailors.
However, as he moved away from illustration, Yeats's art
became increasingly more abstract, fluid and introverted, and
the later works, painted in vivid unmixed colours, show a free
expressivity as he communicates the spirit of the individual in
landscapes of chaos and wild beauty.

the tension between Yeats's urge to portray the contemporary scene with all its life and colour and a desire for more abstract creativity becomes increasingly apparent. Even as early as 1930 he conjures up a tremendous sense of freedom and light in the minor landscape painting *Power Station*. Among the 1940s collection, *The Gay Moon* and *And so my brother, hail and farewell for evermore* offer evocations of turbulent inner lives imaged through nature, the latter a particularly striking example in which the single, foregrounded figure appears to communicate with the abstract colour and form of a landscape. The height of Yeats's expressivity is reached in works of the later 1940s and early 1950s such as *The Singing Horseman* and *For the Road*, spirited paintings in which the subject appears to be trying to break free from the canvas, and *Grief*, a chaotic abstraction of anguish.

Level 1: The Beit Wing

Reynolds' most elaborate caricature from his 1751
visit to Rome is on show in Room 25 – see p.72.

The ground floor of the Beit Wing is largely devoted to **British art**, most of it from the eighteenth century. In Rooms 10 and 9, superb large-scale portraits by the great rivals **Reynolds** and **Gainsborough** vie for attention, and there's a delightfully wistful portrait of *The Mackinen Children* by **Hogarth** in Room 10. Other notable works include portraits of the aristocracy by **Francis Wheatley**, which constituted his bread-and-butter until debts and a scandalous love affair forced him to seek refuge in Ireland, where he painted *The Dublin Volunteers on College Green* (showing how much College Green has changed since then; Room 8). In the same room, look out also for one of

THE NATIONAL GALLERY

Henry **Raeburn**'s finest paintings, *Sir John and Lady Clerk of Penicuik*; bathed in strong back-lighting, it skilfully depicts the couple's easy-going intimacy. Room 7, which contains a rather haphazard collection of British and American art to the 1920s, is notable chiefly for **Augustus John**'s marvellously animated portrait of Seán O'Casey. Opposite, *The Goose Girl* by **Stanley Royle**, a realistic Victorian scene treated with a post-Impressionist's feel for composition, vibrant colours and dappled light, has proved irresistible to greeting-card publishers.

Level 2: The Beit Wing

The lion's share of the gallery's **Spanish art** collection is on display in Rooms 33 and 32. A highlight in the first room is *Kitchen Maid with the Supper at Emmaus*, the earliest known picture by **Velázquez** (c. 1617–18) – Christ and his disciples are in the background and attention is focused on the Moorish maid, her startled pose perhaps suggesting that she too might convert to Christianity. In Room 32, works by **Goya** include *Lady in a Black Mantilla* and *El Conde del Tajo*, an unusually austere portrait of an unknown Spanish nobleman, while **Murillo**'s *Holy Family* manages to convey the homely detail of the scene without veering into the cutesy sentimentality of his nearby *Infant St John the Baptist*.

You can quite happily avoid making the acquaintance of the anonymous early German and Netherlandish masters in Room 31, but the first room of **Italian art** (Room 30) is far more compelling, especially as it covers more than its designation, "The Early Renaissance in Florence", suggests. An elegant portrayal of the *Annunciation* by **Jacques Yverni** is here, a rare survivor of the fifteenth-century Avignon school which developed around the papal court during the Great Schism. There's a fine Sienese triptych, *The Virgin and Child with SS Mary Magdalen and Peter*, by

Jacopo del Pisano, while *SS Cosmas and Damian*, a panel by **Fra Angelico**, the fifteenth-century Florentine master, shows the medical saints miraculously surviving trial by fire. The nearby panels of *The Battle of Anghiari* and *The Taking of Pisa* are notable for their sophisticated narrative detail (read them both from left to right) and for the depiction of Pisa's bell tower, which was already three centuries into its famous lean when these paintings were made in the 1460s. **Paolo Uccello**'s obsession with perspective is evident in his *Virgin and Child*, which shows an animated baby Jesus trying to scramble away from Mary's hands and out from the plane of the picture.

A poignant, glowing *Pietà* by **Perugino** hangs in Room 29, along with a superb **Mantegna**, *Judith with the Head of Holofernes*, painted in monochrome to simulate a marble relief. In the same room, look out for **Filippino Lippi**'s lively *Portrait of a Musician*, in which the subject carefully tunes his lyre to illustrate the inscription on the back, "never start before the time". Progressing into Room 28 and the sixteenth century, you'll come face to face with **Tintoretto**'s wizened *Portrait of a Venetian Senator*, bracketed by a pair of **Titians**: the delicately composed *Supper at Emmaus* and a severe portrait of the diplomat and writer Baldassare Castiglione. Room 27 contains some fine examples of the Bolognese school of painting of the sixteenth and seventeenth centuries, which left behind Mannerism for more spontaneous handling of emotions. Especially notable are the sharply observed *Portrait of a Man* by **Annibale Carracci**, one of the school's prime movers; and *Jacob Blessing the Sons of Joseph* by **Guercino**, who despite the disadvantages of being self-taught and having problem eyesight (hence his name, meaning "Squinter"), demonstrates here his outstanding feel for colour and naturalism.

Unless you've acquired the taste for Italian Baroque art, you can quite safely ignore Room 26 and pass through to

25, which covers "Art in Rome in the eighteenth century" with plenty of local interest. Among some diverting views of Rome and various Irish gentlemen who had themselves immortalized in the Eternal City, don't miss **Reynolds'** fascinating *Parody of Raphael's "School of Athens"*, which purveys some familiar Irish stereotypes to ridicule the Grand Tourists. Replacing Diogenes the Cynic in Raphael's famous Vatican fresco, Joseph Henry, who commissioned the painting, is shown reclining on the steps reading a book called *Larry Grog*, while the future Earl of Charlemont (see p.205) and his friends' music session has been substituted for Euclid and his mathematics pupils. Henry's uncle and cousin, later the 1st and 2nd Earls of Milltown, appear at the back of Reynolds' caricature – the father with an eyeglass in the role of Plato, staring across at his spindly son – but look scarcely less ridiculous in their nearby portraits by **Pompeo Batoni**, Rome's most sought-after painter during the second half of the eighteenth century.

Russborough House, for which the 1st Earl of Milltown collected art and antiquities in Rome, is covered on p.224.

Level 2: The Milltown Wing

From Room 25 it makes sense to continue the Italian theme into 42 and 43, before going Dutch and Flemish in Rooms 37–41. **Caravaggio's** *The Taking of Christ* is the highlight of Room 42. All the dynamic violence of the act is conveyed in the powerful movement of the soldiers' gestures, with Christ a figure of spiritual stillness at the centre of it all; Caravaggio portrayed himself on the right of the picture holding a lamp and spectating passively. Among several harmoniously restrained cityscapes by **Canaletto** and his nephew **Bellotto** in Room 43, the dynamic *Allegory of* *the Immaculate Conception* by **Tiepolo** shouts out for attention. It's only a study for a larger work that seems never to have been executed, but is fraught with religious meaning: crowned with a triangular halo signifying the Trinity, God welcomes, with open arms, the Virgin, who is drowning under images associated with her role as Lady of the Apocalypse – the obelisk, the crescent moon, the globe, the snake of Original Sin, the palm and the angel holding a mirror.

Backtracking through the Caravaggio Room, you'll find the highlight of the **Dutch collection** in Room 40: **Vermeer**'s *Woman Writing a Letter, with her Maid*, one of only 35 accepted works by the artist. Characteristic white light from the window plays up the heated emotions of the woman (who has thrown a love letter and her letter-writing manual on the floor), but gives the maid a statuesque calm, while a painting of *The Finding of Moses* on the wall behind provides a reminder to trust in Divine Will to resolve matters. Look out also for the mysterious *Rest on the Flight into Egypt* nearby, **Rembrandt**'s only night landscape.

Vermeer's *Woman Writing a Letter* has been stolen and recovered twice – first by Bridget Rose Dugdale in 1974 to raise money for the IRA, and again in 1986 from Russborough House.

Otherwise, the best of the Low Countries is in Room 37, a wildly varied collection of **Flemish art**. The knee-tremblingly bawdy *Peasant Wedding* by **Pieter Brueghel the Younger** will raise a smile, but your eye is more likely to be drawn to *A Boy Standing on a Terrace* – in this, the most elaborate of his portraits of children, **van Dyck** skilfully juxtaposes the young Genoese nobleman's haughty, grown-up stance with the vulnerability of his cherubic expression. Van Dyck's teacher, **Rubens**, contributed to

THE NATIONAL GALLERY

the nearby portrayals of two saints, Dominic and Francis of Assisi, but his most interesting work here is on *Christ in the House of Martha and Mary*. He painted the elegantly animated main figures, while **Jan Brueghel II** contributed the intricate still life in the foreground, suggesting the theme of mortality, and the peaceful landscape, which features the French château of the possible sponsors, Spanish regents Albert and Isabella.

Level 2: The Dargan Wing

Lofty Room 44 is where over-sized, and generally over-stuffed, **Baroque** masters have found their rest. Only *St Peter Finding the Tribute Money* by **Rubens** demands attention, a beautifully observed portrayal of middle-aged men in robust discussion. It tells the story from St Matthew's Gospel of Peter finding money for taxes in the jaws of a fish, a rare subject which was probably commissioned by the fishermen's guild.

From here, take the left-hand set of stairs up to Room 48 to get a chronological take on the collection of **French art**. Among several fine paintings by **Poussin**, the master of restrained classicism, *The Lamentation over the Dead Christ* stands out: this unusually emotive work, heightened by the use of intense colours, was painted by the ageing artist as a meditation on death, with a nod to the imminent Resurrection in the new shoots on the bare tree in the background. Room 47 traces the eighteenth century's abandonment of Baroque grandeur in favour of the frivolous, decorative effects of the Rococo style – look no further than **Fragonard**'s impossibly fey *Venus and Cupid* for illustration.

The next room fortunately brings back a sense of realism with the Barbizon School, who left their Paris studios to paint directly from nature, taking inspiration from the seventeenth-century Dutch landscapists and providing it for the Impressionists who followed. Works by **Millet**, **Corot** and **Courbet** amply illustrate what this meant in practice, while **Couture**'s *La Peinture Réaliste* is a satirical counterattack on the theory from the classical establishment: with his behind parked on a sculpted head of Jupiter, the Realist sketches a pig's head, with an old lantern, a shoe and a cabbage on the wall for further inspiration.

To finish off, Room 45 gives a whirlwind tour of Impressionism and the movements that came in its wake. Both **Claude Monet**'s *Argenteuil Basin with a Single Sailboat* and his under-rated friend **Alfred Sisley**'s *The Banks of the Canal du Loing at St-Mammès* beautifully capture the transitory effects of light. Those that followed attempted to reintroduce structure as a key element: the bright dots and dashes of **Paul Signac**'s *Lady on the Terrace* seem strangely cold and stilted, but Fauvist **Kees van Dongen**'s *Stella in a Flowered Hat* and Expressionist **Emil Nolde**'s *Two Women in a Garden* harness vibrant, emotive colours far more successfully. By the time of **Picasso**'s exuberant *Still Life with a Mandolin* and fellow-Cubist **Juan Gris**' melancholic *Pierrot*, structure has firmly won the day.

THE NATURAL HISTORY MUSEUM

Map 4, G7. Tues–Sat 10am–5pm, Sun 2–5pm; free.

Across the Leinster Lawn from the National Gallery, the **Natural History Museum** preserves the essence of Victorian museums like a fly in amber, being virtually unchanged since the explorer and missionary Dr David Livingstone delivered its inaugural lecture in 1857. A statue of a rifle-toting naturalist with his foot on an animal skull on the lawn – Surgeon Major T.H. Park, the first Irishman to travel the breadth of Africa – presages the orgy of taxidermy and taxonomy within. The ground-floor **Irish**

Room opens with three skeletons of the giant Irish deer which, despite having the largest antler span, at 13ft, of any deer ever with which to intimidate rivals and impress females, became extinct around 9000 BC. Upstairs, the **World Collection** on the first floor includes rhinoceroses, mooses and other appealing creatures, as well as the Barrington collection of birds, many of which were hapless enough to crash into Irish lighthouses. The **lower gallery** on the second floor, the last resting place of a stuffed dodo, is the best spot to view the skeletons of two whales stranded on Irish shores, one of them a twenty-yard fin whale, and to stare into the eyes of a wretchedly moth-eaten giraffe. The third-floor **upper gallery** includes the amazing Blaschka collection of glass models of marine creatures, masterpieces of the glassmaker's art; look out also for a pair of cosy golden gloves, knitted from threads secreted by the fan mussel.

The Natural History Museum puts on a variety of lectures and special events, as well as guided tours – usually at 3.30pm, but phone ⊕677 7444 in the morning to check.

GOVERNMENT BUILDINGS

Map 4, F8. Guided tours Sat 10.30am–3.30pm (last tour). Free tickets from the National Gallery on the day.

Beyond the Natural History Museum looms the Edwardian colossus of the **Government Buildings**. The last great edifice erected by the British, its domed centrepiece was inaugurated by George V as the Royal College of Science in 1911, and lectures proceeded despite eleven more years of noisy construction work. No sooner was it finished than the north wing was occupied by the Free State government, whose ministers lived and worked there during the

Civil War, for fear of assassination. (Kevin O'Higgins was nearly killed by a sniper when he went onto the roof at night to smoke.) After the Royal College vacated in 1989 the whole complex was refurbished to suit the government. Besides the stylish decor, it's fascinating to see the lair of the powers-that-be, with their odd perks and quirks, in a forty-minute **guided tour** shadowed by a gimlet-eyed security man.

You'll start by mounting the **Ceremonial Staircase** – the square holes in the balustrades are a trademark of Angela Rolf, who designed much of the furniture. Though Charles Haughey vetoed moving Cabinet meetings into the **Sycamore Room**, he was happy with the **Taoiseach's Office**, complete with a private lift to a rooftop helipad and a limo in the basement. The historic **Cabinet Room** is the only part of the building that's still in old-fashioned style, hung with portraits of Wolfe Tone, Parnell, Markievicz and other Irish heroes.

That most English of Irishmen, Arthur Wellesley, Duke of Wellington, may have been born across the road at no. 24 Merrion Street Upper (now a hotel) – though evidence also points towards Trim in County Meath. The Duke was reticent about his Irish origins – on one occasion when reminded, he retorted, "Being born in a stable doesn't make one a horse."

THE RHA GALLAGHER GALLERY

Map 4, F9. Tues–Sat 11am–5pm, Thurs until 8pm, Sun 2–5pm; free. ⓦwww.royalhibernianacademy.com.

Cross Baggot Street at the top of Merrion Street Upper and you find yourself in **Ely Place**, a charming Georgian residential lane. Here, while completely at odds with the Georgian houses that surround it, stands the **Royal Hibernian Academy of Arts Gallagher Gallery**. The

Royal Hibernian Academy of Arts was established in 1823 and its annual exhibition soon became an important feature of the city's cultural calendar. Although the Academy's buildings in Abbey Street Lower were destroyed during the 1916 Rising, it continued to hold its annual exhibition at alternative venues. Former academicians include Nathaniel Hone, Walter Osbourne, John Butler Yeats, Jack B. Yeats and Charles Lamb. The Gallagher Gallery, built for the RHA in 1988, is a discreet modern building providing an excellent airy space for viewing painting and sculpture. It's one of Ireland's most important galleries for modern art, hosting several major Irish and international contemporary shows each year.

Temple Bar and the old city

Nowhere is Dublin's economic transformation over the last decade more evident than in **Temple Bar**, the area sandwiched between Dame Street and the Liffey. Marketed, with a fair dose of artistic licence, as Dublin's "Left Bank" – it's on the right bank as you face downstream – Temple Bar gained a name as the city's arty quarter in the early 1980s, when its cobbled streets and old warehouses were redeveloped in a way that was intended to retain much of the area's unique character. However, the bullish 1990s saw Dublin property prices soar, especially here, resulting in a change of emphasis from culture to entertainment. Nowadays Temple Bar has the city's greatest concentration of **restaurants**, **pubs** and **clubs**, as well as **galleries** and **arts centres**. Indeed, such has been the proliferation of alco-tourists packing its pubs, that hen and stag parties have been banned from licensed premises within Temple Bar, in an attempt to reverse its reputation as a

---

Map 6 at the back of the book covers Temple Bar.

---

bacchanalian rather than a bohemian centre. As property prices continue to rise and Temple Bar's narrow streets become ever more crowded, the tide of development has swept westwards, through the newly tagged shopping district of the "Old City" on the west side of Parliament Street, towards Wood Quay. Here stand the hugely controversial civic offices, locally known as "the bunkers", which were built over the extensive remains of Viking Dublin.

The **historic core** of the city to the west and south of Temple Bar is roughly triangulated by Dublin Castle and the cathedrals of Christ Church and St Patrick's. Although few old buildings remain, many streets in this area follow contours staked out by the Vikings in the ninth century, when a main axis ran east–west along the ridge (now Castle Street, Christchurch Place and High Street) and lanes divided by wattle fences descended to the quays. The Anglo-Normans took and fortified this area in the early thirteenth century, building the castle, enclosing Dublin with walls, towers and gateways, and founding both **Christ Church** and **St Patrick's Cathedral**. From nearby Cook Street you can see a massive section of the Norman city walls, and there are curios to be found in **St Werburgh's** and **St Audoen's** churches. **Marsh's Library**, near St Patrick's, is a wonderfully archaic scholar's den from the time of Jonathan Swift, who was dean of the cathedral for many years.

Near the end of Dame Street stands **Dublin Castle**, the former centre and symbol of British authority. Only since independence have Dubliners been able to enjoy its architecture and tour the State Apartments where the viceroys once held court. Today the castle grounds enclose one of the jewels in Dublin's crown, the **Chester Beatty Library**, a world-class collection of manuscripts and prints amassed by a thoroughly multinational mining magnate. In front of the castle is the **City Hall**, which at times – especially under the mayorship of the Liberator, Daniel O'Connell, in the 1840s – was able to impose checks on British power; its neoclassical rotunda has been beautifully restored while its vaults shelter a slick exposition of Dublin's political history.

TEMPLE BAR

Until the dissolution of the monasteries in 1537, the land on which **Temple Bar** stands was the property of the Augustinian order. It owes its name not to the friars, however, but to Sir William Temple, who bought the plot in the late sixteenth century. During the eighteenth century, this area was a centre for Dublin's lowlife, while in the nineteenth it attracted small businesses and traders.

The land was acquired in the 1960s by CIE (the state transport company at the time), whose aim was to build a new central bus terminal to replace the one on the other side of the river. As CIE procrastinated and uncertainty over the future of the area grew, small shops, studios and offices took on cheap short-term leases in Temple Bar. In the 1980s a movement to preserve the district gained momentum, and under pressure from politicians, most notably Charles Haughey, CIE abandoned its plan, paving the way for Temple Bar's development as Dublin's "cultural quarter".

This section highlights some of the major galleries and exhibitions in the area, but for a comprehensive list of restaurants, shop, pubs and other venues, check the Listings section of this guide. It's also worth dropping in to **Temple Bar Properties** at 18 Eustace Street (ⓦwww.templebar.ie) for their compendious, free visitors' guide to the area.

If you're approaching Temple Bar from the Ha'penny Bridge, you enter through **Merchant's Arch** (Map 6, F3), a dark alleyway that gives you an idea of how Dickensian Temple Bar must have looked a century ago, when many of

TEMPLE BAR

the streets beside the quays had such archways. Straight ahead of you is **Crown Alley** (Map 6, G4), which leads to the Central Bank on Dame Street. About halfway down to your right is the *Bad Ass Café* (see p.264), where Sinéad O'Connor once worked as a waitress while singing with Ton Ton Macoute.

Dublin's financial centre since the eighteenth century, **Dame Street** lies at the opposite end of Crown Alley to Merchant's Arch. The street was named after a dam which linked the hilltop Viking settlement to the outlying *Thingmount* (see p.27), and has a flush of Victorian banking houses now trumped by the **Central Bank** (Map 6, F5). Designed by controversial architect Sam Stephenson in 1978, the bank is an outsized stack of concrete slabs which, in a recent architectural survey, was voted one of the most hated as well as one the most loved buildings in the city.

The heart of Temple Bar

You won't have to wander far to find an arts centre of some kind in Temple Bar. Ultramodern **Curved Street** (Map 6, E5), off Temple Lane (once known as Dirty Lane), is flanked by the **Arthouse**, a multimedia centre for the arts (closed at the time of writing due to financial difficulties, its future uncertain) and the state-of-the-art **Temple Bar Music Centre**, a major gig venue (see p.298) that's also home to recording and television studios. A passageway links to **Eustace Street** (Map 6, D5), where you'll find **The Ark**, a cultural centre for children (℡670 7788 or ⓦwww.ark.ie for details of its programmes and festivals of music, theatre, literature, visual arts and new media), and the coolly minimalist **Irish Film Centre** (see p.313). Its two screens show art-house and special-interest films, and its bar and restaurant attract a trendy crowd.

TEMPLE BAR

THE EAGLE TAVERN AND THE HELLFIRE CLUB

Before it was demolished by the Wide Streets Commission in 1757, the Eagle Tavern was among the foremost roistering spots of Georgian Dublin. Standing beside the equally popular *Lucas Coffee Shop*, it allowed gentlemen-about-town to spend day and night in dissipation without having to walk far. It was at the *Eagle* that the notorious Hellfire Club was founded in 1735 by the Earl of Rosse, Buck Whaley, Colonel St Leger and the artist James Worsdale. Dedicated to gambling, whoring and profanity (they walked all the way to Jerusalem and played handball against the Wailing Wall to win a bet of £15,000) rather than black magic *per se* – though the Devil is said to have appeared at one of their parties – their main meeting place was outside Dublin at Speaker Connolly's hunting lodge on Montpelier Hill. The scandal they caused eventually forced them to quit Ireland, but in 1755 the Club was re-established at Medmenham Abbey in England by Sir Francis Dashwood. He was later to become Chancellor of the Exchequer but made such a hash of it that he was retired to the Lords, and the Hellfire Club languished as its members succumbed to bankruptcy or cirrhosis.

Sadly, for those seeking any relic of the club in Dublin, the location of the tavern is uncertain, due to a missing portion of the original surveyor's map. Although a plaque on the wall of Eustace Street states that it occupied the site of the Quaker meeting-hall where Wolfe Tone later founded the Dublin United Irishmen, most sources place the tavern on Cork Hill, where much was levelled to create Parliament Street and City Hall, so *Thomas Read* pub or *Da Pino* restaurant may be closer to the mark.

On the other side of Eustace Street, **Meeting House Square** (Map 6, D4), named after the Quaker meeting-hall, hosts a Saturday food market (see p.333) as well as a wide variety of outdoor events throughout the summer. Facing onto the square are the **Gallery of Photography**, which shows contemporary photoworks from around the world (℡671 4654, ⓦwww.irish-photography.com); the **National Photographic Archive** (℡603 0200, ⓦwww.nli.ie), which puts on exhibitions from the photographic collections of the National Library; and Ireland's premier drama school, the Gaiety School of Acting.

Diversions is a free outdoor festival of all manner of cultural events, running from May to September in Meeting House Square and Temple Bar Square.

Turning right from Eustace Street or Meeting House Square will take you along Temple Bar itself to the **Original Print Gallery** (Map 6, E3; ℡677 3657, ⓦwww.originalprint.ie), where you can catch the work of emerging and established Irish and international printmakers, and to **Temple Bar Gallery and Studios** (Map 6, F3; ℡671 0073), one of the largest of its kind in Europe, with thirty studios for contemporary artists and a cutting-edge exhibition space. South of here beyond Temple Bar Square, in a small alley off Cope Street, the word "Art" flashes on a neon sign outside a converted warehouse, home of the **Graphic Studio Gallery** (Map 6, G4; ℡679 8021, ⓦwww.graphicstudiodublin.com), another leading print gallery.

Temple Bar Square (Map 6, F3) hosts a lively book market on Saturdays and Sundays.

TEMPLE BAR

If you turn left instead of right at the top of Eustace Street, along Essex Street East, you'll find the **DESIGNyard** (Map 4, C4; see p.320), a showcase for contemporary jewellery, as well as some furniture and interior design. Opposite lies the bright-blue flagship of the contemporary art scene, **Project Arts Centre** (Map 6, C5; ☎679 6622, ⓦwww.project.ie), which began life as an art project in the foyer of the Gate Theatre, but now hosts theatre, dance, film and live music as well as the visual arts. Further up on the same street, U2 spent millions on the *Clarence* hotel (Map 6, B4; see p.239) and have turned it into Dublin's coolest establishment, with a rooftop penthouse used by the likes of Björk and Jack Nicholson. Before the Custom House moved downriver in the 1780s, this was the site where a crane used to unload ships – hence Crane Lane, nearby.

Broad **Parliament Street** (Map 6, A3–4) was the first of the new roads cut through the old city after the formation of the Wide Streets Commission in 1757. Despite the results it achieved within a decade, the Commission was much hated at the time, since tenants who ignored its compulsory purchase orders had their roofs removed overnight to force them to quit. Fortunately, it spared what is now Dublin's oldest shop, at no. 4. Thomas Read has been a cutlers since 1670 and contains its original display cabinets and furniture (the *Thomas Read* pub is next door).

On the corner of Parliament Street which faces Grattan Bridge stand the **Sunlight Chambers**, whose exterior has beautiful bas-relief friezes of men making their clothes dirty through honest toil, and women washing them. Its unusual theme is explained by the fact that Sunlight was the brand of soap manufactured by Lever Brothers (now the Unilever conglomerate), who commissioned the building at the turn of the century.

CITY HALL

Map 6, B6. ⓦwww.dublincity.ie/cityhall.

Parliament Street slopes slightly uphill towards the **City Hall** on Dame Street. Built between 1769 and 1779 as the Royal Exchange, it has been occupied by Dublin Corporation since 1852 and is still the venue for council meetings. It's definitely worth walking in to view the gleamingly restored neoclassical rotunda, where creamy Portland stone columns, interspersed with statues of O'Connell and other worthies in Roman garb, bathe in wonderful natural light from the dome. Among the Arts and Crafts murals under the dome tracing Dublin's history is one depicting Lambert Simnel being carried through the streets after his mock coronation (see p.99). The civic coat of arms on the floor shows three burning bastions, symbolizing resistance to invaders, but the motto *Obedientia Civium Urbis Felicitas* ("Happy the City whose Citizens Obey") suggests that rebellion was a greater worry for Dublin's rulers. During the Easter Rising, City Hall was seized by the insurgents, who sniped at British forces in the castle from its roof. In 1922, as headquarters of the provisional government during the Civil War, City Hall witnessed the lying-in-state both of Arthur Griffith, the first president, and, just a week later, of the assassinated Michael Collins – for which the 16ft statue of O'Connell was dramatically swathed in black robes.

The excellent *Queen of Tarts* café (see p.269)
has a small branch in the City Hall vaults.

The vaults beneath the rotunda now shelter **The Story of the Capital** (Mon–Sat 10am–5.15pm, Sun 2–5pm; €4), a fascinating multimedia journey through Dublin's history and politics – with occasional hints of self-promotion for the exhibition's sponsors, the city council. The story is told through exhaustive display panels, slick interactive databases and a series of videos, complemented by an entertaining audioguide narrated by Sinead Cusack with snippets from leading historians. There are few exhibits as such, a notable exception being the intricate city seal and its strongbox, which was instituted after the seal was stolen in 1305 and required the presence of all six keyholders. To make up for the lack of hard evidence on show, however, the enterprising curators have commissioned a series of artworks, including *Utopian Column*: a stack of glass plates engraved with historical scenes and flooded with light.

Diagonally opposite the City Hall is the stained-glass
porte-cochere of the Olympia Theatre – see p.312.

DUBLIN CASTLE

Map 4, B6. Tours of state apartments Mon–Fri 10am–5pm, Sat & Sun 2–5pm; €4. It's advisable to ring ahead, as tours don't run on state occasions (℡677 7129). ⊚www.dublincastle.ie.

For seven hundred years, **Dublin Castle** embodied English rule as the headquarters of the viceroy. Built by the Anglo-Normans in the early thirteenth century, it was the key element of their walled city and served their successors well, withstanding all attempts to take it by force.

Its gravest test was in 1534, when besieged by Silken Thomas Fitzgerald, Henry VIII's Lord Deputy, who had renounced his allegiance to the English crown. The castle was formally handed over to Michael Collins and the Irish Free State on January 16, 1922. The story goes that the last viceroy complained, "You're seven minutes late, Mr Collins", to which he replied, "We've been waiting seven hundred years, you can have the seven minutes." Today, denuded of menace, it could be mistaken for a private

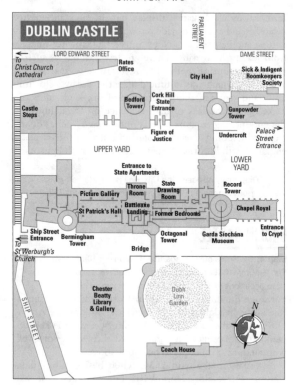

college. Its palatial interior is revealed only on guided, 45-minute **tours** of the State Apartments, though you can look around the courtyards and the Chapel Royal for free.

Above the main gate into the Upper Yard, the Cork Hill State Entrance, is a **figure of Justice** that turns her back on Dublin – an apt symbol of British justice, Dubliners said. Moreover, the scales of Justice tilted whenever it rained, till the authorities ensured even-handedness by drilling holes in the scale-pans. The nearby **Bedford Tower** is an eighteenth-century clock tower built upon the base of a Norman gate-tower. It was from here that the Irish "Crown Jewels" – a diamond St Patrick Star and Badge, together with other insignia – were stolen shortly before the state visit of Edward VII in 1907. Nobody was caught and the jewels have never been recovered.

The **Upper Yard** marks the extent of the original medieval castle, which was ravaged by fire in 1684. Surveyor-General Sir William Robinson took the opportunity of creating a larger complex of residential and administrative buildings, the arcaded appearance of which closely resembles his design for the Royal Hospital, Kilmainham (see p.124). It's hard to imagine the same place heaped with the bodies of rebels, brought into the city on carts after the British crushed the Rebellion of 1798 – or the castle's defenders being slain and buried here in shallow graves during the Easter Rising.

The State Apartments

You'll begin your tour of the **State Apartments** by ascending a grand staircase leading to the Battleaxe Landing, where the viceroy's ceremonial bodyguards stood. During World War I the **bedrooms** served as a Red Cross hospital – the wounded James Connolly, one of the leaders of the Easter Rising, was held here before his execution at Kilmainham Gaol. Famous names like Nelson Mandela, Chancellor Kohl and Mrs Thatcher (who insisted cable TV be installed) have slept in the Queen's Bedroom. Across the corridor, the Drawing Room was reconstructed after a fire in 1941, and contains a mirror bought for £5 by a farmer who used it for a headboard for 25 years; it would now be

DUBLIN CASTLE

worth something like €100,000.

In the **Throne Room**, the 1801 Act of Union is embodied in a chandelier combining the rose, shamrock and thistle, and in a throne belonging to William of Orange. Viceregal portraits line the **Picture Gallery**, with Cornwallis, who not only lost the American colonies, but also faced rebellions as viceroy first of India then of Ireland (1798), hung in disgrace behind the door. Next comes the blue, white and gold **St Patrick's Hall**, which once hosted ceremonies of the Knights of St Patrick (an order created in 1738) and is now used for presidential inaugurations and funerals. Ceiling paintings depict George III's coronation, Henry II receiving the surrender of the Irish chieftains, and St Patrick lighting the Paschal Fire on the Hill of Slane, watched by suspicious Druids.

Tours finish at an **undercroft** beneath the Lower Yard exposing a wall and gunpowder tower of the Norman castle and part of the original Viking ramparts.

The Lower Yard and the rest of the grounds

In the **Lower Yard**, the dramatic juxtaposition of the Record Tower and the Chapel Royal is marred by a modern tax office. Beefed up with battlements in Victorian times, the **Record Tower**, a rough-hewn mass dating back to 1258, originally served as a prison. In 1592, Red Hugh O'Donnell made two celebrated escapes from here; first by climbing down a rope, and then via a privy. The adjoining **Chapel Royal** is a neo-Gothic gem by Francis Johnston; look out for the viceroys' coats-of-arms carved on the balcony rail and around the altar. Mindful of the underground river that had undermined two earlier chapels, Johnston made it as light as possible by using plaster-coated brick rather than stone.

**The Crypt arts space and theatre (see p.311)
is underneath the Chapel Royal.**

A small door at the rear of the Record Tower gives access to the **Garda Síochána Museum**, relating the history of Ireland's police force (irregular hours – ring the bell; free); none of the exhibits are very compelling, but there are good views over the complex from the room at the top. Beyond, overlooked by the Chester Beatty Library, lies the pretty **castle garden**: now adorned with a swirling motif taken from the passage grave at Newgrange, it marks the site of the "Dark Pool" (*Dubh Linn*) which gave the city its English name.

THE CHESTER BEATTY LIBRARY

Map 4, B6. Tues–Fri 10am–5pm, Sat 11am–5pm, Sun 1–5pm; free. ⓦwww.cbl.ie.

Housed in former revenue offices in Dublin Castle's eighteenth-century Clock Tower Building, the **Chester Beatty Library** preserves a dazzling collection of books, manuscripts, prints and *objets d'art* from around the world. Superlatives come thick and fast here: as well as one of the finest **Islamic collections** in existence, containing some of the earliest manuscripts from the ninth and tenth centuries, the library holds important **Biblical papyri**, including the earliest surviving examples in any language of Mark's and Luke's Gospels, St Paul's Letters and the Book of Revelations. Elegantly displayed in high-tech galleries, the artefacts are used to tell the story of religious and artistic traditions across the world with great ingenuity, a formula which won the CBL the European Museum of the Year award in 2002.

The collection was put together over the course of sixty

years by the remarkable **Sir Alfred Chester Beatty**, a mining magnate born in New York in 1875 into a family of Ulster-Scots, English and Irish ancestry. At about the same time as he moved to London in 1911, Beatty began collecting, buying only works of the utmost rarity and highest quality, and always comparing them against similar material in the British Museum or the Bibliothéque Nationale in Paris. In the 1920s he began paying annual retainers to British Museum curators to advise him of suitable purchases, contacts which were usual at the time but which would probably be considered unethical these days. Although he became a naturalized British subject in 1933 (and was later knighted), after World War II Beatty grew disillusioned with Britain under the new Labour government, holding in contempt what he saw as their socialist bureaucracy – and, in particular, their strict foreign exchange rules. He cut a deal with the Irish government to gain exemption from their currency limits (then 60 guineas, whereas Beatty liked to travel with no less than $10,000), from import taxes on his artistic purchases and from estate duties on his collection after his death. In the early 1950s, Beatty moved himself and his works to Dublin, in 1957 he was made the first honorary citizen of Ireland, and when he died in 1968, he was given a state funeral and bequeathed his collection to the state.

It's well worth timing your visit to coincide with lunch at the Chester Beatty Library's excellent *Silk Road Café* – see p.269.

Most of the CBL's vast holding is accessible only to scholars via the reference library, with just two percent on show in the public **galleries** at any one time – though that's more than enough to keep you occupied for a few hours. Consequently, and to protect the delicate artefacts, the examples on display are changed every six months, but the gist of the exhibition's narrative remains the same. Engaging free **guided tours** run on Wednesdays at 1pm and Sundays at 3pm and 4pm, and there's a full programme of **events**, including artists' demonstrations, talks, workshops and concerts (☎407 0750 for details). **Temporary exhibitions** have included Japanese wood-block prints and "Holy Show", presenting the responses of contemporary Irish artists to the Old Testament in the context of the collection.

Spiritual Traditions

It makes sense to start with the second-floor gallery, which covers **Spiritual Traditions**, divided into Christianity, Islam and Eastern Religions; among the AV presentations is a fascinating ecumenical programme on religious practice around the world. At the time of writing, **Christian** highlights included a ropy-looking fragment of the Book of Deuteronomy, produced in Egypt around 150 AD, which, until the discovery of the Dead Sea Scrolls in the 1940s, was the earliest extant manuscript of the Bible; and a beautifully illuminated page of the twelfth-century Walsingham Bible, an important example of English Romanesque art. **Islam** is represented by gorgeous Qur'ans written in swirling calligraphy on gold leaf, colourfully illustrated poetry books and guidebooks for pilgrims, amulets intricately inscribed with holy verses, and an ingenious indicator, with pointer, map and compass, to determine the direction of Mecca. Finally, the diversity of the **Indian religions** and the branches of **Buddhism** is illustrated with everything from jolly paintings of Krishna stealing butter to embroidered mandalas and serene Burmese statues of the Buddha.

THE CHESTER BEATTY LIBRARY

Artistic Traditions

The first-floor gallery deals with Western, Islamic and Eastern **Artistic Traditions**, complemented by AV programmes showing some of the techniques involved. Chester Beatty was particularly interested in the dramatically detailed and strangely modern-looking engravings and woodcuts of **Albrecht Dürer**, and collected his early-sixteenth-century Biblical illustrations of *The Apocalypse*, *The Passion of Christ* and *The Life of the Virgin*. The collection also contains title pages by **Rubens** – the pay was low, but he did them in his spare time for his publisher friend, Balthasar Moretus. Elsewhere, keep an eye out for lavish examples of Viennese imperial binding, etchings by **Goya**, and **Matisse** calligraphy and illustrations. Even more elaborate bindings, using leather, silk and lacquer, can be found in the **Islamic section**, along with gorgeous Mughal illustrations and Persian books of poetry and paintings. Highlights of this part of the collection include the earliest existing example of a Qur'an in cursive script, and a book of poems, the *Divan of Hidayat*; produced in Iran in the fifteenth century, it's acknowledged as one of the finest Islamic manuscripts in the world, adorned with gold, blossoms in primary colours and exquisite binding.

The **Eastern room** is stuffed with beautiful Chinese, Japanese and Thai manuscripts, paintings and prints, as well as some more unusual artefacts. The Library holds one of the world's largest collections of rhino-horn cups, with over 200 of these intricately carved ceremonial drinking vessels; their appeal to Chester Beatty is clear to see, as Chinese scholars of the fifteenth to nineteenth centuries collected the cups for themselves or gave them as gifts. Books made of jade, which is traditionally associated with immortality but would have taken months to carve, show the vainglory of the Chinese emperors, who sought in this way to preserve their thoughts – even on quite mundane matters – forever. To end the exhibition, the extensive collection of Chinese snuff bottles carved from precious and semi-precious minerals harks back to Chester Beatty's prized boyhood collection of rocks.

ST WERBURGH'S

If you're heading towards Dublinia and Christ Church Cathedral from the Chester Beatty, your best bet is to nip out of Dublin Castle's Ship Street gate, along Ship Street, then right up Werburgh Street. This will take you past **St Werburgh's** (Map 4, B6), which has been lacking its spire since it was removed after Emmet's rising of 1803, for fear that future rebels would use it as a sniper's nest. Founded by the Normans in 1178, it was named after the daughter of the king of Mercia, the Abbess Werburgh. One of the leaders of the 1798 Rebellion, Lord Edward Fitzgerald, who was betrayed by spies and died of wounds sustained during his arrest, lies in the Fitzgerald vault; his captor, Major Henry Sirr, is buried in the yard. Rebuilt in 1715 and again in 1750, the church has an elegant Georgian interior that comes as a surprise after the dour exterior, should you manage to gain entry (Sun 10am for Church of Ireland services).

If you're hungry after all that walking, *Leo Burdock's* (see p.268), opposite St Werburgh's and just down the road from Christ Church, serves the best fish and chips in town.

DUBLINIA

Map 4, A6. April–Sept daily 10am–5pm; Oct–March Mon–Sat 11am–4pm, Sun 10am–4.30pm; €5.75, €7 for combination ticket with Christ Church Cathedral. ⓦwww.dublinia.ie.

As "a bridge to the medieval past", **Dublinia** falls short of virtual reality but conveys lots of impressions and facts with a light touch. The exhibition occupies the ex-**Synod Hall** of the Church of Ireland, connected to Christ Church Cathedral by an elegant bridge across which visitors exit the exhibition. Though both were created in Victorian times, the hall incorporates a medieval tower and stands on the site of the palace of the last Viking ruler, Hasculf, who was chased out by the Normans in 1170.

On the **ground floor**, Dublinia runs through themes like crime and punishment, plague and the medieval fair, with life-size tableaux, sound effects and lots of fun interactive possibilities, such as wearing medieval costume, throwing balls at a criminal in the stocks and brass rubbing. **Upstairs**, a timber-framed merchant's house and a quayside give a sanitized view of medieval life, which the captions admit was anything but salubrious.

The first floor's centrepiece is a panoramic **model of Dublin** c. 1500, showing the walled city dominated by Christ Church and surrounded by extensive undefended suburbs amid tracts of open land, with just one bridge across the Liffey to Oxmanstown. Wall-maps trace Dublin's subsequent evolution well into Georgian times. The **excavations at Wood Quay** are reconstructed in the next room, followed by a museum of artefacts found there, which are employed to illustrate everything from medieval food preparation to music and games. Highlights are the thigh of a stone effigy from Fishamble Street, which may come from the original tomb of Strongbow at Christ Church (see p.98); and the skeleton, alongside a complete facial reconstruction, of a woman found buried with her two children in a humble grave.

Before crossing the bridge on the second floor over to Christ Church, it's worth taking a look at the **Great Hall** where the Church of Ireland bishops convened until 1982, and climbing **St Michael's Tower**, a lofty relic of the fifteenth-century Church of St Michael and All Angels, for a great view of Dublin and the Wicklow Mountains on fine days.

CHRIST CHURCH CATHEDRAL

Map 4, A6. Cathedral: Mon–Fri 9.45am–5pm, Sat & Sun 10am–5pm; €3, free with Dublinia combination ticket (see above). @www.cccdub.ie.

In medieval times, **Christ Church Cathedral** would have soared above the city's wooden houses from its commanding site on the brow of Dublin Hill. Today, the view is generally obscured by buildings till you get nearby, and the Church of Ireland cathedral has been isolated from its surroundings by the traffic system.

A small Celtic church, Cill Céle Christ, may have stood on this site as early as 600 – long before the coming of the

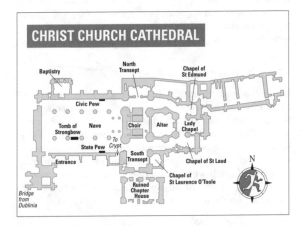

Vikings, who probably pillaged it. In 1028 their ruler Sitric IV ("Silkenbeard") converted to Christianity and requested that Bishop Dúnán found a cathedral on these grounds. Judging by Viking churches in Norway, Sitric's Christ Church was made of wood and probably decorated with pagan as well as Christian symbols, since both faiths co-existed for decades. When the Normans ousted the Vikings, their leader, Richard de Clare "Strongbow", made an agreement with Archbishop Laurence O'Toole to demolish the old cathedral and replace it with one symbolizing their joint glory. Work began in 1172 but was not completed until 1240. Unfortunately, the structure had been built on a bog, and in 1562 the south wall collapsed, pulling down half the cathedral. The rest continued as a church (and a tavern and market) but steadily deteriorated until the distiller Henry Roe lavished £230,000 to finance its restoration in the 1870s. Architect George Street refaced the exterior and transformed the cathedral's outward appearance by adding flying buttresses. The interior was also renovated, but it preserves more of its original character: the choir and transepts belong to Strongbow's cathedral, to which the nave was added in 1234.

The church

Close to the entrance lies the curious **tomb of Strongbow**. The original was destroyed by the collapse of the south wall, but was substituted with an effigy of an earl so that Dublin landlords could resume their practice of collecting rents around it. Depending on which version you want to believe, the smaller figure alongside is a fragment of the original tomb which may contain Strongbow's bowels – or an effigy of one of his sons, whom he cut in two for cowardice on the battlefield.

In Norman and Tudor times Christ Church was used for swearing in the viceroy, until the building of the Chapel Royal in Dublin Castle usurped its role. In 1487, the cathedral witnessed the pseudo-coronation of ten-year-old Lambert Simnel as "Edward VI"; within a month the Yorkist revolt of which he was the figurehead was crushed by the Lancastrian king, Henry VII, who amused himself by sparing Simnel's life to employ him as a kitchen-scullion. At one side of the nave the **Civic Pew** for Dublin's Lord Mayor has brass supports for his Great Sword and Mace (rarely used today), and on the other side the **State Pew**, used by the Irish president, still bears the royal arms of the Stuarts.

The **choir** contains oak stalls for the canons and choristers, and the lofty archbishop's throne. Turning back to face the nave, you'll be startled by the "**leaning wall of Dublin**" – ever since the south wall collapsed, the north wall has leaned outwards.

Christ Church's excellent choir may be heard at Choral Evensong (usually Wed & Thurs 6pm, Sat 5pm, Sun 3.30pm). There are also programmes of concerts, mostly in the evening, and free lunchtime lectures (☎677 8099 for details).

In the **north transept**, look for the Romanesque carvings on the capitals of the archways: a troupe of musicians as you go in, and two human faces being absorbed by griffins (symbolizing wealth) at the exit into the aisle of the choir. The **south transept** is notable for its tiered tomb of the nineteenth earl of Kildare. There are also two medieval effigies in the adjoining Chapel of St Laurence O'Toole (see below), one of whom is reputed to be the wife or sister of Strongbow.

In the ambulatory, look out for a **mummified cat and rat** known to generations of Dublin kids – the cat chased

CHRIST CHURCH CATHEDRAL

the rat into an organ pipe in the 1860s, where both perished. Of the three chapels extending off the choir, the right-hand one is the **Chapel of St Laud**, named after the fifth-century bishop of Coutances in Normandy. On the wall of Laud's chapel is a heart-shaped iron casket containing the heart of Archbishop Laurence O'Toole, the patron saint of Dublin, canonized after his death in Normandy. The original medieval floor tiles in the chapel were copied by the Victorians throughout the cathedral. The central chapel, dedicated to the Blessed Virgin Mary, is adorned by a tiny bronze *Virgin and Child* by contemporary artist Imogen Stuart, while to the left is the Chapel of St Edmund, dedicated to him by Strongbow and his knights.

The crypt and Treasures of Christ Church

Descend the stairs by the south transept to reach the **crypt**, the purest remnant of the twelfth-century cathedral (you can still see parts of the timber frame used during construction); formerly a storehouse for the trade in alcohol and tobacco, it's one of the largest crypts in Ireland and Britain. The grumpy-looking Charles I and II statues came from the city hall that stood opposite the cathedral until 1806, and the punishment-stocks remained in use in Christ Church Yard till 1870.

Part of the crypt is taken up with the **Treasures of Christ Church** exhibition (Mon–Fri 9.45am–5pm, Sat 10am–4.45pm, Sun 12.30–3.15pm; €3; pay at the turnstiles), which includes an interesting AV presentation on the history of the cathedral, as well as a miscellany of manuscripts and church crockery. Look out for a ropey-looking tabernacle and pair of candlesticks made for James II on his flight from England in 1689, when, for three months only, Latin Mass was again celebrated at Christ Church (the existing cathedral paraphernalia was hidden by quick-thinking Anglican officials under a bishop's coffin). In extravagant contrast is a chunky silver-gilt plate, around a yard wide, presented by King William III in thanksgiving for his victory at the Battle of the Boyne in 1690.

THE VIKINGS

The first Vikings to turn their attention to Ireland, in the eighth century, were Norwegian. Having overrun the Picts in the Hebrides, their first recorded raid on Ireland was in 795, and in 837 sixty longships sailed up the Liffey to attack inland; four years later the fortified port that was to become the town of Dyflin, an important trading post, was created. Though the settlement was plundered by Danish Vikings, and the Norsemen were forced out by the king of Leinster in 902, they returned fifteen years later, this time reinforcing their position by building defences at the base of the high ground around the "Dark Pool" and houses on the hillside above the quays.

Intermarriage with the Irish (the name Doyle, for example, derives from *Dubh Gaill*, meaning "dark-haired foreigners") encouraged the growth of a Hiberno-Norse culture, consolidated by the Norse king Sitric IV's conversion to Christianity (Brian Ború, king of Munster, despite being credited with "driving out the Danes" at the battle of Clontarf in 1014, valued the Norse trading links and let Sitric remain in Dyflin). Meanwhile, Danish Vikings were forging the Duchy of Normandy into a formidable power. Having conquered England in 1066, the Normans were invited by the Gaelic chieftain Diarmuid Mac Murchada to invade Ireland and restore him to the throne of Leinster, in return for making it subject to the king of England. The offer proved irresistible, and by 1170 they had routed the Hiberno-Norsemen from Dyflin, obliging those that remained to live in Oxmantown, across the river, where they gradually lost their ethnic identity and merged into the general population.

WOOD QUAY AND FISHAMBLE STREET

The most populous part of **Viking Dublin** covered the hillside by **Wood Quay** (Map 4, A5), in the area behind Christ Church that's now occupied by the gigantic **Civic Offices** of Dublin Corporation, a much-loathed lump known as "the bunkers". As layers of medieval timber structures were being destroyed by mechanical diggers, archeologists won an injunction allowing them to conduct an excavation of the site before remains of tenth-century Viking houses and quay walls, as well as the finds currently on show in the National Museum, were lost forever. As a token apology, the bunkers are surrounded by ornamental references to the Norsemen, with a wooden longship and brass images of axe-heads and other artefacts embedded on Wood Quay, and the outlines of a Viking house picked out on the slope behind Christ Church.

Twisting downhill from the cathedral, **Fishamble Street** has followed the same route for a millennium. A fish market for much of that time, it was the birthplace of Archbishop Ussher (of Trinity fame) and Henry Grattan, the founder of the Irish Parliament. Between the *Handel Hotel* and the *Chorus Café*, a white arch and a low red-brick wall are all that's left of **Neal's Music Hall**, where Handel conducted the combined choirs of Christ Church and St Patrick's in the first performance of his *Messiah* in 1742. Ladies were asked not to wear hoops in their crinolines so that more people could attend, since proceeds went to charity. Swift's verdict was, "Oh, a German, a genius, a prodigy". In the private garden beyond the white arch, Handel's reward is a statue of him conducting in the nude, perched on a set of organ pipes. Excerpts from the *Messiah* are performed here on the anniversary of the event (April 13, throughout the day).

ST AUDOEN'S

Map 5, E7. Church of Ireland St Audoen's May Sat & Sun
9.30am–5.30pm; June–Sept daily 9.30am–5.30pm; last admission
4.45pm; €1.90.

Just to the west of Christ Church and Dublinia, on the corner of High Street and Bridge Street, stand two churches
dedicated to St Audoen (in French, Ouen, seventh-century
bishop of Rouen and the patron saint of Normandy). The
Protestant **St Audoen's**, built around 1190, is now partly
administered by Dúchas, the Heritage Service, as an
intriguing tourist site, though there are still services every
Sunday at 10.15am – the church has been continuously
used for worship for over eight centuries, longer than any
other in Dublin.

The most fascinating aspect of a visit is seeing the physi-
cal evidence of how the church's fortunes waxed and waned
over the centuries. As it prospered through close association
with the city's guilds, a **chancel** was built onto the original
single-naved church around 1300; then, in 1431, **St Anne's
Guild Chapel** was added, making a two-aisled nave. The
latter is now the main exhibition area, with interesting displays on the parish and the guilds and, on the south wall, a
panoramic panel highlighting the architectural features from
different eras, from a fifteenth-century window built to
shed extra light after the building's extension to a simple
nineteenth-century grave slab.

A quirky series of leaflets, available at the information desk,
gives potted biographies of sixteen of the leading figures
interred at St Audoen's, as "companions during your visit".

In 1455 the addition of the large **Portlester Chapel**
marked the zenith of the church's size and fortune. Around
this time, St Audoen's was the top parish church among

Dublin's leading families, who sought to worship and be buried here. After the Reformation, however, many members of the all-important Guild of St Anne refused to become Protestant and withdrew money from the church. The congregation declined and by the nineteenth century St Audoen's had retreated to its original single nave, by the simple expediency of removing the roofs from the other parts of the church and letting them rot. You can now poke around the open-air chancel and Portlester Chapel, where, before the building was declared a national monument, locals would hang their washing out to dry.

A guide will escort you into the present (and original) parish church, which includes a fine, scalloped **font** from the time of the church's founding. Beyond the deeply moulded Romanesque **doorway** (also original) stands the big crowd-pleaser, the **Lucky Stone**: this unprepossessing ninth-century grave slab has been credited with all manner of powers – glowing, groaning, rolling and even assuming human form – and has been worn down to a smooth sheen over the centuries with supplicants stroking and kissing it for luck.

After the Catholics were displaced by the Reformation, they used a chapel on Bridge Street until the Emancipation enabled them to build their own St Audoen's on the adjacent hilltop in 1846. As Maurice Craig wrote, "It looks like some impregnable fortress of the faith, its rugged calp masonry battened like a medieval castle to its base, pierced only by windows at the very top and crowned with the cross which breaks up the silhouette against the sky." The door is flanked by two giant turtle shells from the South Pacific, given by a sea captain to his brother, the parish priest. Catholic St Audoen's celebrates Mass at 11am on Sundays.

Behind the Protestant church, steps descend to thirteenth-century **St Audoen's Arch**, the only remaining gate in the **Norman city walls** – a dramatic, though heavily restored remnant stretching for 219yd along Cook Street, 23ft high and tipped with battlements.

TAILOR'S HALL AND ON TO ST PATRICK'S

At St Audoen's you're well-placed to continue westwards to the Guinness Storehouse in the Liberties (see p.122), or you can continue your exploration of the old city by crossing High Street and heading down Back Lane, before turning right onto Nicholas Street towards St Patrick's Cathedral. On Back Lane stands Dublin's last surviving guildhall, **Tailors' Hall** (Map 5, F8). This modest brick structure, built between 1703 and 1707, was rescued from demolition when An Taisce (the Irish Heritage Trust) bought the building in 1966 and restored it as their headquarters. Its assembly hall contains a plaque listing the masters of the tailors' guild from 1491 to 1841 and a gallery from which Wolfe Tone and Napper Tandy addressed the "Back Lane Parliament" in 1792 (see box on p.116). The building is not open to the public.

The slums around St Patrick's were considered among the worst in Europe prior to their demolition in the 1890s, when they were replaced by the **Iveagh Buildings**, a model housing estate built by the Guinness family. Its decorative main block stands on the east side of **St Patrick's Park** (Map 4, A7), once the cathedral green, where Cromwell's troops planted cabbages and thereby introduced them to Ireland.

ST PATRICK'S CATHEDRAL

Map 4, A8. March–Oct daily 9am–6pm; Nov–Feb Mon–Fri 9am–6pm, Sat 9am–5pm, Sun 10am–3pm; €3.50. ⓦwww.stpatrickscathedral.ie.

ST PATRICK'S CATHEDRAL

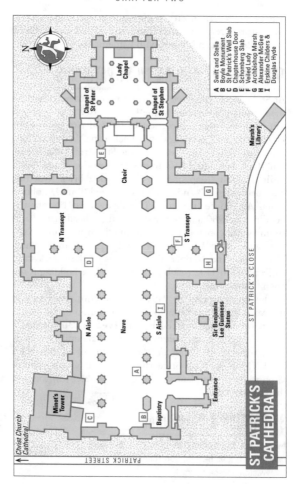

ST PATRICK'S CATHEDRAL

A Swift and Stella
B Boyle Monument
C St Patrick's Well Slab
D Chapterhouse Door
E Schomberg Slab
F Veiled Lady
G Archbishop Marsh
H Alexander McGee
I Erskine Childers &
   Douglas Hyde

Like Christ Church, **St Patrick's** was restored by the Victorians, though it seems closer to its origins than Christ Church and is altogether quirkier, thanks to its array of odd memorials. The cathedral stands on one of Dublin's earliest Christian sites, where St Patrick is said to have baptized converts in a well (c. 450). Bishop John Comyn founded St Patrick's in 1191 in order to create his own diocese beyond the city walls. However, it was Archbishop Henry de Londres who raised it to cathedral status and entirely rebuilt it (1220–70) at the same time as completing Christ Church. In 1544 the vaulting of the nave collapsed, and in 1649 it was used as a stable by Cromwell's cavalry, hastening St Patrick's decline into separate chapels serving different communities. Eventually, in the 1860s, Sir Benjamin Guinness – who is commemorated by a prominent statue outside the main door – commissioned Thomas Drew to reconstruct the cathedral, setting a precedent for the restoration of Christ Church.

The sombre **exterior** is dominated by the fourteenth-century **Minot's Tower**. Oddly misaligned with the rest of the cathedral, the tower seems to have been built for defence, a precaution necessitated by St Patrick's exposed location outside the city walls.

The interior

St Patrick's is the longest medieval church in Ireland, and its **interior** is majestically proportioned, the nave and transepts scrutinized by enigmatic **figures** carved on the pillars of the aisles. (Don't miss the Veiled Lady in the south transept or the gruesome monsters dotted along the nave.) Most visitors make a short beeline for the **graves of Jonathan Swift and Stella**, Swift's long-term partner, beneath brass tablets in the nave, just to the right of the entrance. On the nearby wall of the south aisle are a bust of Swift and two

ST PATRICK'S CATHEDRAL

plaques bearing their epitaphs, penned by him. She is remembered in English as "Mrs Esther Johnson, better known to the world as Stella, under which she is celebrated in the writings of Dr Jonathan Swift, Dean of this cathedral." His is in Latin but a translation reads:

Here is laid the body of
Jonathan Swift, Doctor of Divinity,
Dean of this Cathedral Church,

JONATHAN SWIFT

Born at Hoey's Court near Dublin Castle in 1667, Jonathan Swift could read by the age of three, and at fifteen was accepted as a student at Trinity College. On graduating, he worked for the diplomat Sir William Temple and subsequently for the Church of England, hoping to secure "a fat deanery or a lean bishopric". This ambition clashed with his activities as a political pamphleteer, from 1704 onwards; as his pen had been deployed on behalf of the Tories, the incoming Whig administration of 1714 bore a grudge against Swift, who felt it wise to return to Dublin and take up the post of Dean of St Patrick's, which he had accepted the previous year.

Back home his commitment to Ireland and his social conscience grew, as expressed in a series of anonymous tracts during the 1720s. An early advocate of economic independence, Swift's *Proposal for the Universal Use of Irish Manufactures* argued that the Irish should burn all English imports, except coal. *The Drapier's Letters* exposed shady business deals, and *A Modest Proposal* bitterly suggested that the Irish poor could solve their problems by selling their babies to the rich, as food. He is now chiefly known for *Gulliver's Travels*, a dazzlingly diverse satire now too often misperceived as a children's story.

Besides his increasingly vitriolic writings, Swift was famous

Where fierce indignation can no longer
Rend the heart.
Go, traveller, and imitate, if you can
This earnest and dedicated
Champion of liberty.

There's also a copy of a tribute to Swift by his friend Alexander Pope, with whom he planned to share a home in retirement. Among other Swift memorabilia in this area are

for his eccentricities and his mysterious relationship with Esther Johnson, known as "Stella". The daughter of Sir William Temple's housekeeper, she was variously rumoured to have been Swift's niece or sister, his secret bride or his platonic companion. Whatever the truth, Swift was heartbroken by her death in 1728, finishing his *Journal to Stella* in the darkened cathedral on the nights following her burial.

His final years were overshadowed by a malady causing giddiness, which Swift mistook for symptoms of insanity. Eventually he did go mad, hailing the viceroy as "you fellow with the Blue String" and assaulting two clergymen in a carriage. As soon as Swift's death, in 1745, became public, admirers burst into the Deanery and cut off all his hair, carrying the locks away as souvenirs. In his will, he left money to build a mental hospital, St Patrick's, which was one of the first in Europe when it opened in 1749.

Given Swift's reputation as a Dubliner and a patriot, he was astonishingly rude about both, calling Dublin "the most disagreeable place in Europe, at least to any but those who have been accustomed to it from their youth", in which case "a jail might be preferable"; and averring that "no man is thoroughly miserable unless he be condemned to live in Ireland".

ST PATRICK'S CATHEDRAL

his pulpit and table, his death mask and a cast of his skull: both his and Stella's bodies were exhumed by Victorian phrenologists, studying the skulls of the famous.

Heading clockwise from Swift and Stella's graves, you can't miss the gigantic **Boyle monument**, which teems with painted figures of the fifteen children borne by Katherine Fenton, the "dearest, dear wife" of Richard Boyle, Earl of Cork. Erected in 1632, it originally stood near the altar but was moved after the viceroy objected to churchgoers being forced to pray "crouching to an Earl of Cork and his lady. . . or to those sea nymphs his daughters, with coronets upon their heads, their hair dishevelled, down upon their shoulders". The earl got his revenge years later by engineering Viceroy Wentworth's execution.

His heir, **Robert Boyle**, is given a niche of his own on the monument. Robert is famous above all for formulating Boyle's Law on the relationship between the pressure, volume and temperature of gases. He is less well-known for leaving a legacy to fund eight sermons a year, refuting "Atheists, Theists, Pagans, Jews and Mohammedans".

In the northwest corner of the nave lies a stone **slab** with a Celtic cross that once marked the site of St Patrick's well in the park alongside the cathedral. Marble statues and plaques commemorating such luminaries as the Marquis of Buckingham, the first Grand Master of the Knights of St Patrick, portrayed in the extravagant robes of the order, and the harpist Turlough Carolan, the "last of the Irish bards", are ranged along the north aisle.

At the junction with the north transept is a curious **wooden door**, which once belonged to the cathedral's chapterhouse. In 1492, so the story goes, a quarrel arose between soldiers of the earls of Kildare and Ormond. Ormond barricaded himself in the chapter house, where-upon Kildare, eager to end hostilities, cut a hole in the door and stuck his arm through, inviting Ormond to shake hands. Peace was restored, and so the expression "chancing your arm" entered the English language. The north transept itself is hung with flags of the Irish regiments of the British army; 49,400 Irishmen died in World War I alone.

Until 1869 the **choir** was used for investitures of the Knights of St Patrick – hence the helmets, swords and banners above the stalls, scathingly described by Thackeray as "tawdry old rags and gimcracks" representing a "humbug of chivalry". A plain black slab in the north aisle of the choir honours Duke Frederick **Schomberg**, who advised William of Orange to come to Ireland in 1686 but was slain at the ensuing Battle of the Boyne. As the tablet above relates, his heirs didn't care to erect a memorial, so his admirers had to make amends; in Swift's words, "The renown of his valour had greater power among strangers than had ties of blood among his kith and kin." On the opposite side of the choir in the **Chapel of St Stephen**, you can see the armchair used by William at the thanksgiving service after his victory at the Boyne. Also note the plaque commemorating Sir Benjamin Guinness's daughter, beneath a window inscribed "I was thirsty and ye gave me a drink."

The **south transept** (once the chapter house where Kildare chanced his arm) contains magnificent stained-glass **windows** and various opulent funerary monuments – that of Archbishop Marsh (see p.112) is the finest surviving carving by Grinling Gibbons in Ireland. In one corner of the transept is a small tablet dedicated by Swift to his manservant, Alexander McGee, "in memory of his discretion, fidelity and diligence in that humble station". McGee's discretion in the libel case arising from *The Drapier's Letters* (purportedly written by a humble tailor) saved Swift from financial ruin.

Returning to the **south aisle** you'll find memorials to eminent Irish Protestants of the twentieth century, starting with a bust of Erskine Childers (Irish president 1973–74), whose father was executed by the Free State during the Civil War. The label relates how Childers never spoke of the war because his father made him promise on the eve of his execution not to do anything that might promote bitterness among the Irish people. The adjacent plaque in Irish honours Douglas Hyde, the founder of the Gaelic League, who became Ireland's first president. At his funeral service in 1949, former government colleagues waited outside St Patrick's in their cars, adhering to a ruling which forbade them to enter a Protestant cathedral.

MARSH'S LIBRARY

Map 4, A8. Mon & Wed–Fri 10am–12.45pm & 2–5pm, Sat 10.30am–12.45pm; €2.50. ⓦwww.marshlibrary.ie.

Beside St Patrick's Cathedral, a crenellated wall with an arched gateway surrounds a Georgian edifice half faced in stone to match the cathedral. This is **Marsh's Library**, the oldest public library in Ireland, opened to "All Graduates and Gentlemen" in 1707. Its founder, Archbishop Narcissus Marsh, was a scholar and scientist who translated the Old Testament into Irish and first used the word "microphone" in his own works on acoustics. The core of the library is the collection of Edward Stillingfleet, archbishop of Worcester, whose entire accumulation of 10,000 books Marsh bought for £2500; donations by other clerics and bibliophiles have boosted the tally to 25,000 printed books and 300 manuscripts.

Built by Sir William Robinson (the architect of Dublin Castle), Marsh's is a charming example of an eighteenth-century scholar's library, consisting of two L-shaped rooms whose oak bookcases have carved and lettered gables crowned by a bishop's mitre, and three alcoves, or "cages", where readers were locked in with rare books. The middle one contains a cast of Stella's skull, and a case displays books owned by Swift, including a *History of the Great Rebellion*, with pencilled notations disparaging the Scots. The bindery for the conservation and repair of antique books (featured in *Ulysses*) has had the odd task of treating bullet-marks, as Marsh's Library was peppered by shots aimed at the nearby Jacob's Biscuit Factory during the Easter Rising.

AUNGIER STREET

Between Marsh's Library and St Stephen's Green is an area of run-down flats bisected by **Aungier Street** (Map 4, C8), the seedier continuation of South Great George's Street at the Temple Bar end. Aungier Street is named after Francis Aungier, who developed this area on land seized from the Whitefriars Priory in 1537. An anonymous pamphlet of 1725 (possibly written by Swift) describes a throng of "Bawds with band-boxes, borrowed smocks, and scoured manteaus", apothecaries carrying "purges and potions" and "lap-dogs cleaning and dressing to go to church with their ladies". Comparatively little has changed today, as Chinese herbalists jostle with dodgy gentlemen's sporting clubs and adult shops, though the Whitefriars are back.

Raised in 1827 on the site of the dissolved Carmelite priory, **Whitefriar Street Carmelite Church** (Map 4, C7; Mon–Fri 8am–3.15pm, Sun 8am–7pm, bank holidays 10am–1pm) caters to a wide cross-section of Catholic worshippers, with a panoply of shrines and kitsch statuary. **Our Lady of Dublin**, a life-size, fifteenth-century oak statue of the Virgin and Child, takes pride of place by the entrance, the only wooden image to have survived the sack of Ireland's monasteries. Hollowed out and used as a pig trough, it was rescued in the 1820s by Father Spratt, the priest who re-founded the church, from a junk shop near St Mary's Abbey, whence it probably came. There was no sign, however, of the statue's silver crown, which was said to have been used for the mock coronation of Lambert Simnel (see p.99), but has now been replaced by a gaudy, multi-coloured affair. Whitefriar Street is also the scene of many romantic pledges, as a casket on the north side of the church supposedly enshrines the remains of St Valentine, donated by Pope Gregory XVI in 1835.

The Liberties and Kilmainham

To the west of St Patrick's Cathedral lies the sprawling district of the **Liberties**, named after the patchwork of parishes with charters giving its residents "freedom from toll, passage, portage, lestage, pavage, quayage and carriage". Originally the area was known as Meath's Liberty, after the Earl of Meath who invited Huguenot refugees from France to settle in the quarter known as The Coombe in 1650. Over the following sixty years the 10,000 Huguenots who settled here had a profound effect on the small and undeveloped city, introducing poplin- and silk-weaving, founding a horticultural society and encouraging the wine trade. However, the area's prosperity was severely undermined during the late seventeenth century by the imposition of hefty duties on Irish exports to Britain. Conditions worsened even further during the 1770s, when the area's textile industry encountered competition from imported Indian muslin and French silks – over 19,000 weavers faced unemployment. To protect their jobs, they formed gangs who went about cutting "every foreign dress worn by man or woman, no matter of what rank" and kid-

WOLF TONE, THE UNITED IRISHMEN AND THE REBELLION OF 1798

The French Revolution of 1789 had a profound effect on Ireland, where the credo *Liberté, Egalité, Fraternité* inspired a Protestant barrister, Theobald Wolfe Tone, to issue *An Argument on Behalf of the Catholics in Ireland* (1791), urging all denominations to unite in the cause of Irish freedom. Within months of its publication, societies of United Irishmen were formed in Dublin and Belfast, aiming to achieve the emancipation of Catholics and Dissenters. Though their "Back Lane Parliament" avowed change by constitutional means, the movement turned towards revolution after Wolfe Tone, forced to flee Ireland in 1795 to escape a charge of treason, travelled to the new republics of the USA and France seeking support for an insurrection.

Tone secured French governmental support for an invasion, and a force under General Hoche set sail in the winter of 1796. However, atrocious weather conditions prevented the landing at Bantry Bay in County Cork and the invasion was aborted. Undeterred, Tone and the French planned a second attempt to coincide with the rebellion of 1798. This was to be the first major rising against British rule since the seventeenth century, and it set a precedent for future attempts. Nevertheless, plans for the revolt were dealt a severe blow when, in March of 1798, most of the leaders of the National Directory of the United Irishmen were arrested in Dublin on the word of spies who had infiltrated their movement. The leader, Lord Edward Fitzgerald, a radical aristocrat who had renounced his title, evaded arrest – but his freedom was shortlived as two months later he was

napping haberdashers, dragging them through the mud to Weaver's Square where they were tarred and feathered. Such interventions mattered little, except to the victims, captured and mortally wounded. With rebellious sentiments mounting, martial law was imposed, but nonetheless, local uprisings took place in County Dublin, County Mayo, County Antrim and particularly County Wexford, where rebels made progress towards Dublin before being defeated in the town of Arklow. These local rebellions were virtually over when an 1100-strong French invasion force landed near Killala in County Mayo in August. After some success, the Franco–Irish army was defeated in County Longford on September 8. More than 11,000 Irish fell in battle and 2000 were hanged or deported; the British lost 1600 men. In November a second French force, with Wolfe Tone on board, was intercepted in Lough Swilly, off Donegal. Sentenced to death and denied the honour of a firing squad, Wolfe Tone cut his throat with a penknife to avoid being hanged, drawn and quartered as a traitor.

Henceforth revered as the founder of Irish Republicanism, Wolfe Tone was buried at Bodenstown in County Kildare – a place of pilgrimage for many Nationalists. On the anniversary of his birth (June 20, 1763), members of the Fianna Fáil party travel here to pay their respects. In Dublin itself, Tone's death mask is on display in the crypt of St Michan's Church (see p.116).

In contrast, critics of Wolfe Tone argue that his actions destroyed any chance of the Anglo–Irish ruling class conceding reforms, for in response to the 1798 Rebellion Britain engineered the Act of Union, which dissolved the Irish Parliament and fettered Ireland to Britain more strongly than ever.

and the Liberties deteriorated rapidly to slum level. As an American doctor wrote sarcastically: "Winds and rain have *liberty* to enter freely through the windows of half the houses

– the pigs have *liberty* to ramble about – the landlord has *liberty* to take possession of most of his tenements – the silk-weaver has *liberty* to starve or beg."

Although the slums have long been cleared, the Liberties have maintained their traditional self-sufficiency, and many families are able to trace their local roots back for generations. However, there's little in the way of "sights" to attract tourists beyond the **antique shops** on Francis Street. Conversely, the area further west – **Kilmainham** – has less atmosphere but several bona fide attractions. The **Guinness Storehouse** off Rainsford Street reveals all you might wish to know about the famous stout produced at the adjacent Guinness Brewery. Further out, the former Royal Hospital Kilmainham houses the **Irish Museum of Modern Art**, a venue for temporary exhibitions of contemporary work. Nearby is **Kilmainham Gaol**, a prison indelibly associated with the struggle for Irish independence and now a fascinating museum of penal and revolutionary history.

WEST FROM FRANCIS STREET

Francis Street (Map 5, E8) has become one of the centres of Dublin's **antiques** trade, with numerous shops down the road past the defunct **Iveagh Market Hall**. As its name suggests, this was another bequest by Lord Iveagh of the Guinness family, who is said to have been used as the model for the winking face that's among the stone heads carved above the arches of the hall.

At the bottom of Francis Street you'll find **The Coombe** (Map 3, E6), an ancient route and still one of the Liberties' main thoroughfares. Slum clearances have spared the **gateway** of the old Coombe Maternity Hospital, founded in 1826 as a result of the plight of two poor women and their newborn babies, who died in a blizzard while attempting to reach the Rotunda Hospital on the northside. Inscribed in concrete behind the gateway is an odd list of nicknames of well-known Dublin characters including Bang Bang, a shell-shocked veteran famous for "shooting" people with an imaginary gun, who died in 1981. Other intriguing names include Jembo No Toes, Damn the Weather and Johnny Forty Goats. **Meath Street**, across the road from the gateway, is the site of an indoor **market** (Thurs–Sat 10am–5pm) for cut-price clothes and tat – nothing to get excited about, but a good place to imbibe the atmosphere of the Liberties. Meath Street itself is replete with the kind of old-fashioned, useful shops (including a surprising number of butchers) that have long died out in more fashionable parts of the city.

At the north end of Meath Street you'll come to **Thomas Street West** (Map 5, D8), leading from High Street to the Guinness Brewery, on the middle section of which stands the **Church of SS Augustine and John**, possessor of Dublin's tallest spire; it was designed by Edward Pugin, whose father, Augustus, played a leading role in Britain's Gothic Revival. A discreet plaque some 200 yards away on *Iaws Pub* commemorates the arrest of Lord Edward Fitzgerald, a leader of the 1798 Rebellion, who died of wounds received in the struggle.

THE GUINNESS BREWERY AND STOREHOUSE

Thomas Street West becomes James's Street as it passes the **Guinness Brewery** (Map 5, B7), whose chimneys, tanks and wonderful aroma dominate the neighbourhood. The St James's Gate Brewery, as it's sometimes known, covers 64 acres, making it one of the largest in the world. However, when 34-year-old Arthur Guinness leased the derelict brewery in 1759, the industry in Dublin was at a low ebb; ale was notoriously bad, and whiskey, gin or poteen were preferred

WEST FROM FRANCIS STREET

ROBERT EMMET

The Thomas Street West area is associated with a brief insurrection in 1803, led by 24-year-old Robert Emmet. The youngest son of a distinguished Dublin doctor and brother of Thomas Emmet, a leading United Irishman, Robert was too young to take part in the 1798 rebellion, but in that year he followed in his brother's footsteps by becoming the leader of the United Irish movement at Trinity College. In protest at a clampdown on United Irish activities at the college, Emmet took his name off the college register and began to formulate plans for his own uprising. He sought help from the French and in an effort to secure weapons sailed to France in 1802, only to be frustrated by the French leadership's lack of commitment to his cause.

He returned to Ireland in October of the same year and set about executing a plan for rebellions in Dublin and Ulster. Having abandoned the idea of staging an insurrection to coincide with a French invasion of Britain, on July 23, 1803, Emmet put into action a plan to take Dublin Castle, which held the British forces' arsenal. The consequent killing of popular Chief Justice Lord Kilwarden and his nephew lost Emmet a lot of support, and the rebellion soon degenerated into a drunken fiasco, with Emmet's forces failing even to reach the Castle. Emmet was forced to flee, but rather than leave the country he returned to see his lover Sarah Curran, and was captured in a house near Harold's Cross in Dublin. Sentenced to death, Emmet assured his immortality with an eloquent oration which ended: "when my nation takes her place among the nations of the earth, then, and not till then, let my epitaph be written." Emmet was hanged and decapitated outside St Catherine's Church on Thomas Street West on September 20, aged 25.

throughout rural Ireland. Although he began by brewing ale, Guinness soon switched to producing a new black beverage called "porter" (because of its popularity with the porters at London's Covent Garden and Billingsgate markets). His new formula proved so successful that it was being exported to England within a decade; by the nineteenth century brewing had become such a major industry in Ireland and Britain that brewers were elevated to the House of Lords. An old joke has an outraged peer of ancient lineage asking about an ennobled member of the Guinness family "Who is this fellow Moyne, anyway?" the reply being "Moyne's a Guinness". Today, the Guinness Brewery produces around 2,500,000 pints a day, constituting about sixty percent of Ireland's total production, and is the world's largest exporter of beer, exporting some 300 million pints a year.

**The Guinness Storehouse is open daily 9.30am–5pm;
€12. It's reachable on bus #51B, #78A or #206 from
Aston Quay, and #123 from O'Connell St or Dame St.**

Sadly, the brewery is not open to the public, but you can learn all about the company and its products at the **Guinness Storehouse** (Map 5, C8), a seven-storey building off Rainsford Street (parallel to Thomas Street West), which has been converted into a shrine to the dark stuff. The building's design, in which glass, escalators and stainless steel predominate, is strangely reminiscent of the Pompidou Centre in Paris. The **first floor** guides visitors through the brewing process, emphasising the stout's four ingredients (water, barley, hops and malt) and covering areas such as the lost art of barrel-making – there were once some 250,000 casks in the Guinness cooperage yard, stacked in massive wooden pyramids – and the export of the brew around the world; there's also a surviving engine from the yard's own railway system. The **second floor** has some of the most intriguing exhibits, including an array of Guinness's award-winning **advertisements**, from the work of John Gilroy, whose animal cartoons and painful puns are still used to this day, to modern masterpieces such as the surfing ad (which led the Irish singer-songwriter Christy Moore to ponder "how yer man stayed up on that surfboard after fourteen pints of stout"). Also present is the **Downhill Harp**, an example of the old brass-strung form of the instrument, plucked with the fingernails, upon which the Guinness logo is based – this particular harp is noteworthy for having been played by Denis Hempson (or Hempsey) at the 1792 Belfast Harp Festival. Skip the third floor (which houses the Guinness learning centre – a business and conference suite) and the fourth (unless you want to join the visitors from around the world who've left messages on the so-called "Home" noticeboard) and take the lift to the Gravity Bar on the **top floor**. Here you'll be poured a pint of what is arguably the best Guinness in Dublin – arguably because the honours traditionally went to *Mulligan's* pub in Poolbeg Street, which still has its supporters (see p.291). Whatever the case, you can savour your drink while enjoying superb panoramic views of Dublin and its surrounding country-side.

If you fancy a further pint, there's another bar and a restaurant on the fifth floor, while the ground floor shop stocks all manner of souvenirs bearing the company logo.

To the north of the Storehouse, across Thomas Street West, rises the 150ft **St Patrick's Tower**, the tallest smock windmill (ie with a revolving top) in the British Isles. Originally used to facilitate work at Roe's Distillery on the other side of Watling Street from the Guinness Brewery, it's topped with a St Patrick's weathervane, but no longer has any sails.

ST PATRICK'S AND ST JAMES'S HOSPITALS

Further along Thomas Street West, the road forks at an obelisk that's optimistically equipped with four sundials. The road to the right, Bow Lane West, leads off to **St Patrick's Hospital** (Map 5, A7), known as "Swift's Hospital", having been founded for the care of the mentally ill by **Jonathan Swift** in 1749 (see p.108), whose bequest included a witty explanation: "He gave the little wealth he had, to build a house for fools and mad: And shew'd by one satiric touch, No nation wanted it so much." The larger **St James's Hospital** (Map 3, C5), off nearby James's Street, incorporates part of the old South Dublin Union, a nineteenth-century workhouse that was a rebel stronghold during the Easter Rising. Before becoming a workhouse it had been a foundling's hospital, where conditions were so wretched that over forty thousand babies died in thirty years.

IRISH MUSEUM OF MODERN ART

Map 3, B5. Tues–Sat 10am–5.30pm, Sun and Bank Holidays noon–5.30pm; free. ⊛www.modernart.ie.
Bus #78A, #79 or #90 from Aston Quay.

To get to the **Irish Museum of Modern Art** (IMMA), it's best to follow Bow Lane West as far as *Murray's* bar, from where you follow the road opposite, Irwin Street, which leads to the back entrance of the museum. Much criticized when it opened in 1991, the IMMA is now acknowledged to have proven its worth. The project was backed by the government of Charles Haughey, but many felt that the IR£20 million spent on converting a derelict hospital into a gallery could have been better used for buying artworks, and the end result was reviled as a blank space which denied the character of the building. Criticism has faded as IMMA has increased its holdings through bequests and loans and asserted its stature with bold exhibitions. There is no permanent display, only temporary shows, often half a dozen or more at a time, some being sited in the newly converted Deputy Master's House just outside the museum's east wing.

Free guided tours of IMMA exhibitions are available on Wednesdays and Fridays at 2.30pm, and Sundays at 12.15pm.

You can usually expect several **exhibitions** of paintings and sculptures on loan, and others selected from IMMA's holdings. Items on long loan from other galleries include works by Picasso, Miró and Braque, and contemporary artists like Gilbert and George, Damien Hirst, Tracey Emin, Julian Schnabel and Rachel Whiteread. Irish artists, such as Oisín Kelly, Felim Egan and Brian Maguire are usually well-represented. There's a good **bookshop** and a fine **café** in the basement of the north wing.

IMMA occupies the former **Royal Hospital Kilmainham**. Built in 1680–87 by Sir William Robinson (who restored Dublin Castle), this was one of the first classical-style public buildings in Ireland. Austerely elegant in shades of grey, it was modelled on Les Invalides in Paris and served as a home for retired veterans. Its rules decreed that if any inmate "presumed to marry, he be immediately turned out of the house and the hospital clothes taken from him". Near IMMA's main entrance in the south wing, a small **heritage exhibition**, including a video presentation, recounts some of the Royal Hospital's history. Group tours (Tues–Fri 10am, 11.45am, 2.30pm & 4pm; free; places must be booked two weeks in advance on ☎612 9900) are available of the north wing, whose lofty chapel has a magnificent Baroque ceiling and woodcarvings by the Huguenot master James Tarbery. You'll also see the panelled

IRISH MUSEUM OF MODERN ART

Great Hall, hung with portraits of monarchs and viceroys, and the Master's Residence.

When leaving the IMMA, depart by the arch in the west wing and aim for the **Kilmainham Gate** (Map 3, A5) at the end of a tree-lined avenue. Formerly the Richmond Tower and sited at Watling Street Bridge near the Guinness Brewery, it was moved here in 1846 to improve access to Heuston Station. The avenue passes by **Bully's Acre**, one of Dublin's oldest cemeteries, where the son and grandson of Brian Boru (see p.356) were reputedly buried after the victory over the Danes in 1014, and brings you out across the main road from Kilmainham Gaol – the greatest attraction in this part of town.

KILMAINHAM GAOL

Map 3, A6. April–Sept daily 9.30am–4.45pm; Oct–March Mon–Sat 9.30am–4pm; Sun 10am–4.45pm; €4.40. ⓦwww.heritageireland.ie. Bus #51, #51B, #78A or #79 from the city centre.

A forbidding hulk on Inchicore Road, **Kilmainham Gaol** is enshrined in Irish history as a symbol of political martyrdom and oppression. Opened in 1796, Kilmainham replaced an earlier prison that epitomized the evils criticized by the English penal reformer John Howard, whose improvements were first applied in Ireland. Howard advocated the separation of prisoners to prevent criminal associations and encourage individuals to repent in solitude, a policy adopted at Kilmainham. In accordance with his stress on hygiene, the new jail was sited on a hill to ensure good ventilation. Unfortunately, it was built from a limestone that weeps in wet weather, so perennial damp and cold took a heavy toll on prisoners' health.

Over the 128 years of Kilmainham's existence, some 100,000 men and women passed through its gates. Between 1845 and 1847, at the height of the Great Famine, it was

swamped with destitute folk jailed for stealing food or beg-
ging, resulting in **wretched conditions** that made a
mockery of Howard's intentions. Only after the Famine had
abated did reformers build a new east wing. Turned into a
military detention barracks in 1911, Kilmainham later held
insurgents from the 1916 Easter Rising. Even the end of
British rule brought no respite, for 150 Republican women
were interned here during the Civil War, including the
daughter and the widow of two of the martyrs of 1916.
The last prisoner to be released by the Free State in 1924
was Éamon de Valera – subsequently elected prime minister, then president, of Ireland.

Shut down after the Civil War, Kilmainham was left to
rot till 1960, when volunteers (many of them ex-inmates)
began to restore it as a memorial. Now one of Dublin's best
museums, it can be visited only on **guided tours** (every
45min, until 1hr 15min before closing). While waiting to
start the tour, visit the **exhibition** behind the reception
area. The ground floor exhibits cover conditions at
Kilmainham, crime in the nineteenth century (including an
early "mugshot" camera) and the development of hanging.
It was a Dublin surgeon, Samuel Haughton, who devised
the "long drop" method, which the Victorians saw as an
improvement on the old "short drop" technique which
slowly asphyxiated victims. Altogether, over 140 hangings
took place at Kilmainham, 24 of them involving political
prisoners. Upstairs covers the struggle for independence,
with numerous items relating to the Fenians, the Easter
Rising and the IRA, including a letter instructing under-
Secretary Burke (one of the men assassinated in Phoenix
Park – see p.175) to release Charles Stewart Parnell, and a
list of Michael Collins' agents in the Dublin postal service
entitled "Friends of Kathleen Ní Houlihan" (her name
being one of the many euphemisms for Ireland). Look out

also for the small gallery which contains a bust of the Republican leader Ernie O'Malley – who actually managed to escape from the gaol in 1921.

The tour

The **guided tour** begins in the **East Wing**, a lofty hall flanked by tiers of cells and walkways. Like many Victorian prisons, Kilmainham was based on philosopher Jeremy Bentham's "Panopticon", a layout that maximized light (thought to be morally uplifting) and enabled constant surveillance of prisoners. Its architect, John McCurdy, had previously refurbished the *Shelbourne Hotel*.

In the Catholic **chapel** you'll hear the moving story of Joseph Plunkett and Grace Gifford, who were married here on the eve of Plunkett's execution. British soldiers stood by with fixed bayonets as the vows were read. Immediately afterwards the newlyweds were separated; later they were granted ten minutes together – timed by a stopwatch – before Plunkett was taken out and shot. A short, emotive **film** on the history of Kilmainham and the struggle for independence leaves you in no doubt as to who the heroes and villains were, gliding over the moral and political ambiguities of the Civil War.

The prison's conditions become evident in the crumbling **West Wing**: there was no glass in the windows nor any heating (there still isn't), while an hour of candlelight each evening was the sole concession to comfort. Occasionally, certain prisoners were accorded privileges – when Parnell was jailed for sedition, he had a room with a fireplace and armchairs and was allowed to give interviews. Most, however, were obliged to do hard labour, oakum-picking or stone-breaking; the practice of "shot-drill" – passing cannonballs from one man to another – ceased after a prisoner

KILMAINHAM GAOL

threw one at the governor. Among those held here were Robert Emmet, the "Invincibles", and fourteen leaders of the Easter Rising on the night before their executions.

You will also see the **yacht** *Asgard*, used by Erskine Childers and his sister Molly to run guns into Ireland in 1914. Despite being half-English, Childers was a devoted Republican and opposed the treaty which established the Irish Free State. In 1922 he was captured and executed by the Free State authorities at Beggar's Bush Barracks (see p.183) for the possession of a revolver given to him by Collins, when the two were still allies.

The inner northside

M uch of Dublin's **inner northside** was developed
in the eighteenth century by Luke Gardiner, a
banker who married into the Mountjoys and
Blessingtons, both prominent (and related) Anglo-Irish
families, and bought land – which had once belonged to St
Mary's Abbey – from families who had fallen on hard times.
Profits from commercial premises near the quays were used
to finance **Henrietta Street**, a luxury development on
Constitution Hill (then open country), followed by
Gardiner's Mall (now **O'Connell Street**). With the establishment of the Wide Streets Commission in 1757,
Gardiner's schemes became the blueprint for a whole new
city of elegant terraces and squares for society's elite. Soon,
however, rival developments on the southside began to
entice them away, and the Act of Union sank the property
market after Gardiner's grandson had invested heavily in
Mountjoy Square. This proved to be the swan song of the
dynasty, and of the northside too.

Although the present-day northside has many inner city
problems, it also displays a vitality often missing in the more
sedate southside. Certainly not as well preserved as its counterpart across the river, the northside's significance lies more
in its associations with events and movements central to
Dublin and Ireland's history – the **GPO**, which played a

seminal role in the history of independent Ireland, is probably its most important landmark. And as home to the **Abbey Theatre**, **Dublin Writers Museum**, **Hugh Lane Municipal Gallery of Modern Art** and **Croke Park GAA Museum**, the northside offers plenty of cultural interest too.

O'CONNELL STREET LOWER

Map 4, D3.

The commercial hub of the northside and Dublin's main axis, O'Connell Street was laid out by Luke Gardiner in the 1740s. Originally envisaged as an exclusive residential square, it became a public highway following the completion of Gandon's Carlisle Bridge (1794), causing Dublin's centre of gravity to shift eastwards from the old axis of Capel Street. Renamed Sackville Street after the British viceroy, the avenue was almost 50 yards wide (one of the broadest in Europe) and lined with grand edifices that predated the Parisian boulevards of Haussmann by a century. Today the street's facades are marred by neon and plastic (leading one wag to describe its architectural style as "neon classical"), particularly near the Liffey along **O'Connell Street Lower**, where buildings were destroyed in the Easter Rising of 1916.

At the southern end of the street near O'Connell Bridge stands the imposing statue of "The Liberator", **Daniel O'Connell** (Map 4, E4). Smack in the centre of the street and staring proudly towards the river, O'Connell is flanked at ground level by winged figures symbolizing his patriotism, courage, eloquence and fidelity (closer inspection of "courage" reveals a bullet hole gained during the War of Independence). Born in 1775 near Cahirciveen in County Kerry, O'Connell was elected MP for Clare in 1828 but barred from entering parliament on the grounds of his

Catholicism. He was re-elected in 1830 after Emancipation, becoming MP for Dublin two years later and, subsequently, the city's first Catholic Lord Mayor in 1841 (the same year that he lost his seat, but won a new one in Cork). Having secured the backing of Dublin Corporation for the repeal of the Union in 1843, he then organized mass rallies to put pressure on Westminster. These alarmed the British to such an extent that 35,000 troops under the command of Wellington were dispatched to Ireland and, early the following year, O'Connell and five of his supporters were jailed for conspiracy to raise sedition. Though he was released after a few months, O'Connell's health was failing; the Famine decimated his rural following, and in 1847 he left Ireland, dying in Genoa on his way to Rome. His statue (financed by subscription) was unveiled in 1882, and his name was bestowed upon the new, wider bridge that replaced the Carlisle. Soon, Dubliners began to call Sackville Street "O'Connell Street", though its name was not officially changed until 1924. Directly below the O'Connell statue you can see one of the city's first public examples of nationalist iconography in the female figure of Erin, unshackled and pointing towards her liberator.

Further north, where the street is crossed by Abbey Street, the central strip is graced by smaller statues of two lesser nineteenth-century figures: William Smith O'Brien, leader of the Young Ireland Party, and Sir John Gray, the publisher of the influential *Freeman's Journal*. More arresting is the statue of **Jim Larkin**, the trade unionist who led Dublin's workers during the lock-out strike of 1913 (see p.363). It shows Larkin haranguing a crowd, as he did from a window of the *Imperial Hotel* across the road (now the site of Clery's department store – see p.331), shortly before mounted police charged the demonstrators, killing two and injuring hundreds. The figure's huge hands, outstretched in a classic oratorical pose, give a sense of Larkin's imposing physicality; a larger-than-life demagogue, he made a formidable opponent – as Dublin's employers found out. At the foot of the statue is a poetic inscription in Gaelic, which, roughly translated, means "the great appear great because we are on our knees; let us rise". Larkin was actually deported from the USA in 1923 on the grounds of alleged anarchism, but continued to head the Irish Transport and General Workers' Union before he was expelled from that a year later. He remained a forceful activist until his death in 1947.

THE ABBEY THEATRE

Map 4, E3.

On the eastern side of O'Connell Street Lower on Abbey Street Lower stands the **Abbey Theatre** – the present structure, a much-maligned piece of 1960s Modernism made slightly more distinguished by the addition of a portico in 1991, is a replacement for the original Abbey, which burned down in 1951. Ireland's national theatre, the Abbey has its beginnings in the Irish Literary Society founded by **W.B. Yeats** and **Douglas Hyde**, which, in 1899, became the Irish Literary Theatre. The site on Abbey Street (formerly a morgue) was bought by the English tea heiress Lady Gregory, the patron of Yeats and a driving force behind the Irish cultural revival at the turn of the nineteenth century, and the playhouse itself opened in 1904, with Yeats and Lady Gregory as its first directors. Their 1907 production of John Millington Synge's tragi-comedy *The Playboy of the Western World* caused outrage – one critic called it "the outpouring of a morbid, unhealthy mind ever seeking on the dunghill of life for the nastiness that lies concealed there" – and nightly affrays needed up to five hundred policemen to prevent bloodshed. In 1926 there was an equally fierce reaction to Seán O'Casey's *The Plough and the Stars*, which

SEÁN Ó RIADA AND THE CHIEFTAINS

A Cork-born classically trained composer, arranger and musician who had worked for Raidió Éireann, Seán Ó Riada served as musical director at the Abbey Theatre in the late 1950s. During his stint, he began to incorporate traditional themes into his compositions, most notably in his music for the film *Mise Éire*. He experimented with various musical settings and worked with a range of musicians before settling upon an ensemble, which adopted the name Ceoltóirí Chualann, to accompany the Abbey's plays.

During the 1960s, Ó Riada continued to work with the nucleus of this group on subsequent – and often significant – works, including the soundtrack to the film version of *The Playboy of the Western World*. In 1963 the group's uilleann piper and whistler, Paddy Moloney, was asked by the head of Claddagh Records (see p.328) to record an album. Moloney recruited fellow members of Ceoltóirí Chualann to record *The Chieftains*, never realizing that they were about to embark on a career spanning, to date, forty years and more than fifty albums and film soundtracks. The Chieftains went on to become an international byword for Irish traditional music, popular in places as far-flung as China and South America, though only two of the original members (Paddy Moloney and the fiddler Martin Fay) remain. In contrast, Ó Riada opted for an academic career, lecturing in music at University College Cork, though he continued to compose and, occasionally, perform with Ceoltóirí Chualann until his death in 1971.

took a cynical view of the Easter Rising and displayed the Free State flag in a pub frequented by prostitutes – as the audience booed on opening night, Yeats rebuked them, "You have disgraced yourselves again. Is this to be an ever-recurring celebration of the arrival of an Irish genius?"

As time went on, a general uneasiness about one theatre receiving the lion's share of state subsidies became widespread – a conviction that would lead to the establishment of the Gate Theatre (see p.141). The Abbey still produces dazzling drama, with two auditoriums and companies on the premises: the Abbey, devoted to the Irish classics and contemporary dramatists like Brian Friel and Frank McGuinness; and the **Peacock Theatre** (see p.313), which shows new experimental drama. There are hour-long backstage **tours** of the Abbey most Thursdays at 11am (€6; for further info and to book call ☏887 2223).

**For information on performances
at the Abbey Theatre, see p.000.**

THE GPO

Map 4, D3.

Back on O'Connell Street Lower, beyond Larkin's statue, looms the **General Post Office** (**GPO**) designed by Francis Johnston – the building's huge Ionic portico is still scarred by gunfire from the Easter Rising (see box, p.136), when it was used as the insurgents' headquarters. From its porch, Pádraig Pearse read the Proclamation of the Irish Republic to onlookers bemused by the sight of his men smashing windows and sandbagging them with mailbags. For six days they held out against British attacks, until the GPO was set ablaze and survivors retreated to nearby Moore Street, where Pearse and Connolly agreed to surrender (see p.139). Their subsequent martyrdom conferred iconic status on the Rising and on the GPO itself, which is still a focal point for political protests.

In the foyer, the building's historical significance is reinforced by a sequence of **paintings** by contemporary Irish artist Norman Teeling, depicting scenes from 1916. Near the foyer's main window stands the city's finest public **sculpture**, a bronze statue entitled *The Death of Cúchulainn*. Exquisitely wrought, it was created by Oliver Sheppard in 1935 and depicts the last moments of the mythical warrior. Legend has it that Cúchulainn tied himself to a tree so that he could fight even when dying – his enemies were so afraid to approach him they only did so when a raven rested on his shoulder, proving beyond doubt that he was actually dead. The statue also features in a hilarious episode in Samuel Beckett's *Murphy*, where one character attacks Cúchulainn's buttocks (though in reality the sculpture only depicts the top half of the warrior's body).

O'CONNELL STREET UPPER

North of the GPO, after the intersection of Henry Street and Earl Street North, is **O'Connell Street Upper** (Map 4, D2). At one time this section of O'Connell Street was dominated by **Nelson's Pillar**, located at the crossroads themselves and execrated by W.B. Yeats as "that monstrosity that destroys the view of the finest street in Europe". Erected 32 years before Nelson's Column in London's Trafalgar Square, this symbol of British imperialism survived several attempts to destroy it, until a bomb on the fiftieth anniversary of the Rising left it so damaged that it had to be demolished. Nelson's head now lies in Collins Barracks (see p.135), and the monument's demise put paid to an old joke that O'Connell Street had statues honouring three notorious adulterers: O'Connell, Nelson and Parnell (see p.143). The site of the pillar is intended to be occupied by a huge, illuminated stainless-steel spike, designed by London architect Ian Ritchie. It's meant to represent Dublin's hopes for the new millennium, but many commentators have argued that a city with a chronic heroin

THE EASTER RISING

The heroic Easter Rising of April 1916 was one of the key events leading to Irish self-government. At the time however, most Dubliners saw it as a calamity: many Nationalists regarded it as a botched and futile attempt, while Loyalists reckoned it high treason, fermented by Imperial Germany.

The Rising was conceived by the Irish Republican Brotherhood (IRB) or "Fenians", a revolutionary organization dating back to 1858, led by a new generation of activists including Pádraig Pearse and Joseph Plunkett. For manpower and arms they relied on support from two legal militias: the Citizen Army under James Connolly, who helped in drawing up the battle plan and was given operational command; and the Irish Volunteers headed by Éoin MacNeill, who only agreed to commit his forces after Pearse showed him a forged document from Dublin Castle, ordering the suppression of the Volunteers. The final element was a shipment of arms from Germany, whose delivery was to be arranged by Sir Roger Casement, a Sandycove-born ex-British diplomat turned Irish rebel.

Things started to go wrong quickly. The ship arrived prematurely and left without delivering its cargo, and Casement was caught by the British. MacNeill, on learning that he had been duped, revoked the mobilization order by placing notices in the Sunday papers, which resulted in only a minority of the 10,000 Volunteers turning up the next day. Though both mishaps foredoomed the Rising, its strategy was already flawed by Connolly's belief that "a capitalist government would never use artillery against private property". While the exact number of

problem doesn't need a steel needle as its focal point. Local wags have already dubbed it "the stiletto in the ghetto", continuing a tradition for caustic rhyming couplets. At the

O'CONNELL STREET UPPER

insurgents is uncertain (somewhere between 700 and 1750), the British ultimately committed over 20,000 troops to crush them.

The first shots were fired at noon on **Easter Monday**. A group of insurgents assaulted the castle, other units seized the GPO, the Four Courts and sites such as Jacob's Biscuit Factory and Jameson's Distillery, which overlooked the routes from British barracks into the centre. As Pearse emerged from the GPO to read the Proclamation of the Irish Republic, his comrades were fortifying their positions against a British response. Initial attacks were beaten back, but the tide turned once reinforcements arrived from England with artillery. After six days of bitter fighting, which destroyed Sackville Street and other areas, the insurgents surrendered and were led away through jeering crowds.

This reaction was perhaps to be expected, since the Rising left 1351 people dead or gravely wounded, 179 buildings smouldering, and much of Dublin's population needing aid. The hostility towards the rebels was exacerbated by the fact that the Rising occurred on the first anniversary of the battle of Gallipoli, when many Dublin families were in mourning for the menfolk who had perished there.

However, the British decision to execute the Proclamation's seven signatories and all the Volunteer leaders (except Éamonn de Valera, who received life imprisonment being technically stateless thanks to his American birth and Spanish father) completely backfired and catalysed new calls for Home Rule.

time of writing, the Spike had not yet been constructed and, indeed, rumour suggested that it might only eventually be half-built, leading one newspaper correspondent to

O'CONNELL STREET UPPER

write that, like the concept itself, the project would ultimately be "completely pointless".

In the 1980s the Corporation commissioned two other monuments along more whimsical lines, only one of which now remains in place. With its rakishly tilted hat and carefree air, the **James Joyce statue** outside *Café Kylemore* just down Earl Street North (Map 4, D3) captures the style of a writer who was always dapper despite his indigence. The other, the recumbent **Anna Livia Fountain**, representing Joyce's personification of the River Liffey in *Finnegans Wake*, used to sit on O'Connell Street Upper, but has been removed to make way for The Spike.

On the central strip of O'Connell Street Upper (Map 4, D2) stands a **statue of Father Matthew** (1790–1856), the "Apostle of Temperance", whose Pioneer Total Abstinence Movement, founded in 1838, persuaded five million Irish (out of eight million) to take a pledge of teetotalism, and reduced the production of whiskey by half; its influence is still widespread in a country that, despite the stereotypical image, has a higher percentage of non-drinkers than any other in Europe.

Many bus tours of the city and further afield (see pp.17 & 216) start at the offices of Bus Éireann and Dublin Bus, opposite the Father Matthew statue at no. 59 O'Connell St Upper.

On the corner of O'Connell Street Upper and Cathal Brugha Street, the **Gresham Hotel** (see p.245) is Dublin's finest after the *Shelbourne* and surpasses it for nostalgia. This was where Michael Collins often met his agents during the War of Independence. After the Nationalists split over the Anglo-Irish Treaty, the anti-Treaty "Irregulars" led by Cathal Brugha and de Valera made it their headquarters during the insurrection of July 1922. Following a week of fighting that left central Dublin in ruins for the second time in six years, Brugha ordered his men to surrender but refused to do so himself, and was mortally wounded outside the hotel. The building itself was destroyed in the fighting and rebuilt in the late 1920s.

O'Connell Street Upper ends at a crossroads, where the **Parnell Monument** proclaims in gold letters: "No man has a right to fix the boundary to the march of a nation. No man has a right to say to his country, Thus far shalt thou go and no further . . . "

MOORE STREET

Turn left off O'Connell Street Lower at the GPO and you're into Henry Street, an earthier version of Grafton Street, where black-market cigarettes are openly touted in front of department stores. Off to the right lies Moore Street, which from Monday to Saturday is more or less taken over by **Moore Street Market** (Map 4, D3; see p.332), where the loquacious vendors revel in their reputation as "true" Dubliners. The street also has historical significance; no. 16 was the site where survivors from the GPO laid up in the back of a fish-and-chip shop – they decided against a fighting retreat through Henry Street and Ormond market to avoid further civilian casualties and gave themselves up to British soldiers. Henry Street, Moore Street and Earl Street are all named after **Henry Moore, Earl of Drogheda**, who even managed to squeeze in a lane called "Of Lane" (now Moore Lane) leading into Drogheda Street, so that his name and title would be blazoned across maps of Dublin.

ST MARY'S PRO-CATHEDRAL

Map 4, E2. Daily 8am–6.30pm, Sun until 7pm.

On the other side of O'Connell Street Upper, and running parallel to it, Marlborough Street is home to **St Mary's Pro-Cathedral**. In 1814, Dublin's Protestants were up in arms about the plan to build a Catholic cathedral on O'Connell Street (where the GPO now stands), so the Castle decreed that St Mary's Pro-Cathedral be tucked away down a side road, with its facade, based on the Temple of Theseus in Athens, facing away from O'Connell Street. It was here, in 1847, that funeral rites were performed over the body of Daniel O'Connell, brought back from Genoa for burial in Prospect Cemetery (see p.204); crowds lined the streets all the way from the Custom House to the Marlborough Street Chapel (as it then was). St Mary's is Dublin's principal Catholic church and every Sunday at 11am you can hear Latin Mass sung by its famous male **Palestrina Choir**, where the tenor John McCormack began his career in 1904; otherwise, there's nothing to tempt you into the rather functional interior.

PARNELL SQUARE AND AROUND

At the end of O'Connell Street Upper lies **Parnell Square** (Map 4, C1), one of the few on the northside which wasn't begun by Luke Gardiner. The credit goes to Sir Benjamin Mosse, the surgeon who founded the **Rotunda Maternity Hospital**, which, when it opened in 1748, was the first purpose-built maternity hospital in Europe. Designed by Cassels, the architect of Leinster House, it retains a gorgeous Baroque chapel which, with the tarnished glory of the west facade, suggests how fine it must have once looked. Mosse funded the project by laying out a pleasure garden and organizing fancy dress balls and concerts to be held there, including the premiere of Handel's *Messiah*. The gardens fell out of fashion as the northside declined, but the Rotunda on the corner remained a concert hall until it became the Ambassador cinema (see p.297). (It had also previously witnessed the birth of Sinn Féin, founded by Arthur Griffith at a public meeting there in 1905.)

The Gate Theatre

Since 1930 the Assembly Rooms, to the east of the Square, have been home to the **Gate Theatre** (Map 4, D1), founded in 1928 by Hilton Edwards and Micheál MacLiammóir. Life-long partners, Edwards and MacLiammóir were in fact English; the latter (real name Michael Wilmore) started his career as a precocious young actor on the London stage before becoming enamoured with Ireland and its literary heritage (he also founded Taibhdhearc na Gaillimhe, a theatre dedicated to Irish language drama). Aside from setting up the theatre, MacLiammóir is also known for his portrayal of Wilde in one of the most famous productions to be staged at the Gate – the one-man show *The Importance of Being Oscar*, which ran from 1960 to 1975, with MacLiammóir performing the role 1384 times. Having been established as a showcase for European drama (it opened with *Peer Gynt*), the Gate quickly became a great rival to the Abbey (see p.132), which featured a predominantly Irish repertoire – the two theatres were nicknamed "Sodom and Begorrah" in some quarters, in reference to the Abbey's fondness for kitchen sink Irish drama and the sexuality of the founders of the Gate.

For more on the Gate, see p.312.

PARNELL SQUARE AND AROUND

CHARLES STEWART PARNELL

"There is something vulgar in all success. The greatest men fail, or seem to have failed." So said Oscar Wilde of Charles Stewart Parnell, the "uncrowned king of Ireland".

Parnell was born into the Anglo-Irish Protestant hierarchy in Avondale, County Wicklow, in 1846. His great-grandfather was Chancellor of the Irish Exchequer, and his mother the daughter of an American admiral, a connection that would subsequently bring financial rewards. Parnell's nationalism came to the fore early with his devotion to the Home Rule movement, calling for the restoration of Irish self-government. This ensured his election to parliament in 1875, where his approach was one of obstruction – to delay and interfere with the passing of Bills – a policy much approved by the militant Fenians. The latter's support lost him favour in certain circles, but led to his commitment to the cause of land reform – Parnell recognizing that the move towards Ireland's autonomy would never prosper while the rights of tenant-farmers lay unprotected – and in 1879 he became president of the Irish National Land League. He sought financial backing in the USA, raising the colossal sum of £70,000 and the next year, on re-election, became the leader of the Irish Home Rule Party.

The Phoenix Park Murders in 1882 (see p.175) marked a major turning point for the affairs of the Home Rule movement. Parnell had already found himself imprisoned in Kilmainham jail that year on charges of sedition for his Land League activities (the League was later declared illegal after urging tenants to withhold payments of rent to absentee landlords, but was revived in 1884) and attempts were made to implicate him in the murders. He denounced the crime in parliament and, in so doing, revitalized his own popularity at home, but Gladstone's Liberal government reacted by hurrying through a Prevention of Crimes Act, which, by temporarily abolishing trial by jury and increasing police powers, further diminished Ireland's administrative scope.

The Liberals' proposal to renew the Crimes Act in 1885 prompted Parnell to negotiate with the Tories, but the relationship didn't last long, and, with his support returned to the Liberals, he flung the Irish vote behind Gladstone, resulting in the fall of the short-lived first Salisbury administration. Returned to power, Gladstone was now committed to Home Rule but when the bill was put to parliament, his own party members defected and it was defeated. A consequent appeal to the country was overwhelmingly rejected and a new Tory government was elected in 1886 with a Unionist majority of more than a hundred. Parnell and the Irish Party no longer held the balance of power.

The affair that finally deposed Parnell, however, was personal rather than political. Named as co-respondent in a divorce case brought by Captain William O'Shea against his wife Katherine in 1890, his relationship with Kitty O'Shea became public knowledge. The decree was granted with costs against Parnell – public disgrace followed and he lost the chair of his party. Parnell now carried what was left of the fight back to Ireland but, with clerical condemnation there too, his credibility was destroyed. He died suddenly in 1891, five months after his marriage to Kitty, and, despite the notoriety of his latter years, 200,000 people jammed Dublin for his funeral.

PARNELL SQUARE AND AROUND

Around Parnell Square

Turning left at the Ambassador cinema and heading towards the west of Parnell Square you'll find **Patrick Conway's Pub** (Map 4, C2); established in 1745, it's the oldest on the northside and has been a haven for nervous fathers-to-be since the hospital opened. Originally named *Doyle's*, it was another of Collins' local haunts – having survived the Easter Rising, he surrendered to the British on the corner right outside the pub. This area has traditionally been a focal point for republicans, as evinced by the **Sinn Féin Bookshop** (Mon–Sat 11am–4pm) at 44 Parnell Square West; the basement at no. 46 next door was once used by Collins to brief his hit-team, "The Apostles". On the other side of the road stands the part of the Rotunda that still functions as a Maternity Hospital; in January 1922 the hospital briefly became the "Irish Soviet Republic" when it was seized by a band of dockers and the writer Liam O'Flaherty, protesting against unemployment. Their republic fell in three days without a shot being fired.

On the northern side of the square lies the **Garden of Remembrance** (Map 4, C1), dedicated to those who died for Irish freedom. The garden was created in 1966, the fiftieth anniversary of the Easter Rising, and carries its ideology very heavily. Celtic and Christian symbols are employed around the railings, while the pond in the middle is in the shape of a crucifix. The redeeming factor is the *Children of Lir* statue that adorns the western end of the garden. Hoping to create a new kind of nationalist iconography when he was given the commission for this statue, Oisín Kelly chose the myth of Lir, lord of the sea, whose four children by his first wife were turned into swans by her jealous sister Aoife, his second wife; the statue depicts the point at which they are transformed. Kelly felt that the swan, as an ideal of isolation and perfection, was a suitable symbol for contemporary Ireland.

During the 1760s and 1770s, Parnell Square North was Dublin's poshest address, nicknamed "Palace Row" and inhabited by the earls of Ormond and Charlemont. The needle-spired **Abbey Presbyterian Church** (Map 5, H3) on the corner is known as "Findlater's Church" after the grocer and brewer Alex Findlater, who financed its construction in 1864.

Hugh Lane Municipal Art Gallery

Map 5, G3. Tues–Thurs 9.30am–6pm, Fri & Sat 9.30am–5pm, Sun 11am–5pm; entrance to gallery free; Francis Bacon Studio €7.60. ⓦwww.hughlane.ie.
Bus #10, #11, #13, #16, #19, #121 and #122 from O'Connell St.

Former residence of the Earl of Charlemont, the **Hugh Lane Municipal Art Gallery** on Parnell Square North occupies a grey-stone townhouse designed by the Scottish architect Sir William Chambers. The gallery was founded in 1908 by Sir Hugh Lane (a nephew of Lady Gregory), who had intended to bequeath his entire collection, but – piqued by the Corporation's refusal to build a special gallery – added a codicil leaving just 39 works to "the nation", before dying aboard the *SS Lusitania* when it was sunk by a German U-boat in 1915. With Ireland's independence, the question of exactly *which* nation arose, and an unseemly wrangle began. It wasn't resolved till the 1980s, when the Irish and British governments agreed that half of Lane's bequest should remain in Dublin.

Though the mansion works well as a gallery, its modest size means that well-known pictures often disappear to make room for temporary exhibitions. The first room ahead of you after you enter the gallery includes works by **Pissarro** and **Monet** together with **Renoir**'s characteristic and expansive *Les Parapluies*. The most marked contrast in

PARNELL SQUARE AND AROUND

works is provided by the hanging of **Roderic O'Connor**'s splendidly insalubrious *Boulevard Raspail* adjacent to the stark realism provided by **Degas**' insouciant *Breton Girl*. To the left, the only other room currently devoted to the permanent collection features a number of nineteenth-century Italian paintings together with works by **Courbet** and **Corot**.

The Hugh Lane Gallery also hosts free classical music **concerts** at noon on Sundays during the winter, and offers lectures throughout the year.

The Francis Bacon Studio

Right at the very rear of the gallery lies the **Francis Bacon Studio** (tickets purchased in the gallery shop), transported from its original location at Reece Mews in London's South Kensington, where the artist lived and worked for the last thirty years of his life (he died in Madrid in 1992). Bacon was born in Dublin, at 63 Baggot Street Lower; after he died, his studio was donated to the gallery by his sole heir, John Edwards, and reconstructed here with astonishing precision.

A video of an interview with Melvyn Bragg, originally shown on *The South Bank Show*, introduces the artist at work in his studio, of which he aptly comments "This mess here around us is rather like my head". It isn't possible to enter the studio reconstruction itself, but its extraordinary clutter and some of the myriad objects present can be viewed through windows. Amongst the apparent debris is an old Bush record-player, empty champagne boxes and various books and photographs, together with the huge tins of matt vinyl which Bacon favoured, whose fumes exacerbated his asthma.

The surrounding rooms hold displays of memorabilia and details of the database of items found in the studio, but the crowning glory is unquestionably his five unfinished **paintings**, of which the subject of one, *Study after Velazquez 1950*, bears an uncanny resemblance to Ronald Reagan.

Dublin Writers Museum

Map 5, G3. Mon–Sat 10am–5pm, Sun & bank holidays 11am–5pm, July & Aug Mon–Fri until 6pm; €5.50. ⓦwww.visitdublin.com.

Two doors along from the Hugh Lane Gallery, the lovely Georgian mansion at 18 Parnell Square North houses the **Dublin Writers Museum**, a combination of tourist crowd-puller and serious literary venue. The ground-floor rooms constitute a whistle-stop tour of Irish literature from the first Gaelic rendition of the Old Testament (1645) to twentieth-century greats such as Shaw, Joyce and Beckett. Though the exhibits are fairly dull (a typewriter belonging to Brendan Behan – see box, overleaf – which he once threw through a pub window in a fit of rage, is as good as it gets), an accompanying guide tape canters through literary fashions and the lives of the writers in a light-hearted way.

Upstairs, the house itself is the main attraction. A staircase with stained-glass windows of the Muses and allegories of art, science, literature and music leads to a resplendent white and gold salon, the **Gallery of Writers**. The ceiling is by Michael Stapleton, Dublin's finest stuccoist, who learnt his art from the Swiss-Italian Francini brothers, while the door panels feature figures representing the months of the year and the quarters of the day, accompanied by aphorisms such as "Work is the great reality, Beauty is the great aim." Another room contains the **Gorham Library** of books by writers featured in the museum, and downstairs there's a well-stocked bookshop and a pleasant café. In the summer

PARNELL SQUARE AND AROUND

there's also a Zen garden, and *Chapter One* in the basement (see p.282) is one of the northside's best restaurants.

Next door is the Living Writers Centre, with an ongoing programme of lectures and seminars.

BRENDAN BEHAN

Born in 1923 and raised in Dublin's slums, Brendan Behan came from a family of learning and talent. While his mother had a full repertoire of rebel songs, his father read extensively, introducing his children to literature from an early age. Brendan's grandmother gave him a taste for alcohol before he was ten, and the Gaelic clubs around Parnell Square fuelled his passionate political ideals. Republican-inspired acts of violence landed him with hefty prison sentences throughout his early adult years, and while incarcerated he learned Irish and gathered material for his writing.

Success came with the 1956 London production of *The Quare Fellow*, a play depicting events in a prison the night before an execution. Behan's drunken tie-in interview with the BBC's Malcolm Muggeridge made him internationally notorious, and in both England and America he became a media star – the big, burly Irish wit, drunk and rebellious and outrageously entertaining. This same personality comes through in *The Hostage* and in the autobiographical *Borstal Boy*, both written in 1958. Ultimately, however, his image was to overshadow him, and Behan collapsed into alcoholism, his creative output dwindling along with his health. At his death in 1964 obituaries lamented the tragic loss of talent, but Dublin has always remembered him with affection – and numerous bars around the city sport photographs of the man as he was in his heyday.

THE JAMES JOYCE CULTURAL CENTRE

Map 5, H3. Mon–Sat 9.30am–5pm, Sun & Bank Holidays
12.30–5pm; €4.50. ⓦwww.jamesjoyce.ie.

From the Dublin Writers Museum, walk along Gardiner
Row and its continuation, Great Denmark Street, and turn
into North Great George's Street. Here, at no 35, the
James Joyce Centre taps deeper into the life of Dublin's
most celebrated author, whose formative years were spent
on the northside. His life and genius are the subject of
guided tours of the beautifully restored Georgian townhouse – which has a regular programme of films and lectures, runs walking tours of Joyce's haunts, and organizes
the Bloomsday celebrations (see p.338). One of the directors, Ken Monaghan, is a nephew of Joyce and gives talks
on their family life by arrangement.

Copies of Joyce's cherished **family portraits** are on display around the centre (the originals are held by Buffalo
University), while on the top floor is a **Ulysses portrait
gallery** featuring some of the three hundred characters
who appear in the novel. In the tea room at the back of the
house you can see the front door of 7 Eccles Street, home
of Leopold Bloom. The **Guinness Library** of Joycean literature is available to visitors, along with audio-readings of
his works, so aficionados can really get stuck in.

The **house** itself, with its superlative stucco mouldings
by Stapleton, was restored following a campaign in the
1980s, led by the Joyce scholar Senator David Norris, to
save it from demolition. It was built for the Earl of
Kenmare's annual visits to Dublin to attend parliament, but
was promptly sold after the Act of Union. At the turn of
the twentieth century, the ground floor was leased by Denis
Maginni, a well-known dancing teacher (really named

A JOYCEAN WALK ON THE NORTHSIDE

Having been reared by governesses and sent to an exclusive Jesuit boarding school when he was six, James Joyce was unprepared for the misfortunes that struck him at the age of eleven. Shortly after he was withdrawn from school with his fees unpaid, the family quit their last fashionable address in Blackrock, and two caravans transported all their possessions across the "gloomy foggy city" to the impoverished northside. As an adult, Joyce occupied several flats in the neighbourhood before leaving Ireland for good in 1912.

The James Joyce Centre is only a few doors downhill from 38 North Great George's Street, the last residence of the Trinity Provost John Pentland Mahaffy, who loathed Joyce, describing him as "a living argument in favour of my contention that it was a mistake to establish a separate university for the aborigines of this island – for the corner-boys who spit into the Liffey."

Were it not for the intervention of a Jesuit priest, Joyce might not have gone to university at all. Initially, he and his brother Stanislaus attended a local Christian Brothers school, before his old teacher, Father Conmee, arranged for them to study for free at Belvedere College – one of the most prestigious schools in Ireland. The college is on Great Denmark Street, at the top of North Great George's Street (Map 5, H3).

The Joyce family occupied a series of properties, moving on

Maginnis; he dropped the "s" to sound sophisticated) who makes six appearances in *Ulysses*. After his departure it continued as a ballroom run by Dickie Graham (whose grandson is a director of the Centre), a popular place with British officers, who never suspected that the basement was an arms dump for a Nationalist group that secretly met upstairs. It's said that de Valera was once smuggled into the house disguised as a woman.

THE JAMES JOYCE CULTURAL CENTRE

as they fell behind with the rent. One of the first was a boarding-house at **no. 29 Hardwicke St** (Map 5, H2), recalled as "a kip" run by Mrs Mooney, who connived to pimp her daughter in *Dubliners*. At the end of the street, **St George's Church** (now deconsecrated) is a frequent landmark in Joyce's stories.

Across Dorset Street Lower on nearby Eccles Street (Map 5, H2), Joyce confided to his friend J.F. Byrne about his fears that his wife Nora had been unfaithful. Byrne assured him that it was untrue, and in gratitude Joyce honoured her fidelity by making 7 Eccles St the fictional abode of Leopold and Molly Bloom. *Ulysses* fans must be satisfied with a plaque, as the house was demolished in 1982 to build an annexe to the Maternity Hospital. Following Dorset Street Lower downhill turn right into Gardiner Street Upper (Map 5, H1) and you'll pass the **Jesuit House** where Stephen Dedalus "wondered vaguely which window would be his if he joined the order"; it's beside the Church of St Francis Xavier, where Father Conmee was a priest.

Finally, turn off the northeast corner of Mountjoy Square to find **14 Fitzgibbon Street** (Map 5, I2), the "bare cheerless house" that was the Joyces' first home on the northside in 1894. There is nothing to mark their stay, for the house lay derelict until 1997, but it is now being renovated and may eventually sport a plaque.

THE NATIONAL WAX MUSEUM AND THE BLACK CHURCH

Map 5, G3.

To the northwest of Parnell Square, on the corner of Granby Row and Dorset Street, Dublin's **National Wax Museum** (Mon–Sat 10am–5.30pm, Sun noon–5.30pm;

€4.40) is a good way to while away a wet afternoon if you have kids to entertain. There are over 300 exhibits, from Irish writers and rock stars to the Teletubbies and the Simpsons. Young children will enjoy the crawl-through tunnels and the hall of mirrors, while older kids will get a kick out of the chamber of horrors. Some of the tableaux now seem quite dated, though the presence of an extremely sinister-looking Charles Haughey in a gathering of *Taoisigh* (Prime Ministers) might seem prescient considering various allegations regarding his involvement in financial scandals, while other exhibits, such as the sports and music sections (where Bob Geldof looks strangely uncomfortable between Michael Jackson and Garth Brooks) could be improved by new additions. However, it's all pretty enjoyable and there's a chance to see the actual Popemobile used by John Paul II on his visit to Ireland in 1979.

Across Dorset Street, the spiky finials of the **Black Church** brood over St Mary's Place on the brow of the hill. Built of black Dublin calp, this former St Mary's Chapel of Ease is associated with two legends. One holds that it was designed to be turned into a redoubt should the Catholics rise up (as the Protestants feared in the 1820s); the other is that you can summon up the Devil by walking three times around the outside of the church. It has now been deconsecrated and serves as an office.

TO KING'S INNS AND BEYOND

Head downhill into Bolton Street (the southern continuation of Dorset Street Upper) and you enter a world far from the current gentrification of the northside's Georgian squares. The Corporation estates which replaced the worst of the old tenements in the 1960s and 1970s have themselves become a blighted area, where **Henrietta Street** (Map 5, F4), dowdy as it is, comes as a pleasant respite. Laid

MOUNTJOY PRISON

Built in 1847 as a holding centre for transportees to the Australian penal colonies, Mountjoy Prison (Map 3, F1), north of Parnell Square over the North Circular road, is the oldest working jail in Dublin, and the most notorious. Early last century its notoriety was due to the political prisoners held here, first by the British (1916–21) and then by the Free State (1922–23). It was here that the Irish Republican Brotherhood leader Thomas Ashe died after being force-fed during a hunger-strike in 1917 – one of the first instances of what would become a favoured method of protest by imprisoned Republicans. In 1939, Mountjoy also saw the first hunger-strike by IRA men demanding to be recognized as political prisoners, a status that the Free State refused to concede, and one which the British would later refuse in Northern Ireland. After the IRA sprung three prisoners by landing a hijacked helicopter in the yard in 1973, most Republican inmates were moved to the high-security jail at Portlaoise. Nowadays, Mountjoy is Dublin's main jail for remand prisoners and convicted felons, and such is the scale of drug-related crime that you don't have to spend long on the northside to meet people who've served time or have friends or relatives in "The Joy". Its most famous inmate was Brendan Behan (see box on p.148), who was sentenced to fourteen years for the attempted shooting of a policeman but amnestied after five years in 1946. During his time inside Behan penned his ballad *The Auld Triangle*, recorded by The Dubliners amongst others, which describes prison conditions.

out by Gardiner between 1730 and 1740, it was the first street in Dublin to contain aristocratic mansions, and it remained a most fashionable address until the 1800s. Its residents included three earls, an archbishop of Ireland and the Speaker of the House of Commons; Gardiner himself lived at no. 10. In 1908, many houses were stripped and turned into tenements by Alderman Meade, who managed to squeeze seventy tenants into the huge four-bay house at no. 7 alone. As Joyce recalled in *Dubliners*, a "horde of grimy children . . . stood or ran in the roadway, or crawled up the steps before the gaping doors, or squatted like mice upon the thresholds".

The street ends at the rear gate of **King's Inns** (Map 5, F4), crowned by the British lion and unicorn. The third of James Gandon's great edifices, it was designed in 1795 but work on it was delayed for seven years due to residents' objections that it would spoil their view; when completed in 1817 it was unanimously praised. The Inns are the home of Irish Bar, where Ireland's barristers are trained. During daylight hours you can walk through the courtyard to see the allegorical reliefs out front and the view of Dublin from **Constitution Hill**. It was at Glasmanogue (as the hill was anciently called) that St Patrick is said to have stopped on his way north after converting Dubliners to Christianity and, looking back on the settlement, prophesied, "Although it's small and miserable now, there'll be a big town here in time to come. It will be spoken of far and near and will keep increasing until it becomes the chief town of the kingdom."

Having come this far, there are two routes back to the river and the centre of town, with a few sights along the way. The easiest and most obvious route to take is to head west along King Street North, turning down Church Street (Map 5, E5–E6) past St Michan's Church to the Four Courts – for details of both, see Chapter six. Alternatively, before reaching Church Street by this route, turn down Halston Street, past the former **Black Dog Debtors Prison** (Map 4, A3). Built in 1760, it had a window on the pavement where prisoners could beg for alms, and stood right beside the Green Street Court where Robert Emmet, the Young Irelanders and the "Invincibles" were later tried. This street leads on to Little Britain Street, which has a lively **fruit and veg market** early in the morning (daily), and, on the corner with Halston Street, the most recent incarnation of *Barney Kiernan's* pub, the setting for the "Cyclops" chapter of *Ulysses*.

THE GAA MUSEUM, CROKE PARK

Map 3, H1. Museum: May–Sept daily 9.30am–5pm; Oct–April Tues–Sat 10am–5pm, Sun noon–5pm; open to New Stand ticketholders only on match days; €5. ⓦwww.gaa.ie.
Bus #3, #11, #11A, #16, #16A or #123 from O'Connell St to Clonliffe Rd.

The **GAA Museum**, located on what is effectively the inner northside's boundary, is part of Dublin's famous Gaelic sports ground, **Croke Park**. Somewhat surprisingly, considering the amateur status of matches staged here, the impressive stadium itself has the fourth largest capacity in Europe (following Barcelona's Nou Camp, Real Madrid's Bernabeu and the San Siro in Milan), holding around 85,000 spectators. Housed under the New Stand, the **museum** is one of the finest in Dublin and holds much interest even if you know little or nothing about the sports organized by the GAA (Gaelic Athletic Association).

Tours of the GAA museum and stadium are available
daily at 12.30pm & 3pm; but call ☏855 8176
for information on weekend availability.

From its formation in 1884, the history of the GAA has been inextricably linked with that of Irish nationalism. Indeed, for a time in 1887 the Irish Republican Brotherhood took control of the organization, and in 1918

it was banned for several months by the British government. The GAA still prohibits "foreign" matches from taking place on its grounds and recently, amid some controver-
sy, refused to amend its rules to allow Ireland's national
Association Football team to play at Croke Park. The
importance of the GAA in the political arena is highlighted
in several of the museum's displays, most notably the audio-
visual presentation "**National Awakening**" which relates
the details of one of the great tragedies of Irish history,
Bloody Sunday. On November 21, 1920, the notorious
Black and Tans opened fire on the crowd and players at a
match being played in Croke Park, in reprisal for the killing
of fourteen members of the so-called Cairo gang – British
Secret Service agents – by Michael Collins' men. Twelve
people were killed, including Tipperary captain Michael
Hogan, after whom one of the stands in the stadium is
named.

The museum also has a wealth of exhibits relating to the
tradition of Gaelic sports, ranging from a cast of a tenth-
century High Cross panel depicting David slaying the lion
(featured for its inclusion of a hurling ball and stick), to
interactive stands testing one's mastery of the fundamental
skills of **hurling** and **Gaelic football**. Other displays highlight such sporting luminaries as Jack Lynch, an adept player
of both hurling and Gaelic football for Cork, who remains
the only person to have won six successive All-Ireland
Senior medals and became more widely known as a politi-
cian, twice becoming *Taoiseach* (in 1966 and 1977). There is
also a complete computer database of all the All-Ireland
finals which allows you to watch the highlights of any
match from 1931. Your visit ends with a high-tempo fifteen-minute film entitled *A Day in September*, which captures all the excitement, colour and energy both on and off
the field on finals day in Croke Park.

The Quays: the Custom House to Phoenix Park

Temple Bar isn't the only area in Dublin to reflect the changing economic face of the city; **the quays** on the Liffey's north bank also give a very visible indication of the amount of money currently being invested in urban renewal, with traditional working-class areas the focus of intense **property speculation** and **development**. From the Sheriff Street area in the east to Smithfield and Stoneybatter in the west, you can see the awkward coexistence of old and new, with beggars and barristers, Georgian piles and Corporation sink-estates standing cheek-by-jowl. Nevertheless, this stretch along the river has much to recommend it, not least the fact that it boasts two of Dublin's architectural masterpieces, the **Custom House** and the **Four Courts** – remnants of the city's Georgian heyday. A walk along the north-bank quays can also be a very pleasant experience (endless streams of noisy trucks aside), and offers plenty of interesting detours: **St Michan's Church** for its ghoulish "mummies", **Smithfield** for its monthly horse sales, and, for anyone who enjoys a tipple, the **Old Jameson Distillery**.

THE LIFFEY AND ITS BRIDGES

The distance from the source of the Liffey in the Wicklow Mountains to its outlet in Dublin Bay is just 13 miles as the crow flies, but the river itself meanders for over 80 miles. Over the thousand years of Dublin's history, the Liffey has become narrower and deeper as channels have been dredged, land reclaimed and the harbour moved eastwards. The River Poddle, which once joined the Liffey at the "Dark Pool" which gave Dublin its name (Dyflin), now runs underground for three miles, to trickle from a grating on the south bank, downstream from the Grattan Bridge.

Dublin's early settlements grew around the river and from it the city derives its Gaelic name Báile Áth Cliath ("Ford of the Hurdles"). The oldest bridge still standing dates from 1764; formerly Queen's Bridge, it is now known as Mellowes Bridge, named after the IRA "Irregular" Liam Mellowes (other Nationalists so honoured are Sean Heuston, Rory O'Moore and O'Donovan Rossa). While each bridge had localized effects, the Carlisle (now O'Connell) Bridge changed Dublin's axis from east–west to north–south, which had profound consequences for the city's development. Today fifteen bridges of varying shapes and sizes cross the Liffey, including the universally loved Ha'penny Bridge (1816) – which derives its name from the halfpenny toll that was levied on pedestrians wishing to cross until early last century – and the adjacent Millennium footbridge to the ugly railway Loop Line Bridge, which ruins the view of Gandon's Custom House.

Exploration further west by catching a bus (#25, #25A, #26, #66 or #67 from Wellington Quay) along the quays will take you to the **Collins Barracks**, home to the decorative arts collection of the National Museum of Ireland, and, further out, the huge expanse of **Phoenix Park**, one of Europe's largest urban parks and home to the Irish president, Ashtown Castle and Dublin Zoo.

THE CUSTOM HOUSE

Map 4, F3.

The majestic **Custom House**, just east of Eden Quay, has surveyed Dublin's waterfront for the past two hundred years. James Gandon, an English architect of Huguenot extraction, was considering going to work in St Petersburg when he received the commission for the building in 1781. Gandon went on to create the Four Courts and the Carlisle Bridge, and spent the rest of his life in Ireland, dying at his home in Lucan at the age of eighty.

Plans for the Custom House were opposed by dockers and merchants, who resented moving from the old customs point near Crane Lane, and by the genteel residents of Gardiner Street Lower, who feared contagion by a "low and vulgar crowd with the manners of Billingsgate". When petitions failed, objectors resorted to violence (Gandon wore a sword to work) and took heart that the proposed site was on a submerged mudflat where it seemed impossible to lay foundations. Gandon, however, confounded everyone by building atop a layer of four-inch-thick pine planks. The Custom House took ten years to construct and cost the unheard-of sum of £500,000 sterling; nine years later the Act of Union made it redundant by transferring customs and excise to London. In 1921 the building was set alight by Sinn Féiners and totally gutted. Initial rebuilding by the new Irish government later that decade radically

THE CUSTOM HOUSE

MONTO

The fears of residents of Gardiner Street Lower proved justified after the docks moved east and the area west of where Connolly Station now stands declined into "one of the most dreadful dens of immorality in Europe". Known as Monto, after Montgomery (now Foley) Street, its seedy terraces were once inhabited by some 1600 prostitutes, who were tolerated by the police, provided they kept within the quarter. Among the flashy houses on Railway Street were Mrs Arnott's, Mrs Meehan's and Mrs Cohen's – all of which feature in the *Nighttown* section of *Ulysses*.

Although the departure of British troops in 1922 hit trade badly, Monto was dealt its fatal blow during Lent in 1925, when Catholic vigilantes and the Garda raided the area, resulting in 120 arrests (including a member of the Dáil). The following morning the Legion of Mary arrived on the scene, pinning holy pictures on brothel doors and offering succour to penitent prostitutes.

During the 1930s much of the area was swept away and replaced by Corporation flats, now among the most run-down in Dublin. Bloomsday tours skip "Nighttown", and you'd be wise to do the same.

altered its internal structure and made some significant changes to its facade; however, further reconstruction work in the 1980s sought to restate the splendour of Gandon's initial design. Since its restoration, the building has housed government offices.

The Custom House displays some of the most elaborate **architectural detailing** in the city: its embankment facade, 114 yards long, is flanked by arcades culminating in pavilions crowned with the arms of Ireland; around the building are fourteen heads representing Ireland's rivers (only the Liffey is a goddess, above the main door), and cattle heads symbolizing the beef trade; the Four Continents (Africa, America, Asia and Europe) decorate the rear portico; and the 115-foot-high dome, modelled upon Wren's design of Greenwich Hospital, is topped by a figure of Commerce.

The **visitor centre** (mid-March to Nov Mon–Fri 10am–12.30pm, Sat & Sun 2–5pm; Dec to mid-March Wed–Fri 10am–12.30pm, Sun 2–5pm; €1) occupies the only part of the interior to survive the fire, on the first floor. The displays on transport and revenue collection in Ireland are pretty insipid, but it's worth paying the entrance fee to enjoy the beauty of Gandon's original decor.

AROUND THE CUSTOM HOUSE

After viewing the Custom House you can make a loop around it by walking up **Beresford Place** (Map 4, F3), the first road upriver. Downstream, the tall edifice of **Liberty Hall** rises above the city's skyline; built in the 1960s, it's home to the country's largest trade union, SIPTU (the Services, Industrial, Professional and Technical Union). Facing Liberty Hall, near the Custom House railings, you'll see a statue to the father of Irish trade unionism, **James Connolly**, with the flag of the Irish Citizen Army ("the Plough and the Stars") in the background, proclaiming that "the cause of labour is the cause of Ireland: the cause of Ireland is the cause of labour". A little further along, where the road meets with Abbey Street Lower, the forecourt of the Irish Life building holds the *Chariot of Life* sculpture by Oisín Kelly – the struggle between the charioteer and his horses is Kelly's interpretation of the fight between reason and passion. Continuing round as Beresford Place becomes Memorial Road, **Busáras**, Dublin's central bus station, comes into view; in 1953 it was the city's first unashamedly

MATT TALBOT

Born in 1856, Matt Talbot grew up in Dublin's Monto district and started work at the age of twelve at a wine merchant's, where he began to steal ale – by the time he was sixteen he was working at the Custom House docks and drinking whiskey. Alcoholism was rife in Dublin, and Talbot spent much of his early life alternating between work and drink, funding his habit by pawning possessions and stealing.

One day in 1884, having forgone his usual visit to the pub, he returned home sober, and so commenced a period of abstinence that would last the rest of his life. He took the oath of Temperance (see p.138), attended Mass daily (partly to avoid his drinking friends) and started donating to charity. Self-denial became a defining feature of Talbot's fervent piety: he fasted, remained on his knees for long periods, and slept on a plank, with a wooden block for a pillow. He would often be found, trance-like, with arms spread in the shape of a Cross, but the extent of his devotions came to light when, having been ill for some time, he collapsed and died outside his church in June 1925. The coroner, on removing his clothing, found large chains wrapped around his body – Talbot's sign of his "slavery" to God. For many, the discovery confirmed Talbot as a truly holy man. In 1931, his cause for canonization was brought before the pope, and is still under consideration today.

Modernist building, but it has since been overshadowed by a younger contender, the Financial Services Centre (Map 4, H3). Designed in 1987, this monument to Ireland's economic success provides the backdrop to a group of figures commemorating the country's greatest economic and human catastrophe, the **Great Famine**.

At the end of the loop is the Talbot Memorial Bridge (Map 4, G3), on the other side of which you'll find the **City**

Arts Centre; its gallery (daily 11am–5pm; free) features socially related exhibits by amateur and professional artists, while the centre also hosts a mix of music, theatre and dance. Opposite the building is a statue of **Matt Talbot** (see box, opposite), after whom the bridge is named.

O'CONNELL BRIDGE TO THE FOUR COURTS

West of **O'Connell Bridge** (Map 4, E4), the **quays** really come alive: cars and pedestrians jostle for position, while red-headed children try to make some change by posing for tourists' photographs and street vendors try to do the same by selling posters of Irish Republican heroes.

Bachelor's Walk (Map 4, D4) was laid out in 1678 as an extension of the Ormond Quay, ending at Bagino Slip, where a ferry used to cross the Liffey. It's chiefly associated with a violent clash in 1914, when British troops fired on a crowd, killing four of them and wounding thirty-eight. Near the corner of Liffey Street (Map 4, C4) are The Winding Stair Bookshop (with a laid-back café where you can sit and gaze over the Ha'penny Bridge; see p.270) and a pair of life-size **statues** of two housewives taking a rest from shopping, irreverently known as the "Hags with the Bags".

Ormond Quay (Map 4, A5–C4) bears the name of one of the few viceroys who actually liked Dublin and is well remembered here. James Butler, the Duke of Ormond, served two terms (1662–69 and 1677–85) and did much to restore Dublin's pride after a century of intermittent war. Exiled in France when Cromwell was in power, Ormond was inspired by continental city planning and longed to tear down the old city and build anew. He then took advantage of the new Essex Bridge and laid out three quays along the north bank, which were to form the east–west axis of the city. This development spurred the growth of an extensive **market quarter** behind the quays.

Between Ormond's terms of office, the job was held by Arthur Capel, Earl of Essex, after whom a new bridge was named in 1676. Further downstream than the others, **Capel Street Bridge** (Map 4, B5; now Grattan Bridge) became the main crossing point over the Liffey and was to remain the marker for Dublin's north–south axis until the Carlisle Bridge was built, its role then being usurped by Sackville (now O'Connell) Street. The well-to-do left the area, which soon assumed a more proletarian character owing to the nearby Ormond market. It still caters for tradesmen, and in and amongst the development blocks you'll spot dozens of tool shops, builders' merchants and greasy-spoon cafes.

Two blocks inland, the former **St Mary's Church** (Map 4, B3), built in 1697 on Mary Street, is now being redeveloped as a bar and restaurant complex. The church's history is associated with various Dublin personalities, though: here, Richard Brinsley Sheridan and Seán O'Casey were baptized, Arthur Guinness got married, John Wesley preached his first sermon in Ireland and Lord Norbury, the Hanging Judge of 1798, was buried. Wolfe Tone, one of the leaders of the 1798 Rebellion, was born opposite the church, where the Guardian Life Assurance building now stands. It's also strange to imagine that Joyce opened Ireland's first cinema at 45 Mary Street in 1909 – the Volta's diet of continental films was not to Dubliners' tastes, however, and his Italian backers sold out after a few months.

Turning west off Capel Street down Mary's Abbey, look out for a tiny cul-de-sac, Meetinghouse Lane, harbouring what's left of **St Mary's Abbey** (Map 4, B4; mid-June to mid-Sept Wed & Sun 10am–5pm; €1.20; ⓦwww .heritageireland.ie). The vaulted chamber of the chapter house is all that remains, but there's a model of how the complex once looked. Founded by the Benedictines in

1139 and transferred to the Cistercians eight years later, St Mary's was one of the most important monasteries in the country until the Reformation, when meetings of the Council of Ireland were held here. It was during such a meeting in 1534 that Silken Thomas Fitzgerald renounced his allegiance to Henry VIII and stormed out to raise a rebellion, only to be captured and executed the following year. The monastery was dissolved in 1539 and turned into a quarry in the seventeenth century, when its stones were used to build the Essex Bridge.

Returning to the quays you'll find the *Ormond Hotel* (Map 4, A5) whose bar and restaurant retains the name *Sirens*, since its erstwhile barmaids were likened to the alluring creatures by Joyce in his *Ulysses*.

The Four Courts

Map 5, E6.
Ormond Quay leads west into Inns Quay, site of the second of Gandon's masterpieces on the northside, the **Four Courts** – a perfect foil to the Custom House, were it not for a slight bend in the river that makes it impossible to view both buildings together from O'Connell Bridge. Built between 1786 and 1802 at a cost of £200,000 sterling, the courts provoked criticism of lawyers' "contemptible vanity" for having "the grandest building in Europe, in the world, to plead in". This failed to stop Gandon from undertaking another commission for the legal profession, King's Inns (see p.154). The courts and inns were originally located south of the river, but the latter moved to the site of the present-day Four Courts after Henry VIII gave the legal society land stolen from a Dominican convent; the courts moved north in the seventeenth century, whereupon the Society of Lawyers got their own premises on nearby Constitution Hill.

Like the GPO, the building is virtually synonymous with a specific event that was to have momentous consequences for Ireland – not the Easter Rising (when it fell to the insurgents without a shot being fired), but the **seizure of the Four Courts** by anti-Treaty Republicans in July 1921, an event that marked the onset of hostilities that led to the Civil War. Michael Collins saw it as a direct challenge to the Free State and shelled the rebels into submission. Before surrendering, they blew up the Public Records Office with two lorry-loads of gelignite, sending scraps of historic documents floating above Dublin. In an unwelcome message of congratulation to Collins, Churchill wrote: "The archives of the Four Courts may be scattered, but the title deeds of Ireland are safe."

If you're curious to observe a trial, the courts are open to the public (Mon–Fri 11am–1pm & 2–4pm).

ST MICHAN'S CHURCH

Map 5, E6. April–Oct Mon–Fri 10am–12.45pm & 2–4.45pm, Sat 10am–12.45pm; Nov–March Mon–Fri 12.30–3.30pm, Sat some hours; guided tours of the vaults €3.
Bus #134 from Abbey St Lower.

St Michan's Church stands on Church Street, the first street upriver from the Four Courts. Built by the Danes and named after one of their saints, it dates from 1095 – the oldest surviving building on the northside. For five hundred years it was also the only church north of the river, ensuring it the largest parish in Dublin and sufficient funds for a complete rebuild in 1685. Since then its fortunes have declined and its roof has long required costly repairs – hence the exploitation of the "mummies" in its vaults.

Strictly speaking, the dozen **bodies** have not been

mummified – they've been preserved by the constant temperature, the limestone masonry that absorbs moisture from the air, and methane gas secreted by rotting vegetation beneath the church. The "best" ones are 300–700 years old – a woman who may have been a nun, a man missing a hand, possibly a thief-turned-monk, and another thought to have been a Crusader – one of his fingernails has been dramatically elongated by the regular rubs of visitors seeking good fortune. Later burials are better accounted for, with the brass-studded coffins of a hated family of landlords in one vault, and the Sheares brothers, who were executed for their part in the 1798 Rebellion, in another, alongside the death mask of Wolfe Tone (see p.116). It's said that Robert Emmet, the leader of the 1803 rising, is buried in an unmarked grave at the back of the cemetery; a priest from St Michan's attended him on the scaffold.

Outwardly dour, the church is dominated by the one element that was not part of the seventeenth-century revamp – a grim **tower** from medieval times. Its much-remodelled interior contains an early eighteenth-century **organ** which was reputedly played by Handel; the organ gallery is dominated by a superb carving of seventeen musical instruments cut from a single piece of wood, made by an unknown apprentice as his examination piece. Flanking the organ are the eighteenth-century pulpit and the font in which Edmund Burke was baptized – he was born nearby at 12 Arran Quay. In the corner near the altar you'll notice a pew known as the **Penitents' Pew** (facing out toward the congregation) because at one time erring parishioners knelt at this and confessed their sins publicly. Although the **stained-glass windows** of the church were shattered during the shelling of the Four Courts, they have been tastefully replaced; the middle one, inspired by the *Book of Kells* and installed in 1958, is particularly eye-catching.

ST MICHAN'S CHURCH

SMITHFIELD VILLAGE

The **Smithfield Village** (Map 5, D6) area, just to the west of St Michan's Church, was formerly famous only for its horse sales, but it has undergone significant redevelopment in recent years and ongoing building works continue to litter the area. The mixture of old and new is very apparent here, with exhibitions such as the **Old Jameson Distillery** and its adjacent **Chimney** observation platform alongside modern Temple-Bar-like establishments such as *Chief O'Neill's* hotel (see p.245) and *The Cobblestone* (see p.300), probably Dublin's best bar for traditional music.

The village is centred on the cobbled expanse of **Smithfield** itself (Map 5, D5–6), just west of Bow Street. The city's largest civic space, it bears resemblance to an unfinished football stand, and it was here that U2 received the freedom of Dublin in 2000. For a time during the eighteenth century Smithfield became quite a fashionable place to reside, but eventually returned to its original function as a venue for horse and cattle fairs and assorted markets. The first Sunday of every month still sees the renowned Smithfield **horse sales**, although these are not as busy as they once were thanks to the Control of Horses Act, which limited the ownership of horses in an urban setting. Nevertheless, the area is completely transformed on sale days, with horse-boxes arriving in a continuous stream from 9am, so that by noon the market is buzzing. Though there's nothing glamorous about the event, there's plenty to watch: blacksmiths shoeing horses at mobile forges, kids riding bareback on ponies, and weatherbeaten farmers spitting into their palms and clapping their hands together to seal agreements.

The Old Jameson Distillery

Map 5, E6. Tours daily 9.30am–6pm (every 30min); last tour
5.30pm; €6.50.
Bus #25, #25A, #66 and #67A from Wellington Quay, or #68, #69
and #90 from Aston Quay.

Though it's a blatant plug for Ireland's distillers, you'd have
to be a vehement teetotaller not to enjoy the museum in
the **Old Jameson Distillery** on Bow Street. Taking its
name from the Irish *uisce beatha* (water of life), **Irish
whiskey** is almost as integral to Dublin's pub culture as
Guinness, and quite distinct from Scotch whisky in that it's
distilled three times rather than only twice. The oriental art
of distillation was probably brought to Ireland by
Phoenician traders or missionary monks in the sixth century; the exhibits on the tour explain the modern-day malt-
ing, fermenting, distilling and maturing processes, how
proof value is assessed and mature whiskeys are blended
("nosed" and left to "marry", as they say in the trade). An
audiovisual show fills you in on the pioneering whiskey
families – the Jamesons and the Powers in Dublin, the
Murphys of Midleton in County Cork and the Bushmills in
the North – now amalgamated as the Irish Distillers Group,
which produces all the well-known brands at its ultramodern Midleton distillery.

Tours finish with a ritual **tasting** of five types of whiskey,
Scotch and bourbon, and the presentation of a "taster's cer-
tificate". Tots are watered down, as the Irish believe that
this brings out the flavour, but neat refills are available on
request and connoisseurs are rewarded with a dram or two
of vintage stuff. To sober up, read the rules of the lodging
house for distillery workers; their minutely detailed laundry
allowance ends, "and once every fortnight, one night-
shirt". The complex also has a fine souvenir shop and
popular restaurant.

SMITHFIELD VILLAGE

The Chimney Viewing Tower

Map 5, E6. Mon–Sat 10am–5.30pm, Sun 11am–5.30pm; €6.
Bus #25, #25A, #66 and #67A from Wellington Quay, or #68, #69
and #90 from Aston Quay.

Just next to *Chief O'Neill's* hotel stands the old distillery
chimney, originally constructed in 1895 and recently
redeveloped as a **viewing platform**. A glass-panelled lift
attached to the chimney's side whisks visitors up to the observation area at the top, where a panoramic view of central
Dublin awaits. Whether it's worth the price is debatable
and, arguably, the view is by no means as good as that from
the Guinness Storehouse's *Gravity* bar (see p.122), but it
certainly does offer a sense of being in the heart of a
bustling city.

THE COLLINS BARRACKS AND THE CROPPY'S ACRE

Map 5, B6. Bus #25, #25A, #66 and #67A from Wellington Quay or
#68, #69 and #90 from Aston Quay.

Further along the quays towards Phoenix Park, the imposing grey-stone **Collins Barracks** (Tues–Sat 10am–5pm,
Sun 2–5pm; free) are an annexe of the National Museum.
The Barracks themselves date from 1701 and until being
decommissioned in 1997 claimed to be the oldest continuously inhabited barracks in the world, with the largest drill
square in Europe – it could hold six regiments.

The **museum** itself houses decorative artefacts, both
Irish and otherwise, ranging from glassware and china to
textiles and musical instruments. If time is limited head
straight for the superb **Curator's Choice** room on the first
floor of the west block, where museum curators from all
over Ireland have chosen items of particular interest. While

every one of the 25 objects on display is fascinating, three that stand out for their superlative craftsmanship and historical significance are the seventeenth-century Fleetwood cabinet given by Oliver Cromwell to his daughter on her wedding day – it's decorated with scenes from Ovid's *Metamorphoses*, erotic verses which were highly popular at the time. Look also for the William Smith O'Brien Gold Cup, named after an Irish patriot who was one of the leaders of the abortive Young Ireland rebellion of 1848 and was exiled to Australia. The cup was given to him on release from jail in Australia in 1854. There's also a hurdy-gurdy, made in Coleraine in 1775, a fascinating example of what is probably the earliest stringed instrument to be equipped with keys.

The adjacent room, entitled **Out of Storage**, contains a huge miscellany of artefacts, from Samurai suits of armour to early Edison phonographs; putting this eclectic mix into context is made easy by the excellent interactive touch-screen computers, which offer information on every item. The **Irish Silver Room** is also recommended, housing examples of early Irish silverware – such as the 1494 de Burgo Chalice – as well as various exuberant nineteenth-century pieces. The south block of the Barracks houses less interesting displays of furniture. while the top floor of the west block is used for temporary exhibitions.

Between the barracks and the river lies a railed-in plot of grass called **The Croppy's Acre**, with a monument made of Wicklow granite at its southern edge marking the location where many of the executed rebels of 1798 were buried. During the Great Famine, Ireland's largest soup-kitchen was set up on the esplanade, and policemen supervised mass feedings from a three-hundred-gallon pot. The quay is now named Wolfe Tone Quay, after the Rebellion's leader (see p.116).

THE COLLINS BARRACKS AND THE CROPPY'S ACRE

CHAPTER FIVE

PHOENIX PARK

Map 3, A3. Parkgate St entrance and Islandbridge Gate: bus #25, #25A, #26, #66 and #67 from Wellington Quay or #68 and #69 from Aston Quay. Chapelizod Gate: bus #25, #25A, #26, #66 and #67 from Wellington Quay. North Circular Rd entrance: bus #10 from Suffolk St or O'Connell St. Ashtown Gate and Castleknock Gate: bus #37 from Abbey St Lower.

A rolling landscape over twice the size of London's Hampstead Heath or New York's Central Park, **Phoenix Park** is a pleasure to visit at any time of year – but be sure to leave before dusk, as it's unsafe after dark. Since the attractions are scattered over seven hundred hectares, it's also wise to conserve your energy by getting there by bus – though if you've already walked as far as the Collins Barracks, it's only another ten minutes to the main entrance off Parkgate Street.

Ryan's pub at no. 28 Parkgate St is the ideal
place to take a break for refreshments; see p.294.

Landscaped in the English fashion, the park harbours three hundred **deer** which bask on the Fifteen Acres area or roam the woods nearby. Frequented by joggers and dog-walkers every day, and families at the weekends, it's also a venue for **cricket**, **football** and **hurling** matches in season, and occasional pop concerts over summer.

The name "Phoenix" is a corruption of the Irish *fionn uisce* ("clear water"), from the pre-Reformation days when this land belonged to St John's Priory in Kilmainham. After the Restoration of Charles II in 1660, the duke of Ormond supervised the construction of a viceregal lodge which remained a private preserve until 1747, when it was opened to the public by Lord Chesterfield. For decades, Head Ranger Nathanial Clements ensured that "every impropriety

PHOENIX PARK

172

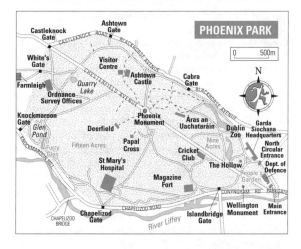

was vigorously expelled", but after his death in 1777 the "gates were opened wide to Tag, Rag and Bobtail" and the Sabbath was profaned by hurling matches "productive of blasphemous speaking, riot, drunkenness, broken heads and bones". Eventually, up to three hundred tents were pitched on the Fifteen Acres for gambling and drinking on Sundays – a fitting spot for a Temperance rally in 1875. A tradition of political meetings going back to 1792 reached its zenith with the Land League demonstration of 1880, whose 30,000-strong crowd set a record only surpassed by religious events, with 500,000 at the Eucharistic Congress of 1932, and over twice that number attending Papal Mass in 1979.

On entering the park at the main gate you'll find the 1980s **People's Garden**, the only part with formal flowerbeds and hedges, which merges into the hillocks and ponds landscaped in the 1830s by Decius Bruton, who also

PHOENIX PARK

laid out **Chesterfield Avenue**, which runs the length of the park. Near the Parkgate Street entrance, you'll also find the **Wellington Monument**, a 184-foot-high granite obelisk which bears reliefs cast from cannons captured at Waterloo, depicting the triumphs of the "Iron Duke".

Off the avenue to the right, **Dublin Zoo** (Mon–Sat 9.30am–6pm, Sun 10.30am–6pm, Nov–Feb closes at dusk; €9.80, children €6.15; ⓦwww.dublinzoo.ie) dates back to 1830 – the second oldest in Europe. In recent years the zoo's decline led to a public campaign for its closure, but it was granted IR£15 million in the mid-1990s to refurbish and extend its premises into something fit for the new millennium. The formerly tired-looking buildings were modernized, and conditions for many of the animals improved, while the "African Plains" section doubled the zoo's size – it now extends over 60 acres and is home to more than 700 species of animals and birds. Where the zoo once boasted of having bred MGM's trademark lion, it now lays stress on breeding endangered species for subsequent release into the wild. Thanks to regular new-born arrivals, and resulting photo opportunities, the zoo's popularity has increased, and it now makes for a fairly absorbing visit, particularly if you've young children in tow.

Heading up Chesterfield Avenue past the Army and Garda athletic grounds, the cricket pitches and the Nine Acres polo fields, you'll see the Palladian **Áras an Uachataráin** (Presidential Residence), which was built in 1751 as the viceregal lodge. Queen Victoria stayed here during her first visit to Ireland in 1849, and appeared not to notice the Famine at all, while the young Winston Churchill spent three years at the nearby "Little Lodge" when his father was secretary to his own father, the duke of Marlborough. The lodge, which became the home of the Irish president in 1937, proudly flies the Harp from its flagstaff and, since the presidency of Mary Robinson, keeps

THE PHOENIX PARK MURDERS

The Phoenix Park Murders of 1882 shocked society on both sides of the Irish Sea. One Saturday evening in May, the viceregal Chief Secretary Lord Frederick Cavendish and Under-Secretary T.H. Burke were strolling home along Chesterfield Avenue when four men jumped out of a hansom cab, stabbed them to death and escaped towards Chapelizod. The killings struck fear into every official in Ireland, where cold-blooded assassination had never been encountered before. The *Illustrated London News* blamed a "foul conspiracy of the enemies of civilized society – Nihilists or Anarchists, or Fenians, or by whatever name they may be called", aiming "to subvert all regular Government, for the purpose of Communistic plunder". Most Irish nationalists were equally appalled, as Parnell had just been released from jail after making a pact with Gladstone, and the murdered Chief Secretary was Gladstone's nephew. Parnell offered to resign, to forestall any imputation of support for the murders, but was dissuaded by Gladstone. It was discovered that the assassins belonged to a Fenian splinter group, the Invincibles, when one of their comrades turned state's evidence. (He was later killed by Fenians aboard a boat bound for South Africa, where he hoped to start a new life.) A plaque on the roadside of the Polo Grounds marks the spot where the murders took place; the four Invincibles were executed at Kilmainham and are now remembered by a monument in Glasnevin cemetery.

a candle burning in its window for "the Irish Diaspora". The latest occupant, Mary McAleese, has had a much lower profile than her predecessor since taking office in November 1997, but became the first incumbent to open the Residence to **tours** (Sat: April–Sept 10.30am–4.30pm, Oct–March 10.30am–3pm; free; tickets from the Visitor

PHOENIX PARK

175

Centre, see below), allowing visitors to ogle the State Reception Rooms and the President's Office.

All of Dublin's open-top-bus city tours (see p.17–18) stop at the Phoenix Monument in the centre of the park.

A spur road from Chesterfield Avenue leads to the 92ft-high stainless steel **Papal Cross**, erected on the spot where John Paul II celebrated Mass on September 29, 1979. Further along the Avenue, at a crossroads, Lord Chesterfield's **Phoenix Monument** resembles an eagle more than a mythical bird and obfuscates the origin of the park's name. One road leads towards Deerfield, the US Ambassador's residence; the other to a **visitor centre** (Jan to mid-March & Nov–Dec Sat & Sun 9.30am–4.30pm; mid- to end-March daily 9.30am–5pm; April–May daily 9.30am–5.30pm; June–Sept daily 10am–6pm; Oct daily 10am–5pm; €2.50; ⓦwww.heritageireland.ie). This features a reconstruction of the Knockmaree cist grave found on the Fifteen Acres in 1838, which is older (3500–3000 BC) than the famous Neolithic passage tomb at Newgrange (see pp.230–231), as well as various displays on the park's history and habitats, including designs rejected for the Wellington Monument.

The ticket for the centre includes a tour of the adjacent **Ashtown Castle**, a slender seventeenth-century tower-house built to safeguard the family and assets of a distant ancestor of Daniel O'Connell. The tower has such defensive features as a "murder hole" by the door and a spiral staircase with a "trip step" on the threshold of the living quarters.

Farmleigh and the rest of the park

For rather more contemporary opulence, head for White's Gate on the park's northwestern fringe. From here, there's access to one of the most splendid buildings in the city, **Farmleigh** (Map 2, D4; Easter–Oct Sun & bank holidays: house 11am–4pm; grounds 10.45am–5pm; free), set in equally impressive eighty-acre grounds and well worth making a special effort to see. Originally constructed in 1752 for the Trench family, the building was purchased by Edward Cecil Guinness, the first Earl of Iveagh, as a rustic residence offering easy access to his brewery. James Franklyn Fuller (who also designed Ashford Castle at Cong, Co. Mayo, for Sir Arthur Guinness) was employed to extend the house in the 1880s, and the Guinness family remained in residence until the death of the third earl in 1992. The house was then purchased by the Irish government as a state guesthouse and, consequently, **tours** may not be available if a visiting delegation is in residence (call ☎815 5900 in advance to check).

The informative guided tours, rich with anecdote and colour, commence in the **dining room**, whose unusual decorations include statues of Bacchus either side of the fireplace and a clock inlaid in its centre, all set off by seventeenth-century Italian silk tapestries made for the Duke of Milan. In the **hall** look out for eighteenth-century Flemish tapestries, Bohemian chandeliers made from Waterford crystal and a pair of debtors' chairs in which the sitting pauper's legs would be trapped until he or she had agreed to pay their debts. The house's original entrance hall was converted by Fuller into a **library**, which now contains 4000 items on loan from the Iveagh Collection, including a first edition of *Ulysses* and books dating back to the twelfth century. The **Blue Room**, dedicated to Ireland's Nobel Prize winners, causes a double-take, thanks to another strange fireplace – this one situated below a window. However, the real treat is the **ballroom**, added in 1897, whose Irish oak floor was constructed of wood originally intended for Guinness barrels. Delicate linen portieres fringe doors

PHOENIX PARK

leading out to a massive, plant-stocked and astonishingly warm conservatory. Behind the house there's a tearoom in the stable block and an extremely pleasant walled garden.

Returning from Farmleigh, a path south of White's Gate heads off past the Ordnance Survey Offices to the secluded **Glen Pond** and **Furry Glen** on the edge of the Fifteen Acres, a huge meadow once used for military manoeuvres.

Beyond St Mary's Hospital (formerly the Hibernian Military School), the path continues to the derelict **Magazine Fort**, dug into a hilltop in 1734. "Lo, here's proof of Irish sense / Here Irish wit is seen / Where nothing's left worth defence / They build a magazine", quipped Swift. After the British left, the fort became the main arms depot of the Irish Army until a daring raid by the IRA in 1939 got away with over one million rounds of ammunition, since when its bunkers have been impregnably secured against interlopers and abandoned to the elements.

The Grand Canal and the southern suburbs

Although it hasn't been used commercially for over twenty years, parts of Dublin's **Grand Canal** are still very pleasant for a stroll – the stretch between Mount Street Lower and Leeson Street Lower is especially attractive, with some good places to stop for a drink around Portobello Bridge. There are a few low-key tourist attractions along the way too: the **Waterways Visitor Centre** and the **National Print Museum** towards its eastern extreme and **Shaw's birthplace** and the **Irish Jewish Museum** off Portobello Road.

To the southeast of the Grand Canal lies leafy middle-class Ballsbridge and its adjacent **suburbs**. The Royal Dublin Society (see p.342) and Lansdowne Road (see p.345) are in this part of town, but unless you're going to a sporting event at one of these venues, or are staying in

THE GRAND AND ROYAL CANALS

True Dubliners, it's said, are born within the confines of the city's two canals: the Grand Canal, which makes a 3.5 mile loop around south Dublin, and the Royal Canal, which performs a similar loop through the northside.

The Grand Canal, which was intended to link Dublin to a vast area of central Ireland, had two branches: one joined the River Barrow to extend navigation to Waterford, the other met up with the great natural waterway of the River Shannon. Work began in 1756 but proceeded so slowly that only 12.5 miles had been dug by 1763, when the Dublin Corporation took over the project to speed things up, handing it back to private investors in 1772. Nine years later the first cargo barges began operating between Dublin and Sallins, and passenger services started the following year. Boats terminated at the St James's Street Harbour near the Guinness brewery until the Circular Line opened, encircling the southside to meet the Liffey at Ringsend. The inauguration of the Grand Canal Basin locks in 1796 marked the completion of the longest canal system in Ireland and Britain, extending for 341 miles (of which the Shannon and Barrow account for about 155 miles).

While much of its revenue came from shipping turf (Dublin's fireplaces burnt 40,000 tonnes a year), the Grand Canal Company had horse-drawn barges that could carry up to

accommodation hereabouts, it's not a district you're likely to explore. In the southern suburb of Rathfarnham, however, you'll find a couple of minor sights that merit a brief

eighty people, and ran five hotels along the route to accommodate them. By 1852 however, passenger services had been killed off by the railways, though cargo was transported by barge for a further century – the last haulage company went bust in 1950. A decade later Guinness stopped transporting its stout by barge from St James's Street Harbour, which was filled-in in 1974.

The Royal Canal was a later rival venture by John Binns, a director of the Grand Canal who quit after taking offence to a jest, and vowed to wreck its business. The Grand Canal Company claimed breach of charter but failed to stop it, though they did win a stipulation that it maintain a distance of four miles from their own canal once it had advanced fourteen miles from Dublin. Unfortunately, the Duke of Leinster, a major backer, also put restrictions on the canal's route, insisting it run past his mansion near Maynooth. As a result, construction was longer and costlier than anticipated, and it never made a profit; in 1840 it was bought by a railway company as a route (their line still runs alongside the canal today), and in 1961 it was closed for navigation, as so much of it had dried up. Since realizing its tourist potential, the stretch between Dublin and Mullingar has been restored, and work on the next section is in progress.

excursion: the **Pearse Museum** and **Rathfarnham Castle**; while to the southwest of the city lies the miniature medieval tower house of **Drimnagh Castle**.

Around the Grand Canal

If you need a break from the sometimes frenetic pace of Dublin's city centre, then a walk along the banks of the **Grand Canal** is an ideal way to while away a couple of hours, especially during sunny weather. The canal is no more than twenty minutes' walk from the centre, but we also detail bus services in the individual accounts.

WATERWAYS VISITOR CENTRE

Map 3, J5. June–Sept daily 9.30am–5.30pm; Oct–May Wed–Sun 12.30–5pm; last admission 45min before closing; €2.50.
Bus #2 or #3 from O'Connell St or Townsend St; DART to Grand Canal Dock Station.

Raised on stilts above the water of the Grand Canal by Pearse Street bridge, in the manner of an ancient bogland settlement, the **Waterways Visitor Centre** is a purpose-built tourist attraction that strives to convey the beauty of Ireland's rural waterways from a Dublin backwater. It's no substitute for a holiday on the Shannon, but if you're considering such a trip the centre is worth a visit, as it provides a good overview of Ireland's extensive inland waterways (a video monitor upstairs runs through the scenic highlights) – and sells navigation charts, books and towpath trails. There's plenty to absorb enthusiasts of canal engineering, including a working model of a barge going through lock gates, along with pictorial displays covering history and ecology. Having fallen into disuse in the 1950s, the canal system has been revived since the 1970s thanks to tourism, so it's unfortunate that the romantic image of the waterways conjured up

by the centre is weakened by the grimy vista of the Grand
Canal Basin and its downstream locks from the rooftop
viewing platform.

NATIONAL PRINT MUSEUM

Map 3, J7. May–Sept Mon–Fri 10am–5pm, Sat, Sun and bank
holidays noon–5pm; Oct–April Tues, Thurs, Sat & Sun 2–5pm;
€3.17.
Bus #5, #7 or #7A from Trinity College.

It's possible to walk from the Waterways Centre to the leafi-
er stretches of the Grand Canal in about ten minutes; alternatively, you can take a detour to the **National Print
Museum**, set in the former garrison chapel of the Beggars'
Bush Barracks on Haddington Road. The guided tour
commences with a fifteen-minute video outlining the history of printing, while the **collection** itself traces the
development of printing presses from an eighteenth-century
"handcaster" through the nineteenth-century keyboard-
operated "Linotype", revolutionary in its day, down to the
earliest Apple word-processors, most of which are still in
working order. There's also material on bookbinding and
changes in design and typefaces.

Built by the British in 1830, the barracks themselves
were constructed in an effort to control a lawless area on
the edge of Dublin – **Beggars' Bush** – and were the first
barracks to be handed over to the Free State in 1922. It was
here that Erskine Childers was executed for possessing a
revolver during the Civil War – an ironic end for someone
who became a Nationalist hero for smuggling 900 rifles
into Ireland in 1914. The barracks are now mainly private
housing but also contain the Irish Labour Court.

MOUNT STREET TO PORTOBELLO BRIDGE

From the National Print Museum, Northumberland Road crosses over the canal to become **Mount Street Lower** (Map 3, I6); the verdant stretch of canal between here and Portobello Bridge that isn't far from the centre of town and has a choice of approaches. One is from Merrion Square along **Mount Street Upper**, past the pepperpot church of St Stephen's; another is by **Baggot Street Lower** (Map 3, I7).

The stretch of **canal** by Baggot Street Lower is 3–6 yards wide at this point, and shaded by trees that once provided cover for prostitutes and their clients (it was here that Joyce lost his virginity). In the 1950s and 1960s, Parson's Bookshop by Baggot Street Bridge (now a café) was a meeting place for writers like Brendan Behan and the poet Patrick Kavanagh; the latter lived nearby and produced a short-lived "journal of literature and politics" called *Kavanagh's Weekly*, written largely by himself (with contributions from Behan and Flann O'Brien). After Kavanagh's death in 1967, his home on Pembroke Road was found to contain little more than a bed, and his friends erected a plain memorial **seat** opposite the *Mespil Hotel* on the Mespil Road side of Baggot Street Bridge in accordance with his wish: "O commemorate me with no hero-courageous/Tomb – just a canal-bank seat for the passer-by". Sadly, the seat's wood is now decaying, while the life-size **statue of Kavanagh** (Map 3, H7), musing on a bronze bench on the other side of the canal, is tarnished by verdigris.

Just under a mile west of Kavanagh's statue you'll reach a trio of **pubs** as the canal dwindles to a ditch near the Portobello Bridge (Map 3, F8): The *Barge Inn*, on Charlemont Street, The *Portobello*, just by Portobello

RAGLAN ROAD

Though Patrick Kavanagh was both an accomplished poet and novelist, many now remember him for just one song, Raglan Road, a story of lost love which begins on the leafy street of the same name, southeast of the Grand Canal in Ballsbridge.

On Raglan Road on an Autumn Day
I saw her first and knew
That her dark hair would weave a snare
That I may one day rue

Set to the traditional air *The Dawning of the Day*, the song is one of Ireland's most recorded numbers, though probably the best-known version was released by Van Morrison and The Chieftains on their *Irish Heartbeat* collaboration album.

Bridge, and The *Lower Deck*, around the block from **Portobello House**. Originally a hotel for passengers at the terminus of the Grand Canal, Portobello House was Jack B. Yeats's residence from 1950 until his death in 1957, and now serves as a college.

THE SHAW BIRTHPLACE

Map 3, F7. May–Sept Mon–Sat 10am–5pm, Sun & bank holidays 2–6pm; €5.50. ⊚www.visitdublin.com.
Bus #16, #19 or #122 from O'Connell St or Dame St.

There are two places of interest in the side streets northwest of Portobello Bridge, whose houses are minor versions of the Georgian edifices of Dublin's centre. The first, at no. 33 Synge Street, is the **birthplace of George Bernard Shaw**, and has been painstakingly restored to provide a picture

GEORGE BERNARD SHAW

Born in Dublin in 1856, George Bernard Shaw was technically a member of the privileged Ascendancy, but his father's failed attempt (after leaving the civil service) to make money meant that Shaw grew up in an atmosphere of genteel poverty and, by the age of sixteen, was earning his living in a land agency. When his mother left his father for a singing teacher and took her two daughters with her to London, Shaw soon joined them and set about educating himself. Subsidized by his mother's meagre income, he spent his afternoons in the British Museum's reading room and his evenings writing novels.

Shaw's novels were unsuccessful, but his plays were a different matter entirely and he was soon acclaimed the most important British playwright since the eighteenth century. However, Shaw recognized his foreignness as being a big part of his success: "the position of foreigner with complete command of the same language has great advantages. I can take an objective view of England, which no Englishman can." In the 1890s, influenced by the drama of Ibsen, he began to write plays hinged on moral and social questions rather than romantic or personal interests – *Man and Superman*, *Caesar and Cleopatra*, *Major Barbara*, *St Joan*, and, of course, *Pygmalion*, from which the musical *My Fair Lady* was adapted. As well as a dramatist he was an active pamphleteer, critic, journalist and essayist, on subjects ranging from politics and economics to music. In 1925, Shaw was awarded the Nobel Prize for literature, but donated his prize money to the establishment of the Anglo-Swedish Literary Foundation. He died in Hertfordshire, England, in 1950.

of Victorian domestic life. Shaw lived here until he was ten and recalled that "neither our hearts nor our imaginations

THE SHAW BIRTHPLACE

were in it". This "loveless" atmosphere arose from his parents' failing marriage and the strain of keeping up appearances when the family was sinking into debt – a mood conveyed by the claustrophobic rooms and a terse inscription acknowledging that "Bernard Shaw, author of many plays", lived here.

THE IRISH JEWISH MUSEUM

Map 3, F8. May–Sept Sun, Tues & Thurs 11am–3.30pm; Oct–April Sun only 10.30am–2.30pm; closed on Jewish holy days; free.
Bus #16, #19 or #122 from O'Connell St or Dame St.

Further west along the widening canal, you can turn into Kingsland Parade and take the second turning on the left to find the other place of interest hereabouts, the **Irish Jewish Museum** at 3–4 Walworth Road. Opened in 1985 by President Chaim Herzog of Israel, who was born in Belfast and educated in Dublin, the museum relates the history of the Jewish community in Ireland (the first were Portuguese and Spanish Jews, fleeing the Inquisition), who established a synagogue in Crane Lane, opposite Dublin Castle, in the 1720s. The house itself functioned as a synagogue from 1915 until the mid-1970s, when its congregation moved to the suburbs. Ireland's Jewish population has been declining steadily over the last fifty years and now numbers less than two thousand.

The museum's **downstairs** section charts the social and cultural history of Irish Jews, covering subjects as wide as sport, trade, a typical late nineteenth-century kitchen and Jewish references in *Ulysses*. **Upstairs** the original synagogue is on view and you can see a wedding canopy, circumcision instruments and other artefacts of Judaic culture.

The southern suburbs

A few of Dublin's less well-known attractions are situated in the **suburbs**, though each is readily accessible by a twenty- to thirty-minute bus ride from the centre. The green, almost village-like suburb of **Rathfarnham** lies close to the city's southern fringe, and holds the absorbing Pearse Museum, while the neat crescents and cul-de-sacs of **Drimnagh** are situated to the southwest.

RATHFARNHAM CASTLE

Map 2, F6. May–Oct daily 9.30am–5.30pm, last admission one hour before closing; guided tour €1.90. ⓦwww.heritageireland.ie. Bus #16 or #16A from O'Connell St or Dame St.

Rathfarnham Castle has been undergoing restoration since 1987, and work is still far from finished, but if you're interested in historic monuments and their conservation, the **guided tour** is worthwhile. Built around 1583 by Adam Loftus, Rathfarnham appears today as an impressive semi-fortified mansion. Loftus was a Yorkshireman who came to Ireland as the Lord Deputy's chaplain and went on to become both Archbishop of Dublin, the first Provost of Trinity College and Lord Chancellor of Ireland – clearly a man of considerable wealth. The Dublin Hearth Money Roll of 1664 found only twenty establishments in the county with over eight hearths, and with eighteen, Rathfarnham was the largest of these. In the 1720s the battlements were removed and, while the overall exterior retains its sixteenth-century appearance, the interior is that of a stately Georgian residence.

The castle passed through a number of hands in the seventeenth and eighteenth centuries, but in 1767 it was bought by Nicholas Loftus, second earl of Ely, a descendant of the archbishop and something of an eccentric, who erected a triumphal arch at the north entrance to the grounds. At one point he was nearly judged insane, but escaped committal thanks to his uncle, **Henry Loftus**, who defended him in court and inherited Rathfarnham after his death. It was Henry who made Rathfarnham a byword for luxury and refinement, hiring Sir William Chambers and James "Athenian" Stewart to remodel the rooms, and installing aviaries and menageries in the grounds. In subsequent years the castle fell into decline, and in 1913 part of the land was sold off for a golf course – the castle itself was bought by the Jesuits.

Today the kitchen wing has been fully restored and although conservation work is still ongoing in the eighteenth-century apartments, they do give you some sense of the scale of Rathfarnham's former grandeur.

PEARSE MUSEUM

Map 2, F7. Daily: Feb–April & Sept–Oct 10am–1pm & 2–5pm; May–Aug 10am–1pm & 2–5.30pm; Nov–Jan 10am–1pm & 2–4pm; free.
Bus #16 from O'Connell St, Dame St or Rathfarnham Castle.

If you're interested in the background to the 1916 Easter Rising, it's worth visiting the **Pearse Museum** in former St Enda's School, off Grange Road in Rathfarnham. The school was run by Pádraig Pearse from 1910, and set about promoting Gaelic culture by teaching its curriculum in Gaelic and encouraging students to take part in sports such as hurling, Gaelic football and handball. Sadly, the school attracted fewer pupils than Pearse had hoped for and in 1916, facing bankruptcy, it closed down. It was from here that Pearse and his brother Willie went out to fight on

PEARSE MUSEUM

Easter Monday of that year. As a signatory to the Proclamation of the Irish Republic, Pearse was one of the first leaders to be executed at Kilmainham Gaol (see p.125) and was subsequently buried in a quicklime grave at Arbour Hill.

A visit to the **house** best begins in the rooms to the rear where displays focus on Pearse's background, including his birth in 1879 on Great Brunswick Street (now Pearse Street). Other rooms recount the school's history and Pearse's educational philosophy, including "special attention to character building and the development of those elements which promote true manhood, honour and good citizenship". Upstairs, the dormitory's original straw mattresses and bedframes suggest that bodily comfort was not one of those essential elements. Pearse was also a reasonably successful playwright, but whether he was a good teacher was certainly questioned by James Joyce, who took Pearse's Irish classes at University College but left after three months, deploring his tutor's attempts to elevate the Irish language by denigrating English.

The museum also has tearooms and a nature study centre with a self-guiding trail around **St Enda's Park** (daily: Feb-March 10am-5.30pm, April & Sept-Oct 10am-7pm, May-Aug 10am-8pm, Nov-Jan 10am-4.30pm), which features riverside walks, a waterfall and a walled garden where outdoor concerts are held during the summer (call ☏493 4208 for details).

DRIMNAGH CASTLE

Map 2, E5. April–Oct Wed, Sat & Sun noon–5pm; Nov–March Wed noon–5pm, Sun 2–5pm; last tour at 4.15pm; €3.50.
Bus #56A from Eden Quay.

Drimnagh Castle is well worth the bus journey through

the pebble-dashed suburb of Drimnagh, five miles south-west of the centre. Visible from Long Mile Road, behind a Christian Brothers School, the castle's rugged profile attests to eight hundred years of inhabitation and alterations.

The **tower house** was built in the thirteenth century by the Anglo-Norman Barnewall family, who occupied it for nearly four hundred years, but its defensive role declined as the lawless clans of the Wicklow Mountains were subdued. Sir Adam Loftus of Rathfarnham Castle leased Drimnagh in the seventeenth century, replacing some of the arrow-slit windows with mullioned ones, adding a rooftop fumerelle for smoke to escape, and a front staircase to supersede the low, ground-floor entrance beneath a "murder hole", designed to force attackers to stoop as lime or boiling water was poured on their heads.

Over the centuries there have been sightings in various parts of the castle of the ghost of Eleanora, Hugh de Barnewall's niece, who is said to have killed herself on hearing that she was destined to marry her cousin.

Inside, the **spiral staircase** turns – unusually – anti-clockwise (stairways were built to favour the defender's sword-hand, and Sir Hugh Barnewall was left-handed). At the top is a garderobe (toilet) sited conveniently near the **Great Hall**, which was an all-purpose living room and sleeping quarters. Its floor would originally have been strewn with rushes, but restorers have surfaced it with tiles bearing the coats of arms of the Barnewall, Loftus and Lansdowne families. The Jacobean-Tudor minstrels' gallery and the hammer-beamed roof of Roscommon oak are modern replicas – some of the craftspeople involved in their creation were honoured by statues in medieval guise, carved on the beams. The chandeliers come from the film

DRIMNAGH CASTLE

Excalibur, which was shot in Ireland at the Powerscourt Estate (see p.218).

Behind the house are a small seventeenth-century French-style **garden** with bay hedges, and a **poultry-run** for diverse breeds of fowl. The aim is to restore the grounds to something of the self-sufficiency that prevailed in medieval times and persisted as late as 1954, when Drimnagh was vacated by the Hatch family, who lived here and ran a dairy business.

The outskirts

Though a huge arc of coastline has effectively become part of the greater Dublin metropolitan area, you'll still feel like you're leaving the city behind as you head **south along the coast**. You'll pass **Dún Laoghaire** with its great harbour overlooked by the Martello tower at **Sandycove**, immortalized in Ulysses and now a museum to Joyce, and the charming seaside towns of **Dalkey** and **Killiney**, with the Wicklow Mountains on the outskirts of **Bray**, further south.

All of these places are accessible from Dublin by frequent DART trains, making it easy to visit several in a day's outing. The DART isn't quite as useful for **northern outskirts**, but a bus ride will take you to **Glasnevin**, home to the National Botanic Gardens and Prospect Cemetery, to the exquisite Casino in **Marino**, and further east, towards the grasslands and seabirds at **North Bull Island**, just offshore from Clontarf.

The headland of **Howth**, at the end of the DART line, is the scenic highlight of this part of Dublin, with a cliffside walk as fine as any. Beyond Howth, **Malahide** deserves a visit for its delightful castle, while **Donabate** is home to the quirky Newbridge House and a traditional farm. Both are accessible by regular suburban trains from Dublin.

South along the coast

The DART line **south** follows the course of Ireland's first railway, opened in 1834, which ran from Dublin to Kingstown (as Dún Laoghaire was then called) where, at the townsfolk's insistence, it terminated on the outskirts. After their intolerance had abated, the railway was extended to Dalkey along the route of a quarry-railroad called "The Metals", and finally right down to Arklow – though the DART itself terminates at Greystones.

Boarding a train in the centre of Dublin, you'll catch a first glimpse of the sea on the horizon at **Sandymount**. Two stops later, the track starts to trail along beside Dublin Bay, past the UNESCO-designated bird sanctuary of Booterstown Marsh, whose wading birds are visible from the station platform. Glimpses of the sea alternate with views of the railway as you pass through Blackrock and Monkstown, till **Dún Laoghaire** harbour comes into view.

Map 7 at the back of the book covers the
coast from Dún Laoghaire to Killiney Hill.

DÚN LAOGHAIRE

Map 2, I6. Dún Laoghaire DART station.

The seaside town of **DÚN LAOGHAIRE** (pronounced "Dunleary") is virtually a suburb of Dublin, but there's still a residue of a resort atmosphere here. The harbour, now a port for ferries from Britain and the base for lightships and yacht clubs, was built to hold a great fleet within its two-mile-long granite piers, and was the largest artificial harbour in the world at the time of its construction (1817–42). However, now that the National Maritime Museum has closed indefinitely for maintenance work, there's little to detain you in Dún Laoghaire other than taking a harbourside stroll.

The **East Pier** has all the requisites for an edifying constitutional, a popular pastime among locals on Sundays in particular: a bandstand, a lifeboat memorial, a compass pointer, and an anemometer for measuring windspeed (one of the first in the world when installed in 1852). Along the landward side are the crusty members-only Royal Irish Yacht Club (dating from 1850), Royal St George Yacht Club (1863) and National Yacht Club (1876) – with the non-elitist National Sailing School over on the **West Pier**.

Just inland from the Carlisle Pier, which is within the harbour, stands an odd **monument to George IV** (commemorating his state visit of 1821), which was described by Thackeray as "a hideous obelisk, stuck upon four fat balls, and surmounted by a crown on a cushion". The king had been expected to disembark here, but landed, visibly drunk, at Howth instead, though he tried to make amends by departing from Dún Laoghaire. One of the balls is newer than the others; the original was blown away by the IRA, who also put paid to a statue of Queen Victoria that stood nearby. A little way uphill is Andrew O'Connor's sculpture **Christ the King**, which the civic fathers purchased in 1949 but kept in storage till 1979 because Church authorities objected to it.

For accommodation in Dún Laoghaire see p.252.

SANDYCOVE

Map 7, E3. Sandycove & Glasthule DART station, then a 10min walk to the James Joyce Tower, or a 20min walk from Dún Laoghaire.

A short way along the seafront from the East Pier, Dún Laoghaire merges into **SANDYCOVE**, a quieter suburb whose most famous son was **Roger Casement**, the British diplomat turned Irish rebel. Casement made his name as a consul championing the rights of indigenous tribes in the Belgian Congo and the Peruvian Amazon, and retired with a knighthood, convinced that Irish freedom was his next cause. In 1914 he travelled to Berlin to enlist German support; he returned by U-boat shortly before the Easter Rising, but was soon captured. Charged with high treason, Casement was stripped of his honours and hanged at Pentonville prison in London. Unfortunately, his legacy has been overshadowed by an unseemly, essentially homophobic argument about his sexuality: republicans, unable to accept the graphic details of homosexual activities in his "Black Diaries", have maintained that the diaries were forged by British secret services, but recent forensic examination has established, hopefully once and for all, that they are genuine.

Today, Sandycove is more widely associated with James Joyce, who for a brief period lived in the **Martello tower** – now a Joyce museum and the starting point of the Bloomsday pilgrimage. Originally it was just one of 21 such towers built against the threat of French invasion in 1804–06. Their walls are 2.5 yards thick and an armoured door 3.9 yards off the ground is the sole means of entry, making them almost impregnable – but they never fired a shot in anger. You'll see other Martello towers at Dalkey, Bray, Howth and Sandymount.

The Sandycove Martello tower is called the **James Joyce Tower** (April–Oct Mon–Sat 10am–1pm & 2–5pm, Sun 2–6pm; €5.50, not so much for its association with his life – Joyce spent barely a week here in September 1904, a month before eloping with Nora Barnacle – but more because it features so prominently in the opening chapter of *Ulysses*. The characterization of "stately, plump Buck Mulligan" was Joyce's revenge on his host, Oliver St John Gogarty. On the sixth night of Joyce's stay, a fellow guest, Samuel Chenevix Trench, had a nightmare about a panther and fired some shots into the fireplace; Gogarty seized the gun and shot down a row of saucepans above Joyce's head, shouting, "Leave him to me!" Joyce took the hint and left promptly.

All of the items on show are donations to the museum, which was opened in 1962 by Sylvia Beach, who first published *Ulysses*. An edition illustrated by Matisse vies for attention with a plaintive letter from Joyce to Nora, accusing her of "treating me as if I were simply a casual comrade in lust", and such odd exhibits as a pandybat of the kind with which Joyce was beaten for "vulgar language" at school. In the first-floor guardroom, Gogarty's abode has been re-created complete with a life-size ceramic panther representing Trench's *bête noire*. The spiral staircase emerges on the rooftop gun-platform where Buck Mulligan does his ablutions at the start of the novel.

From there you can see right over the back yard of **Geragh**, a Constructivist seaside villa which the architect Michael Scott built for his family in the 1930s. Beyond it lies a knobbly brown headland with a famous bathing place known as the **Forty Foot Pool** (so called not for the pool's size but because of a forty-feet-deep fishing hole off the coast here). The pool was long reserved for male nude bathing: nowadays both sexes can use it but "Togs must be worn" – though nude bathers still get away with it before 9am. If you're tempted to join them, bear in mind the water temperature only varies by about 5°C throughout the year, so you'll find it pretty chilly.

SANDYCOVE

DALKEY AND KILLINEY

Map 2, I7–8. Dalkey and Killiney DART stations. Dalkey is a 15min walk from Sandycove.

Just down the coast from Sandycove is the charming seaside town of **DALKEY** (pronounced "Dawky"), immortalized in Flann O'Brien's satirical novel *The Dalkey Archive*. On sunny days, the narrow streets and cliffside villas here have an almost Mediterranean lushness that makes Dublin itself seem a little cold and grey. Historically, Dalkey has thrived on comparisons with the capital: for two hundred years, it was the only natural **harbour** on the east coast of Ireland. Goods unloaded here filled Dalkey's warehouses and swelled its coffers, until the dredging of the Liffey in the sixteenth century wiped out its business and Dalkey dwindled to a village. In time, though, Dalkey's beauty ensured that fresh comparisons were made, as well-to-do Dubliners built seaside homes and the advent of the railway brought day-trippers with it. Today, its nostalgic old quarter merges into a commuter-belt hinterland under the cover of forested slopes and azaleas.

Restaurants in Dalkey are covered on p.283.

From Dalkey DART station it's a short walk down Railway Road to Castle Street, distinguished by two fortified warehouses from the fifteenth century, when Dalkey was dubbed the "Port of the Seven Castles". **Goat Castle**, across the way from **Archibold's Castle**, serves as Dalkey's town hall, with a **Visitor Centre** (Sat & Sun 11am–5pm, plus April–Oct Mon–Fri 9.30am–5pm; €5) that features detailed exhibits on the town's history, set within the castle's impressive interior. If you're walking from Sandycove to Dalkey, you'll pass a third fortification, **Bullock Castle**, built by the Cistercians in 1180 to protect Bullock fishing harbour.

From Castle Street you can take a lovely walk down **Coliemore Road**, past Georgian houses and Victorian villas, to Coliemore Harbour facing Dalkey Island, from which you can then head south towards Killiney along the cliffside **Vico Road** to view the fabulous coastline. In summer there are daily **boat trips**, weather permitting, from this harbour (☎283 4298; €5 return) to **Dalkey Island**, 300yd offshore, although it is advisable to phone in advance as even when the weather is fine the service can be a little erratic. First inhabited 8500 years ago (the dwelling sites are marked by thickets of nettles), the island was known in Gaelic as Deiliginish (from which Dalkey derives), a name which recalls a spiked wooden fort (*Deilig* means "thorn" or "spike") that once existed there. Here you'll find another Martello tower and the ruins of the medieval St Begnet's Oratory on the far side of the saddle-shaped island.

Dalkey Hill is definitely worth climbing; steps and a path ascend steeply from Vico Road, or there's an easier route off Sorrento Road via Knocknacree Road and Torca Road. On the latter road, Shavians can track down **Torca Cottage**, where George Bernard Shaw spent much of his boyhood; the house is privately owned, but a plaque on the wall acknowledges Shaw with his words, "The men of Ireland are mortal and temporal but the hills are eternal." En route to the summit, with its crenellated former telegraph station and fine views over Dublin Bay, you'll pass Dalkey **quarry**, where the granite blocks that form the walls of Coliemore Harbour and the great piers of Dún Laoghaire were hewn.

To give your lungs a further workout, follow the partly wooded ridge up to **Killiney Hill**, where a stone obelisk enjoys even more glorious **views**, north to Howth and south to Killiney Bay and the Wicklow Mountains. From here, you can quickly descend to the park gate on Killiney Hill Road and refreshment at the cosy *Druid's Chair* pub;

DALKEY AND KILLINEY

and then head down Victoria Road and Vico Road through the leafy and exclusive borough of **KILLINEY**, to reach the Killiney DART station in around fifteen minutes. The wide grey beach in front of the station runs along the length of the four-mile bay to Bray.

BRAY

Map 1, F6. Bray DART station.

Beyond Killiney the coast relapses into humdrum suburbia, but things pick up as you cross the border into County Wicklow and approach **BRAY**, whose rugged headland contrasts with the softer flanks of the Wicklow Mountains. Its fine surroundings make amends for the resort, which is a poor relation to Dalkey and Killiney. Though the amusement arcade and places to eat and drink are open all year round, Bray only really comes alive in the summer, especially during the **International Festival of Music and Dance** (see p.337) in August. The **Oscar Wilde Autumn School** (see p.340) in October marks the end of the festive calendar. Details of both events are available from the **tourist office** (Mon–Fri 9.30am–4.30pm, until 5pm June–Aug, Sat 10am–3pm; ☎286 6796) in the Old Court House on Main Road, which doubles as a heritage centre (€3) devoted to local history and the achievements of Sir William Dargan, the builder of the Dublin–Kingstown railway and founder of the National Gallery.

- -

The *Tree of Idleness* is Bray's outstanding restaurant (see p.283), while the branch of Temple Bar's *Porterhouse* (see p.292) on the seafront is your best bet for a drink.

- -

One interesting diversion here though, especially if you have children, is the **National Sea-Life Centre** on the seafront (Mon–Fri 10am–4pm, Sat & Sun 10am–5pm;

reduced hours in winter, phone ⓣ286 6939 to check; €8, children €5.50), an aquarium specializing in Irish marine life that is both entertaining – the touch pool, full of crabs and starfish, is a particular favourite – and educational, with a strong emphasis on the need for conservation.

There's an excellent two- to three-hour **walk** from Bray seafront south across **Bray Head** to **Greystones** (Map 1, F7), a small commuter town at the end of the DART line. You can follow the comparatively flat cliff path that runs above the rail tracks for most of the way, giving close-up views of rocky coves and slate pinnacles, lashed by magnificent waves on windy days. Alternatively, take on the steep climb over the top of Bray Head for great views of Killiney Bay and the cone-shaped hills inland known as Little Sugar Loaf and Great Sugar Loaf, with a distant backdrop of the Wicklow Mountains: the route ascends rapidly from the end of Bray seafront through pine woods and over gorse slopes to a large cross, 656ft above sea level; from here a track winds across the ridge below the 860ft summit of Bray Head, before you turn sharp left down to join the cliff path which will bring you into Greystones.

The leeward side of Bray Head partakes of the softness of Wicklow, the "Garden of Ireland", where trees and plants from five continents flourish in gardens that throw open their gates during the **Wicklow Gardens Festival** (May to late July, see p.336). A full list of the gardens and viewing days is available from the Bray tourist office; the easiest to reach is the seventeenth-century French-style **garden of Killruddery House** (April–Sept daily 1–5pm; €4.50), off the Southern Cross Route on the edge of Bray (bus #84 from Main Street or a twenty-minute walk from Strand Road). By paying €2 extra you can tour Killruddery House itself (May, June & Sept daily 1–5pm), the Tudor Revival seat of the earls of Meath, which was a famous hunting-lodge for generations.

BRAY

The northern outskirts

Heading northwards from the centre of Dublin, you won't catch sight of the sea from the DART until you're nearly at Sutton, and there isn't much time to enjoy the view before the line terminates at **Howth**, the rugged northern headland of Dublin Bay. Aside from Howth, the bay's only real seaside spot in this direction is **Dollymount Strand**, a few miles from the centre. The other main attractions are in the suburbs of **Glasnevin** and **Marino**, and out beyond Howth in **Malahide** and **Donabate**.

Buses are the only way to get to Glasnevin, while Malahide and Donabate can be reached by **train** from Connolly Station. You'll need to catch a suburban train bound for Drogheda, which can also be boarded at Howth Junction – an interchange between the DART and suburban lines (not to be confused with Howth, the DART terminus). Until 1959, Dubliners enjoyed riding the famous Hill of Howth trams, which crested the summit of the peninsula; bus #31B does the same today, sans romance – though the view is still pretty spectacular.

GLASNEVIN

Map 2, F3. Bus #13, #19 or #19A from O'Connell St Upper, or #134 from Middle Abbey St.

A village on the cattle-road from Meath, **GLASNEVIN** remained quite bucolic until the establishment of two civic amenities catalyzed its evolution into a genteel suburb of pebble-dashed maisonettes and B&Bs. It now coexists uneasily alongside Finglas, a sprawl of new estates built to rehouse inner-city slum-tenants, which is rough enough (so locals joke) for the Alsatian dogs to walk around in pairs.

The Botanic Gardens' glasshouses shut earlier than the rest
of the gardens. Most close 12.45–2pm for lunch, all close at
3.15pm on Thursdays, and the Alpine House is closed on
Saturdays. Call ☏857 0909 for full details.

The National Botanic Gardens

Mon–Sat 9am–6pm, Sun 11am–6pm; winter Mon–Sat
10am–4.30pm, Sun 11am–4.30pm; free.

As you head off Botanic Road on to Glasnevin Hill you'll
see the gates of the **National Botanic Gardens**, founded
by an act of the Irish Parliament in 1795. Ireland's mild climate makes it an excellent place for growing exotic
species, and its Botanic Gardens were the first in the world
to raise orchids from seed, and the first in Europe to grow
pampas grass and the giant waterlily. Some 20,000 species
and varieties flourish over nineteen hectares of gardens,
rockeries and arboretums by the River Tolka, and in cast-
iron glasshouses that are early masterpieces of the genre.
The **Curvilinear Range** was fabricated from 1843
onwards by Richard Turner, a Dublin ironmaster who
built the Palm House at Kew Gardens in London; its newly
restored ironwork is sublime. The new **Alpine House** is a
worthy addition to Turner's legacy, while the Palm House
and Orchid House are due to open early in 2004 after
extensive renovation.

Guided tours of the Botanic Gardens run on Sundays
at 2.30pm (€1.90), and there's a varied programme of
temporary exhibitions, talks, demonstrations and
other events in the visitor centre.

GLASNEVIN

Glasnevin Cemetery

Mon–Sat 8am–4.30pm, Sun 9am–4.30pm; free;
ⓦwww.glasnevin-cemetery.ie.

Fifteen minutes' walk from the Botanic Gardens (down Glasnevin Hill and Botanic Road, before turning right into Prospect Way and Finglas Road) lies the entrance to **Glasnevin Cemetery**, aka **Prospect Cemetery**, a place ennobled by the remains of national heroes. Established as a burial place for Catholics by Daniel O'Connell in 1832, its jungle of Celtic crosses, shamrocks, harps and other patriotic iconography is elucidated by ninety-minute **guided tours** (Wed & Fri 2.30pm; free).

The 164ft-high **Round Tower** by the entrance is a monument to O'Connell, whose corpse was interred in its crypt in 1869, having been brought home from Genoa in 1847 (in fact, not all of his body is here: his heart was buried in Rome). Similar pomp attended the burial of Parnell – he asked to be buried in a mass grave among the people of Ireland, beside which a huge granite boulder carries his name (to the left of the round tower). Other historical figures among the 1.2 million dead at Glasnevin include Roger Casement, Michael Collins, Arthur Griffith, Jim Larkin, Countess Markievicz and Éamon de Valera; from the arts, Gerard Manley Hopkins, Maud Gonne MacBride, Brendan Behan, Alfred Chester Beatty and Phil Lynott of Thin Lizzy. To the right of O'Connell's tower is the **Republican plot**, with a memorial to hunger strikers, from Thomas Ashe who died in 1917 to Bobby Sands in 1981, while in front of the tower lie the recent graves of eighteen-year-old Kevin Barry and eight other Volunteers hanged by the British during the War of Independence; originally buried in Mountjoy Prison, their bodies were moved here with the full honours of a state funeral in

October 2001 (a tenth Volunteer was reburied in his home town of Ballylanders, Co. Limerick).

One of the city's finest old pubs, *Kavanagh's* (aka *The Gravediggers*), stands by the former cemetery entrance on Prospect Square, where it has consoled mourners, and changed little, since 1833; it's best reached by retracing your steps along Finglas Road and taking the first small lane on the left along the cemetery walls.

THE CASINO AT MARINO

Map 2, F4. Guided tours June–Sept daily 10am–6pm; May & Oct daily 10am–5pm; April Sat & Sun noon–5pm; Jan–March, Nov & Dec Sat & Sun noon–4pm; €2.50.
Bus #20B from Eden Quay, #27 from Talbot St, #27B or #42 from Beresford Place, #42A or #42B from Abbey St Lower or #123 from Thomas St; or DART to Clontarf, then a 15min walk.

Three miles northeast of O'Connell Street and just under two miles east of Glasnevin, **MARINO** originally enjoyed a sweeping view of Dublin Bay that made it an ideal location for a stately home. It was here that the **Earl of Charlemont** endeavoured to bring the civilization of ancient Rome and Renaissance Italy to Ireland by creating a splendid park and a mansion to display the antiquities he had collected during his nine-year Grand Tour of Europe. While nothing remains of Marino House, you can still admire the elegant summer residence that was the *pièce de résistance* of his 200-acre estate, the **Casino** (*casino* being the diminutive version of *casa*, the Italian word for "house"). Regarded as one of the finest Neoclassical buildings in Ireland, its construction preoccupied Charlemont from 1757 to 1778. In later years, Charlemont was able to give rein to his belief in Irish self-government, becoming the first commander-in-chief of the Irish Volunteers and even leaving his deathbed to vote against the Act of Union in the last session of the Grattan Parliament.

The Casino cost £20,000 sterling (equivalent to about €5 million today) and was designed by Sir William Chambers – the architect of Charlemont's town house on Parnell Square (now the Hugh Lane Gallery – see p.145). Its most remarkable feature is the way Chambers plays with your perception of its scale, so that what outwardly seems to be a one-roomed pavilion actually contains three floors of rooms, each designed, using tricks such as hidden doors, coffered ceilings and sky-blue domes, to appear larger than it is. To maintain the illusion, the main **entrance** is a monumental pedimented affair, though only two half-height door panels open, and the large windows are masked to hide the fact that they illuminate two levels, with curved panes of glass to reflect the outside world. With equal ingenuity, the downpipes that carry rainwater into underground cisterns are hidden in the columns (with bronze chains inside to reduce the noise of the falling water), and the chimney flues are disguised as urns. The whole of the **exterior** is covered in exquisite and remarkably well-preserved carving in Portland stone, which reflects, notably in the ox skulls symbolizing animal sacrifice, the Enlightenment's preoccupation with pagan antiquity.

The very high standards of craftsmanship continue **inside**, with ornate plasterwork and beautiful wooden floors inlaid in geometric patterns. While the Casino's exterior was designed to ornament the landscape, nothing was allowed to mar guests' views from the inside out. To this end, the entrance doors convert into a window, and a series of tunnels were built under the surrounding land, including one that ran to the main house so that the servants wouldn't blot the landscape. On the top floor is the earl's extravagant **state room**, with a screen of gilded columns separating a reception area from the bed.

If you're catching a bus back into town, try to sit upstairs on the left for a view of **Marino Crescent**. This elegant row of Georgian houses was once nicknamed "Ffolliot's revenge" after the man who built the crescent out of spite, to block Charlemont's view of the sea. To further upset him, Ffolliot ensured that the side facing Marino House was an unsightly jumble of chimneys and sheds. No. 15 (still privately owned) was the birthplace of Bram Stoker, the author of *Dracula*.

BULL ISLAND

Map 2, H4. DART to Raheny, then a 30min walk to the interpretive centre, or bus #130, from Lower Abbey St in the city centre or from Fairview/Clontarf Road near Marino, to Dollymount, then a 30min walk.

In fine weather it's pleasant to stroll along **Dollymount Strand**, the three-mile beach on the seaward side of **North Bull Island**, now designated a UNESCO Biosphere Reserve. Originally no more than a sandbank visible at low tide, the island grew in the tidal shadow of the North Bull Wall, which was built along with the South Bull Wall in 1821 at the suggestion of Captain Bligh of HMS *Bounty* fame to prevent Dublin Harbour from silting up. Besides golfers and day-tripping Dubliners, the island provides winter accommodation for up to 40,000 migrating **birds** from more than 50 species, including a sixth of the world's population of Brent geese – it's one of the most northerly sites in Europe where the foreshore doesn't freeze. In summer, you'll still see cormorants, curlews and oystercatchers wading on the mudflats. As well as a rich and varied **flora** – notably thrift, a mass of pink flowers in June, and several orchids – the grasslands behind sustain foxes, shrews, badgers, rabbits and one of the few remaining large indigenous **mammals**, the much-harassed Irish hare. You can find out

BULL ISLAND

●

more at the **interpretive centre** (Mon–Thurs 10.15am–1pm & 1.30–4pm, Fri 10.15am–1.30pm, Sat & Sun 10.15am–1pm & 1.30–5.30pm; closes 4.30pm Sat & Sun in winter) by the beach in the centre of the island, at the end of the causeway road from the mainland.

Map 8 at the back of the book covers Howth.

HOWTH

Map 8. DART to Howth station, or bus #31 or #31B from Lower Abbey Street or Howth Road (near Marino).

A rugged peninsula at the northernmost point of Dublin Bay, **HOWTH** derives its name from the Old Norse *hofuth*, or "cape", and is pronounced to rhyme with "both". While the DART gives you a glimpse of the northern coast of the peninsula, the #31B bus crosses the summit, with views right across Dublin Bay to the Wicklow Mountains, and even the Mountains of Mourne on fine days.

For the best places to stay in Howth see p.249;
for the nicest places to eat see p.284.

Howth **village** is a sleepy place of steep streets and dramatic views. Poised above Harbour Road but accessible by Church Street, the Gothic shell of **St Mary's Abbey** dates from the fourteenth to the sixteenth centuries and traces its origin to the first church founded by the Norse king Sitric, in 1042. You can see a fair bit of the interior without going to the trouble of obtaining the keys from Mrs O'Rourke at no. 3 Church St opposite, but will need them to view the fifteenth-century double tomb of Lord and Lady Howth. St Mary's offers a fine view of Howth harbour and Ireland's Eye, and there's food and log fires to be enjoyed at the sixteenth-century *Abbey Tavern*, on Abbey Street below. Windy **walks** along the harbour's east pier are a popular way to blow away the Guinness-induced cobwebs, giving you the chance to stare out **Ireland's Eye**, a rocky island and sea-bird sanctuary that shelters the ruins of a sixth-century monastery and a Martello tower; during the summer, **boats** from the east pier (€8; ☎831 4200 or 087/267 8211) run across to Ireland's Eye when they have enough takers.

To the west of the harbour, **Howth Castle**, built in 1564 and now the oldest inhabited house in Ireland, is a weather-beaten and battlemented veteran of numerous restorations. For many years the St Lawrence family kept open house at mealtimes, a custom said to have arisen from an incident in 1575, when Grace O'Malley, the "Uncrowned Queen of the West", was turned away because the family was at dinner, and reacted by kidnapping their eldest son and holding him until Lord Howth promised to keep his gates open at mealtimes in the future. Although the castle isn't open to the public, you can wander along to a barn in the grounds that enthusiasts have turned into a **National Transport Museum** (June–Aug Mon–Fri 10am–5pm, Sat & Sun 2–5pm; Sept–May Sat & Sun 2–5pm; €2.50), with vehicles from buses to fire engines, armoured cars and a Hill of Howth tram. In spring, don't miss the **rhododendron glades** behind the Deer Park golf club, where four hundred species flourish in the peaty soil below Mud Rock. Just downhill is a prehistoric dolmen, its gigantic 91-tonne capstone balanced on a dozen smaller rocks.

On a fine day you can enjoy Howth's famous **Cliff Walk**, with imposing rockscapes and superb **views** south past the mouth of the Liffey to the Wicklow Mountains, and north to the flatlands of the Boyne. The footpath runs for some five miles (allow 2hr 30min) almost right around the peninsula to Shielmartin Road, where you can catch bus #31A to Sutton Cross near Sutton DART station or all

HOWTH

the way back to Abbey Street; bus #31B runs parallel and above for much of the way, along Carrickbrack Road, so you can bail out of the walk if you feel like it. You first head out east along Balscadden Road to the Nose of Howth, before the path turns south, crossing the slopes above the cliffs, which are covered in colourful gorse and bell heather in season, towards the **Baily Lighthouse** on the southeast point. Built in 1814 on the site of a Celtic fort (*baile*), it was, until March 1997, the last manned light-house on Ireland's coastline. The path along the south-facing coast of the peninsula is the most spectacular part of the walk, providing close-up views of cliffs, secluded beach-es and rocky islands. If all that doesn't sound strenuous enough, you could add on a long detour to the peninsula's highest point, which despite its large radio mast offers panoramic views: leave the Cliff Walk to the north of the Baily Lighthouse and head up through the area known as The Summit, which has a pub and a café, to the actual summit, the 512ft **Ben of Howth**.

MALAHIDE

Map 1, E4. Bus #42 from Beresford Place (or Marino), or suburban train from Connolly Station or Howth Junction.

A few miles up the coast from Howth, the old feudal estate of **MALAHIDE** lends its name to a commuter village of pretty houses and quiet streets sloping gently down to a yachting marina. It's a fifteen-minute walk from the station through pretty Malahide Demesne to a cluster of tourist attractions, chief among them **Malahide Castle** (guided tours Mon–Sat 10am–12.45pm & 2–5pm, Sun 11am–12.45pm & 2–6pm; Nov–March closes 5pm Sun; €5.50), a twelfth-century tower-house that was modified and expanded over the eight hundred years that it was owned by the Talbot family. The Talbots were of Anglo-Norman origin but remained Catholic until the eighteenth century; dispossessed while Cromwell was in power, they regained Malahide after the Restoration, and it stayed in the family until the death of Lord Milo in 1973, after which the estate was acquired by Dublin County Council. Its charm lies in its disparate styles, as it evolved from a defensive to a domestic building while retaining the look of a romantic turreted castle.

Bon Appetit, 9 James Terrace (☎845 0314), is recommended for a lunch splurge in Malahide, or there's a cheaper restaurant in the castle, which stays open over the lunch break.

The **first room**, whose stone walls are hidden behind dark sixteenth-century panelling carved in swirling floral patterns, was the principal one in the tower house. The panels on one wall incorporate copies of Raphael's Vatican frescoes of Adam and Eve and Joseph and his brothers, while the Virgin carved over the fireplace was the family totem and is said to have disappeared during the years that Malahide was given to Cromwell's general, Myles Corbet, as a reward for his signature on the death warrant of Charles I.

You then pass on through the **drawing rooms** of the west wing, with their beautiful Rococo cornices, to the family **bedrooms** upstairs, featuring an eighteenth-century four-poster bed which is said to have belonged to the actor David Garrick. From there you descend to the **Great Hall**, whose oak hammer-beam ceiling and minstrels' gallery date from 1475. The low door in the corner is known as "Puck's Door", after the ghost of a servant who fell asleep on the night when invaders attacked, and hanged himself in shame. It's said to appear whenever there are changes Puck dislikes and made its last appearance in 1975, when the contents of

MALAHIDE

the castle were auctioned. A picture of the Battle of the Boyne is flanked by portraits of the Earl of Tyrconnell, "Fighting Dick" Talbot, who led the Jacobites, and other family members who fought with him. The tour ends in a small **library** with Flemish floral wall-hangings and an exquisite inlaid table. In 1928, many of the papers of James Boswell (the great-grandfather of Emily Boswell, who married the fifth Lord Talbot) were found here, including an unexpurgated draft of his *Life of Johnson*.

Having seen the castle, most visitors make a beeline for the **Fry Model Railway** (April–Sept Mon–Sat 10am–5pm, Sun 2–6pm; €5.50), installed in the old Corn Store nearby. The nation's largest model railway layout (covering 287 square yards), it represents Ireland's transport system in all its diversity, from canal barges to the DART and ferry services.

Pride of place in the Craft Courtyard behind the model railway goes to **Tara's Palace and the Museum of Childhood** (April–Oct Mon–Sat 10am–1pm & 2–5pm, Sun 2–6pm; Nov–March Sat & Sun 2–5pm; €2, with proceeds going to Irish children's charities). Downstairs is a display of toys from 1720 to 1960, including a rare travelling dolls' house, and houses from the collections of Oscar Wilde's mother, Speranza, and Vivien Greene, wife of author Graham. The first floor shelters Tara's Palace, a meticulous re-creation of an eighteenth-century mansion, including chapel and billiards room, at one-twelfth scale, based on Leinster House, Castletown House and Carton House.

Finally, there's the twenty-acre **Talbot Botanic Gardens**, laid out by Lord Milo, which contain a walled garden, conservatory and 5000 species from Australia, New Zealand and Chile (May–Sept daily 2–5pm; €3; guided tours Wed 2pm).

MALAHIDE

NEWBRIDGE HOUSE

Map 1, E3. April–Sept Tues–Sat 10am–1pm & 2–5pm, Sun 2–6pm;
Oct–March Sat & Sun 2–5pm; house €5.50, farm €1.50.
Suburban train to Donabate from Connolly Station, Howth Junction
or Malahide.

Next stop along the Malahide line is **DONABATE**, a trim
commuter village that is graced by **Newbridge House**, a
solid brownstone edifice with a fine Georgian interior, built
around 1737 for Charles Cobbe, archbishop of Dublin from
1742 to 1765. It remained in the Cobbe family until 1985,
when the estate was sold to the county council (though the
Cobbes retain an apartment upstairs). From the station, it's a
fine fifteen-minute walk across Newbridge Demesne to
reach the house.

Guided tours begin in the **dining room**, which has a
lovely Rococo ceiling commissioned by society hostess Lady
Betty Beresford, who married the archbishop's son. Off the
adjacent library – which also sports fine Rococo plasterwork, depicting the four seasons – lies the family's **Museum
of Curiosities**, containing all sorts of weird artefacts from
around the world, including an intricate Kashmiri sari box
and some ostrich eggs laid in Dundalk. In the inner hall
beyond, the stairway features a portrait of one of Swift's
beloveds, either Stella or another woman called Vanessa (it's
not known which). The magnificent **Red Drawing
Room**, dominated by its crimson curtains, wallpaper and
carpet, was added to the back of the house around 1760 and
has been left almost exactly as it was after its 1820s redecora-
tion. Finally, you descend to the basement, where the **laundry** features a manually operated washing machine and an
early vacuum cleaner, while the **kitchen** is crammed with
more fascinating devices, such as a duck-press for squeezing
juice from poultry, and a mousetrap that drowned its victims. The house remained unelectrified until the 1960s,

when it was wired up for the filming of *The Spy Who Came in from the Cold*.

Attached to the house is a **traditional farm**, home to various breeds of sheep, fowl, pigs and cattle. In the coach house you can see the extravagantly gilded ceremonial coach made in 1790 for "Black Jack" Fitzgibbon, who was such an unpopular Lord Chancellor that someone once threw a rat through the window during a procession. Work is afoot in the grounds to restore the nineteenth-century walled fruit and vegetable garden, which will include a vinery, ornamental glasshouse and herb garden.

Day-trips from Dublin

t's feasible to travel to most parts of the country in less than a day from Dublin, making the list of possible **excursions** endless. In this chapter we've concentrated on six places within a short range of the capital which represent a geographical and historical cross-section of what's on offer, covering an arc from the Wicklow Mountains to the Neolithic sites of the Boyne Valley.

To the south, the **Wicklow Mountains** are modest in height (the highest peak is under 3000ft), but have remained very sparsely populated – for many centuries they were bandit country. From a tourist's point of view, three attractions stand out from the rest: the **Powerscourt Estate**, famous for its splendid gardens; the early monastic site of **Glendalough**; and **Russborough House**, renowned for its decoration and art collection.

The landscape is less inspiring to the west, with small towns and villages fast becoming suburbs of Dublin. But if you're interested in stately homes and the lifestyle of the old Anglo-Irish Ascendancy, it's worth taking a suburban bus out to Celbridge to explore **Castletown House**, which

TOURS OUT OF THE CITY

There's a plethora of one-day and half-day tours available from Dublin and, given the limitations of public transport, they're well worth considering. Most need to be booked a day or two in advance during high season – the Tourism Centre (see p.6) can do this for you for all of the operators listed below. Note that all tour prices include admission charges to sites and attractions, and that many companies offer discounts for children and students.

Bus Éireann (☎836 6111; @www.buseireann.ie) runs excursions to Glendalough and the Wicklow Mountains (mid-Jan to March & Nov to mid-Dec Wed, Fri & Sun; April–Oct daily; €20), and Newgrange and the Boyne Valley (mid-Jan to March & Nov to mid-Dec Thurs & Sat; April–Sept Mon–Thurs, Sat & Sun; €20). Coaches depart from Busáras at 10.30am for the Glendalough/Wicklow Mountains tour, and 10am for Newgrange and the Boyne Valley.

Dublin Bus (☎873 4222; @www.dublinbus.ie) runs a "South Coast Tour" (daily 11am & 2pm; €17) which takes in fine coastal scenery, as well as views of the Sugarloaf mountain. Their "Coast and Castle Tour" (daily 10am; €17) takes in Howth and Malahide Castle. Tours depart from the Dublin Bus office at 59 O'Connell St Upper and run throughout the year.

Gray Line (☎676 5377; @www.grayline.com) runs half-day tours to Glendalough (Sat 10am; €22), Newgrange (Mon & Tues 10am, Sat 2.30pm; €24), Knowth (Thurs 10am; €22) and the North Dublin coast (Mon & Thurs 2.30pm; €19). Full-day tours (€38) also run to Newgrange (Fri 10am) and Glendalough and the Wicklow Mountains (Sun 10.30am) plus a combined Glendalough and Powerscourt trip (Wed 10am). Tours depart from outside the Dublin Tourism Centre on Suffolk Street and run from the end of March to the end of October.

Irish City Tours (☎872 9010; ⒲www.irishcitytours.com) run a "Coast and Garden" morning tour (€20), which includes Dalkey and the Powerscourt Estate, departing from the *Camden Court Hotel*, Camden Street and an all-day Wicklow tour (€28), covering Glendalough, departing from the *Burlington Hotel*, Leeson Street Upper. Both tours operate daily throughout the year, and depart at 9am with pickups outside the Dublin Tourism Centre on Suffolk Street and the *Gresham Hotel* on O'Connell Street Upper.

Over the Top Tours (☎838 6128 or freefone reservations only ☎1-800 424 252; ⒲www.celticbustours.com) operate minibus trips that are specifically designed to reach the places not covered by the larger tourist coaches. Their Wicklow and Glendalough tour (€18) runs daily throughout the summer. Tours depart at 9.20am from outside the Dublin Tourism Centre on O'Connell Street Upper.

Railtours Ireland (☎856 0045; ⒲www.railtoursireland.com) run a combined rail and coach tour which leaves from Connolly Station at 1pm (Mon–Sat; €29) and whisks you to Rathdrum and thence by coach through the Vale of Clara to Glendalough. Tours run all year, but not on bank holidays.

Wild Coach Tours (☎280 1899; ⒲www.wildcoachtours.com) offer fun, sociable all-day tours of the wilds of Wicklow (8.50am; €28), taking in Glendalough and stupendous scenery, while their morning "Castle" tour (9.15am; €20) takes in Howth and Malahide, and there's an afternoon tour to Powerscourt (1.30pm; €20). Tours run daily all year round, and pick up from the *Shelbourne Hotel*, St Stephen's Green, Dublin Tourism on Suffolk Street, and the *Gresham Hotel*, O'Connell Street Upper; the prices include all admission charges.

was founded by William Connolly, one of the most influential figures of Dublin's golden age. If you're travelling around by car, you may want to visit the award-winning but remote **Larchill Arcadian Gardens**, one of Ireland's most fascinating artificial landscapes.

The Boyne Valley in County Meath, north of Dublin, has the distinction of being Ireland's richest pastureland. The area known as the **Brú na Bóinne** (Palace of the Boyne) is the site of three prehistoric passage graves – **Newgrange**, **Knowth** and **Dowth** – that are among the most remarkable archeological structures in Europe. We haven't covered Dowth in this chapter as it's currently closed to the public.

While most of these places can be reached by public **transport**, in some cases – especially Brú na Bóinne, Glendalough and Powerscourt – you may want to take an **organized tour** from Dublin, which makes for a smoother day out (see box on p.216).

POWERSCOURT ESTATE

Map 1, E7. Gardens daily: March–Oct 9.30am–5.30pm; Nov–Feb 9.30am to dusk; €6. House daily: March–Oct 9.30am–5.30pm, Nov–Feb times may vary; €2.50. Waterfall daily: summer 9.30am–7pm; winter 10.30am–dusk; €3.50. ℗www.powerscourt.ie. Bus #44 from Hawkins St (off Burgh Quay) or #185 from Bray DART station to Enniskerry.

Nestled in the foothills of the Wicklow Mountains, the village of **ENNISKERRY** originally belonged to the **Powerscourt Estate**, which was owned by a dynasty founded by one of James I's generals, Richard Wingfield. The great house, half a mile south of Enniskerry's main square, is one of the largest Palladian mansions in Ireland, but its real attraction are the magnificent formal gardens which are blended into the backdrop of the Great Sugarloaf and other Wicklow peaks.

The grey-stone **house**, with its twin copper domes, was designed by Richard Cassels for the first Viscount Powerscourt and took a decade to build (1731–41). From afar it still looks impressive; inside, however, only shadows of its former glory remain. Although gutted by fire in 1974 (on the eve of a party to celebrate the completion of extensive renovation) you can at least get some sense of its past grandeur from the smoky brickwork remains of the double-storey **ballroom**, based on Palladio's version of the "Egyptian Hall" designed by Vitruvius. Photographs of the room before the fire, with its classical columns and lavish gilt decoration, survive and are on display in the exhibition by the house's entrance, where you can also take in an interesting audiovisual display on the history of Powerscourt.

The ceremonial entrance to the ten-acre walled garden is the gilded, ironwork **Bamberg Gate**, which originally belonged to Bamberg Cathedral in Bavaria. Infront of the house, the great **stone terrace**, with winged figures of Fame and Victory, was designed in 1843 by Daniel Robertson, who used to be wheeled about in a barrow, clutching a bottle of sherry while working on the job. When his creative powers were exhausted and the bottle was empty, he'd call it a day. The black and white stones which form the mosaics below were gathered from Bray beach, while the various statues on display around here and elsewhere in the gardens were collected by the sixth and seventh viscounts during their travels around Europe. In the 1850s, the seventh viscount began the terraced **Italian Gardens**, which accompany a grand staircase leading down to the circular **Triton Lake** with its central eponymous statue (based on Bernini's fountain in the Piazza Barberini

POWERSCOURT ESTATE

in Rome) firing a jet of water one hundred feet skywards. From here the view up the terraces towards the house is staggering, a colossal amphitheatre populated by winged horses and assorted statuary.

At the far end of the terrace the land falls away sharply, enhancing the beauty of the North American conifers planted by Robertson. Behind the **Pepper Pot Tower** (which can be climbed to view the surrounding valley) is the **Killing Hollow**, where one of the last of the O'Toole bandit clan, whose forebears had once owned these lands, was beheaded. Reputedly, a nineteenth-century descendant of the O'Tooles used to regularly turn up drunk outside Powerscourt House and demand the return of his family's property – and often ended up before the local magistrate, who happened to be the then Viscount Powerscourt. A little further down lies a very fragrant Edwardian **Japanese Garden** of Japanese maples, azaleas and Chinese Fortune Palms, built on reclaimed bogland. Skirting the Triton Lake, you can carry on to the **Pet Cemetery**, where the graves of family dogs and horses are accompanied by that of a cow which produced seventeen calves and over 100,000 gallons of milk during her lifetime. Back at the house, the **terrace café-bar** and **restaurant** make an ideal spot from which to enjoy views over the gardens to the Wicklow Mountains.

The famous **Powerscourt waterfall** lies three miles from the house: turn right as you exit the main gate and follow the signs along the road. At almost four hundred feet, it's the highest in Ireland, leaping diagonally down the rockface into a valley where it joins the River Dargle.

Returning to Dublin from Powerscourt, you may want to pass through Glencullen, three miles from Enniskerry, to visit *Johnnie Fox's*, a popular pub which was once Daniel O'Connell's local.

GLENDALOUGH

Map 1, D8. Daily: mid-March to mid-Oct 9.30am–6pm; mid-Oct to mid-March 9.30am–5pm; free. Visitor centre same hours, last admission 45min before closing; €2.50.

Deeper into the Wicklow Mountains lies **Glendalough** (the "valley of the two lakes"), a magical setting for one of the best-preserved monastic sites in Ireland. Despite the car parks and the coach parties, there's a sense of peace and spirituality around here that makes it easy to imagine how hermits and monks once lived. The **visitor centre** features photographic displays and a video setting Glendalough in the context of ancient monasteries elsewhere in Ireland, as well as a model of how the monastery probably looked when it was at the height of its activity. The centre's entry price also includes an informative **guided tour** of the site, which is well worth taking in order to learn about some of the less visible aspects of the remains.

St Kevin's bus service (℡281 8119; €15 return) runs daily from Dublin to Glendalough, leaving from outside the Royal College of Surgeons, St Stephen's Green at 11.30am and returning from Glendalough at 4.15pm.

The monastery's foundation is attributed to **St Kevin**, a scion of the royal house of Leinster who studied under three holy men before retreating to Glendalough to fast and pray in solitude. His piety attracted followers, and in 570 he became abbot of a monastic community. As a centre of the Celtic Church, the monastery became famous throughout Europe for its learning, and despite being sacked by the Vikings, Normans and English, it was restored each time, until being dissolved during the Reformation. However, as the pope decreed that seven visits to Glendalough would procure the same indulgence as one pilgrimage to Rome, pilgrimages continued until 1862, when a local priest banned gatherings thanks to the activities of the pilgrims, whose abstemious devotions on St Kevin's day (June 3) were often followed by more licentious behaviour.

You enter the grounds through a double stone archway that was once surmounted by a tower. The nearest ruin is the site's largest remain, the impressive **Cathedral**, dating from the early ninth century, whose roofless nave and chancel contain numerous grave slabs. Among the tombs outside stands **St Kevin's Cross**, one of the best remaining relics from the period, consisting of a granite monolith decorated with an eighth-century carving of a Celtic cross superimposed upon a wheel; it's thought to have been left unfinished, in that, unusually, the quadrants of the cross have not been pierced. Nearby is a small **Priest's House** from the twelfth century, above the door of which are carved three barely discernible figures, thought to represent Kevin and two abbots. Further downhill is the two-storey **St Kevin's Church**; its steeply pitched roof and bell-turret so resemble a chimney that the building is also known as St Kevin's Kitchen; it was probably an oratory, however. The most impressive structure is the 89ft-high *Cloigtheach* or **Round Tower**, which served as a belfry, watchtower and place of refuge – the doorway high above the ground would have been reached by a ladder that could be pulled up in times of danger. (Such towers were a distinctive feature of Irish monasteries.) Further west, outside the enclosure, you'll see the remains of **St Mary's Church**, which is believed to have been the first building in the lower valley, and may mark the site of Kevin's grave.

Downhill from St Kevin's Church is a footbridge, on the far side of which is the hollowed-out **Deerstone**, so-called after a legend claiming that tame deer squirted their milk

THE WICKLOW WAY

If you prefer to explore the Wicklow Mountains on foot, there are plenty of opportunities for hiking, and the Wicklow Way, following a series of sheep tracks, forest firebreaks and bog roads, at a height of more than 1600ft for most of the way, provides access to some of the choicest spots. Running 82 miles from Marlay Park in the Dublin suburbs to Clonegal on the Wexford border, the whole route can be walked comfortably in ten to twelve days. If you want to do this, Marlay Park is accessible via the #16 bus from O'Connell Street or Dame Street. If you're short of time, the best part to walk is probably the three-day section between Knockree, three miles west of Enniskerry, and Glendalough; the path reaches its highest point at White Hill (2073ft), from which you can get a view of the mountains of North Wales on a fine day. Take the #44 bus from Hawkins Street (Map 4, E4) to Enniskerry, and pick up St Kevin's bus service at Glendalough for the return journey. Alternatively, try one of the circular walks detailed in *Easy Walks Near Dublin* by Joss Lynam (see p.386).

Low as they are, the Wicklow Mountains are notoriously treacherous, and even if you're planning on spending no more than a day walking, you should make sure you have the Ordnance Survey's map no. 56 (Wicklow/Dublin/Kildare; 1:50,000). If you begin your explorations at Glendalough, call in to the Wicklow Mountains National Park information centre (April & Sept Sat & Sun 10am–6pm, May–Aug daily 10am–6pm), situated at the eastern end of Glendalough's Upper Lake, for advice on routes and conditions. Bad weather can close in rapidly, and all the customary warnings about mountain walking apply; in addition to this you should avoid areas marked on the OS map as rifle ranges.

into it to feed the motherless twins of one of Kevin's followers. By following the signposted "Green Road" skirting the Lower Lake, you'll come to the tiny, ruined **Reefert Church**, dating from the late tenth century, whose small cemetery is thought to contain the graves of local chieftains, and the start of a path to **St Kevin's Cell**, where the remains of a typically Celtic, corbel-roofed hut resembling a beehive hut mark the spot where he slept on a promontory overlooking the Upper Lake. He later moved into a cave halfway up the cliff – dubbed **St Kevin's Bed** – to avoid the advances of a maiden called Kathleen. She eventually found his hiding place and, awaking one morning to find her beside him, he reacted with the misogyny characteristic of the early church fathers by throwing her into the lake, where she drowned. (Kevin himself is said to have died in 617 or 618, at the age of 120.) The cave is only accessible by boat from the far shore of the lake in summer.

RUSSBOROUGH HOUSE

Map 1, B7. April & Oct Sun & bank holidays 10.30am–5.30pm; May–Sept daily 10.30am–5.30pm; tours €6.
Bus #65 from Eden Quay.

Three miles south of the village of Blessington stands the classic Palladian structure of **Russborough House**, designed, like Powerscourt and both Leinster House and the Rotunda Maternity Hospital in Dublin (see pp.37 & 140), by the German architect Richard Cassels (with the assistance of Francis Bindon). The house was constructed for Joseph Leeson, son of a rich Dublin brewer who became MP for Rathcormack then **Lord Russborough** in 1756. In its grandiose extravagance Russborough House epitomizes the great flowering of Anglo-Irish confidence before the Act of Union deprived Ireland of its parliament, much of its trade and its high society.

The lake in front of Russborough provides the house
with an idiomatically eighteenth-century prospect – but
it's actually a thoroughly twentieth-century reservoir
(created by damming the Liffey) which provides Dublin
with twenty million gallons of water a day.

The chief reason why Russborough is so firmly on the
tourist trail is its collection of **paintings**. The German
entrepreneur Alfred Beit (1853–1906), co-founder with
Cecil Rhodes of the De Beers Diamond Mining Company,
poured the fortune he derived from that enterprise into
amassing works of art. His nephew, Sir Alfred Beit,
acquired Russborough in 1952, and donated many of his
most valuable paintings to the National Gallery (see
pp.61–75) in 1988. Only a fraction of his extraordinary collection of Dutch, English, Flemish and Spanish masterpieces are on display at Russborough at any one time (the
bulk are at the National Gallery), but you're likely to see
works by artists such as Hals, Gainsborough, Goya and
Rubens.

Russborough has been **burgled** twice: first in 1974,
when an Englishwoman, Rose Dugdale, stole sixteen paintings to raise money for the IRA (her booty, worth £18
million, was recovered undamaged from a farmhouse in
County Cork a week later); and again in May 1986 in an
operation orchestrated by one of Dublin's most notorious
criminals, Martin Cahill; the robbery subsequently became
a central element in John Boorman's 1997 film *The General*,
which takes its title from Cahill's nickname. Some of the
paintings taken in this second heist have since been
retrieved in the Netherlands, though in a damaged condition. Nowadays, security is tight; the forty-five-minute
guided tour limits study of the paintings in detail, but for all
that the house is still well worth a visit.

RUSSBOROUGH HOUSE

CASTLETOWN HOUSE

Map 1, B5. Easter–Sept Mon–Fri 10am–6pm, Sat, Sun & bank holidays 1–6pm; Oct Mon–Fri 10am–5pm, Sun & bank holidays 1–5pm; Nov Sun 1–5pm; last admission one hour before closing; tours €3.80. @www.heritageireland.ie.
Bus #67 or #67A from Wellington Quay to Celbridge.

Some thirteen miles west of Dublin, on the upper reaches of the River Liffey, the village of Celbridge is the site of one of Ireland's great Palladian mansions, **Castletown House**, a building remarkable both for its size and ostentation.

Castletown was built for **William Connolly**, a publican's son from Donegal who made his fortune by dealing in forfeited estates after the Battle of the Boyne, as legal adviser to William III. Unanimously elected Speaker of the Irish House of Commons in 1715, he was acknowledged as the richest man in Ireland by the 1720s. He later joined the Hellfire Club (see p.83), holding sessions of debauchery at his hunting lodge outside Dublin. Castletown was begun in 1722, in a somewhat haphazard fashion, and the interior was still unfinished when he died seven years later. Work on the house didn't resume until his nephew, **Tom Connolly**, inherited it in 1758. The driving force was his wife, **Lady Louisa**, who was only fifteen years old when she assumed responsibility for the job, which carried on into the 1770s. Castletown was sold by the Connolly family in 1965, and would have been demolished to build houses if the property developer owners hadn't gone bust. **Desmond Guinness** stepped in to buy the house on behalf of the Irish Georgian Society, which used Castletown as its headquarters until 1994. In 1979, ownership was assigned to the **Castletown Foundation**, who began a process of maintenance and restoration that continued once the house was transferred to State care in 1994 and underwent a £5 million restoration programme.

The **guided tour** starts in the Main Hall, where some of the characteristically ornate stucco work of the Italian Francini brothers is on view, and moves on to the pine-panelled Brown Study, the only room to retain the house's original plain decorative style. During the 1760s Sir William Chambers, the architect of Somerset House and the Kew Gardens pagoda in London, was commissioned by Lady Louisa to remodel much of the ground floor and his designs remain intact on walls of the **Red Room**, which are covered in torn French damask, and in the viridescent silk decoration and use of gilded filet in the adjacent **Green Room**. The **Print Room**, next door, is the only surviving example in Ireland of the eighteenth-century fad for glue-ing prints of the works of old masters onto walls. A splendid yellow-and-blue-silk canopied bed dominates the **State Bedroom**, beyond.

The grand cantilevered **staircase**, with what's thought to be the first set of brass banisters in Ireland, has wonderful plasterwork by the Francini brothers on the walls and a painting of bears being savaged by hunting dogs. Upstairs the highlight is the **Long Gallery**, with its Pompeiian murals and gilded sconces bearing busts of poets and philosophers, an overall effect somewhat marred by grotesque glass chandeliers from Murano, near Venice. One oddity here is a of doors on the south wall, only one of which is real – the false one exists simply to provide symmetry.

From the gallery's windows you can see the **Connolly Folly**, two miles to the north. This bizarre structure consists of a 130ft-high obelisk, balanced precariously on the top of a stack of arches, and was commissioned by Katherine Connolly as a memorial to her husband, William. She also commissioned the **Wonderful Barn**, three miles northeast of the house, a weird conical tower with an external stairway, which can be seen from the N4

CASTLETOWN HOUSE

motorway just west of the Leixlip junction. Both projects were set up to provide relief work for estate labourers hit by the famine-ridden winter of 1739. Unfortunately, the land on which both follies stand is privately owned and so not accessible to the public.

LARCHILL ARCADIAN GARDENS

Map 1, A4. Daily May–Sept noon–6pm; €6.50.
Bus #66 from Wellington Quay to Kilcock.

If you're exploring this area by car, **Larchill Arcadian Gardens**, around eight miles northwest of Castletown House, or three miles north of Kilcock off the N4, is well worth a detour. Painstakingly restored, Larchill is the only surviving example in Ireland or England of a *ferme ornée*, a type of garden (literally an "ornamental farm") that represents a midway point between the true landscaped garden and the rigorously formal style of garden that preceded it. These attained a degree of fashionabilty amongst wealthy landowners during the latter half of the eighteenth century, inspired by the influence of Marie Antoinette at the Palace of Versailles.

A fifteen-minute circular walk through avenues of beech trees links ten classical and Gothic **follies**, the most notable of which are the fortified island named **Gibraltar** and the curious **Foxes' Earth**. The latter was built on the instruction of a Mr Watson who, convinced he would be reincarnated as a fox, wanted to be sure of a bolt-hole from the hounds in his next life – it appears today as a grass-covered mound with tunnels for escape, topped by a cluster of rubble-rough columns. The ten acres of **parklands** are stocked by rare breeds of farm animals, especially sheep, some of which are kept in a string of recently constructed buildings which form a new *ferme ornée*. An attractive **walled garden** holds a variety of unusual plants, as well as a herb garden and a pergola, and these new projects are explained in the pleasant **tea-room**, where there's interesting material on the conservation project here.

BRÚ NA BÓINNE

Map 1, B1–C1. Visitor centre and Newgrange daily: March, April & Oct 9.30am–5.30pm; May & mid- to end-Sept 9am–6.30pm; June to mid-Sept 9am–7pm; Nov–Feb 9.30am–5pm; last tours 1hr30min before closing. Knowth: same times but May–Oct only. Visitor Centre €2.50; combined ticket with Newgrange €5; combined ticket with Knowth €3.80; all three €8.80. @www.heritageireland.ie. Suburban train from Pearse St, Tara St or Connolly stations to Drogheda, then bus #163 to Donore.

Around thirty miles north of Dublin, caught within a curve of the River Boyne between Tullyallen and Slane, is the area known as **Brú na Bóinne**, an extraordinary landscape which retains forty or so related prehistoric tombs, vestiges of Neolithic settlements that sprang up here as a result of the valley's rich soil; the sheer imposing solidity of these remains leaves a lasting impression. The three most important sites, **Dowth** (which is still being excavated), **Knowth** and **Newgrange**, are **passage graves** – high round mounds raised over stone burial chambers. All access to Newgrange and Knowth is channelled through the visitor centre, in **DONORE**, from which you're whisked by minibus to begin your guided tour of the sites.

As one of Ireland's major attractions, Brú na Bóinne draws a huge number of visitors, especially during the summer months, and because the graves can only hold a limited number of people at any one time (and the total is restricted to just six hundred per day), it's advisable to arrive early in the morning or be prepared for what can be a very long

BRÚ NA BÓINNE

wait. Sadly, the site's popularity can leave you with the sense of being herded about, but it's impossible not to be overawed by the sheer magnificence of these Neolithic achievements. Although you can't book a tour in advance of your arrival, you can do so once at the **visitor centre**, where well-constructed and informative displays provide some background on the sites' significance, both religious and social, as well as explaining, in detail, the original construction process.

Newgrange

About eight miles west of Drogheda, **Newgrange** Neolithic tumulus is an artificial mound built between 3500 and 2700 BC, when stone was the only material available for use as tools. The mind boggles at the effort required to transport the building materials, which amounted to 450 giant boulders and over one million sackfuls of small stones – a task believed to have taken forty years. Though evidently important, its purpose remains unclear: a burial place, a cenotaph, a solar temple or a kind of astronomical chart have all been suggested as functions.

To confuse matters, the mound is surrounded by later additions, such as the **Great Circle** of massive standing stones, of which a dozen of the estimated 35 originals remain upright. There is also a series of concrete **slabs** and wooden **stakes**, the former representing the remains of a satellite passage grave which has largely been destroyed over the centuries, the latter marking the centre-point of deep pits whose purpose remains unknown.

The grass-covered mound itself covers about an acre. Around 250ft in diameter and rising gradually to a height of just over 40ft at its centre, it has the look of a grounded, green flying saucer. The white quartz **retaining wall** gives some hint of the power this stone must have had for the builders, since the nearest source is the Wicklow Mountains. The base is girdled by a ring of 97 granite **kerbstones** weighing between four and eight tonnes apiece. These were quarried in the Mourne Mountains of County Down – it's estimated that it would have taken eighty men four days to drag one from the quarry to the river, whence it was transported by boat to Newgrange.

The most important feature, and one which distinguishes Newgrange from Dowth and Knowth, is the **roof-box** above the entrance, containing a slit through which the light of the rising sun penetrates the tomb on the **winter solstice** (December 21). At 8.58am, the rays start edging their way slowly up the passage, to illuminate the chamber at the far end with an orange glow, which fades away fifteen minutes later. Guided tours feature a speeded-up "re-creation" of this phenomenon, using electric light; there's a nine-year waiting list to witness the real event, though the effect is almost as good a couple of days before or after the solstice.

The **passage** extends for twenty yards into the tumulus (about a quarter of its depth), sloping gently upwards so that the floor of the chamber at the end is the same height off the ground as the roof-box. The **chamber** is roughly cross-shaped with a corbelled roof of huge slabs that stands exactly as it did some five thousand years ago, without renovation or repair. When the chamber was excavated in 1967 the charred bones of four or five people were found, which some take as proof that only priests and rulers were buried here – others argue that is where bodies were merely laid out before being interred elsewhere (a theory given credence by the discovery of hundreds of cremated remains in other tumuli).

BRÚ NA BÓINNE

Knowth

Major excavations have been going on at **Knowth** since 1962, but since the mid-1990s about a third of the complex has been opened to the public. Though there's less to see for visitors here, the discoveries have already surpassed what was excavated at Newgrange. At Knowth alone, about 250 decorated stones have been found: over half of all known Irish passage-grave art.

Several periods of occupation by different cultures have been identified, from the **Neolithic**, when the original passage tombs were built (around 3200 BC), through occupation by the Beaker people (2000–1800 BC) – so-called because of a distinctive beaker left with each of their dead – and a late **Celtic** settlement in the early centuries AD. Early **Christian** occupation has been identified from the eighth to twelfth centuries, bringing a glut of souterrains (underground passages and chambers), followed by **Norman** usage during the twelfth and thirteenth centuries.

The main passage tomb is about twice the size of that at Newgrange – with a tunnel almost 100ft long leading to the central chamber – and even more richly decorated. There's also a smaller second passage tomb within the main tumulus, and up to seventeen **satellite tumuli**. Structurally the main mound is similar to the one at Newgrange, with a cruciform chamber, high corbelled roof and richly decorated stones. However, unlike Newgrange, evidence (such as bronze and iron workings) has been found here of settlement around the mound, while the discovery of a circle of large holes suggests that a wood-henge might once have stood here.

LISTINGS

Accommodation

Although new places continue to spring up around Dublin's city centre, the ever-rising demand for **accommodation** means that there's hardly a slack season. Unless you're willing to risk a frustrating search for a bed, it's necessary to make **reservations** if you're arriving at the weekend (Fri–Sun) any time of year; on weekdays over summer; or around St Patrick's Day (March 17), Easter or major sporting or musical events. How far in advance you make your booking depends: one or two weeks should be OK in February or November, but one or two months is more appropriate for peak times. If you arrive without a reservation, it's possible to book on the spot at any of the Dublin Tourism offices (see p.6). With a credit card, this can also be done by phone (see box below), or by using the touch-screens outside tourist offices.

If you book directly at the tourist office or over the phone using the numbers in the box above, an €3 charge is levied; using the touch-screen is free. However all three services require you to pay a **deposit** of ten percent of your hotel or guesthouse bill in advance – you pay the balance at the establishment. Alternatively, you can run through the listings here and phone around yourself, or use the **USITNow** discount student travel agency on Aston Quay, opposite O'Connell Bridge (Mon–Wed & Fri 9.30am–6.30pm,

BOOKING ACCOMMODATION BY TELEPHONE

For **telephone accommodation reservations** anywhere in Ireland call the Gulliver freephone ☏ 1800/6686 6866. International freephone calls can also be made from the UK, France, Belgium, Germany, Switzerland, Norway, Sweden, Finland, Denmark, the USA, Canada, Australia and New Zealand. Use the international access code (00) plus your country's freephone code, e.g. from the UK call ☏ 00 800/6686 6866, from the USA call ☏ 011 800/6686 6866. From all other countries call ☏ 00353/6697 92082.

Thurs 9.30am–8pm, Sat 9.30am–5pm; ☏ 602 1600; ⓦ www.usitnow.ie), which can book you a B&B during the summer, as well as running its own hotel and hostel; like the tourist centre, it can get busy and operates a ticket waiting system.

The telephone code for the Dublin area is ☏ 01.
Calling Dublin from abroad (or Northern Ireland), dial
☏ 00-353-1, followed by the subscriber's number.

The accommodation in this chapter is divided into the following categories: **hotels and B&Bs**, **hostels**, **student accommodation** and **camping**. Our listings are divided geographically, starting in the centre and moving, first northwards and then southwards, through the suburbs to the outskirts. Central Dublin is split into the southside and Temple Bar, and the inner northside. The **southside** has traditionally been the focus for the capital's top-quality accommodation, and the best establishments around Merrion and Fitzwilliam squares and St Stephen's Green share the elegance and charm of the surrounding streets; **Temple Bar**, by contrast, is home to some of the newest hotels and hostels, but as the area is packed full of young revellers, it can be exceedingly noisy unless your room has soundproofed windows. Accommodation on the **inner northside** is concentrated around Gardiner Street, which used to be a little dingy but has, in places, improved of late. That said, take care with your bags here and avoid walking back alone late at night.

The suburbs to the north of the city, **Clontarf, Drumcondra and Glasnevin**, are quiet areas easily accessible from the airport and served by regular buses into the centre. To the south are **Ballsbridge, Donnybrook and Sandymount**. Ballsbridge and Donnybrook are affluent suburbs with plenty of decent accommodation – again all three are served by regular buses, and Sandymount, situated on the coast, is also accessible by DART (Sandymount or Sydney Parade stations).

The seaside towns on the outskirts of Dublin, **Howth** in the north and **Dún Laoghaire**, **Dalkey and Killiney** in the south, are all attractive places to stay and are served by DART, making commuting into the centre very easy.

ACCOMMODATION PRICE CODES

Accommodation prices vary throughout the year, with the highest rates between June and September, over Christmas, Easter and St Patrick's Day, and during events such as international rugby matches. Our listings for hotels, guesthouses and B&Bs have been graded according to a code (eg ⑤) which represents the price of the cheapest double room in high season, including breakfast (unless otherwise stated), as follows:

① Under €50   ④ €90–110   ⑦ €160–200
② €50–70   ⑤ €110–130   ⑧ €200–300
③ €70–90   ⑥ €130–160   ⑨ Over €300

ACCOMMODATION

HOTELS, GUESTHOUSES AND B&BS

Hotels in Dublin (especially those on the southside) are generally quite expensive, though it's worth bearing in mind that many – particularly those geared towards the business market – offer competitive weekend rates. **Guesthouses** and **B&Bs** are in abundance, ranging from an extra room in a family home to luxurious properties that are hotels in all but name (and which charge similar prices) – again, the pick are on the southside, although you'll find some good deals in the suburbs.

THE SOUTHSIDE AND TEMPLE BAR

Adams Trinity Hotel
Map 6, F6. 28 Dame Lane ⓣ670 7100, ⓔadamshtl @indigo.ie.

Small, welcoming hotel near Dublin Castle, with comfortable rooms equipped with double-glazing and Victorian reproduction furniture. Breakfast is served on a gallery overlooking the bar, there's no private lounge, and as street noise is inevitable, this isn't ideal if you want to unwind at the end of the day. Reductions available at weekends and on triple rooms. ❻

Bewley's Principal Hotel
Map 4, E5. 19–20 Fleet St ⓣ670 8122, ⓦwww.bewleysprincipalhotel .com.

Cosy, friendly and recently refurbished three-star hotel on the edge of Temple Bar, with old-style decor in keeping with the famous café below. There's a pleasant lounge and breakfast is served on a small gallery overlooking the café till 9.30am, after which it is available all day in the self-service section downstairs. Some rooms are air conditioned. Secure parking nearby. ❼

Burlington Hotel
Map 3, H8. Leeson St Upper ⓣ660 5222, ⓦwww.jurysdoyle.com.

A massive modern four-star in a pleasant location within walking distance of the city centre. Particularly well-equipped for conferences and tour groups hence the Irish cabaret several nights a week. **9**

Buswell's Hotel
Map 4, F7. 23–27 Molesworth St ⊤614 6500, ⊛www.quinnhotels .com.
This superb Georgian town-house offers comfortable three-star accommodation in a prime, quiet location near Leinster House. Decorative plasterwork, ornamental fireplaces, and antique furniture in the lobby and brasserie ensure a sense of tradition; the homely bedrooms have been recently refurbished. No car park. **7**

Central Hotel
Map 5, H8. 1–5 Exchequer St ⊤679 7302, ⊛www.centralhotel.ie.
Refurbished nineteenth-century establishment (part of the Best Western group) on the corner of South Great George's Street, near both

Dublin Castle and Temple Bar. Pleasant, cheery rooms with soundproofing; plus comfortable Victorian bars and a lounge enlivened by contemporary Irish paintings. Secure parking nearby. **7**

The Clarence
Map 6, B4. 6–8 Wellington Quay ⊤407 0800, ⊛www .theclarence.ie.
Ultra-stylish, five-star Temple Bar hotel owned by U2, containing the award winning *Tea Room* restaurant (see p.274), as well as penthouse suites used by sundry rock stars. All rooms come with video, candles and Egyptian linen. Rates don't include breakfast. **8**

Fitzwilliam
Map 4, G9. 41 Fitzwilliam St Upper ⊤662 5155, ⓔfitzwilliamguesthouse @eircom.net.
A plush, twelve-bedroom southside guesthouse on the corner of Baggot Street Lower, with a restaurant, bar and en-suite rooms with TV and phone. Parking available, as are discounts for children. **6**

The Georgian Hotel

Map 4, G9. 18–22 Baggot St Lower ⊤ 634 5000, ⓔ info @georgianhotel.ie.

A fine Georgian townhouse with a new extension, a short walk from St Stephen's Green. Breakfast is served in the ancient cellar, and the 47 en-suite bedrooms are immaculately furnished. Parking available, and discounts for children. ❼

Harcourt Hotel

Map 4, D10. 60 Harcourt St ⊤ 478 3677, ⓌⓌⓌ.harcourthotel .ie.

Pleasant three-star hotel not far from St Stephen's Green; George Bernard Shaw once had a flat in one of the houses that have been knocked together to form the hotel. All rooms are en suite, and there's the *Tomato* bar on site, noted for its traditional music sessions, restaurant and nightclub (see p.308). Discount for children. ❼

Harding Hotel

Map 4, A6. Copper Alley, Fishamble St ⊤ 679 6500, Ⓦ www.hardinghotel.ie.

Attractive two-star USITNow hotel facing Christ Church Cathedral. Bright and cheerful rooms with en-suite facilities, and a good-value flat rate of €92 applying to twin, double and triple rooms. The wood-panelled bar/restaurant *Darkey Kelly's*, named after the keeper of a notorious eighteenth-century brothel on Copper Alley; often has live rock music at night, making this a lively place to stay. ❹

Harrington Hall

Map 4, D10. 70 Harcourt St ⊤ 475 3497, Ⓦ www.harringtonhall.com.

Deservedly popular and elegantly furnished Georgian guesthouse, with 28 comfortable, well-equipped en-suite rooms whose windows have been soundproofed against street noise. Superb breakfasts are served in a bright and airy basement. Secure parking. ❽

Jury's Inn Christchurch

Map 4, A6. Christchurch Place ⊤ 454 0000, Ⓦ www.jurysdoyle.com.

A three-star eyesore opposite

Christ Church. Comfortable, modern rooms accommodate up to three adults, or two adults and two children, so their flat rate of €91 (€96 at weekends) represents good value. Bar and restaurant; rates don't include breakfast. ❹

Kilronan Guesthouse

Map 3, G7. 70 Adelaide Rd ⑦475 5266, ⓦwww.dublinn .com.
Excellent, family-run Georgian guesthouse in a quiet setting within walking distance of St Stephen's Green. Ten en-suite bed-rooms with plenty of facilities and, best of all, orthopaedic beds. Private car parking and splendid breakfasts. ❻

Leeson Inn

Map 4, F10. 24 Leeson St Lower ⑦662 2002, ⓦwww.leesoninn.com.
Elegant four-storey Georgian townhouse just off St Stephen's Green that makes a delightful southside option. The bedrooms, all en-suite, are thoughtfully designed around original Georgian

sash windows with natural colours and contemporary furnishings. Breakfast is a continental-style buffet. Friendly staff. Attractive low-season rates (❹) available; as is parking. ❻

Longfields Hotel

Map 4, H9. 9–10 Fitzwilliam St Lower ⑦676 1367, ⓦwww.longfields.ie.
A haven of peace within walking distance of the National Gallery, *Longfields* stands on one of Dublin's finest Georgian streets, and has a real air of gentility. Bedrooms vary in size, but all are comfortably furnished with lavish drapes and large firm beds, some four-posters. Renowned for its excellent gourmet restaurant, *Kevin Arundel@Number 10.* ❼

Le Meridien Shelbourne

Map 4, E8. 27 St Stephen's Green North ⑦663 4500, ⓦwww.shelbourne.ie.
Dublin's most prestigious hotel, and a society watering-hole. Elegantly furnished period interiors and a buzzing social life (afternoon

HOTELS, GUESTHOUSES AND B&Bs

tea in the Lord Mayor's Lounge is a Dublin tradition), plus an excellent restaurant, bar (see p.289), swimming pool and health club. Rates do not include 15 percent service charge. ⑨

The Merrion Hotel

Map 4, G8. Merrion St Upper ⓣ603 0600, ⓦwww.merrionhotel.com. This five-star hotel, replete with top-hatted doorman, is housed in four restored eighteenth-century townhouses and offers every modern amenity including its own spa and pool, plus the exclusive *Patrick Guilbaud* restaurant (see p.279). ⑨

Mont Clare Hotel

Map 4, G7. Merrion Square North ⓣ607 3800, ⓦwww.ocallaghanhotels.ie. Smart, glossy-fronted three-star hotel near the National Gallery, with generously proportioned, well-furnished rooms. Popular with middle-aged tourists, but with none of the stuffiness associated with that market niche. Facilities include room ser-

The Morgan

Map 6, H3. 10 Fleet St ⓣ679 3939, ⓦwww.themorgan.com. This small, style-conscious hotel, whose frontage is more like a Parisian haute couture establishment, was the birthplace of youthful rebel Kevin Barry, hung by the British and the subject of a ballad song still popular amongst Nationalists. Minimalist bedrooms come with just about everything covered in cream cotton, except the occasional abstract, plus TV, CD player and tape deck. Continental breakfast is served either in your room or the *A1 Sports Café* next door – a bit of a shock after the tranquillity within. ⑧

Number 31

Map 4, F10. 31 Leeson Close, off Leeson St Lower ⓣ676 5011, ⓦwww.number31.ie. A stylishly converted stable block forms the sitting and breakfast areas of this seclud-

vice, valet parking and fitness centre. Good weekend discounts available. Bar and restaurant. ⑧

ed, family-run Georgian guesthouse, the former home of architect Sam Stephenson – the sunken lounge, turf fires and ethnic rugs give it the air of a country retreat in the heart of the city. Comfortable rooms, excellent breakfasts and great hospitality. ⑦

Paramount Hotel

Map 6, A5. Parliament St ⑦417 9900, ⓦwww.paramounthotel.ie. Set in a prime location on the western fringe of Temple Bar, the *Paramount* dates from the 1930s, but you'd never guess this from its modish, en-suite bedrooms nor the lively bar/bistro. Rooms come with every imaginable facility and there are substantial reductions midweek. ⑦

Staunton's on the Green

Map 4, F8. 83 St Stephen's Green East ⑦478 2300, ⓦhttp://indigo.ie/~hotels. One of the swankiest guesthouses on the southside: an elegant Georgian house overlooking the Green, with its own private garden. All rooms are en suite with

phone and TV, and there's a bar and parking. Family-friendly, with discounts for children. ⑦

The Temple Bar Hotel

Map 6, H3. 13–17 Fleet St ⑦677 3333, ⓦwww.towerhotelgroup.ie. A spacious lobby of tasteful prints and generous sofas sets the tone for this superior three-star hotel with its popular *Buskers* bar. Breakfast is served in a light-filled, glass-roofed dining room; comfortable bedrooms each with TV, phone and en-suite bathroom. Front rooms can be noisy. Triples available; under-12s stay free; reductions for weekend breaks. ⑦

The Westbury Hotel

Map 4, D7. Harry St, off Grafton St ⑦679 1122, ⓦwww.jurysdoyle.com. Lavish five-star hotel, where facilities include underground parking, fitness centre, restaurant, bistro and elegant lounge-bar. Luxurious throughout – you can even watch TV while having a soak, since bathrooms have

HOTELS, GUESTHOUSES AND B&Bs

screens blended into their mirror-lined walls. Reductions available at weekends. **9**

Westin Dublin

Map 4, E4. Westomoreland St ⓣ 645 1000, ⓦ www.westin.com. Opened in September 2001, this swish, five-storey temple of excellence hides behind the nineteenth-century facade of the old Allied Irish Bank building just north of Trinity College. Its 163 bedrooms are designed with character and elegantly equipped, while the bar is housed in the former bank's vaults, and the lounge has a stunning glass roof. **9**

THE INNER NORTH-SIDE

Anchor Guest House

Map 4, F2. 49 Gardiner St Lower ⓣ 878 6913, ⓦ www.anchorguesthouse.com. All rooms in this tastefully refurbished Georgian house are en suite with TV and phone. Limited parking is available, but ring ahead, as on-street parking in this area is not recommended. Infants free; discount for children. **4**

Celtic Lodge Guesthouse

Map 4, F2. 81–82 Talbot St ⓣ 677 9955, ⓔ celticguesthouse @eircom.net. Housed in a converted Victorian residence, this businesslike guesthouse has brightly decorated and comfortably furnished en-suite bedrooms overlooking the street, all with TV. Breakfast is served in an even brighter canteen; there's a bar downstairs, but no residents' lounge. However although it's just a short walk into town, the location is unattractive. **5**

Charleville Lodge

Map 3, D2. 268–272 North Circular Rd, Phibsborough ⓣ 838 6633, ⓦ www.charlevillelodge.ie. A fine, family-run guesthouse in a Victorian terrace near Phoenix Park with well-furnished and extremely comfortable bedrooms. The owners can arrange a round at a local golf club, if you fancy

ACCOMMODATION

bringing your clubs. Price includes an excellent breakfast. Babysitting service; parking available. **5**

Chief O'Neill's Hotel

Map 5, D6. Smithfield ☎ 817 3838, ⊛ www.chiefoneills.com. Ultramodern hotel deploying minimalist styles. Bedrooms combine bold contemporary design-pieces with cool light and lines, plus en-suite showers, TV, CD players and tea-making facilities. Similarly-styled lounge and bars occupy the lower floors, and are used for live music shows at the weekends. Centrally located, but take care coming back at night as this isn't the safest part of town. Special weekend rates; limited parking. **8**

Clifden Guesthouse

Map 5, H2. 32 Gardiner Place ☎ 874 6364, ⊛ www.clifdenhouse.com. Set in an old Georgian street just off Mountjoy Square, *Clifden* has extremely helpful owners and fourteen pleasant en-suite rooms (single, double, twin, triple and family), each with TV. Child discount

and midweek reductions are available, as is a babysitting service and private car parking. **5**

Comfort Inn

Map 4, E2. 95–98 Talbot St ☎ 874 9202, ⊛ www.comfort-inn-dublin.com. A recently converted, centrally located northside guesthouse, close to O'Connell Street and the Liffey. All rooms are en suite and non-smoking, with cable TV and phones. Discounts for children, and cots available. **7**

The Gate Hotel

Map 4, D1. 80–82 Parnell St ☎ 872 2500. Popular northside hotel, thanks to its score of comfortable en-suite bedrooms, all equipped with TV, and extremely economical prices. Family-friendly. **3**

The Gresham

Map 4, D2. 23 O'Connell St Upper ☎ 874 6881, ⊛ www.gresham-hotels.com. Dublin's oldest hotel, and one of the classiest, comprising 288 luxury bedrooms and six

HOTELS, GUESTHOUSES AND B&Bs

even more opulent penthouse suites. The grandiose lobby, with its crystal chandeliers, decorative stucco work and potted palms, makes the perfect spot for afternoon tea. Comfortable, recently refurbished rooms (some with oversized beds), and a huge range of amenities including restaurant and bar, room service, valet parking and a well-equipped business centre. Family-friendly. ❽

Hotel Isaacs
Map 4, G3. Store St ☏ 855 0067, ⓦ www.isaacs.ie.
The upmarket sister to *Isaacs* hostel (see p.258), situated right next to Busáras, offering 58 brightly furnished en-suite rooms, all with TV as well as its own Italian restaurant, *Il Vignardo*, and the associated *Isaac Butt* pub (see p.299) next door. Prices rise by €10 at weekends. ❻

Marian Guesthouse
Map 5, H2. 21 Gardiner St Upper ☏ 874 4129.
The best budget B&B near the city centre, with six rooms, shared bathrooms and

a garden. Unlike other nearby options there are no price hikes at peak times, so this is recommended for lone travellers on a budget who want a basic, clean, private room. ❶

Morrison
Map 4, C4. Ormond Quay Lower ☏ 887 2400, ⓦ www.morrisonhotel.ie.
A minimalist *tour de force*, this is one of Dublin's most stylish new hotels. Perfectly proportioned throughout, the decor here (John Rocha was design consultant) utilizes natural Irish materials with dark ash brown fittings and cream stone floors; the penthouse is utterly stunning. Aside from offering aesthetic bliss, bedrooms have en-suite bathrooms plus mod cons including CD players and ISDN links. On site are a very mellow bar and the *Halo* restaurant (see p.282). ❽

Ormond Quay Hotel
Map 4, A5. 7–11 Ormond Quay Upper ☏ 872 1811, ⓦ www.ormondquayhotel.com.
Historic hotel (it features in

HOTELS, GUESTHOUSES AND B&BS

Ulysses) on the north bank of the Liffey, offering bright and cheerful recently refurbished rooms. The hotel has its own art gallery, and the *Sirens* bar and restaurant is a popular spot; there's no separate sitting-room, but guests looking for a more relaxed evening can use the fairly spacious and comfortable lobby. No car parking. ❻

Othello Guesthouse

Map 4, F2. 74 Gardiner St Lower Ⓣ855 4271, Ⓔothello1@eircom.net.
One of the area's longest-established guesthouses, bedecked with pleasant window-boxes and floral displays. Twenty-two en-suite bedrooms with TV and telephone; family rooms are available at good rates. The Irish breakfast is very good. Secure parking available; child-friendly. ❹

The Townhouse

Map 4, F2. 47–48 Gardiner St Lower Ⓣ878 8808, Ⓔgtrotter@indigo.ie.
A snazzily refurbished Georgian house that once belonged to the playwrights Dion Boucicault and Lafcadio Hearn, and definitely the classiest guesthouse on the northside, with a hostel (see p.257) attached. All rooms are en suite with TV, fridge and tea-maker. Fine healthy breakfast. Secure parking. Higher rates at weekends. ❻

CLONTARF, DRUMCONDRA AND GLASNEVIN

Clontarf Castle Hotel

Map 2, G4. Castle Ave, Clontarf Ⓣ833 2321, Ⓦwww.clontarfcastle.ie.
This superbly renovated four-star hotel, occupying a castle which dates back in part to 1172, boasts exquisitely and individually designed bedrooms, a swimming pool, two bars and a bistro. To cap it all, service is highly efficient and friendly. ❽

Mary Dunwoody

Map 2, G4. 19 Copeland Ave, Clontarf Ⓣ833 909, Ⓔcdunwoody@eircom.net.
A long-established, semi-

detached guesthouse in the vicinity of the Casino. Mrs Dunwoody's welcome is as warm as ever, and the three rooms (two en suite) are clean, well-equipped and represent good value for money. Non-smoking. Open March–Nov. ❷

Egan's Guest House
Map 2, F3. 7–9 Iona Park, Glasnevin ⊤ 830 3611, ⓦ www.eganshouse.com.
Situated in a quiet road near the Botanic Gardens, this friendly, family-run guesthouse is an excellent option – all bedrooms are en suite with TV and telephone. Car parking is available at the front of the house, and there are child-minding facilities. ❹

Hedigan's
Map 2, G4. 14 Hollybrook Park, Clontarf ⊤ 853 1663, ⓔ hedigans@indigo.ie.
Fine detached, listed Victorian house just off Howth Road next to Clontarf Golf Club. *Hedigan's* is well furnished (rooms are

themed according to different countries), and offers secure parking, child-minding facilities, a small playground and reductions for children and pensioners. ❹

Kathleen Hurney
Map 2, F4. 69 Hollybank Rd, Drumcondra ⊤ 837 7907.
Four comfy rooms with TV, two of them en suite, in a terraced house near the bus stop for easy access to the centre. Discounts for children. Non-smoking. ❷

The White House
Map 2, G4. 125 Clontarf Rd, Clontarf ⊤ 833 3196, ⓔ info@family-homes.ie.
Very friendly house near to Dublin Bay that offers excellent value for money, including a substantial breakfast, and is on the #130 bus route into the centre. Three bedrooms: one double, one twin and one family. Booking early is essential for the summer months. ❷

HOTELS, GUESTHOUSES AND B&BS

HOWTH

Margaret & Michael Campbell

Map 8, 93. Highfield, Thormanby Rd ☎832 3936. Up towards The Summit, this late-Victorian guesthouse has three rooms with TV, two of them en suite (the front rooms offer views of Malahide). Families are especially welcome. Child discount; cot available. ❷

Hazelwood

Map 8, 94. 2 Thormanby Woods, off Thormanby Rd ☎ & ℻839 1391. A large modern bungalow set in its own extensive grounds, one mile away from the seafront near Howth Golf Club. Four en-suite, non-smoking bedrooms with fifty-percent child discounts; plenty of parking space. ❷

King Sitric's Restaurant

Map 8, F6. East Pier ☎832 5235, ℮info@kingsitric.ie. A piscivore's ultimate fantasy, with eight well-appointed en-suite rooms, all with sea views, slap bang by the harbour and above one of the area's finest seafood restaurants. Closed Christmas and the last two weeks in January. ❼

BALLSBRIDGE, DONNYBROOK AND SANDYMOUNT

Aaronmor Guesthouse

Map 2, G5. 1B–1C Sandymount Ave, Ballsbridge ☎668 7972, ℮aaronmor @indigo.ie. Elegant red-brick house on the road leading from Ballsbridge to Sandymount, with large, comfortable en-suite rooms, excellent service and great breakfasts. ❺

Aberdeen Lodge

Map 2, G5. 53–55 Park Ave, Ballsbridge ☎283 8155, ⓦwww .halpinsprivatehotels.com. Luxurious four-star accommodation in an Edwardian house in landscaped gardens, set on a quiet street running parallel to the coast and near

HOTELS, GUESTHOUSES AND B&Bs

249

to Sandymount and Sydney Road DART stations. A cut above the average guesthouse, *Aberdeen Lodge* offers, amongst other things, suites with a private jacuzzi and four-poster beds, elegant lounges and a license to sell alcohol. ❻

Anglesea Town House

Map 2, G5. 63 Anglesea Rd, Ballsbridge ☎ 668 3877, ℻ 668 3461.

First-rate accommodation in an elegant Edwardian family house on the road leading from Ballsbridge to Donnybrook. Beautifully restored period rooms, many with the original fireplaces still intact, and a great, award-winning breakfast made entirely from home produce. Free parking available; child-friendly. Closed Christmas and New Year. ❺

Berkeley Court Hotel

Map 2, G5. Lansdowne Rd, Ballsbridge ☎ 660 1711, ⓦ www.jurysdoyle.com.

Hideous exterior, but the interior of this prestigious hotel combines conservative

elegance with utter luxury. Five-star facilities include mini-gym and business centre. ❾

Mrs Maureen Bermingham

Map 2, G5. 8 Dromard Terrace, off Seafort Ave, Sandymount ☎ 668 3861.

Family-run, value-for-money guesthouse in an ivy-covered period house a minute's walk from the beach; reachable from the centre via bus #2 and #3 or Sandymount DART station. Old-fashioned comfort with three non-smoking bedrooms, one en suite. Open May–Sept. ❷

Bewley's Hotel

Just off **Map 3, J8.** Next to the RDS, Merrion Rd, Ballsbridge ☎ 668 1111, ⓦ www.bewleyshotel.com.

Excellent-value, comfortable rooms (all one price, no matter how many occupants) in a beautiful red-brick Victorian edifice – fronted by an elegant terracotta fountain and entered through a grand lobby – which started life as a masonic school for orphan

HOTELS, GUESTHOUSES AND B&BS

girls. Catering facilities have improved somewhat since then, in the form of the top-notch *O'Connell's* restaurant (see p.278). ❹

Camelot

Map 3, I8. 37 Pembroke Park, Ballsbridge ☎668 0331.
One of several excellent options in a pleasant street that's only a five-minute bus ride from the centre (#10 and #46A), *Camelot* has friendly owners, well-appointed en-suite rooms with TV, excellent breakfasts and parking on the fore-court. ❸

Lansdowne Hotel

Map 3, I7. 27–29 Pembroke Rd, Ballsbridge ☎668 2522, ⓦwww.lansdownehotel.com.
Popular with rugby fans due to its proximity to Lansdowne Road stadium, this well-equipped forty-bedroom hotel, including two suites, is set in pleasant leafy surroundings within walking distance of the cen-tre. Sports memorabilia deco-rate the *Den* bar, and *Druids*

restaurant is designed in a "Celtic" style. ❼

Merrion Hall

Map 2, G5. 54 Merrion Rd, Ballsbridge ☎668 1426, ⓦwww.halpinsprivatehotels .com.
Sister establishment to *Aberdeen Lodge* (see p.249), *Merrion Hall* shares all the same luxurious facilities, though is set in a busier loca-tion on the main road to Dún Laoghaire. There's a library, comfortable drawing rooms, superbly furnished suites and bedrooms and a private car park and gardens. ❻

Montrose House

Map 3, I8. 16 Pembroke Park, Ballsbridge ☎668 4286.
Some rooms in this elegantly furnished townhouse are almost suite-like in size. Most are en-suite with TV and there are plenty of books available if you're short of reading matter. Breakfast is taken communally around the same table. On-street parking requires a disc available from nearby machines. ❸

HOTELS, GUESTHOUSES AND B&BS

St Jude's Guesthouse

Map 3, I8. 17 Pembroke Park, Ballsbridge ☎668 0928, 🖷668 0483.

Comfortable en-suite accommodation in a quiet location; all rooms have TV and there's parking on the house's forecourt. The excellent breakfast is taken in a pleasant downstairs room. ❸

Stonehaven

Map 2, G5. 9 Claremont Rd, Sandymount ☎ & 🖷668 2028.

Cosy, ivy-clad Victorian townhouse in Sandymount village, ten minutes' walk from the sea and Lansdowne Road DART station. The house has three comfortable and neatly furnished en-suite rooms, maintained well by the friendly owner. Open March–Nov. ❸

DÚN LAOGHAIRE

Gresham Royal Marine Hotel

Map 7, B3. Royal Marine Rd ☎280 1911, 🖦www.gresham-hotels.com.

Sister to the famous *Gresham* on O'Connell Street (see p.245), this grandiose nineteenth-century hotel is set in spacious grounds overlooking Dublin Bay. Rooms are comfortable and facilities include a bar, restaurant, 24hr room service, laundry service, babysitting and parking. Reductions of up to fifty percent available some weekends. ❽

Kingston Hotel

Map 7, C3. Adelaide St ☎280 1810, 🖦www.kingstonhotel.com.

The facade doesn't do justice to the interior of this large, family-run Victorian hotel; bedrooms are decorated in pale green and fitted with comfortable dark-wood furniture. Ask for a room overlooking the bay. The cheerful and popular bar serves food daily till 9.30pm. Limited parking. ❻

Lynden

Map 7, C3. 2 Mulgrave Terrace ☎280 6404, 🖂lynden@iol.ie.

A friendly family-run

Georgian guesthouse, five minutes' walk from the car-ferry terminus, with four comfortable rooms (two en suite). The helpful owners offer a value-for-money service, including early morning breakfasts for those catching the ferry. Secure parking available. ❷

Windsor Lodge
Map 7, D3. 3 Islington Ave ☎284 6952, @winlodge@eircom.net.
Ideally located on a small street leading from the coast, near to Sandycove & Glastule DART station, this non-smoking house with four en-suite rooms is especially suitable for families, as it offers a childminding service and generous concessions for older children. Secure parking. ❸

DALKEY AND KILLINEY

The Court Hotel
Map 2, I8. Killiney Bay, Killiney ☎285 1622, @book@killineycourt.ie.

Large Victorian mansion set in pleasant gardens overlooking Killiney Bay. Bedrooms have en-suite bathrooms and TVs, and some have sea views. Two restaurants, one specializing in fish dishes, and a bar. Very handy for Killiney DART station; good weekend rates, midweek specials and child discounts. ❼

Fitzpatrick Castle Hotel
Map 2, I8. Killiney ☎284 0700, @www.fitzpatrickhotels.com.
Former stately home complete with battlements, set in a landscaped garden below Killiney Hill with views overlooking Dublin Bay, that's now a comfortable four-star hotel, whose antique furnishings give it a traditional character. Facilities include indoor pool, sauna, gym and crèche. Child discounts. ❽

Ms Betty MacAnaney.
Map 2, I8. 70 Avondale Rd, Killiney ☎285 9952, @www.macananey.com.
A pleasant modern bungalow in a quiet road, ten minutes' walk from Glenageary DART station, consisting of three

HOTELS, GUESTHOUSES AND B&BS

en-suite double rooms and one standard. Open Feb–Nov. ❷

Tudor House
Map 7, G3. Off Castle St, Dalkey ☏ 285 1528, ⓔtudorhousedalkey@hotmail .com.

Listed manor house set in its own grounds, offering six individually and stylishly decorated en-suite rooms with views over Dublin Bay. Elegant throughout, this family-owned establishment offers real seclusion from the Dublin bustle. ❺

HOSTELS

Although Dublin has always had its fair share of budget options, the recent increase of young tourists has boosted the amount of upmarket **hostels** you'll find around the city – while some of these offer a very high standard of shared accommodation, they do lack something of the traditional communal feeling you associate with hostelling. Hot showers, luggage rooms, payphones and TV lounges are standard; other facilities vary.

Hostel **prices** vary considerably, depending on season, location, facilities and demand. The high season price of a dorm bed per person ranges from €11.50 to €34, but, on average, you should expect to pay €22 to €25 in high season. Bear in mind, though, that some hostels charge a weekend supplement of €2 to €4. Nearly all the hostels affiliated to **Independent Holiday Hostels of Ireland** (IHH; ⓦ www.hostels-ireland.com) operate a price range system which guarantees that at least twenty percent of their beds are at the lowest price stated. Naturally, these fill up early, so it's advisable to book ahead where possible; all hostels listed below belong to IHH unless otherwise stated. Hostels affiliated to **Independent Hostel Owners Ireland** (IHO; ⓦ www.holidayhound.com/ihi) don't operate the same system, though most will still have a range of prices. Prices for all hostels will be a few euro higher for beds in smaller four- or six-bed dorms, and substantially more in twin- or double-bedded **private rooms** – we've given price codes for the private rooms within the listings. Unless otherwise indicated, every hostel listed below is open twenty-four hours and includes breakfast and bed linen in its rates.

THE SOUTHSIDE AND TEMPLE BAR

Ashfield House
Map 4, E4. 19–20 D'Olier St ⓣ 679 7734, ⓔ ashfield @indigo.ie.
Spacious, clean and friendly 104-bed hostel occupying a converted church near Trinity College. Consists mostly of small four- or six-bed dorms (plus seven double rooms; ❷), with en-suite facilities throughout plus a kitchen and laundry.

Avalon House
Map 4, C8. 55 Aungier St ⓣ 475 0001, ⓔ info@avalon-house.com.
Friendly, traditional 281-bed hostel in a former medical school five minutes' walk from St Stephen's Green and Temple Bar, with sixteen

double rooms (❸), mostly en-suite. Pleasant café – excellent for hanging out and meeting people – plus a large self-catering kitchen, tip-top security and internet access.

Barnacles Temple Bar House
Map 6, E4. Temple Lane South ⓣ 671 6277, ⓦ www.barnacles .ie.
Custom-made 149-bed hostel right in the heart of Temple Bar and extremely popular as a result, so book early. Excellent en-suite rooms (sleeping four to twelve), as well as a dozen doubles (❸). Efficient and friendly staff.

Brewery Hostel
Map 3, D5. 22–23 Thomas St ⓣ 473 8600, ⓔ brewery@indigo .ie. IHO.
The unfashionable location often means that some of the

HOSTELS

52 beds here are free when other hostels are full. Housed in a converted library a ten-minute walk along Thomas Street from Christ Church, the *Brewery* is friendly and offers good value for its en-suite rooms. Four doubles (❷) are also available.

Kinlay House Christchurch

Map 4, B6. 2–12 Lord Edward St ⓣ679 6644, ⓔkinlay.dublin @usitworld.com.
Cheerful and relaxed 196-bed USITNow hostel near Christ Church Cathedral, which can be a little noisy both from traffic and high-spirited guests. In addition to the dorms, there are thirteen doubles (❷), and a café and kitchen on site; bike hire and laundry are available.

Oliver St John Gogarty's

Map 6, H3. 18–21 Anglesea St ⓣ671 1822, ⓔolivergogartys @hotmail.com.
Comfy and stylish 128-bed hostel situated next to the eponymous pub in the heart of Temple Bar; like the pub itself, it's hugely popular.

Offers triple and four-bed rooms as well as doubles (❷), six- and ten-bed dorms and snazzy one- to three-bed-room rooftop apartments (from ❻) with kitchen, TV and washing machine.

THE INNER NORTH-SIDE

Abbey Court

Map 4, D4. 29 Bachelor's Walk, O'Connell Bridge ⓣ878 0700, ⓔinfo@abbey-court.com.
Just north of O'Connell Bridge this is a modern, blue-fronted, well-equipped and friendly 100-bed hostel. The mostly small rooms are all en-suite (the showers are excellent), fitted with a swipe-card security system and have storage cages under every bed; there are eight doubles, too (❸). Laundry, kitchen and internet facilities are all available.

Abraham House

Map 4, F2. 82–83 Gardiner St Lower ⓣ855 0600, ⓔstay @abraham-house.ie.
A large, well-run 191-bed

hostel with plenty of doubles (**②**), *Abraham House* is handy for both Busáras and Connolly Station. Facilities include a kitchen, laundry, *bureau de change*, excellent hot showers and secure parking. Bus #41 from the airport stops outside.

Celts House

Map 5, G2. 32 Blessington St ☏830 0657, ⓔres@celtshouse .iol.ie.

The bright-yellow Georgian door marks the mood of this friendly hostel on a quiet cul-de-sac north of O'Connell Street. Only 38 beds, including a few doubles (**②**), so a cosier alternative to some of the larger hostels. Prices are very competitive, but breakfast is not included.

Dublin International Youth Hostel

Map 5, G2. 61 Mountjoy St ☏830 1766, ⓔdublininternational @anoige.ie.

Way up near the Black Church and Dorset Street Upper (bus #41 from the airport), this well-equipped 369-bed hostel occupying an ex-convent is the headquarters of An Óige (the Irish branch of Hostelling International). Generally cheaper (€16–€18) than IHH or IHO hostels, though non-members of An Óige or Hostelling International pay a nightly surcharge of €2, and you need to bring or hire a sleeping-sheet.

Globetrotters Tourist Hostel

Map 4, F2. 46 Gardiner St Lower ☏873 5893, ⓔgtrotter @indigo.ie.

Well-run, comfortable 250-bed hostel connected to the *Townhouse* B&B (see p.247) whose cosy, tasteful dorms sleep six to ten people, with security-coded doors and individual bed lights. The breakfast is the best you'll get in any Dublin hostel and the decor and standards are a lot higher, too, plus there's a garden for summer lounging. Well-equipped doubles (**④**) also available.

Goin' My Way

Map 4, F2. 15 Talbot St ☏878 8484, ⓔgoinmyway@esatclear.ie.

HOSTELS

257

Small, family-run, value-for-money 42-bed hostel above a clothes shop, close to O'Connell Street and the river. Breakfast is not included, but there is a kitchen for guests' use. Operates a midnight curfew, so it's one of Dublin's quieter hostels and good for those wanting a good night's sleep. Some doubles (❶) are available.

Isaac's Hostel
Map 4, F3. 2–5 Frenchman's Lane ⊤ 855 6215, ⓔ hostel @isaacs.ie.
Well-run, modern 235-bed hostel housed in a former wine warehouse, just around the corner from the bus station. Comfortable dorms, and some appealing doubles (❸), as well as a laundry, internet facilities, *bureau de change* and bike storage; note that there's a room lockout from 11am–2.30pm. Breakfast isn't included, though there's an excellent café on site.

Jacob's Inn
Map 4, G2. 21–28 Talbot Place

⊤ 855 5660, ⓔ jacobs@isaacs.ie.
Just north of Busáras, this 295-bed sister hostel to *Isaac's* offers comfortable and stylish budget accommodation. Staff are friendly and security is first-rate, with swipe cards and excellent lockers. Breakfast is not included, but there's a kitchen and a café here, plus internet facilities and a *bureau de change*; a dozen en-suite double rooms (❸), too.

Litton Lane Hostel
Map 4, E4. 2–4 Litton Lane ⊤ 872 8389, ⓔ litton@indigo.ie.
Just off Bachelor's Walk, by O'Connell Bridge, this well-equipped 96-bed hostel is housed in a former warehouse which also served time as a major recording studio. Comfortable dorms as well as three cosy double rooms (❷), plus excellent showers, laundry facilities, kitchen and parking.

Mount Eccles Court
Map 5, H3. 44 North Great George's St ⊤ 873 0826, ⓔ info@eccleshostel.com.

HOSTELS

Housed in two converted listed buildings (with most of their original features intact) on a fine Georgian street, ten minutes' walk from the bus station. Breakfast is served in a well-equipped basement kitchen where the walls have been stripped to their original stonework. The comfortable dorm bunks are generally cheaper than other northside options and the four doubles (❷) are reasonably priced, too.

Paddy's Palace

Map 4, F3. 5 Beresford Place, off Gardiner St Lower ☎888 1758, ✉paddyspalace@dublin .com.

Part of the *Paddywagon* backpacker tours empire, this is a small, plain but very airy and economically priced 42-bed hostel whose kitchen and some rooms overlook the Liffey. All dorms are entered by swipe card (some are ensuite), and there are also a few economically-priced doubles (❷) available. Internet facilities and organized tours on offer.

MONKSTOWN AND DÚN LAOGHAIRE

Belgrave Hall

Map 2, H6. 34 Belgrave Square, Monkstown ☎284 2106, ⊕www.dublinhostel.com. IHO.

The best out-of-town option, popular with Irish guests studying at the nearby traditional music academy, offering fine communal dorm accommodation and a few comfortable doubles (❷) in a magnificent building in Monkstown. Both dorms and rooms are spacious and some have period furniture. Bike hire and laundry. Bus #7 and #7A from O'Connell Street and College Green or DART to Seapoint. 50 beds.

Marina House

Map 7, A4. 7 Old Dunleary, Dún Laoghaire ☎284 1524, ✉info@marinahouse.com.
Dublin's smallest hostel (just 30 beds), housed in a renovated stone building next to the DART line and near to Salthill and Monkstown sta-

HOSTELS

259

tion; handy too for the Dún Laoghaire ferry terminal, just five minutes' walk away. Well-furnished and cosy, with very reasonably priced dorm beds, and one double room (❷). Laundry facilities.

STUDENT ACCOMMODATION

As an alternative to staying in a hostel or B&B, you can rent **student accommodation** during the summer holiday (mid-June to mid-Sept). These generally offer better facilities for self-catering than hostels, with a camaraderie arising from the fact that so many of the guests are foreign students attending courses – which makes it imperative to book months ahead.

Dublin City University
Map 2, F3. Larkfield Apartments, DCU Campus, off Ballymun Rd, Glasnevin ☎700 5736, @campusresidences @dcu.ie.

Definitely the most affordable of the campus options, though a little way out of town off Ballymun Road (bus #11, #13 and #19 from O'Connell St). There are 270 en-suite bedrooms consisting of fifty singles (€42 per night) and 200 doubles (€70 per night). Breakfast is served in the restaurant, and rates include use of a nearby sports centre and laundry.

Mercer Court
Map 4, C8. Mercer St Lower ☎478 2179, @www.mercercourt .ie.

Part of the Royal College of Surgeons and just two minutes' walk from Grafton Street, this offers excellent en-suite single (€62 per night) and double (€104 per night) rooms with TV and direct dial telephone. Also has self-catering three- and four-bed apartments (€785 to €920 per unit per week) which sleep up to five people.

Trinity College
Map 4, E5. College Green

STUDENT ACCOMMODATION

⊤608 1177, ⊛www.tcd.ie.
Not cheap, but the setting is unique and utterly central, offering a range of standard or en-suite accommodation in either single, twin- or four-bedded rooms in one of the many halls of residence on campus. Shared kitchen and lounge, breakfast taken in the restaurant. Per-person prices range from €37.50 per night for a standard double to €59.50 per person per night for an en-suite double.

University College Dublin Village

Map 2, F5. Off Stillorgan Rd, Belfield ⊤269 7111, ⊛www.ucd.ie.
A complex of modern single rooms (€35 per night) and four-bed apartments (€110 per night)) with shared kitchens, dining areas and shower rooms. Located on the UCD campus, about four miles south of the centre (bus #46 from Fleet St).

CAMPING

There are two **campsites** on the outskirts of Dublin, one in Clondalkin, the other between Killiney and Bray. Both are mainly aimed at caravaners, and relatively few backpackers use them for the simple reason that by the time you've taken fares into account it's unlikely to be any cheaper than staying in a hostel in Dublin – and involves far more effort.

Expect to **pay** €6–€9 per person per night for a pitch space.

Camac Valley Tourist Caravan and Camping Park

Map 2, A7. Corkagh Regional Park, Naas Rd, Clondalkin ⊤462 0644, ⊛www.irishcamping.com.
On the southwest edge of Dublin off the Naas road (bus #68 from Aston Quay; 40min). An attractive setting of landscaped grounds within a national park, with views of the Wicklow mountains.
Open all year.

CAMPING

Shankill Caravan and Camping Park

Map 1, E6. Off Dublin Rd, Shankill ☎ 282 0011, ✉ shankhillcaravan@eircom.net. South of Killiney and some ten miles from the centre, near the Shankill DART station; direct buses are the #45 and #84 from Eden Quay or #46 from Fleet St; 45min). Handy for the Dún Laoghaire ferry terminal and not far from the sea and secluded beaches. Open all year.

Eating

Dublin may not be the gastronomic capital of the world, but the phenomenal expansion in the range of **places to eat** since the 1980s means that almost any taste is now catered for. Today, Dubliners are far more sophisticated in their eating habits than twenty years ago, creating a virtuous circle of rising expectations and standards that shows every sign of continuing.

Many restaurants, bistros and upmarket cafés offer a **lunchtime** set menu of two to four courses for about half the cost of their evening fare. Alternatively, you could see what pubs have to offer; carvery lunches, seafood, steaks, hearty Irish stew and nourishing soups are typical, but you can find more exotic dishes at trendier bars on the southside. For **dinner**, many establishments have an early-bird menu before 7pm or so, which is often excellent value compared to what you'd pay later on.

In the listings below, **prices** are indicated by the terms "cheap" (under €10 for a main course); "moderate" (€10–15); "expensive" (€15–20); and "very expensive" (over €20). The item most likely to push up your final bill is wine, which is a lot dearer than anywhere else in Europe, owing to the high tax levied by the government.

A lot of restaurants add a **service charge** onto your bill (if it's not clear whether or not it has been included, it's always worth checking); where they don't, a **tip** of 10–15 percent is standard.

CAFÉS AND QUICK MEALS

The distinction between **cafés** and restaurants is often arbitrary: some of the places reviewed here are licensed and open in the evenings; a few establishments listed under "Restaurants" below offer a lighter, café-style menu at lunchtime; and many of the newer places that call themselves cafés are actually restaurants (or at least bistros) in all but name. This section is essentially a run-through of the best places to eat if what you want is a quick, unpretentious bite. All are in the centre of Dublin – the majority of them on the southside.

Bad Ass Café
Map 6, F4. 9–11 Crown Alley.
Daily 11.30am–midnight.
Moderate.
Once deeply hip (Sinéad O'Connor was a waitress here), the *Bad Ass* is still popular with tourists and Dubliners on an evening out in Temple Bar. Snort at the puns on the menu while you work out what kind of pizza, burger, salad or pasta you fancy and see your order whizzed across the room by an overhead pulley.

Beshoff's
Map 4, E4. 14 Westmoreland St.
Daily 11am–11pm.
Map 4, D2. 6 O'Connell St Upper.
Mon–Wed 11am–9pm,
Thurs–Sun 11am–10pm.
Cheap.
A Dublin institution, albeit not as grand as *Bewley's* nor as highly regarded for its fish-and-chips as *Leo Burdock's* (see p.268). Ivan Beshoff was a survivor from the mutiny on the battleship *Potemkin*, who settled in Ireland and opened

a fish shop in Howth and then a café in Dublin. There are now two city-centre *Beshoff's* with counter service and functional tables. The menu varies with the catch, but you can be sure of getting a good fish supper for around €8. The O'Connell Street *Beshoff's* has a fine view from its upstairs windows.

Bewley's Oriental Cafés

Map 4, D7. 78 Grafton St.
Mon–Sat 7.30am–11pm, Sun 8am–11pm.
Map 4, E4. 11–12 Westmoreland St.
Daily 7.30am–7.30pm, Thurs until 8pm.
Cheap.

As integral to Dublin life as Guinness, *Bewley's* cafés have been a meeting place for Dubliners for generations. Founded by a Quaker family in 1840, they embody the ethos of the ordinary made sublime: hearty hot breakfasts and lunches, or sticky buns and cakes, consumed on marble-topped tables in panelled rooms. The Grafton Street branch has lost some of its atmosphere now that it's mostly self-service, but it still retains Harry Clarke's *Birds of Paradise* window. The Westmoreland Street *Bewley's* has a busy, lived-in atmosphere, along with wooden pews and cosy fireplaces.

Café Irie

Map 6, F4. 11 Fownes St Lower.
Daily 9am–8.30pm.
Cheap.

Hippy café that stuffs its bagels, panini, wraps, pitta and plain doorsteps with a tempting variety of copious fillings – "build your own" (one meat, one cheese and salad leaves) gives the flavour of it. Salads available if that all sounds too starchy, as well as healthy breakfasts till 11.30am during the week and all day at the weekend.

Grafton St *Bewley's* plays host to lunchtime plays and cabaret evenings – see p.311.

Café Java

Map 4, E7. 5 Anne St South.
Mon–Fri 7am–7.30pm, Sat
8am–6.15pm, Sun
9am–6.15pm.
Cheap.

Popular breakfast, lunchtime
and coffee stop (with a less
central branch at 145 Leeson
St Upper), offering such light
meals as poached eggs with
bacon, or chicken with
yogurt. The standard of coffee matches that of the food,
and wine is served too.

Cobalt Café and Gallery

Map 5, H3. 16 North Great
George's St.
Mon–Fri 10am–5pm, Sat
11am–4.30pm.
Cheap.

Converted Georgian town-
house whose eighteenth-century elegance and contemporary design – including striking original artworks on the
walls – give it a very relaxing
atmosphere. Light menu
including sandwiches and
cakes, plus cappuccinos,
espressos and tea. Perfect for a
refresher after visiting the
James Joyce Centre.

Cornucopia

Map 4, D6. 19–21 Wicklow St.
Mon–Sat 8.30am–8pm, Thurs
until 9pm.
Cheap.

A small, friendly buffet café
of long standing, somewhat
eclipsed by newer places like
Juice, but still well regarded by
veggies. Their hot breakfast
(till noon) includes vegetarian
sausages, and the excellent
range of salads changes daily.

Dunne and Crescenzi

Map 4, E6. 14 Frederick St
South.
Mon, Tues & Sat 9.30am–7pm,
Wed–Fri 9.30am–10pm.
Cheap.

A cosy Italian deli and wine
shop that's largely been taken
over by its café operation:
croissants and spot-on coffee
for breakfast, and for the rest
of the day, all manner of
Italian sandwiches and excellent plates of *antipasti*, as well
as delicious cakes and
desserts. Packed at lunchtime,
with the few outside tables at
a particular premium in summer.

Fresh ◦

Map 4, D6. 2nd floor, Powerscourt Townhouse Centre, off Grafton St.
Mon–Sat 10am–6pm, Thurs until 8pm.
Cheap.

A great setting, overlooking the shopping centre's glassed-in Georgian courtyard, and a marvellous vegetarian and vegan menu, using organic ingredients wherever possible: soups, salads, pasta, veggie tarts, curries, baked potatoes, pulse dishes and hot-pots; various breads, cakes and desserts; and organic wines, fresh juices and smoothies. Ten percent discount for students and on take-away food.

The Gotham Café ◦

Map 4, D7. 5 Anne St South.
Mon–Sat noon–midnight, Sun noon–11.30pm.
Cheap/Moderate.

This buzzy, child-friendly café just off Grafton Street does a global menu that includes great pizzas and salads, Louisiana crab cakes, Thai vegetable curries and other yummy concoctions.

Govinda's

Map 4, C7. 4 Aungier St.
Mon–Sat noon–9pm.
Cheap.

Great little vegetarian café serving cheap and filling helpings of dahl and rice, samosas, salads, pizzas and burgers, as well as daily specials such as pasta and moussaka. They also do mouthwatering lassis, as well as cakes and other desserts.

Gruel ◦

Map 6, D6. 67 Dame St.
Mon–Fri 7.30am–7.30pm, Sat 10.30am–5.30pm.
Cheap.

Styling itself as a "soup kitchen", this offshoot of the *Mermaid Café* next door doles out a daily-changing menu of excellent sandwiches, salads and soups, as well as snacks such as fishcakes and tortillas. If you're taking away, head for the pretty garden in front of the Chester Beatty Library, across the street in Dublin Castle.

EATING: CAFÉS AND QUICK MEALS

The Irish Film Centre

Map 6, D5. 6 Eustace St.

Daily 12.30–3.30pm &
5.30–9pm.

Cheap.

One of the coolest hangouts in Temple Bar, this is great for lunch or a dinner before the show, whether sitting in the cosy bar or the echoing atrium. Quick meals ranging from sandwiches, fish and chips and lasagne to fish cakes and goat's cheese salad, with lots of veggie options.

Leo Burdock's ๑

Map 5, F8. 2 Werburgh St.

Mon–Sat noon–midnight, Sun 4pm–midnight.

Cheap.

Dublin's best-loved fish-and-chippie (take-away only), near Christ Church Cathedral. Though the coal-powered fryer has gone, everything else remains the same. Great nosh and cheerful service. Queues at lunchtime, after work and during pub hours.

Nude ๑

Map 4, D6. 21 Suffolk St.

Mon–Sat 8am–9pm, Sun 10am–7pm.

Cheap.

Funky canteen-style café with a big open kitchen, serving up hot and cold wraps – try the delicious beef burrito – panini, salads, soups and some weird and wonderful juices and smoothies, to eat in or take away. Organic ingredients are used wherever possible, and there are daily specials and ample choice for vegetarians. This highly successful formula has been repeated on George's Quay, on the first floor of the BT2 store on Grafton Street, and on the corner of Leeson Street and St Stephen's Green (take-away only).

Panem

Map 4, C4. 21 Ormond Quay Lower.

Mon–Fri 8.30am–5pm, Sat 9am–5pm.

Cheap.

Minuscule, stylish café serving excellent French and Italian snacks – fresh soups, filled focaccia, a couple of daily pasta specials, and sweet and savoury croissants.

Probe

Map 4, C6. Market Arcade, South Great George's St.

Mon–Sat 11am–7pm.

Funky little spot with wooden booths and cheerful staff, serving Mexican food, spicy Irish stew, baked potatoes and sandwiches; ten percent discount for students.

Queen of Tarts

Map 6, A6. 4 Cork Hill, on Lord Edward St.

Mon–Fri 7.30am–6pm, Sat 9am–6pm, Sun 10am–6pm. Cheap.

Small, laid-back patisserie-cum-café with an overflow branch in the vaults of City Hall opposite. Bagels and croissants for breakfast; ham, spinach and cheese tarts, Greek salad and all sorts of sandwiches for lunch; and yummy cakes baked fresh on the premises to keep you going between times.

Silk Road Café ♠

Map 4, B6. Chester Beatty Library, Dublin Castle.

Tues–Fri 10am–5pm, Sat 11am–5pm, Sun 1–5pm. Cheap.

Stylish museum café, spilling over into the Library's skylit atrium, that's well worth a journey in its own right. The chef (who's from Jerusalem, one of Chester Beatty's favoured hunting grounds) rustles up mostly Middle Eastern food – lamb moussaka and lasagne, falafels, spinach and feta filo pie and plenty of other veggie options, and very good salads. To round off, as you'd expect, there's great coffee and titbits such as Turkish delight and baklava.

The Stag's Head

Map 5, H7. 1 Dame Court, off Dame St.

Mon–Fri 11am–3.30pm & 5–7pm, Sat 11am–3.30pm. Cheap.

A mosaic of a stag's head on the pavement alerts you to the presence of this delightful Victorian bar. Simple, inexpensive pub grub: Irish stew, ham and cabbage, roast spuds and chips. The hours above refer to when food is available; drinking hours are longer, naturally (see also p.293).

EATING: CAFÉS AND QUICK MEALS

The Steps of Rome
Map 4, D7. 1 Chatham Court, Chatham St.
Mon–Sat 11am–11pm, Sun 11am–10pm.
Cheap.

Just off Grafton Street, this tiny, crammed café with a wine licence serves excellent pizzas made by friendly staff. You'll be lucky to get a table, but if you don't their take-away slices are a treat.

Winding Stair Café ♦
Map 4, C4. 40 Ormond Quay Lower.

Mon–Sat 9.30am–6pm, Sun 1–6pm.
Cheap.

A charming secondhand book emporium on three floors; the staircase that links them (and the bookshop's name) was inspired by a Yeats poem. With crêpes, sandwiches, cakes and very good coffee, their café is good enough to stand on its own merits, and has large windows overlooking the Ha'penny Bridge so you can watch the world go by as you eat.

RESTAURANTS

The majority of Dublin's **restaurants** are on the south side of the river in the city centre, with a tight concentration in Temple Bar. Wherever they're situated, it's always worth **booking** in the evenings.

TEMPLE BAR

♦ Bruno's
Map 6, D4. 30 Essex St East
☎670 6767.
Mon–Fri 12.30–2.30pm & 6–10.30pm, Sat 6–10.30pm.
Expensive.

Excellent French and Mediterranean cuisine with a contemporary edge – dishes such as jasmine-smoked beef with lentils – served in cool, modern surroundings. Early-bird menu Mon–Fri 6–7pm (€18.50 for 2 courses, €21.50 for 3).

EATING: RESTAURANTS

Café Gertrude

Map 6, G2. 3–4 Bedford Row
☎677 9043.

Mon–Fri 10am–10pm, Sat &
Sun 10am–11pm.

Moderate.

Cosy bistro with a convivial
atmosphere and accessible
menu including the likes of
pizzas, spinach cannelloni or
Dublin sausages with red
wine, bacon, onions and
mushrooms, as well as cheap
daily specials; lighter meals
available at lunchtime. Best of
the puddings is a fabulously
sticky hot chocolate-fudge
cake. Wine by the carafe;
early-bird menu daily
3–7.30pm (€11.50 for 2
courses).

Da Pino

Map 6, B6. 38–40 Parliament
St ☎671 9308.

Daily noon–11.30pm.

Cheap/Moderate.

One of the best of the many
Italian restaurants in Temple
Bar. Italians come here to
enjoy spaghetti carbonara,
zuppa di cipolla and other classic dishes. The welcome is
warm and the decor sympa-
thetic. This restaurant possi-

bly stands on the site of the
Eagle Tavern, where the notorious Hellfire Club (see p.83)
was founded.

Eden

Map 6, D5. Sycamore
St/Meeting House Square ☎670
5372.

Daily 12.30–3pm & 6–10pm.

Expensive.

Chic, upmarket but congenial
restaurant in the heart of
Temple Bar, with seats out on
the square during the summer. The menu offers classic
Irish cuisine with a
Mediterranean twist, in dishes such as braised lamb steaks
with olives and lemon barley,
or organic steak with a rich
béarnaise sauce.

Elephant & Castle

Map 6, G3. 18 Temple Bar
☎679 3121.

Mon–Fri 8am–11.30pm, Sat
10.30am–11.30pm, Sun
noon–11.30pm.

Cheap/Moderate.

A hit with Dubliners from
the outset, the panache and
informality of the *E&C* has
had a huge influence on the
culinary scene in Temple Bar,

and Dublin generally. Imagine a neighbourhood diner that just happens to be in the coolest part of town, and does gourmet burgers, breakfasts or late-night meals with a Cajun-Creole or Pacific Rim spin. Big queues on Sundays when clubbers celebrate their hangovers with brunch.

Fitzer's
Map 6, F3. Temple Bar Square
⊕ 679 0440.
Daily noon–4.30pm & 5.30–11pm.
Moderate.
See p.276.

Il Baccaro
Map 6, D5. Meeting House Square ⊕ 671 4597.
Mon–Fri & Sun 6–11pm, Sat noon–3pm & 6–11pm.
Cheap/Moderate.
Lively, informal cellar-osteria serving traditional rustic Italian food. No one minds whether you just fancy a starter or a full meal – wine flows straight from the barrel and the musicians play. A great spot for a party.

La Paloma
Map 6, G2. 17B Asdill's Row
⊕ 677 7392.
Daily noon–midnight.
Moderate.
A cosy, friendly Spanish restaurant just off the main drag in Temple Bar, and a stone's throw from the Liffey. Taped flamenco music and bright primary colours contribute to the Iberian ambience, and there's good tapas, paellas and tortillas on the menu.

The Mermaid Café
Map 6, C6. 69–70 Dame St
⊕ 670 8236.
Mon–Sat 12.30–2.30pm & 6–11pm, Sun 12–3.30pm & 6–9pm.
Expensive.
Airy, chic restaurant with unfussy contemporary furnishings and helpful service. Great food from an eclectic menu might include New England crab cakes with lime mayonnaise or smoked duck with Chinese noodles, and there's an equally well-travelled wine list.

Milano

Map 6, D4. 19 Temple Bar
☎ 670 3384.

Daily noon–midnight.
Cheap/Moderate.

The first venture of the
British *Pizza Express* chain in
Ireland, *Milano* offers a familiar and affordable range of
tasty pizzas and pastas in the
kind of ritzy setting one associates with *Pizza Express*.

Mongolian Barbecue

Map 6, H4. 7 Anglesea St
☎ 670 4154.

Daily 12.30–11pm.
Moderate.

On the strength of this
cheery theme-restaurant, you
can't help feeling that if the
Mongols had eaten this well
at home, they wouldn't have
bothered to maraud across
half of Asia. All-you-can-eat
noodle stir-fries, composed
from a wide range of exotic
ingredients and cooked on
the spot. Great value at
lunchtime (€8.99) or early
evening (4–6pm; €12.99).

Monty's of Kathmandu ♦

Map 6, D5. 28 Eustace St
☎ 670 4911.

Mon–Sat noon–2.30pm &
6–11.30pm, Sun 6–11.30pm.
Moderate.

Authentic Nepalese restaurant
that makes a welcome change
from your run-of-the-mill,
flock-wallpapered curry-
house. Bright, simple decor
and micro-brewed lager complement some deliciously
refreshing starters and main
courses such as succulent tandoori tiger prawns and chick-
en gorkhali, cooked with
yoghurt, chilli, coriander and
spices. If you get your act
together, order the momo
dumplings stuffed with lamb
24hr in advance.

Nico's

Map 6, E6. 53 Dame St ☎ 677
3062.

Mon–Fri 12.30–2.30pm &
6pm–midnight, Sat 6pm–midnight. Moderate/Expensive.

A highly successful Italian
restaurant, popular with the-
atre-goers and courting cou-
ples. The food is good solid
stuff like carbonara and veal
Milanese, but the real secret
of its success is the atmosphere, enlivened by the dramatic flounces of the waiters,

EATING: RESTAURANTS

and piano music as the night wears on.

Tante Zoe's
Map 6, F5. 1 Crow St ☎679 4407.
Daily noon–midnight.
Moderate.
The first Cajun/Creole restaurant to open in Temple Bar, *Tante Zoe's* remains popular for continuing to serve decent food at affordable prices and managing to be fun. Go for the inexpensive lunchtime (Mon–Sat noon–4pm) or early-bird (daily 6–7pm) menu and you won't regret it.

⚬ The Tea Room
Map 6, B4. *The Clarence Hotel*, 6–8 Wellington Quay ☎670 7766.
Mon–Fri 12.30–3pm & 6.30–10.30pm, Sat 6.30–10.30pm, Sun 7am–3pm (brunch) & 6.30–10.30pm.
Very expensive.
Dublin's most stylish hotel, *The Clarence's* (see p.239) fabulous restaurant is one of the coolest places to be seen in town. Its stunning design provides a perfect foil to the

eclectic menu, offering eight different starters and eight main courses, from shellfish lasagne to *magret* of duck with honey-roast parsnips and green beans. Definitely the place for the ultimate splurge.

THE REST OF THE SOUTHSIDE

AYA
Map 4, D7. 48 Clarendon St ☎677 1544.
Daily noon–4pm & 5.30–11pm, closes 9.30pm Sun.
Moderate/Expensive.
Japanese restaurant with Dublin's first sushi conveyor-bar as its focal point – you eat what takes your fancy as it glides past. There's plenty of regular seating, too, for more substantial dishes such as salmon teriyaki and pan-fried duck breast with an orange-soy glaze.

Browne's Brasserie
Map 4, E8. 22 St Stephen's Green North ☎638 3939.
Mon–Fri 12.30–3pm & 6.30–11pm, Sat 6.30–11pm, Sun 12.30–3pm & 6.30–10pm.

Expensive/Very expensive.
Elegant Georgian townhouse
on the north side of the
Green, where you can bask in
the opulent decor of a former
gentlemen's club and enjoy
classy cooking and service.
Carpaccio of beef with wild
mushrooms and truffle oil
vinaigrette will get you off to
a good start, while the main
courses emphasize seafood,
with the likes of seared scallops with black pudding, arti-
chokes and Swiss chard.

Café-Bar-Deli
Map 4, C6. 12–13 South Great
George's St ☏ 677 1646.
Daily noon–11pm.
Cheap/Moderate.
A former *Bewley's Café* that's
been smartly updated without
losing its character: comfy red
booths, bentwood furniture,
brass rails and coathooks. The
menu of simple food well
done is a winner, too, with
some interesting starters, pastas such as rigatoni with gorgonzola, spinach and cream,
Mediterranean salads, thin,
crispy pizzas and mouthwatering desserts.

Café Mao
Map 4, D7. 2–3 Chatham Row,
Chatham St ☏ 670 4899.
Mon–Thurs noon–11pm, Fri &
Sat noon–11.30pm, Sun
noon–10pm.
Moderate.
Slick, trendy spot decorated
with Warhol posters of the
Chairman himself. The menu
follows a successful formula:
great dishes from around
Asia, including such mouth-
watering temptations as
grilled, marinated squid with
watermelon.

The Cedar Tree
Map 4, D6. 11 St Andrew's St
☏ 677 2121.
Mon–Thurs & Sun 5.30–11pm,
Fri & Sat 5.30pm–midnight.
Moderate.
Located in a cavernous basement off Suffolk Street, *The
Cedar Tree* is a great spot for a
lively evening out. Its dazzling array of Lebanese meze
dishes are best appreciated via
sharing with a group of
friends, with lots of wine to
wash it down. The diversity
of dishes based on pulses and
grains makes this a perfect
choice for vegetarians.

Diep le Shaker

Map 4, G9. 55 Pembroke Lane, off Pembroke St Lower ☎661 1829.

Mon–Wed 12.30–2.15pm & 6.30–10.30pm, Thurs & Fri 12.30–2.15pm & 6.30–11pm, Sat 6.30–11pm.

Moderate.

Dublin's best Thai restaurant, with prices that won't break the bank, though drinks are expensive. The surrounds are bright and swanky, and the menu, strong on fish and seafood, offers imaginative takes on thoroughly authentic dishes: try the steamed scallops with garlic and soy sauce, the chargrilled beef sirloin with fish sauce, chilli and lime dressing, or the stir-fried spinach with yellow beans and basil.

East End Tandoori

Map 4, C7. 11 Aungier St ☎478 9774.

Mon–Sat noon–2.30pm & 6pm–midnight, Sun 1–4pm & 6pm–midnight.

Moderate.

Unassuming spot that stands out for its courteous and friendly service and its Indian clientele. Tasty versions of standard dishes – the tandoori fish and vegetable masala are particularly good. Lunchtime special offers and an €11 three-course early-bird menu Sun–Thurs till 7.30pm.

Ely Wine Bar

Map 4, F8. 22 Ely Place ☎676 8986.

Mon–Sat noon–midnight.

Moderate.

Popular, congenial wine bar serving wholesome and unpretentious food to accompany over fifty wines by the glass, as well as some top-notch beers. Choose either a simple dish such as bread and dips, Irish cheeses and salads, or something more substantial like organic lamb kebab and home-made organic sausages and mash.

Fitzer's

Map 4, E7. 51 Dawson St ☎677 1155.

Daily 11.30am–10.30pm.

Map 4, G7. National Gallery ☎661 4496.

Hours variable, but usually restaurant daily noon–3pm, café Mon–Sat 10am–5.30pm,

Thurs until 8.30pm, Sun
noon–5.30pm.
Moderate.
A reliable chain of restaurants,
each with an individual identity. The branch in the heart of
Temple Bar (see above) has a
cool high-tech design;
Dawson Street's attracts a
trendy crowd and has tables
outside in the summer; while
Fitzer's in the National Gallery
(both a restaurant and a cheaper café) revels in the grandeur
of the new Millennium Wing.
Menus change daily, so expect
anything from calamari with
pickled chillies to Cajun bean
casserole. Lots of choice for
vegetarians, and alcohol is
available.

Good World Restaurant
Map 4, C6. 18 South Great
George's St ⓣ 677 5373.
Daily 12.30pm–2.30am.
Moderate.
Sited near several pubs off
Dame Street, *Good World*
attracts a boisterous clientele
with its late hours, and the
reputation of its dim sum
packs patrons in by day.
Dublin's Chinese community
is divided on whether the

Good World or the *Imperial* (see
below) does better dim sum,
but relishes putting both to
the test. Come here early on a
Sunday to get a place upstairs.

Imperial Chinese Restaurant
Map 5, H8. 12A Wicklow St
ⓣ 677 2580.
Daily 12.30–11pm, later on Fri &
Sat.
Moderate.
A large room buzzing with
Chinese customers, who gen-
erally rate it the best restau-
rant in the city centre.
Others, too, have discovered
the joys of its superb dim sum
(served daily 12.30–5pm), and
a Sunday brunch at the
Imperial rivals brunch at the
E&C as a sociable experience.

Juice
Map 4, C6. 73–83 South Great
George's St ⓣ 475 7856.
Daily 11.30–11pm.
Cheap/Moderate.
Chic vegetarian eating place
with not a sweaty sandal in
sight. The imaginative dinner
menu (from 6pm) takes in a
range of vegetarian and vegan
fare, such as stir fries, Thai

EATING: RESTAURANTS

curries, mushroom Wellington and aduki bean Juiceburgers; simpler and cheaper lunchtime dishes might include tabouleh and scrambled tofu. To drink, choose from juices, smoothies and organic wines. Early-bird menu (Mon–Fri 5–7pm) of three courses for €12.60.

La Stampa
Map 4, E7. 35 Dawson St
Ⓣ 677 8611.
Mon–Thurs & Sun 6pm–midnight, Fri & Sat 6pm–12.30am.
Expensive/Very expensive.
A nineteenth-century ballroom extravagantly decked with flowers forms the setting for this much-praised restaurant. The varied European-style menu includes dishes such as salmon with a tomato and olive ragout and aubergine caviar. Early-bird menus are available daily 6–7.30pm (€25 for 2 courses, €32.50 for 3).

Lord Edward Seafood Restaurant
Map 4, A6. 23 Christchurch Place Ⓣ 454 2420.
Mon–Fri 12.30–2.15pm &

6–10.30pm, Sat 6–10.30pm.
Moderate/Expensive.
Around the corner from legendary chippie *Leo Burdock's*, the *Lord Edward* represents the other end of the pescatorial scale. Dublin's oldest seafood restaurant, above a pub opposite Christ Church Cathedral, this is a venerable club-like institution dedicated to simple cooking with the very freshest fish.

Milano
Map 4, E7. 61 Dawson St
Ⓣ 670 7744.
Daily noon–midnight.
Cheap/Moderate.
See p.273.

O'Connells
Just off map 3, J8. *Bewley's Hotel*, Merrion Rd, Ballsbridge
Ⓣ 647 3304.
Mon–Sat 12.30–2.30pm & 6–10.30pm, Sun 12.30–3pm & 6–9.30pm.
Expensive.
Run by Tom O'Connell (brother of Darina Allen, Ireland's most famous celebrity chef), this is a top-notch but pleasantly unpretentious hotel restaurant. The empha-

sis is on letting prime local ingredients speak for themselves, with much use of a woodburning oven and grill, in a mix of Irish and Italian styles. Service is friendly and informal, and in summer you can sit out on the sunken patio. Lunch is buffet-style, and the early-bird menu of three courses for €20.95 (daily 6–7pm) is excellent value.

Odessa

Map 5, H7. 13–14 Dame Court, off Dame St ☎ 670 7634.
Mon–Fri 6–11pm, Sat & Sun noon–4.30pm & 6–11pm.
Moderate.

Cool sounds and outré decor make this one of the city's trendiest restaurants; good for gossiping on the big velour bench seats and sampling pre-dinner cocktails. The menu features dishes such as duck in honey and green pepper sauce as well as a fish of the day; brunch is offered at weekends and there's an early-bird menu from Sun to Thurs 6–7pm (€14.50 for 2 courses).

Pasta Fresca

Map 4, D7. 3 Chatham St ☎ 679 2402.
Mon–Thurs 11.30am–11.30pm, Fri & Sat 11.30am–midnight, Sun 1–10pm.
Moderate/Expensive.

Ireland's first fresh pasta shop when it opened a decade ago, *Pasta Fresca* still delights the ciabatta-loving classes. Informal restaurant with a few tables and chairs in the window, and a menu of fresh pasta, grills, salads, pizzas and daily specials.

Patrick Guilbaud

Map 4, G8. *Merrion Hotel*, 21 Merrion St Upper ☎ 676 4192.
Tues–Sat 12.30–2pm & 7.30–10.15pm.
Very expensive.

An elegant French restaurant that once stunned foodies with its flair and prices, this modestly eponymous establishment still has bags of cachet, not to mention two Michelin stars. Formal and showy in the evenings, "Paddy Giblets" loosens his collar just a little at lunchtime, when the €28 set menu (2 courses plus coffee

EATING: RESTAURANTS

and petits fours) represents amazing value.

🦪 The Rajdoot Tandoori
Map 4, D7. 26–28 Clarendon St ☎679 4274.

Mon–Sat noon–2.30pm & 6–11pm, Sun 6–11pm.
Moderate.

Despite being in the Westbury Mall off Grafton Street, and far plusher than other Indian restaurants, the *Rajdoot* keeps a keen eye on its rivals, so you'll be pleasantly surprised by the prices. Lots of choice for vegetarians, and excellent service.

The Shalimar
Map 4, C6. 17 South Great George's St ☎671 0738.

Daily noon–2.30pm & 5pm–midnight, until 1am Fri & Sat.
Cheap/Moderate.

A long-established rival of the *Rajdoot*'s that's opened a balti house in its basement. You can choose between tandooris, biryanis and other classic Punjabi dishes, or a simpler keema or kofta downstairs – both with lots of options for veggies. Always busy, but especially as the pubs close.

South Street Pizzeria
Map 4, C6. South Great George's St ☎475 2313.

Mon–Thurs & Sun noon–11pm, Fri & Sat noon–midnight.
Moderate.

Sited across the road from Exchequer Street, the *South Street Pizzeria* is one of the most popular hangouts on a road noted for its pubs and restaurants. Relaxed and friendly atmosphere, smashing pizzas, pastas and chargrills and cheap lunchtime specials.

Trocadero
Map 4, D6. 3 St Andrew's St ☎677 5545.

Mon–Sat 5pm–12.30am.
Moderate/Expensive.

Despite looking like an obnoxiously rich trattoria, this is in fact pleasant, friendly and has excellent, though predictable, food. One of Dublin's oldest Italian restaurants, it's decorated with plaudits in the form of signed photographs of visiting showbiz luminaries, and comes into its own late at night when it fills up with theatre folk. There's a pre-theatre

€17.70 menu (vacate the table by 8pm) for those who'd rather save money than socialize.

The Unicorn

Map 4, F8. 12B Merrion Court, off Merrion Row ☎662 4757.
Mon–Sat 12.30–5pm & 6–10.30pm.
Expensive.

This Italian haunt of *bien pensant* media folk and politicos was run for decades by the Sidoli family. Following the trauma of a change of ownership, its regulars are happy to find that the trattoria fare, helpful service and plain, no-nonsense interior haven't altered, and their interactions still make the *Unicorn* what it is – a Dublin institution.

Wagamama

Map 4, D7. King St South ☎478 2152.
Mon–Sat noon–11pm, Sun noon–10pm.
Cheap/Moderate.

Ultra-healthy Japanese-style meat and vegetarian noodle dishes served in a near-clinical atmosphere of long benches, crisp lighting and clean air. Best for noodle soups, dumplings and a wide variety of wholesome juices.

Yamamori Noodles

Map 4, C6. 71–72 South Great George's St ☎475 5001.
Mon–Wed & Sun 12.30–11pm, Thurs–Sat 12.30–11.30pm.
Moderate.

Trendy, fun Japanese restaurant in the heart of publand. Delicious noodles, soups, teriyaki, tempura, sushi and sashimi; in the evenings get there early (or book) to stand any chance of getting a table.

NORTHSIDE

Bond

Map 4, F3. 5 Beresford Place ☎855 9244.
Mon–Wed noon–3pm & 6–9pm, Thurs & Fri noon–3pm & 6–10pm, Sat 6–10pm.
Expensive.

A must for wine buffs, as you can choose your own bottle from over 200 well-priced wines in the cellar. The food's great too, with innovative dishes like guinea fowl, stilton, redcurrant, leek and

EATING: RESTAURANTS

truffle pizza, to go with the airy and bright modern decor.

C-Bar

Map 4, C4. Epicurean Food Hall, 13–14 Liffey St ☎865 6663.
Mon–Wed 12.30–6pm, Thurs noon–9pm, Fri & Sat 12.30–7pm.
Moderate.

Small, tiled fish bar on the north side of Ha'penny Bridge, where the cooking is seriously good and the service friendly and efficient. The good-value, imaginative menu features dishes such as soft-shell crab and citrus risotto and grilled John Dory on a mussel and chickpea broth.

◊ Chapter One

Map 5, G3. 18–19 Parnell Square North ☎873 2266.
Tues–Fri 12.30–2.30pm & 6–11pm, Sat 6–11pm.
Very expensive.

A formal restaurant with an excellent reputation for modern Irish cooking, housed in the atmospheric cellars of the Dublin Writers Museum. The menu includes such temptations as fricassee of lobster, followed by roast sea bass with pistachio and avocado purée. Excellent-value deals at lunchtime (€24.50 for 2 courses, €27.50 for 3) or before a show at the nearby Gate Theatre (Tues–Sat 6–7pm; €27.50 for 3 courses).

Halo

Map 4, C4. *Morrison Hotel*, Ormond Quay Lower ☎887 2421.
Daily 12.30–2.30pm & 7–10.30pm.
Very expensive.

Cutting-edge interior design makes this a very fashionable place to eat. Expect the fresh, crisp flavours of Asian-fusion cuisine, using Irish ingredients wherever possible and delivered with flair. Starters might include baked oysters with smoked bacon and green cabbage; main courses also revolve around seafood, with offerings such as red mullet with spicy couscous or chorizo red pepper stew. Lunchtime set menus bring the price down: €25 for two courses, €27.50 for three.

EATING: RESTAURANTS

101 Talbot

Map 4, F2. 100–101 Talbot St
℡874 5011.
Tues–Sat 5–11pm.
Moderate.

One of the very few good
restaurants on the inner
northside, conveniently close
to the Abbey Theatre. Seedy
Talbot Street is left behind as
you climb the stairs to a lovely spacious dining room,
where flavoursome dishes
with Mediterranean and
Middle Eastern influences
keep meat-eaters and vegetarians coming back. The service never falters.

SOUTH ALONG THE COAST

- - - - - - - - - - - - - - - - - - - -

Guinea Pig Fish Restaurant

Map 7, G3. 17 Railway Rd,
Dalkey ℡285 9055.
Daily 6pm–midnight.
Expensive.

Just downhill from the DART
station, en route to Dalkey's
high street, this award-winning little restaurant offers a
three-course meal of fairly
traditional seafood dishes for

€38. You can pay well over
€50 going à la carte, so it's
certainly a tempting deal, as is
the early-bird menu at €20
for three courses (Mon–Fri &
Sun 6–8pm, Sat 6–7pm).

P. D.'s Woodhouse

Map 7, G2. 1 Coliemore Rd,
Dalkey ℡284 9399.
Mon–Sat 5.30–11pm, Sun
4–9.30pm.
Moderate/Expensive.

A friendly, cosy steakhouse
where meat and fish grilled
over oak wood is the speciali-
ty. They bake their own
bread and do a mean prawn
bisque, and they don't ignore
veggies – try the delicious
halloumi kebabs.

Tree of Idleness

Map 1, F6. The Strand, Bray
℡286 3498.
Tues–Sat 7.30–11pm, Sun
7.30–10pm.
Expensive.

An award-winning Greek-
Cypriot restaurant on the
seafront, serving the freshest
seafood, wonderful moussaka,
smoked lamb and suckling
pig, complemented by a great
wine list, excellent service

EATING: RESTAURANTS

and yummy desserts. Such is its reputation, people travel right out from Dublin to dine here.

HOWTH

Casa Pasta
Map 8, F2. 12 Harbour Rd ☏839 3823.
Mon–Sat 6–10pm, Sun 12.30–9.30pm.
Moderate.
With views of the harbour, good Italian cooking and a buzzing, family-friendly atmosphere, this place has been a big success since it opened in 1993. The menu of pastas, salads and pizzas doesn't stray far from the usual suspects, but it's enlivened by daily specials.

El Paso
Map 8, F2. 10 Harbour Rd ☏832 3334.
Mon–Sat 6–11pm, Sun 2–10pm.
Moderate.
Though it seems a bit incongruous to find a Tex-Mex steakhouse on the seafront of a fishing town, the *El Paso* is the Real McCoy for delicious steaks, nachos, tortillas and all the rest (including vegetarian dishes).

King Sitric's Fish Restaurant
Map 8, F1. East Pier ☏832 5235.
Mon–Fri 12.30–2.15pm & 6.30–10pm, Sat 6.30–10pm; May–Sept Mon–Sat also noon–3pm.
Expensive/Very expensive.
Excellent seafood restaurant with panoramic sea views, specializing in fish landed at the nearby pier, oysters, mussels and lobsters. The €20 two-course lunch menu is a bargain.

Howth boasts an excellent fish-and-chip shop, *Beshoff's*, next door to *Casa Pasta* on Harbour Rd.

Drinking

"Good puzzle would be cross Dublin without passing a pub"

James Joyce, *Ulysses*

Dubliners boast, with ample justification, that the best **pubs** in the world are to be found in their city. The public house stands at the very centre of Irish social life, and any visitor seeking the craic for which Dublin nightlife is so famous should have little trouble tracking it down in one of the city centre's seven hundred pubs and bars.

The economic boom which Dublin has enjoyed of late has had some negative consequences for the city's **pub culture**. A trend towards "quaintification" has seen many modest old pubs gutted and refitted with bulk-purchased turf baskets, moth-eaten books and blackened fire-irons, and practically every fortnight another soulless pastiche opens in Temple Bar or the Grafton Street area. Nevertheless, there are many genuinely historic licensed premises still trading in more or less the same condition that Joyce's hero Leopold Bloom would have found them in 1904.

In recent years these traditional pubs have been joined by a huge array of more youth-oriented and cosmopolitan **bars**. The new and old coexist quite happily, and the compact nature of the city centre means that you can find yourself careering between a succession of nicotine-stained Victorian snugs and ultrahip designer watering-holes in the course of a single riotous evening.

For details of Dublin's highly entertaining pub tours, see p.19.

In general, pubs are **open** from 10.30am or 11.00am to 11.30pm from Monday to Wednesday, until 12.30am Thursday to Saturday, and until 11pm on Sunday. Plenty of places in Dublin have **late licenses**, as noted in the reviews below, which allow them to stay open until 2.30am or so, usually from Thursday to Saturday.

All pubs serve draught beers (a half-pint is invariably referred to as "a glass"), with pride of place being reserved for the city's most famous tipple, **Guinness**, which really does taste infinitely superior in its hometown. It's always granted the requisite two minutes' settling time halfway through pouring, however busy the barman, and however thirsty you are, you should let it settle again once it's fully poured. You'll also find Irish **whiskey** like Paddy's, Powers and Jameson's, as well as a variety of other spirits and, depending on the premises, a range of the imported bottled beers, "alcopops" and wines.

Many of the places listed under "Live Music" (see p.300 onwards) are great places for a drink in their own right, notably *The Brazen Head*, *The Cobblestone*, *Hughes's* and *O'Donoghue's*.

DRINKING

SOUTHSIDE

The Chocolate Bar
Map 4, D10. Harcourt St.
Nestling in the armpit of one
of Dublin's most stylish night-
clubs, this Gaudí-inspired
watering-hole is where the
truly trendy young things
congregate to swig alcopops
and imported bottled beers
before swaggering around to
the club. Mean cocktails and
wonderful sink-into sofas.

Dakota
Map 4, D6. 9 William St South.
A stylish conversion, in
chocolate and orange, of a
fabric warehouse. Table service at the dark leather booths
and armchairs is aimed at
pulling in a late-twenties and
early-thirties crowd, who
duly cram the place at weekends. Late opening (Fri & Sat
till at least 2am).

Davy Byrne's
Map 4, E6. 21 Duke St.
Davy Byrne's "moral pub"
receives a particularly hon-
ourable mention in Joyce's
epic novel as the place where

Leopold Bloom takes a break
from his famous perambula-
tion across Dublin for a
Gorgonzola sandwich and a
glass of Burgundy. Over the
years it's been extensively
redecorated as a lounge bar in
a mix of Art Deco and other
vaguely modernist styles, so
little of its 1904 ambience
remains, but it's still a good
place for a quiet drink and
perhaps a plate of oysters or
other seafood.

The Dockers
Map 3, J4. 5 Sir John
Rogerson's Quay.
Rock fans from around the
world make pilgrimage to
this cosy establishment, located on the somewhat dilapi-
dated quays east of the centre
and just around the corner
from the original site of
Windmill Studios, where U2
recorded their early albums.
Although the studio itself has
now moved, Bono and the
boys are still known to drop
by for the occasional pint
between tours.

DRINKING: SOUTHSIDE

U2 fans may also want to visit the Windmill Lane wall, round
the corner off Creighton St, where, for the past decade,
devotees have been recording their love of the band.

Doheny and Nesbitt
Map 4, G9. 5 Baggot St Lower.
This atmospheric, smoke-filled bar looks as if it's hardly changed since the beginning of the century. Its cosy snugs are packed at weekends, but if you can't stand the pace there, there's a slightly less hectic lounge upstairs.

4 Dame Lane
Map 4, D6. 4 Dame Lane
℗679 0291.
Announced by burning braziers just along the lane from the *Stag's Head*, this airy, minimalist bar-club probably has the stylistic edge over its bare-brickwork-and-wood rivals. Good tunes, too: anything from hip-hop to jazz through chilled ragamuffin, with a dancefloor upstairs. Open till 2.30am every night, with an admission charge after 11pm.

The Front Lounge
Map 6, A5. 33 Parliament St.
One of Temple Bar's runaway success stories, this enormous and airy bar has been thronged since the day its doors first opened a few years ago. The designer watering-hole of choice for arty Dubliners, gay and straight alike, with comfortable leather armchairs and good coffee. As New York as Dublin pubs get. Late opening (Fri & Sat till 1.30am).

The Globe
Map 4, C6. 11 South Great George's St.
Outrageously popular with the sassy and fashion-conscious youth of Dublin, this loud and lively bar is invariably packed at weekends, and busy every night. It's pleasantly dark-wooded and discreetly lit, which makes it the perfect chill-out room for *Rí-Rá* (see p.306).

Grogan's Castle Lounge
Map 4, D6. 15 William St South.
Lively, eccentric traditional

pub where works by local artists hang on the walls, and a new generation of painters and poets nurse their pints, dreaming perhaps of one day being added to the fantastic stained-glass celebration of famous *Grogan's* regulars from the past.

Hartigan's

Map 4, F10. 100 Leeson St Lower.

Resembling an old-fashioned betting shop, with fluorescent lights, lino floor and plastic seating, this bar has made no concessions to the passage of time or modern notions of comfort apart from the odd lick of paint. But what it lacks in decor is more than made up for in history and attitude. And, given the good-natured riotousness that frequently erupts (especially after college rugby matches), the lack of breakable furniture is perhaps understandable.

Hogan's

Map 4, C6. 35 South Great George's St.

Another favoured haunt of the city's bright young things, this large and extremely busy bar is not for those seeking a quiet contemplative drink. The volume of the eclectic music mix often renders meaningful conversation well-nigh impossible, but the lively crowd seem to manage more than adequately with sign language and knowing looks. Late opening (till 2.30am Fri & Sat).

The Horseshoe Bar

Map 4, E8. St Stephen's Green North.

The Horseshoe Bar in the magnificent *Shelbourne Hotel* (p.241) is the place where politicians, gossip columnists and solicitors repair every Friday evening to flirt, swagger and carve up the world. The tightly packed banquettes around the horseshoe can get a bit cosy for comfort, so you may find yourself making a beeline for the back bar, decked with a fascinating gallery of political cartoons.

The International Bar

Map 5, H8. 23 Wicklow St.

On three compact floors, this charming and civilized old pub is an unspoilt gem within a stone's throw of Grafton Street. The magnificent carved shelving behind the ground-floor bar are worth a visit alone, and the gently reclining red velvet seats support the bottoms of both ordinary Dubliners and the comedians and musicians who perform in the tiny and informal venue upstairs.

The Irish Film Centre
Map 6, D5. 6 Eustace St.
Another oasis of calm in the commercial storm: the narrow passageway entrance opens up into an ancient courtyard now covered and converted into a room three storeys high. Spacious and cultured, this is a pleasant spot night or day for a pint, a cappuccino or something to eat (see p.268), and film buffs can browse the specialist bookshop or view cult movies in the adjoining cinema (see p.313).

Kehoe's
Map 4, D7. 9 South Anne St.
Until a few years ago the family whose name adorns this wonderful old establishment lived upstairs, reputedly

the last resident publicans in the city centre. To the collective relief of Dublin's more discerning drinkers, the new owners have scarcely touched the wonderful mahogany interiors, and there are few happier places to be than in the innermost seat of the tiny snug, with a pint settling on the table in front of you.

The Long Hall
Map 4, C7. 51 South Great George's St.
Dark and wonderfully ornate Victorian pub, with deep-red walls and plasterwork, glittering mirrors, and, as you might expect, a very long wooden bar. Friendly staff and a good pint of Guinness.

McDaid's
Map 4, D7. 3 Harry St.
One of Dublin's best known literary pubs, this small, high-ceilinged bar boasts the dubious distinction of having been the preferred watering-hole of Ireland's most famously dipsomaniac writer, Brendan Behan (see p.148). It remains more-or-less intact, and despite now selling its own T-

shirts, it's still highly popular with locals, with overspill seating upstairs for when the crush gets too mighty.

Messrs Maguire

Map 4, E4. 1–2 Burgh Quay. Microbrewery pub that's not quite as classy as the *Porterhouse* (see p.292), but well worth trying out. Centrally placed overlooking the river, with countless floors and mezzanines off a grand, winding staircase. Late opening (till 12.30am Mon, Tues & Sun, 2.30am Wed–Sat).

Modern Green Bar

Map 4, C9. 31 Wexford St. Handy for *Club Mono* (see p.305), this lively, friendly student bar does exactly what it says on the tin, with a splash of primary red paint thrown in. Bright, simple booths, good DJs most nights of the week, and a striking mural of photos of the Liffey.

Mulligan's

Map 4, E4. 8 Poolbeg St. This establishment is generally accepted to be the home of "the best pint in Dublin", an accolade which alone justifies a visit to its rambling premises. A favoured haunt of print workers, journalists and writers, this no-nonsense bar is the genuine article, unaffected by either fashion or prosperity.

The Octagon Bar

Map 6, B4. *The Clarence Hotel*, 6–8 Wellington Quay. As you might expect, the wood-panelled, octagonal bar of *The Clarence* (see p.239) is the epitome of studied cool, eerily illuminated by artificial daylight, however late the hour. This said, it attracts a mixed crowd – though you might spot the occasional celeb who's wandered down from their penthouse suite for a nightcap.

The Odeon

Map 4, D10. Harcourt St. Housed in a converted railway station, this is one of Dublin's trendiest bars, with potted palms, Art Deco fittings and a fabulously ornamental bar salvaged from a Barcelona bank. Heaving most nights, chilled-out on Sunday for brunch or the evening movie show. Late opening with DJ Fri & Sat (till 3am, cover charge Sat after 10pm).

O'Neill's
Map 5, H7. 2 Suffolk St.
This rambling pub with plenty of snugs and quiet corners has been a home from home for generations of students and lecturers from nearby Trinity College. Also much favoured as a lunching spot by office workers, who come for the sandwiches and healthy portions of buffet food.

O'Shea's Merchant
Map 5, E7. 12 Bridge St Lower.
Opposite the more famous *Brazen Head*, the *Merchant* nurtures the atmosphere of a homely, good-natured country pub in the centre of the city, providing sanctuary for culchies from any county, but especially Kerrymen. Regular live music and set dancing, and a good place to watch a GAA game.

The Palace Bar
Map 4, E5. 21 Fleet St.
An elegant and sociable remnant of Old Dublin on the eastern boundary of Temple Bar, this handsome Victorian pub attracts a mixed crowd of drinkers drawn in by the quality of its pint and the relative tranquillity of its ambience compared with the surrounding piped-music tourist traps.

The Porterhouse
Map 6, B5. 16 Parliament St.
Dublin's first microbrewery serves a wide selection of its excellent and playfully monikered own-brand beers – the oyster stout isn't a joke, but tastes a lot better than it sounds – attracting both curious locals and visitors enticed by the bright, bustling interior. Check out a sample tray of all nine beers for €9, a great way to establish your chosen pint before settling in. Live music every night and good food; late opening (Fri & Sat till 2am).

Sosume
Map 4, C6. 64 South Great George's St.

Generations of tellers who worked in this lofty former bank are no doubt turning in their graves at its Oriental-themed reincarnation, and its punning name belongs firmly to the modern Celtic Tiger. But it's a lively enough spot, and the theme, with its Buddhas, dragons and botanical prints, is attractive but not too in-your-face. Late opening (till 2.30am Wed–Sat, 1am Sun).

The Stag's Head
Map 5, H7. 1 Dame Court. One of Dublin's prettiest old bars, favoured by students and workers alike. Its dark woods and stuffed and stained-glassed stags evoke the ambience of a slightly scruffy hunting lodge. Extremely lively at weekends when the crowds overflow out onto the pavements, eventually turning the narrow street into a traffic-impassable beer garden. Decent pub food too.

Thomas Read's and The Oak
Map 6, B6. 1 Parliament St. Two contrasting, intercon-

nected bars. The former is a lively establishment, serving a globe-spanning selection of bottled and draught beers to its youngish regulars; by day, its large windows and strategic location on the corner of Parliament and Dame streets, just opposite the magnificently refurbished City Hall, make it the perfect place to while away a few hours watching the city flow by. *The Oak* next door is a more introverted spot, cosy and traditional, with much of its dark panelling filched from deconsecrated churches. Late opening (till 2.30am Fri & Sat).

Toners
Map 4, G9. 139 Baggot St Lower. Just across the road from *Doheny and Nesbitt*, this Victorian bar is one of Dublin's finest. Dark and cosy with a refreshingly plain exterior, its snugs and glazed partitions are perfect for making and breaking confidences. Amazingly efficient service, despite the crowds.

DRINKING: SOUTHSIDE

NORTHSIDE

Dice Bar

Map 5, D6. Queen St, just off Arran Quay.

Part-owned by Huey from the Fun Lovin' Criminals, along with the *Voodoo Lounge* round the corner, the *Dice Bar* is an ice-cool New York-style place, though it can get wild later in the evening. Long, black bar and black banquettes, lit by church candles, and nightly DJs, playing anything from soukous to lounge funk. Late opening (Thurs–Sat till 2.30am).

Morrison

Map 4, C4. *Morrison Hotel*, Ormond Quay Lower.

Minimalist and extra-chic but nonetheless very mellow bar; a great place to chill out and chat with a view of the Liffey. The clientele is a fairly regular mix of locals and visitors, so don't be put off by the arch-cool exterior.

Pravda

Map 4, C4. Corner of Liffey St and Ormond Quay Lower.

Trendy superbar on the north side of Ha'penny Bridge which might have pleased even Papa Stalin, with its huge Revolutionary murals and industrial theme; balcony seats and tables done out like the dining car of the Trans-Siberian Express mean you can survey the scene in comfort. Decent food available; late opening (Fri & Sat till 2.30am).

Ryan's

Map 5, A6. 28 Parkgate St.

Situated near the entrance to the Phoenix Park, this stately establishment can fairly claim to be the "president of Ireland's local". The quality of its Guinness is legendary, and its regulars hotly dispute the claim of *Mulligan's* of Poolbeg St to the city's finest pint. The sensitive and notoriously travel-sickness-prone liquid, they triumphantly point out, has by far the shorter distance to travel to reach *Ryan's*, the brewery being a mere river-breadth away.

DRINKING: NORTHSIDE

Live music and clubs

D espite enjoying recent international pop success through the likes of Boyzone, B★witched and Westlife, Dublin's **rock music** scene didn't so much swagger as stagger into the new millennium. Gone are the days when agents flocked from London to the capital to sign the next U2 or Sinéad O'Connor, though there are plenty of young hopefuls still plying their trade in the smaller clubs and bars. Nevertheless, there's an abundance of gigs to choose from every week. **Irish traditional music** is in full flower with several bars now offering sessions nightly. While both **jazz** and **blues** have their devotees and a small number of dedicated venues, it's the boom in **clubbing** which has come to dominate Dublin's nightlife. Friday and Saturday nights in particular offer a vast range of possibilities, from funk and samba to Seventies pop and drum 'n' bass. In contrast, there are far fewer opportunities for fans of **classical music** or **opera**, but the quality of the music on offer remains significantly high.

Dublin is well-stocked with medium- and large- sized **venues** for live shows, but, in general, the acts that pack in the punters are from the USA or UK, although stalwarts such as the folkie turned soft-rock singer Mary Black can still draw a crowd. For **information** on Dublin's nightly music performances and clubs, check the publications detailed in Basics, p.7. Traditional music sessions and gigs are also listed in the monthly *Irish Music* magazine (€2.48), widely available in newsagents, while clubs are covered in detail by monthly club-oriented freebie *The Slate*, which you can pick up in record shops, bars and the clubs themselves. For larger shows, you may need to **book tickets** in advance – the ticket shop at HMV on Grafton Street (see p.328) is your best bet; at smaller venues you can generally pay at the door. **Prices** vary from €8 to €30 depending on the act and size of the venue.

Many of Dublin's pubs, live music venues and theatres – notably the Temple Bar Music Centre, Vicar Street and the Gaiety Theatre – turn into clubs on selected nights.

LIVE MUSIC VENUES

The listings below are divided between Dublin's **major venues** (which almost always require advance booking) and **smaller places**, such as pubs and clubs, which regularly feature live music. From spring to late summer, a number of other venues stage **outdoor concerts**, usually advertised in *Hot Press* and *The Event Guide* (see p.7). These include Dublin Castle (see p.87) during the Heineken Green Energy Festival in May (see p.336), Lansdowne Road Stadium (p.345), the National Concert Hall (see p.304) and the Royal Dublin Society's showground in Ballsbridge (see p.342).

MAJOR CONCERT VENUES

The Ambassador

Map 4, D1. Parnell St. Credit card bookings via Ticketmaster ☎1890/925100, ⓦwww.ticketmaster.ie.

Up-and-coming venue in a former cinema at the top of O'Connell Street, whose programme veers towards alternative and leftfield US acts; prices tend to be slightly higher than at other Dublin venues.

The National Stadium

Map 3, E8. South Circular Rd ☎453 3371.

Frequently used medium-size venue holding between 1000 and 2000 people, depending on whether or not the seats are taken out. As you'd expect of an ageing hall designed primarily to host boxing matches, the facilities for audiences are fairly spartan, but the excellent sightlines and acoustics compensate.

Olympia Theatre

Map 6, C6. 72 Dame St ☎677 7744, ⓦwww.olympia.ie.

This wonderful old Victorian theatre is frequently used for live music performances. Established international and Irish acts tend to play early-evening sets, with late-night gigs on Fridays and Saturdays, known as "Midnight at the Olympia", reserved for more good-time performers who entertain an audience drawn in by the promise of the late alcohol licence (see p.312).

Point Theatre

Map 3, J4. East Link Bridge, North Wall Quay ☎836 3633.

The venue of choice for most visiting superstar acts, the cavernous Point Theatre is a huge and charmless converted warehouse on the north bank of the Liffey, about a mile east of O'Connell Street, with a capacity of between 3000 and 5000, depending on whether the show is seated or standing. The acoustics and sightlines are good, but considering its size and status, the venue is surprisingly bereft of facilities for the humble punter.

LIVE MUSIC VENUES

The SFX

Map 5, H1. 28 Sherrard St Upper ☎ 855 4673.

This 1500-capacity hall is one of Dublin's oldest and most popular rock venues, and has hosted some of the city's best rock and pop gigs over the last two decades. The advent of new venues and the *SFX*'s unfashionable location has diminished its popularity somewhat, but it's still a great place to see quality acts.

Temple Bar Music Centre

Map 6, E5. Curved St ☎ 670 9202, ⊛ www.tbmc.ie.

This custom-built facility includes an impeccable, if slightly antiseptic venue for audiences of up to 650, and has a booking policy determinedly geared towards innovation and experimentation. The bar area outside also features frequent free shows by up-and-coming songwriters.

Vicar Street

Map 5, D8. 58–59 Thomas St West ☎ 454 6656.

Despite its rather downtown location opposite John's Lane Church, *Vicar Street* has acquired an estimable reputation for its staggeringly varied programme of gigs, from cool jazz to alt.country, via traditional music and indie rock and the occasional comedian. The arena holds more than 600, and there's a restaurant; *Vicar Street*'s adjacent little brother, *The Shelter*, plays host to less well-known names.

OTHER VENUES

Break for the Border

Map 4, C7. Stephen's St ☎ 478 0300.

This enormous Western-themed restaurant attracts hundreds of good-natured punters in pursuit of rock, indie and dance music, dance, drink and the opposite sex. The mainstream music policy is more than compensated for by the clientele's impressive dedication to the pursuit of a good time. Rock bands usually feature from around 9pm at weekends.

Eamonn Doran's

Map 6, G4. 3A Crown Alley,

LIVE MUSIC VENUES

Temple Bar ☎ 679 9114.
A large, rather soulless joint, but young bands can be heard here most nights, sometimes two or three per evening. You're unlikely to have heard of any of them and equally unlikely to hear of them again, but it can be a good night out on occasions.

The Isaac Butt

Map 4, G2. Store St ☎ 855 5884, ⓦ www.theisaacbutt.com. Nightly gigs from mostly unknown bands and singers, ranging from hardboiled grunge to candy-sweet pop. Some are cracking, others are diabolical, but it's often great fun.

Slattery's of Rathmines

Map 3, F8. 217 Rathmines Rd Lower ☎ 497 2052.
Large and popular bar, a little way south of Portobello Bridge, offering a variable programme of rock, country, traditional music, jazz and blues; usually free.

Slattery's of Rathmines

Just off map 3, F8. 217 Rathmines Rd Lower ☎ 497 2052.
Large, atmospheric traditional bar, a ten-minute walk south of Portobello Bridge (or bus #14, #15 or #83 from the centre), offering a variable programme of rock, country, traditional music, jazz and blues in its upstairs room; usually free, including a lively and well-supported open-mike singer-songwriter night every Tues (from 9.30pm).

Whelan's

Map 4, C9. 25 Wexford St ☎ 478 0766, ⓦ www .whelanslive.com.
With its welcoming 350-capacity, two-level room, this is perhaps the city's best place to see live music up close. The intimate atmosphere makes *Whelan's* particularly good for acoustic and roots music, though it also offers a range of rock and occasional jazz acts.

For more on Irish music, see Contexts, pp.369–372.

LIVE MUSIC VENUES

TRADITIONAL MUSIC PUBS AND VENUES

Traditional Irish music has undergone something of a revival in Dublin of late, with far more pubs now offering regular live sessions than a few years back. Some of these are impromptu, but in the vast majority at least one of the musicians has been paid to appear. The quality of music varies considerably but can sometimes be extraordinarily good, especially if a well-known player decides to drop in. Some bars deliberately gear their music towards the tourist trade with a heavy emphasis on "Oirishness"; we've listed the more worthy venues below. Sessions are, of course, free – you only pay for your drinks – and usually start around 9.30pm and continue until closing time.

The Brazen Head
Map 5, E7. 20 Bridge St Lower ⑦679 5186.
Laying claim to the title of Dublin's oldest pub, the *Brazen Head* opens its doors to musicians every night, though the quality of the sessions can be extremely variable, even if the surroundings are grand.

The Cobblestone
Map 5, D5. 7 King St North ⑦872 1799, ⓦwww.musiclee.ie.
Arguably the best traditional music venue in Dublin (and, some would claim, in Ireland too), this dark, cosy wooden-floored bar at the north end

of Smithfield is also a fine place to sample the hoppy products of the nearby Dublin Brewery Company. High-quality sessions take place downstairs nightly and on Sunday afternoons, while regular concerts (€8–€10), featuring some of Ireland's best-known singers and musicians are staged upstairs several nights a week.

Hughes's Bar
Map 5, E6. 19 Chancery St. Tucked away behind the Four Courts, this renowned bar attracts the cream of the city's traditional musicians to its nightly sessions. Fridays can

draw a large crowd, so arrive early to grab a seat.

The Merchant

Map 5, E7. Merchant's Quay ⊤679 3797

It helps when landlords are fans of traditional music, and this is definitely the case at this popular bar on the corner of Bridge St Lower – high-quality sessions most nights of the week.

Monto

Map 4, F2. O'Shea's Hotel, 19 Talbot St ⊤836 5670.

Dublin's newest traditional music venue, specializing in gigs by some of the bigger names in traditional music, Monto has already garnered a reputation for the quality of its programme. Tickets usually cost around €10.

O'Donoghue's

Map 4, F8. 15 Merrion Row. The centre of the folk and traditional music revival which began in the late 1950s, *O'Donoghue's* will forever be associated with The Dubliners. Nightly sessions draw a considerable crowd, partly because the bar is a notable landmark on the tourist trail.

JAZZ AND BLUES

Although Dublin has never been renowned as a **jazz** centre, the city's increasing cosmopolitanism is reflected in the number of places now hosting gigs or concerts. These include pubs such as *Slattery's of Rathmines* (see p.299), which has weekly jazz (Fri) and blues (Sun); and larger venues such as *Vicar Street* (see p.298) or *Whelan's* (see p.299), both of which sometimes stage concerts featuring visiting jazz and blues stars from Africa, South America, the USA and Europe. Also worth mentioning is the *Gaiety Theatre* (see p.305) which features live jazz and salsa bands in its late-night Friday club. The city's **blues** scene is a lot smaller and revolves around old-stagers such as The Mary

JAZZ AND BLUES

Stokes Band and the singer Rob Strong. However, devotees of electric blues should be satisfied by the offerings listed below.

JAZZ AND BLUES VENUES

Herbert Park Hotel
Map 2, F5. Anglesea Rd, Ballsbridge ☎667 2200, ⓦwww.herbertparkhotel.ie.
Every Sunday (12.30–3pm), the hotel's *Pavilion* restaurant hosts a jazz buffet lunch, with the sounds often provided by one of Ireland's most renowned mainstream musicians, guitarist Louis Stewart, playing solo and accompanying singers.

The International Bar
Map 4, D6. 23 Wicklow St ☎677 9250.
Somewhat of an old-fashioned pub venue (see p.289), the *International* still hosts some great music, usually of the good-time and raunchy variety, including the regular "Dirty Jazz Club" (Tues) and a blues night (Fri). Also noted for the comedy nights

upstairs (Mon, Tues & Thurs).

Irish Film Centre Bar
Map 6, D5. 6 Eustace St ☎679 5744.
The place to go on Friday and Saturday nights if you want to quietly savour the best jazz and blues in the city. After 11.30pm, once the film-goers have departed, the main foyer converts into the perfect venue, where a relaxed and discerning crowd takes in renowned local and international artists.

J.J. Smyth's
Map 4, C7. 12 Aungier St ☎475 2565.
Built on the site of the birthplace of poet and balladeer Thomas Moore (of the nineteenth-century *Irish Melodies* fame), *J.J.'s* offers a feast of contemporary jazz (one of Ireland's best-known saxophonists, Richie Buckley, regularly plays here), a weekly

Irish blues club (Tues) and gigs from the more rumbustious end of the rock spectrum.

Zanzibar
Map 4, C4. 34–35 Ormond Quay Lower ☎878 7212.

This gargantuan African-themed bar on the Quays is usually geared up for the pre-club scene, but offers Sunday relaxation by means of its live jazz residency, usually a modern trio, every week from 5.30–7.30pm.

CLASSICAL MUSIC AND OPERA

The **classical music** scene in Dublin isn't prolific, but in addition to the venues listed below, concerts are often held in the Powerscourt Townhouse Centre (see p.35), the National Museum (see p.41), the Irish Museum of Modern Art in Kilmainham (see p.123) and at the Hugh Lane Municipal Gallery of Modern Art on Parnell Square (see p.145). **Operas** are performed at The Gaiety Theatre (see p.311), while both St Patrick's Cathedral (see p.105) and St Mary's Pro-Cathedral (see p.140) host occasional evening organ and choral recitals. The best sources of **information** about forthcoming events are *The Event Guide* and the *Irish Times*.

CLASSICAL MUSIC VENUES

- - - - - - - - - - - - - - - - - - - -

Bank of Ireland Arts Centre
Map 4, D5. Foster Place ☎671 1488.
A small, 200-seater venue staging an innovative pro-

gramme ranging from choirs to harp virtuosi; tickets usually cost around €10.

Christ Church Cathedral
Map 4, A6. Christchurch Place ☎677 8099, ⊛www.cccdub.ie.
In addition to occasional organ recitals here, the Cathedral Consort sings at

evensong every Saturday at 5pm (free).

National Concert Hall
Map 4, E10. Earlsfort Terrace ☎475 1572.
Dublin's most prestigious classical venue has a full calendar of both lunchtime recitals and evening concerts, the latter often featuring the Radio Telefís Éireann Symphony Orchestra or international singers and musicians; also includes performances by the students of local music schools, and the odd ballet. Expect to pay between €5 and €35 depending upon the type of concert and the performers.

Trinity College
Map 4, E5. College Green ☎608 1120, ⓦwww.tcd.ie.
The Chapel Choir sings the services twice a week (Thurs 5.15pm, Sun 10.45am; free) while there are also occasional concerts in the Chapel or campus buildings (tickets around €6).

CLUBS

For many years, Dublin's **club** scene comprised "The Strip": a cluster of cramped, expensive and mostly unlicensed basements on Leeson Street which still exist to snare the unwary. However, club culture has now arrived with a vengeance, and there are many better options for those looking to keep the night alive, especially around Temple Bar and Dame Street. Venues crop up or disappear so rapidly that the only way to find the hottest draws is to pick up one of the local listings mags (see p.7), and even then quality varies dramatically. The clubs listed below are the pick of the more enduring options. Bear in mind that Ireland's club culture is markedly different to much of Western Europe – drink and dance go hand-in-hand here, and many clubs try to draw in the crowds on slacker evenings by offering drinks promotions.

You can expect to **pay** anything from €8 to €20 for entrance, depending on the coolness of the club and the reputation of the DJ, but on special one-off nights, with an international DJ, you can pay as much as €35.

See p.288 for details of stylish bar-club hybrid, *4 Dame Lane*.

The Gaiety Theatre

Map 4, D7. King St South
☎677 1717.
Fri & Sat 11.30pm–4am.

On Fridays, and Saturdays Dubliners looking for a good night out throng the beautiful old Gaiety Theatre, some enticed by the attraction of the city's latest-serving bars – all five of them. Each night features live bands (Fri salsa and jazz, Sat rock) and DJs playing an assortment of tunes on three different levels, plus film screenings in the array of backstage bars and green rooms.

Lillie's Bordello

Map 4, E6. Adam Court, off Grafton St ☎679 9204.
Mon–Sun 11pm till late.

Rock stars – would-be, has-been and actual – quaff and bitch with supermodels in this velour-bedecked space.

Don't worry unduly if you're asked if you're a member – practically nobody is. Regulars get priority and rarely pay the reasonably hefty entrance fee (€15), but if you beat the after-pub crowd, act relaxed and don't look too dishevelled you should get in easily enough. If you do gain admittance you'll have the dance floor more or less to yourself: the regulars are far too cool to boogie.

Mono

Map 4, C9. 26 Wexford St
☎478 0766.
Daily 10.30pm–2.30am.

Ultra-cool newly redesigned bar and club occupying the premises of the former *Mean Fiddler*, with an extensive programme of club nights including the house-specializing pair of *Saturday* (Sat),

CLUBS

Messy (Sun), plus *Bliss* (Weds) for fans of dancefloor anthems, *Cushi* (Thurs) for drum 'n' bass and, perhaps best of the lot, *Motion* (Fri) featuring guest DJs playing deep house, techno and progressive trance.

POD

Map 4, D10. 35 Harcourt St
☎478 0225, ⊛www.pod.ie.
Wed–Sat 11pm–2.30am.
The phenomenally popular *POD* (short for "Place Of Dance") in Old Harcourt Street train station is a match for anything that New York, Berlin or Tokyo has to offer, boasting ultramodern decor and a tooth-loosening sound system. The most popular venue for international dance acts, it's also home to the hottest local DJs, and is the hangout of choice for many a visiting celebrity. The clientele are intimidatingly chic, and the door policy, especially at weekends, can be tough. Dress to impress and get there early.

Redbox

Map 4, D10. 35 Harcourt St
☎478 0225.

Thurs–Sat 10.30pm–2.30am.
Far more plush than other similar-size dance venues in the city, *Redbox* is a tailor-made, lovingly designed 1000-capacity hall located upstairs from the *POD*, but with a more relaxed and less style-conscious atmosphere. Features what's probably Dublin's largest student night (Thurs) and major DJs (Fri & Sat) playing techno and house, plus occasional live gigs on other nights of the week.

Renard's

Map 4, F6. Setanta Centre, 35 Frederick St South ☎677 5876.
Mon–Sun 9pm–3am.
Popular with Dublin's small but self-important music and media pack, who tend to inhabit the upstairs VIP area. Claustrophobes may find the ground-floor bar preferable to the sweaty basement dancefloor, where the music policy ranges from commercial dance to hardcore funk.

Rí-Rá

Map 4, C6. 1 Exchequer St
☎6774835

Thurs–Sun 11.15pm–3am.

The records spun at *Rí-Rá* (pronounced Ree-Raw) can range from plain commercial disco through world music to hard funk, depending on night and mood: this club manages to be both informal and fashionable and draws an eclectic and friendly crowd.

Shelter

Map 5, D8. *Vicar Street*, 58–59 Thomas St West ☏ 454 6656, Ⓦ www.vicarstreet.com.

Fri & Sat 11pm–3am.

Small but swish, *Shelter* opens its doors to a wide range of different local promoters, so most of the club nights are one-offs. The exception is the fortnightly *Deluxe* (Fri), one of the city's most popular house nights.

Spy

Map 4, D6. Powerscourt Townhouse Centre, Clarendon St ☏ 677 0067.

Mon–Sat 9pm–3am.

Stylishly designed, ultra-cool club spanning three floors, equally enjoyed by lounge lizards and dancefloor divas. Be seen in the *Monochrome Bar*, loll in the *Pink Room* or get down to a wide variety of music courtesy of the resident DJs.

Switch

Map 6, D4. Eustace St, Temple Bar ☏ 668 2504.

Nightly 11pm–3am.

DJs nightly, both downstairs and in the bar of this some-times frenzied venue. *Phunk'dUp* (Sat) is a huge, justifiably popular night of house and tough techno with a strong underground atmos-phere.

Temple Bar Music Centre

Map 6, E5. Curved St ☏ 670 9202, Ⓦ www.tbmc.ie.

Tues–Sat 11pm–2am.

A varied and variable pro-gramme of club nights, including *Soul Riot* (Weds) with a "45s room" playing mainly jazz-funk and a "33s room" for more laid back sounds; an indie night, *Screamadelica* (Thurs) and a range of one-off clubs (Fri). On Tuesdays, doors open at 9pm for *Salsa Villa*, which is preceded by an hour's dance

CLUBS

class for those that need to
freshen up their steps or learn
the basics.

Temple Theatre
Map 5, H2. Temple St North
⊤874 5088,
🌐www.templetheatre.ie.
Fri & Sat 9/10pm–3am.
Housed in an enormous
restored church, spread over
three floors and clearly
inspired by UK mega-clubs
like *Cream* and *Ministry of
Sound*, the Temple has had
some difficulty finding its
feet, not least because of its
unfashionable location.
Nonetheless, the *Rhythm
Corporation* (Fri) has become
an R&B mainstay, bringing
over DJs from the UK, a formula that's repeated on
Saturdays at *Space*.

Tivoli Theatre
Map 5, E8. 135–138 Francis St
⊤670 3771.

Sun, Tues, Fri & Sat
10.30pm–very late.
The city's current "in" venue,
the *Tivoli* has a state of the art
360-degree sound system and
a hefty techno flavour.
International DJs are often
brought in for its *Influx* night
(Sat), while Tuesday's *Genius*
aims at student techno lovers,
and the wildest night is
undoubtedly *Foot Fetish* (Fri).

Tomato
Map 4, D10. *Harcourt Hotel*,
60 Harcourt St ⊤478 3677.
Daily 9pm–3am.
Popular three-room venue,
offering a more downmarket
alternative to nearby *POD*
and *Redbox*, with a range of
different club nights and DJs
throughout the week, including the *Spark* indie night
(Weds), and, for commercial
dance music, *Cheeze* (Thurs)
and *FM104* (Fri).

CLUBS

Theatre and cinema

As befits a city with a rich literary past, **theatre** flourishes in Dublin. The traditional diet of Irish classics at the "establishment" theatres is now spiced by experimental or fringe programmes at newer, smaller venues. Highlights of the year include the **Dublin Theatre Festival** in early October and the Dublin Fringe Festival which runs from late September to mid-October (see pp.337–340 for more on them both). Theatres generally operate from Monday to Saturday; evening performances usually begin at 7.30pm or 8pm, and there may be matinées, too. Credit-card **booking** is widely available – expect to pay €10–20 per ticket for fringe theatre, €15–30 for mainstream. Bookings can also be made through Ticketmaster (☎ 456 9569 or ☎ 1890/925100, ⓦ www.ticketmaster.ie). If you're budget-conscious, it's worth enquiring about low-cost previews and occasional cut-price Monday- and Tuesday-night shows, while students with ID and OAPs can sometimes find good concessionary rates.

As well as the city-centre theatres reviewed below, there are a number of **venues in the suburbs**: the Civic Theatre in Tallaght (☎ 462 7477), Draíocht in Blanchardstown (☎ 885 2622) and the Pavilion in Dún Laoghaire (☎ 231 2929).

THEATRE AND CINEMA

For details of what's on, check the *Irish Times*,
***The Event Guide* or *In Dublin* (see p.7).**

Dublin has numerous **cinemas** showing mainstream films (which are often released earlier in Ireland than in Britain). Most of them are in the suburbs, but there's a couple near the top of O'Connell Street: the Savoy on O'Connell Street Upper itself (Map 4, D2; programme info ☏ 874 8487, booking ☏ 874 6000, ⓦ www.filminfo.net) and UGC on Parnell Street (Map 4, B2; programme info ☏ 872 8400, booking ☏ 872 8444). For more interesting fare, the Irish Film Centre and the Screen, reviewed below, are the chief venues. The **Dublin Film Festival** in late June is well worth checking out (see p.336), as are the outdoor summer screenings in Meeting House Square organized by the Irish Film Centre. All cinemas operate a policy of cheap seats before 5pm (6.30pm in some cases), seven days a week, during which time **tickets** cost €3.50–5.50 – after this they cost €5–8; student discounts are also often available.

THEATRES

The Abbey Theatre
Map 4, E3. Abbey St Lower
☏ 878 7222, ⓦ www.abbeytheatre
.ie.
This is the National Theatre of Ireland (see also p.132), founded by W.B. Yeats and Lady Gregory in 1903 and the first theatre in the English-speaking world to be state-subsidized (since 1925). The original building was destroyed by fire in the 1950s and replaced by the current, much-detested pile in 1966 – it's slated for redevelopment or, more likely, relocation in the near future. It tends to show international and Irish classics (by Synge, Sheridan, O'Casey, Wilde, etc), plus new offerings by contemporary playwrights such as Brian Friel, Marina Carr, Bernard

THEATRES

Farrell and Tom Murphy (see also Peacock Theatre, p.313).

Andrew's Lane Theatre

Map 4, D6. Between St Andrew's St and Exchequer St ℡ 679 5720.

Situated just off Dame Street, the main theatre here puts on generally mainstream plays and musical works by international and touring provincial companies, while the studio upstairs presents a mix of fringe and amateur theatre.

Bewley's Café Theatre

Map 4, D7. *Bewley's*, 78 Grafton St ℡ 086/878 4001.

On the second floor above the café (see p.36), you can often catch an innovative, small-scale production while eating your lunch (€10 including soup and a sandwich); there's also regular evening cabaret (€10–13), at which you can buy wine, soft drinks, tea and coffee.

Crypt Arts Centre

Map 4, B6. Dublin Castle ℡ 671 3387, ⓦ www.cryptartscentre.org.

A small venue in the crypt of

the Chapel Royal, managed by a company called *íomhá Ildánach* (roughly translated as "varied image") who stage a number of plays throughout the year, generally fringe pieces. Occasional art exhibitions are also held here.

Focus Theatre

Map 3, H8. 6 Pembroke Place ℡ 676 3071.

Founded by the late Deirdre O'Connell, a student of Lee Strasberg at the Actors' Studio in New York, this diminutive but important venue stages powerful international modern drama and occasional fringe plays.

Gaiety Theatre

Map 4, D7. King St South ℡ 677 1717, ⓦ www.gaietytheatre.com.

An old-style playhouse with velvet curtains and gilded boxes, which hosts everything from opera and Irish classics to musicals, concerts and other family entertainments. On Fridays and Saturdays after 11.30pm it becomes a nightclub (see p.305).

THEATRES

Gate Theatre

Map 4, D1. 1 Cavendish Row, Parnell Square ☎ 874 4045, ⊛ www.gate-theatre.ie. Founded in 1928 by Micheál MacLiammóir and Hilton Edwards (see p.141) in an eighteenth-century building leased from the Rotunda Hospital, the Gate has a reputation for staging adventurous experimental drama as well as established classics, in a small, elegant auditorium. Over the years, its name has pulled in plenty of star performers, from Orson Welles (who made his stage debut here), to Frances McDormand and John Hurt in recent times.

The Lambert Puppet Theatre

Map 7, A5. 5 Clifton Lane, Monkstown ☎ 280 0974, ⊛ www .lambertpuppettheatre.com. Dublin's only puppet theatre, producing shows of very high quality every Saturday and Sunday at 3.30pm. Great for kids, though there are also performances for adults during the International Puppet Festival in September.

New Theatre

Map 6, C4. Essex St East ☎ 670 3361, ⊛ www.thenewtheatre.com. Seventy-seat theatre in Temple Bar, which puts on three shows a year – classics and new Irish plays – as well as hosting local and international companies.

Olympia Theatre

Map 6, C6. 72 Dame St ☎ 677 7744, ⊛ www.olympia.ie. Somewhat similar to the Gaiety, this old-style music hall has been through many incarnations since it opened in 1749, with a roll-call of luminaries from Charlie Chaplin and Noel Coward to Mary Black and Jack Dee. Nowadays it hosts musicals, stand-up comedy shows and medium-size gigs (see p.297), as well as dramatical crowd-pleasers.

THEATRES

If you've got kids in tow, it's also worth checking out events at The Ark in Temple Bar – see p.82.

Peacock Theatre

Map 4, E3. 26 Lower Abbey St
ⓣ878 7222, ⓦwww.abbey
theatre.ie.

The Abbey's smaller sister theatre, in the basement, produces new Irish drama in both Gaelic and English, and can often be a goldmine for great entertainment and new talent.

Project Arts Centre

Map 6, C5. 39 Essex St East
ⓣ679 6622 or ⓣ1850/260027,
ⓦwww.project.ie.

Renowned for its experimental and often controversial Irish and international theatre, this flagship of the contemporary art scene also hosts dance, film, music and performance art.

Samuel Beckett Theatre

Map 4, E6. Trinity College
ⓣ608 2461.

A small venue used for productions by Trinity College drama students and on a commercial basis by a broad range of theatre, dance and opera companies, both Irish and international.

Tivoli Theatre

Map 5, E8. Francis St ⓣ454
4472.

A modern theatre in the Liberties, with hard seats on three sides of a raised stage, the Tivoli shows everything from mainstream drama and musicals to comedy and dance.

CINEMAS

The Irish Film Centre

Map 6, D5. 6 Eustace St ⓣ679
3477, ⓦwww.fii.ie.

Art-house cinema with two screens, a good bar-restaurant (see p.290) and a film-related bookshop. Films include new, low-budget Irish works as well as a good range of world and gay cinema.

The Screen Cinema

Map 4, E4. D'Olier St ⓣ672
5500.

A fairly old-fashioned, low-key venue with three screens; a good place to catch art-house as well as mainstream films.

CINEMAS

Gay Dublin

As attitudes to homosexuality in Dublin have become increasingly liberal over the last decade, so the capital's **gay** community has grown in confidence, and a small but vibrant scene has now established a niche in the city's social life. The number of permanent fixtures is small but growing; most of the real action happens at the gay nights in the straight venues. Most **pubs** around Temple Bar and South Great George's Street have a mixed clientele and a keen eye on the pink economy, while several mainstream **clubs** have theme nights and gay events.

A good starting point for finding out the latest **information** on gay events and venues in Dublin is the drop-in resource centre at OUThouse, 105 Capel St (Map 4, B3; Mon–Fri noon–6pm; ☎873 4932, ⓦwww.outhouse.ie), which has a café and small library. Alternatively, you could call Gay Switchboard Dublin (Mon–Fri & Sun 8–10pm, Sat 3.30–6pm; ☎872 1055) or Lesbian Line (Thurs 7–9pm; ☎872 9911). It's also a good idea to pick up a copy of the free monthly *GCN* (*Gay Community News*; ⓦwww.gcn.ie), which has detailed listings of upcoming events and all the vital info you need to enjoy yourself. These are stocked in the gay-friendly Books Upstairs (see p.322) or can be picked up in clubs and bars. Alternatively, check out the gay and lesbian listings page of *In Dublin* (see p.7), or the dedicated website ⓦwww.gay-ireland.com.

Dublin's Gay Pride festival usually takes place on the last Saturday in June and features a parade and special events at many of the venues included in our listings. For more info, visit ⓦwww.dublinpride.org.

PUBS AND BARS

Dublin's small number of gay bars aren't just meeting places but fully-fledged entertainment centres, offering a broad range of different events throughout the week from quizzes and singalongs to dance floor delights.

The Front Lounge
Map 6, A5. 33 Parliament St. Not "officially" gay, but popular amongst those who relish its classy, bouffant hair-styled atmosphere and range of entertainment, including karaoke (Tues), lounge music (Wed) and DJs at the weekend. Late opening (till 1.30am Fri & Sat). See also p.288.

The George
Map 4, C6. 89 South Great George's St. Ireland's first gay pub when it opened twenty years ago, *The George* remains as popular as ever. The outside is painted a gaudy purple with a neon-lit sign offering "Bona Polari" (gay-adopted Romany slang meaning "good chat"), while the inside is full of character and offers a range of entertainment including cabaret, quizzes, singalongs and pre-club DJs as well as good meals during the day. Upstairs has four sections linked by *Gone with the Wind* stairways and a small dancefloor where you'll hear house and funk until 3am (Wed–Sun) The downstairs bar opens until 2.30am (Wed–Sat).

Gubu

Map 4, B4. 7–8 Capel St.

Taking its name from the
leading character in Alfred
Jarry's absurdist *Ubu* plays,
this brightly decorated,
relaxed mixed bar hosts probably Dublin's most alternative
cabaret, *G-Spot* (Wed), hosted
by the awesome Busty Lycra
and featuring drag acts, comedy and more (there's an
open-mike policy, if you feel
daring). Other events include
a regular eighties disco (Fri).
Late opening (till 1am Fri &
Sat).

Out on the Liffey

Map 5, F6. 27 Ormond Quay
Upper.

Northside gay pub that's nice
for a relaxed midweek drink
or to warm up for a weekend
session (neat dress code

applies). Equally popular with
gays and lesbians, with late
hours (till 2am Thurs–Sat)
and events (quizzes, karaoke,
etc). The location is not the
most salubrious, so take care
in those backstreets.

The Wig and Pen

Map 3, D5. 131 Thomas St
West.

Dublin's newest gay bar, in a
rather downmarket area of
the city west of Christ
Church. Despite this, it has
proved to be a real hit with
both men and women, with a
happy hour most nights from
6pm to 8pm. Often has DJs
playing house, techno and
funk at the weekends as well
as other entertainment during
the week, including an indie
club night (Tues). Sunday
night is men only.

CLUBS

As yet Dublin has no single dedicated venue for gay clubbers, who rely on usually weekly events in mainstream
clubs. Some of these, however, such as H.A.M. (see p.317)
are now almost scene institutions. Entry prices are usually
pretty reasonable; expect to pay €8–10.

Baby

Map 4, C9. *Mono*, 26 Wexford St ☏478 0766.

Mon 11pm–3am.

Recently relaunched techno night in a revamped venue, featuring resident DJs and a very sociable mixed crowd – a good place to meet people.

Candy

Map 4, F7. *Club Soho*, *Earl of Kildare Hotel*, corner of Nassau St & Kildare St ☏220 1320, ⓦwww.clubcandy.net.

Sat, Sun, Tues & Thurs 11pm–3am.

Four fun nights, including the ever-popular *Lollypop* (Tues) and *Super Handbag* (Thurs), both of which favour commercial dance classics from the Eighties. Often has regular drinks pro-motions and giveaways; neat dress code.

H.A.M. (Homo-Action Movies)

Map 4, D10. *POD*, 35 Harcourt St ☏478 0225, ⓦwww.pod.ie.

Fri 11pm–3am.

Weekly gay night at one of Dublin's trendiest clubs (see p.306), drawing a regular, and often extravagant, mostly male crowd. The music is heavily oriented towards funky house and the Art Deco anteroom is for chilling out and watching movies, usually of the hunky action-man variety. Totally queer door policy – definitely an occasion for dressing up. Drag acts perform on alter-nate Fridays from 10pm.

Hilton Edwards

Map 4, D6. *Spy*, Powerscourt Townhouse Centre, Clarendon St ☏677 0067.

Sun 10pm–3am.

One of Dublin's plushest clubs (see p.307), spread over three floors, *Spy* hosts this enjoyable homosocial Sunday night, devised by the origina-tors of H.A.M; resident DJs playing tracks with a techno edge and an extremely cool lounge.

Libida

Map 5, D6. *Chief O'Neill's Hotel*, Smithfield ☏817 3838.

Last Sat of the month 10.30pm–2am.

GAY DUBLIN: CLUBS

Popular lesbian night with high-energy commercial dance, cool Latin tracks and slower tunes, plus spotlight dancers on the stage and occasional live bands. Swish, modernist surroundings.

Lube

Map 4, H2. *Oslo*, Connolly Station Concourse ☏829 1614, ⓦwww.lube.ie.

Last Sat of the month 9.30pm–late.

Leather Uniform Bear Encounter dress code night for men – see the website for details of suitable apparel.

Muffins

Map 5, E7. *Molloy's Café Bar*, 13 High St ☏677 3207.

First and third Sat of the month 8.30pm–2am.

Women-only night in an elegant bar just west of Christ Church cathedral, featuring three floors of DJs playing everything from commercial dance to Latin grooves, and a chill-out room.

Sharpshooter

Map 6, G4. *Eamonn Doran's*, 3A Crown Alley, Temple Bar ☏679 9114.

Tues 11pm–2am.

Advertised as "Dublin's queer indie night", though the upbeat crowd can be pretty mixed and sometimes struggles to fill this rather cavernous club.

Slam

Map 6, D4. *Switch*, Eustace St, Temple Bar ☏668 2504.

Mon 11pm–2am.

A long-standing Monday night event, playing no-frills, commercial house to a friendly, often exuberant crowd.

Shopping

Dublin's economic boom is most apparent in the development of the city centre's **shops**, but north and south of the Liffey are two distinct areas. The **southside**, focusing on Grafton Street's swish stores and the design culture of Temple Bar, is fashion and form incarnate, while the **north**, based on O'Connell Street and the grid of surrounding streets, is all function. You buy what you need north of the river and what you want on the south. Perhaps the one exception to this rule is Meath Street in the Liberties (see p.119), with its wide range of stores stocking the essentials.

Our listings are grouped into the following categories: art, crafts and design (p.320); books (p.322); clothing and fashion (p.325); jewellery (p.327); records and CDs (p.328); shopping centres and department stores (p.330); and markets (p.332).

Dublin shops generally **open** from 9.30am to 5.30pm or 6pm Monday to Saturday, with late shopping until 7pm or 8pm on Thursday evenings; many places (though not, generally, food stores) also open on Sunday from around noon to 5pm or 6pm. The exception is Temple Bar, where businesses may not open until at least an hour later. Most shops, except small food stores, market stalls and secondhand shops, accept credit cards. Visitors from non-EU countries can claim tax back on most items purchased (see p.351).

ART, CRAFTS AND DESIGN

Dublin's **art and design** scene is thriving, and there are many reliable outlets for buying work of a very high standard, the best of which are listed below. Examples of Irish **crafts** geared specifically towards the tourist market may be found in several of the general gift stores on Nassau Street (Map 4, E6).

The Bridge Art Gallery

Map 4, B4. 6 Ormond Quay Upper ☏872 9702.
Mon–Sat 10am–6pm, Sun 2–5pm.

One of the very best places in Dublin for contemporary art and crafts – including ceramics, hand-blown glass, prints, mirrors, paintings and sculpture – with many pieces very competitively priced.

Monthly exhibitions are displayed in the gallery to the rear.

DESIGNyard

Map 6, C4. 12 Essex St East ☏677 8453.
Mon & Wed–Sat 10am–5.30pm, Tues 11am–5.30pm.

A major showcase for excellence in Irish design, applied art and crafts, including stunning collections of contemporary jewellery and ceramics. A different designer is highlighted each month and this is definitely the place to head for if you want to commission a unique piece of work.

Giles Norman Gallery

Map 4, D6. Ground floor, Powerscourt Townhouse Centre, Clarendon St ☏677 3455.
Mon–Sat 10am–6pm, Thurs till 8pm, Sun noon–6pm.

Collection of black-and-white photographs of Ireland – largely rural subject matter, but does include some atmospheric shots of Dublin.

The Historical Picture Company

Map 4, C4. 5 Ormond Quay Lower ☏ 872 0144

Mon–Fri 10am–6pm, Sat & Sun 9am–5pm.

With its vast range of nostalgic, historical and just plain beautiful photographs from every county in Ireland, organized by town and village, this is *the* place to track down that picture of grandfather's cottage in Ballinskelligs. Photos come ready-mounted or can be framed on the spot.

Kilkenny

Map 4, E6. 6 Nassau St ☏ 677 7066.

Mon–Fri 8.30am–6pm, Thurs till 8pm, Sat 9am–6pm, Sun 11am–6pm.

A superb range of Irish crafts, particularly ceramics and glassware. Look out for decorative pottery by Nicholas Mosse, Bernard Kavanaghs' vibrant blue glazes and Stephen Pearce's classic natural earthenware. Best of the glassware includes colour-dappled Jerpoint Glass and Waterford Crystal. Also stocks an extensive range of clothes by contemporary Irish designers.

Louis Mulcahy

Map 4, E7. 46 Dawson St ☏ 670 9311.

Mon–Sat 10am–6pm, Thurs till 8pm.

Hand-thrown pots, urns and vases from one of Ireland's most famous potters (now based in Dingle, Co. Kerry), plus a selection of hand-woven wool tapestries.

Merrion Square

Map 3, H6.

Sun 10am–6pm (approx).

Original paintings are sold by the artist in person from the railings around the north side of the square. There's no shortage of doe-eyed maidens and dewy glens, but there's a huge range and some of it is very good. Mainly cash transactions (and some artists will accept foreign currency).

Original Print Gallery

Map 6, E4. 4 Temple Bar ☏ 677 3657.

Tues–Fri 10.30am–5.30pm, Sat

SHOPPING: ART, CRAFTS AND DESIGN

11am–5pm, Sun 2–6pm.
A well-run gallery with plenty of variety and work of a very high standard. One of the best places in town for contemporary etchings, lithographs and screen prints, mainly Irish.

The People's Art Hall,
Map 4, D6. Second floor, Powerscourt Townhouse Centre, Clarendon St ☎679 4237.
Mon–Sat 10am–6pm, Thurs till 8pm.
Stocks a wide range of paintings and prints by artists both local (including the owner's own evocative pub scenes) and from elsewhere in Ireland; prices can be very reasonable.

The Solomon Gallery
Map 4, D6. Second floor, Powerscourt Townhouse Centre, Clarendon St ☎679 4237.
Mon–Sat 10am–5.30pm.
Spacious commercial gallery showing predominantly Irish paintings and sculpture, along with a handful of pieces by British artists.

The Source at Urbana
Map 6, E4. 43–44 Temple Bar ☎670 3083.
Mon & Fri 11am–6pm, Tues & Wed 11am–7.30pm, Sat 10am–6pm, Sun noon–6pm.
Crammed to the rafters with novelty household gear, playthings and accessories, ranging from leopardskin cushions to jelly-belly machines.

BOOKS

Dublin's literary life is well-supported by its numerous new and secondhand **bookshops**, ranging from large general stores such as Eason's and Waterstone's to specialist outfits such as Connolly Books.

Books Upstairs
Map 4, E5. 36 College Green ☎679 6687.
Mon–Fri 10am–7pm, Sat

10am–6pm, Sun 1–6pm.
Strong selections of Irish poetry and drama, as well as psychology, philosophy,

women's studies and gay literature. You'll also find keenly priced American imports and a good range of periodicals.

Cathach Books

Map 4, E6. 10 Duke St ☎671 8676.

Mon–Sat 9.30am–5.45pm.

Cathach specializes in rare first editions and antique maps of Irish interest; in the window you might find signed first editions of Yeats's poetry or a 1922 edition of *Ulysses*. The basement is the place to pick up original mounted illustrations at reasonable prices.

Connolly Books

Map 6, B5. 43 Essex St East ☎671 1943.

Mon–Sat 9.30am–5.30pm.

The red frontage and the name give the game away about the nature of this excellent bookshop. Its shelves are filled by works on Irish political history, including a number by James Connolly himself, plus modern fiction, music and the arts. One of the few places in Dublin to stock a wide range of political magazines.

Dublin Bookshop

Map 4, D7. 24 Grafton St ☎677 5568.

Mon–Fri 9am–10pm, Sat & Sun 9am–6pm.

General bookshop offering a broad range of titles, including an extensive Irish section. Specializes in books relating to the mind and body.

Eason's

Map 4, D2. 40 O'Connell St Lower ☎873 3811.

Mon–Sat 8.30am–6.45pm, Thurs till 8.45pm, Fri till 7.45pm, Sun 12.45–5.45pm.

The best general bookshop north of the Liffey, Eason's stocks a wide range of books, cards and stationery, as well as having one of the largest magazine sections in Ireland. There's a branch of Tower Records upstairs and a café on the second floor.

Eason's

Map 4, E6. 27–29 Nassau St ☎677 1255.

Mon–Sat 8.30am–6.15pm, Thurs till 8.15pm, Sun 1–5.15pm.

Formerly Fred Hanna's (one of Ireland's leading independent booksellers), but has maintained its great range of academic titles, books on Ireland and Irish literature since being taken over by Eason's. Good selection of maps and guidebooks.

Greene's

Map 4, G7. 16 Clare St ☎676 2554.
Mon–Fri 9am–5.30pm, Sat 9am–5pm.

Long-standing Dublin book-shop-cum-post-office just around the corner from the National Gallery, selling new and secondhand books. The barrows under its distinctive wrought-iron canopy hold all sorts of treasures.

Hodges Figgis

Map 4, E7. 56–58 Dawson St ☎677 4754.
Mon, Wed & Fri 9am–7pm, Tues 9.30am–7pm, Thurs 9am–8pm, Sat 9am–6pm, Sun noon–6pm.
Founded in 1768, Hodges Figgis is a Dublin institution. Although the breadth of coverage is huge, its emphasis is instantly apparent – directly opposite the door is a comprehensive Irish fiction sec-

tion, while other shelves are dedicated to contemporary and historical Ireland, its language, art and culture. Book bargains and a café are on offer upstairs.

Hughes & Hughes

Map 4, D7. St Stephen's Green Shopping Centre ☎478 3060.
Mon–Sat 9.30am–6pm, Thurs till 8pm.
A long-established family bookshop, with additional outlets in Dublin airport, covering a broad range of categories including children's books and a comprehensive travel section (virtually every book published about Dublin is on the shelves).

Waterstone's

Map 4, E6. 7 Dawson St ☎679 1415.
Mon–Wed & Fri 9am–7pm, Thurs 9am–8pm, Sat 9am–6.30pm, Sun noon–6pm.
Comprehensive bookstore on five levels, with a huge range of fiction, books of general and Irish interest, and academic and business titles, though you may often need to ask staff to direct you to

the specific section required.

The Winding Stair
Map 4, C4. 40 Ormond Quay
Lower ☎873 3292.
Mon–Sat 10am–6pm, Sun
1–6pm.

A pleasantly relaxed secondhand bookshop, particularly
good for Irish literature, with
its own café (see p.270)
where you can settle down
with your recently purchased,
well-worn tomes.

CLOTHING AND FASHION

Grafton Street is the best place in town for **high-street
fashions** and **designer clothes**. British chains such as
Next and Miss Selfridge dominate, but you'll also find
Dublin's most famous department store Brown Thomas (see
p.330), with its superb range of designer labels, and the
nearby Powerscourt Townhouse Centre (see p.331); other
department stores and shopping malls are also worth
exploring. For trendy **secondhand**, **ethnic** and **club gear**,
try Temple Bar or the Market Arcade (see p.332), and for
knitwear and **tweed** shops check out Nassau Street (Map
4, E6); Kilkenny (see p.321) also has a fine selection of
clothes. For cheap, serviceable clothing, Penney's and
Dunnes Stores are hard to beat – branches are on
O'Connell Street (Map 4, D2–3) and in the St Stephen's
Green Shopping Centre (see p.331).

A:Wear
Map 4, D7. 26 Grafton St
☎671 7200.
Mon–Sat 9.30am–6.30pm,
Thurs till 8.30pm, Sun
noon–6pm.
Inexpensive women's fashion
chain geared towards teens
and twentysomethings. Irish

designers Quin and Donnelly
are particularly well represented.

Cleo
Map 4, F8. 18 Kildare St ☎676
1421.
Mon–Sat 9am–5.30pm.
Small shop crammed with

clothes made of traditional Irish textiles, including replicas of Aran waistcoats, hardy wool-lined trousers, casual linen shirts and hand-knitted sweaters. Generally rather expensive.

Coyle's

Map 4, C7. 8 Aungier St ☎475 1416.

Mon–Sat 10am–6pm.

The best specialist men's hatter in Dublin, offering plenty of examples of that old stalwart, the tweed cap, and a variety of other assorted headgear.

Design Centre

Map 4, D6. First floor, Powerscourt Townhouse Centre, Clarendon St ☎679 5718.

Mon–Sat 9am–6pm, Thurs till 8pm, Sun noon–6pm.

The Design Centre's ever-changing panoply of stock represents the cream of young Irish designers of women's fashion, including Louise Kennedy, John Rocha, Helen Cody and Ciarán Sweeney.

The Eager Beaver

Map 6, G4. 17 Crown Alley ☎677 3342.

Mon–Sat 9.30am–6pm, Thurs till 7.30pm, Sun 1–6pm.

Two-storied shop stocking a huge range of secondhand clothing. Garments packing the rails include combats, Seventies gear and leather coats. Discounts for students, the unemployed and senior citizens.

Flip, Sharp's Ville and The Real McCoy

Map 6, F5. 4–6 Fownes St Upper ☎671 4299.

Mon–Sat 9.30am–6pm, Thurs till 7pm.

Trio of secondhand clothes stores, all run by the same people. Items include imports of US workshirts, sports tops, leather jackets and plenty of retro and club gear.

The Harlequin

Map 4, D6. 13 Castle Market ☎671 0202.

Mon–Sat 10am–6pm, Thurs till 7pm.

Stocking a large range of both men's and women's

clothing, The Harlequin specializes in the unusual, so it's a must for that striking party outfit.

The House of Ireland
Map 4, E6. 37–38 Nassau St ☎677 7949.
May–Sept Mon–Sat 9am–7pm, Thurs till 8pm, Sun 10.30am–6pm; Oct–April Mon–Sat 9am–6pm, Thurs till 8pm, Sun 10.30am–5.30pm.
Spacious, quality tourists'

shop stocking Arans, hand-knits, colourful Ireland's Eye sweaters and tailored tweed jackets.

Kevin & Howlin
Map 4, E6. 31 Nassau St ☎677 0257.
Mon–Sat 9.30am–5.30pm.
Tweed heaven for men and women – jackets, caps, waistcoats, hats, ties, suits, all expertly tailored in Donegal tweed.

JEWELLERY

Dublin offers **jewellery** to suit all tastes and budgets. Some of the most expensive outlets cluster along Johnson's Court (which runs between Grafton Street and the Powerscourt Townhouse Centre; Map 4, D6) and off here in Westbury Mall. For the best in contemporary design pieces check out the DESIGNyard (see p.320).

Angles
Map 4, D7. 10 Westbury Mall, off Harry St ☎679 1964.
Mon–Sat 10am–6pm, Thurs till 7pm, Sun noon–6pm.
This tiny store sells intriguing contemporary jewellery, providing a showcase for Irish designers alongside international collections. The emphasis is very much on

design, with many pieces in silver, some with semi-precious stones or gold detailing.

Arkana Design
Map 4, D6. Ground floor, Powerscourt Townhouse Centre, Clarendon St (no phone).
Mon–Sat 10am–6pm, Thurs till 8pm.
Another jam-packed store,

SHOPPING: JEWELLERY

though this time specializing in ceramic jewellery and pieces constructed from crystals, fossils and amber.

Emma Stewart-Liberty

Map 4, D6. First floor, Powerscourt Townhouse Centre, Clarendon St ☎ 679 1603.

Mon–Sat 10am–6pm.
Exclusive designs, using predominantly gold and silver and modern gem-setting techniques – the plain gold bangles and earrings are particularly striking. Specially commissioned work and repairs are undertaken.

RECORDS AND CDS

For a city of its size, Dublin possesses an astonishing array of **record** and **CD** shops. There are branches of chain stores HMV in Grafton Street (Map 4, D7) and Henry Street (Map 4, C3), Tower Records in Wicklow Street (Map 4, D6), and Virgin on Henry Street (Map 4, C3), together with branches of Dublin's own Golden Discs in Grafton Street (Map 4, D7) and St Stephen's Green Shopping Centre (see p.331). For something more esoteric, try the places listed below.

Claddagh Records

Map 6, E5. 2 Cecilia St, Temple Bar ☎ 677 0262,
ⓦ www.claddaghrecords.com.
Mon–Fri 10.30am–5.30pm, Sat noon–5.30pm.
Unquestionably the finest traditional music emporium in Dublin. You can find just about every currently available recording here and, if you're not sure what you're

looking for, the helpful and knowledgeable staff can point you in the right direction. Also stocks contemporary Irish recordings, together with racks of world music, country, blues and Scottish and English folk music.

Disque

Map 6, D3. 29 Wellington Quay, Temple Bar ☎ 671 9455,

@ www.disque.co.uk.
Mon–Sat 10am–8pm, Thurs
until 9pm.

Describing itself as simply "a shop that sells music on vinyl and CD", Disque's tongue-in-cheek minimalism fails to do justice to its splendid stock. This is the place for aspiring DJs, with everything from frenzied hip-hop to the coolest grooves and, thanks to its sister store in London's Chapel Market, often has material unavailable elsewhere in Ireland.

Final Vinyl
Map 4, C10. 40A, Camden St Lower ☎ 475 8826.
Mon–Sat noon–8pm.

A vinyl junkie's paradise, with probably the most extensive range of secondhand LPs and 45s in Dublin, alongside stacks of CDs, T-shirts and assorted memorabilia. Prices are often remarkably low.

Freebird Records
Map 5, I6. 1 Eden Quay ☎ 873 1250, @ www.freebird.ie.
Mon–Wed & Sat 10am–6pm, Thurs & Fri 10am–8pm.

This basement store, just by

O'Connell Bridge, crams an enormous range of new and secondhand indie, rock, drum 'n' bass, techno, jazz and mellow beats into its compact surroundings. Prices are very reasonable.

Road Records
Map 4, C6. 16B Fade St ☎ 671 7340, @ www.roadrecs.com.
Mon–Sat 10am–6pm, Thurs until 7pm.

The ultimate indie, alternative and alternative country specialist, Road is tucked away off South Great George's Street. Certainly the best place to find new releases, as well as an extensive range of leftfield Irish recordings.

Secret Book and Record Store
Map 5, H8. 15A Wicklow St ☎ 679 7272.
Daily 11am–6.30pm.

Probably the best selection of rare vinyl in Dublin, with collector items – mainly rock, punk, folk and blues – from the 1950s onwards. Also has a comprehensive secondhand books section.

SHOPPING: RECORDS AND CDS

SHOPPING CENTRES AND DEPARTMENT STORES

Dublin's redeveloped centre contains several impressive **shopping centres**, the biggest of which is the Jervis Centre on Mary Street (Map 4, C3), replete with British chains, and the most elegant being the Powerscourt Townhouse Centre, worth visiting for the architecture as much as the retail outlets. Dublin's economic boom is also reflected in the number of revamped **department stores**, the most stylish of which is Brown Thomas.

Arnotts
Map 5, H5. Henry St ☎ 805 0400.

Mon, Wed, Fri & Sat 9am–6.30pm, Tues 9.30am–6.30pm, Thurs 9am–9pm, Sun noon–6pm.

The oldest department store in Dublin, recently refurbished. Inside are affordable fashions, for both adults and children, to compete with Grafton Street, plus a large kitchenware department.

Avoca
Map 4, D6. 11 Suffolk St ☎ 677 4215.

Mon–Wed & Fri–Sat 10am–6pm, Thurs 10am–8pm, Sun 11am–6pm.

Astonishingly successful and colourful department store, stocking its own clothing ranges for women, men and children, including various hand-weaves plus lots of accessories, chic houseware and plenty of potential gifts. There's a splendid deli in the basement, stocking Dublin's finest range of breads, plus an equally delightful café on the second floor.

Brown Thomas
Map 4, D6. Grafton St ☎ 605 6666.

Mon–Sat 9am–6pm, Thurs till 8pm, Sun noon–6pm.

Dublin's most prestigious department store, with the emphasis on quality throughout. Amongst the goods on offer are cosmetics, kitchen-ware, furnishings and Irish linen, and there's a particular-ly good range of designer clothing, including Irish labels such as Louise Kennedy and Paul Costelloe, and collections by the likes of Ralph Lauren and Nicole Farhi. A younger, trendy crowd are catered for by Brown Thomas's BT2 store, lower down Grafton Street.

Clery's

Map 4, D3. 18–27 O'Connell St Lower ☏ 878 6000.
Mon–Sat 9am–6.30pm, Thurs till 9pm, Fri till 8pm.
Old department store with a little bit of everything that's still serving customers at a fairly genteel pace while the city revs up all around it; clothing generally for older clients, with younger fashions occupying far less floor space. The small Irish gifts section has assorted machine-knit Aran sweaters.

Powerscourt Townhouse Centre

Map 4, D6. Clarendon St ☏ 679 4144.
Mon–Sat 9am–6pm, Thurs till 8pm, Sun noon–6.30pm.
Once a magnificent Georgian townhouse (see p.35), this elegant southside space now provides a handful of outlets for designer fashions, fine art, a wealth of antiques and some excellent eateries.

St Stephen's Green Shopping Centre

Map 4, D7. St Stephen's Green West (no phone)
Mon–Sat 9am–7pm, Thurs till 8pm, Sun noon–6pm.
A temple to consumerism packed with clothing stores chiefly aiming at the tots to twentysomethings, along with a sprinkling of inexpensive gift shops. It's also home to Dunnes Stores, which has a comprehensively stocked food hall. The café on the top floor has excellent views over the green.

SHOPPING CENTRES AND DEPARTMENT STORES

MARKETS

Dublin's once-thriving street **markets** have all but disappeared, and some of the few that remain have moved into adopted homes under cover. Despite this, all the places listed below are well worth a visit.

Blackrock Market
Map 2, H6. Off Main St (Blackrock DART).

Sat 11am–5.30pm, Sun noon–5.30pm.

A delightful little partially-covered market lurking behind Blackrock's high street that's well worth a browse. Plenty of variety, including rugs, hats, secondhand books, clothes, crafts, plants and CDs, plus an excellent cheap café.

The Liberty Market
Map 3, E5. Meath St.

Thurs–Sat 10am–5pm.

The Liberty's stalls are crammed, maze-like, into a small indoor hall halfway along a vibrant local shopping street. You can buy anything from replica football shirts to WD40, but most people come for the cheap clothing and footwear. On Saturdays stalls spread along Meath Street and out onto Thomas Street West.

The Market Arcade
Map 4, C6. South Great George's St.

Mon–Sat 10am–6pm, Sun 1–6pm.

A covered market with an excellent laid-back, rough-and-rummage atmosphere. Immensely popular for its secondhand book and record stores, used and period clothing and its olive stall – one of the cheapest places to get a nutritious snack. There's also the excellent *Probe* café (see p.269).

Moore Street Market
Map 4, D3. Moore St.

Mon–Sat 10am–6pm.

A long-established, lively and colourful market selling fruit, veg and flowers, this is one of the few places in

SHOPPING: MARKETS

Dublin where you'll catch sight of produce being unloaded off a horse-drawn cart. Moore Street itself has become increasingly cosmopolitan, with a Russian deli alongside shops specializing in Asian, African and Caribbean food.

Temple Bar Market
Map 6, D5. Meeting House Square.

Sat 10am–5pm.

A foodie's delight. Stalls include organic meat and veg, homemade chutneys, Atlantic oysters and an enormous variety of cheeses. Plenty of snacking opportunities too, on anything from potato cakes to sushi or raspberry tartlets.

Festivals and events

Dublin has **festivals and events** for sports fans, lovers of music, drama and cinema, gardeners or devotees of Ulysses – to name only some of the enthusiasms catered for. Though sports events are the only major thing happening in the winter months, there's something for everyone at almost any time of year. For most events, **tickets** can be obtained at short notice through the booking service at Dublin Tourism (see p.6) or the venue concerned – but bear in mind that you'll need to book accommodation well in advance (see p.235). What follows is a calendar of the regular major events. For one-offs, consult The Event Guide, In Dublin (see p.7) or the tourist offices. Sports events are covered separately in the "Sports" chapter of this guide.

MARCH

St Patrick's Day, March 17
"Paddy's Day" sees a parade of floats and marching bands through the centre of Dublin,

starting at St Patrick's Cathedral and finishing at the top of O'Connell Street. Some half a million people usually turn out to watch the parade, and the pubs throng with music and merriment until the wee hours. Such is the enthusiasm for St Patrick's Day that celebrations now stretch over four days (March 15–18 or 16–19 depending on the actual day on which March 17 falls), with plenty of street theatre and traditional music to accompany the usual pub sessions and parade. For further information call ☎ 676 3205.

Dublin Feis Cheoil, second and third weeks

An annual music festival which has been running since 1897. It originally included traditional music and song, but is now concentrated solely on classical music with the exception of various harp competitions. For details of venues and events call ☎ 676 7265.

APRIL

Easter Rising, Easter Sunday

Commemorations on Easter Sunday, with a Republican march from the GPO to Glasnevin Cemetery.

Convergence Festival, second week

Subtitled "exploring a culture for a better world" and firmly centred upon sustainable futures and healthy lifestyles, this annual festival takes place in various locations around Temple Bar. Includes workshops and day-schools and culminates in an "Earth Fair" in Meeting House Square featuring a range of activities, including performances and music. For more details call ☎ 491 2327.

MAY

Heineken Green Energy Festival, first week

Various home-grown and international rock, indie and generally alternative bands and singers appearing at venues such as the Olympia Theatre, Temple Bar Music Centre and Dublin Castle. 2002's programme included Van Morrison, Muse, The White Stripes and The Hives.

Wicklow Gardens Festival, May 1 to July 31

Open days at private gardens throughout County Wicklow (the "Garden of Ireland"), including Russborough, Avondale, Killruddery and Mount Usher gardens. Call ⊤0404 20100 or visit ⓦ www.wicklow.ie for more information.

JUNE

Bloomsday Festival, June 10–16

A week-long celebration of Joyce's *Ulysses* culminating in Bloomsday itself on June 16 (see box on p.338). Organized by the James Joyce Centre (⊤878 8547, ⓦwww.jamesjoyce.ie), which usually produces an associated commemorative magazine, the festival includes dramatizations of some of the more accessible episodes of the book, along with a full programme of talks, readings and

tours celebrating Joyce's life and times, held in various places around the city.

Dublin Film Festival, last ten days

A showcase of the best in home-grown and international cinema, organized by the Irish Film Centre (see p.313) in Temple Bar, which puts on on screenings in a range of cinemas around the city. For details contact the organizing office at ⊤679 1616.

JULY

Anna Livia Opera Festival, second week

A week-long festival of major operatic works staged at the Gaiety Theatre, often featuring international companies. Call ☏ 661 7544, or check ⓦ www.operaannalivia.com.

James Joyce Summer School, mid-July

Annual event dedicated to Joyce and his works, with lectures, seminars and social events held at Newman House (☏ 716 7422) and the James Joyce Centre (☏ 878 8547), usually mid-month.

AUGUST

Bray International Festival of Dance and Music, early August

Three-day festival held in the seaside resort of Bray, with street and indoor entertainment involving Irish dancing and musicians, mummers, Morris dancers and international visiting groups. Call ☏ 286 0080 for more info.

SEPTEMBER

Dublin Fringe Festival, late Sept to mid-Oct

Lively programme of theatre, dance, performance arts and comedy, featuring more than three hundred events and focusing in particular on new Irish writing and innovative production styles. Held in venues all around the city centre; most tickets are under €15. For more info, call ☏ 1850/374 643 or ☏ 677 3850 or log on to ⓦ www.fringefest.com.

FESTIVALS AND EVENTS

BLOOMSDAY

Bloomsday, on June 16, is a unique celebration of a novel, held in the city that it so brilliantly evokes. Joyce's *Ulysses* relates the events of a single day in 1904 (so chosen because it was the day he first "walked out" with his wife Nora Barnacle) with obsessive fidelity to the localities, characters and speech of his native Dublin. As Joyce wrote, "If I can get to the heart of Dublin, I can get to the heart of every city in the world. In the particular is contained the universal." **Performances** from *Ulysses* take place throughout the day outside the James Joyce Centre in North Great George's Street, and the **Bloomsday Lecture** at 2pm is followed by a lively **walking tour** through the inner northside, but for an extensive Bloomsday pilgrimage, you could visit the following:

The Martello tower (Map 7, E2; see p.196) at Sandycove is the location of "stately plump Buck Mulligan's" ablutions at the start of the novel. Joyce himself spent six tense days here with Oliver St John Gogarty, the model for Mulligan, who later noted, "He is planning some sort of novel that will show us all up and the country as well: all will be fatuous except James Joyce."

Sandymount Strand (Map 2, G8). A walk on the mudflats in Dublin Bay gave Stephen Dedalus pause for reflection.

7 Eccles Street (Map 5, G2). The starting point for Bloom's odyssey and the site of Molly's climactic soliloquy; though the house has gone, its front door is preserved in the Joyce Centre on North Great George's Street (Map 5, H3; see p.149).

St Andrew's and Sweny's Chemist Shop (Map 4, G6). On his way into the centre, Bloom drops into Mass at All Hallows Church, now St Andrew's on Westland Row, and carries on to

Sweny's on Lincoln Place (which still exists), where he buys a bar of lemon soap (as one still can).

Glasnevin Cemetery (Map 2, F3; see p.204). Paddy Dignam's funeral passed by Trinity, Parnell Square and Mountjoy Prison, encompassing the noblest and grimmest institutions in Dublin.

The Oval and Mooney's (Map 4, D3, Map 4 E3). As the *Freeman's Journal* and *Evening Telegraph* offices no longer exist, pilgrims can settle for visiting two pubs mentioned in Chapter 5. *The Oval* on Middle Abbey Street hasn't changed much, unlike *Mooney's* on Lower Abbey Street (now the *Abbey Mooney*). In 1988, a series of fourteen pavement plaques tracing Bloom's route from Abbey Street to the National Library was installed.

Davy Byrne's (Map 4, E6; see p.35). Joyce wouldn't recognize this Duke Street pub, which now caters to yuppies and tourists. Nonetheless, it's a fitting place for pilgrims to consume a mustard-and-Gorgonzola sandwich and a glass of Burgundy, in emulation of Bloom.

The National Library (Map 4, F7; see p.40). Its great reading room was the setting for Stephen's impassioned speech on Shakespeare.

The Ormond Quay Hotel (Map 4, A5; see p.246). A plaque celebrates the hotel's role in the "Sirens" chapter at the end of Bloom's walk along Wellington Quay, and the bartenders wear period costume on Bloomsday.

Olhausen's (Map 4, F2). Since the brothel quarter vanished long ago, pilgrims can content themselves with a visit to Olhausen's the butcher's at 72 Talbot St, where Bloom bought a pig's trotter and a sheep's hoof as a snack.

OCTOBER

Dublin Theatre Festival, first two weeks

Major festival featuring around twenty productions, both from abroad and companies including the Abbey and the Gate, held in mainstream theatres around the city. For centralized booking call ⊕874 8525; for information call ⊕677 8439.

Oscar Wilde Autumn School, first or second week

An annual celebration of Wilde's life, works and times, with talks, screenings and performances in Bray. Call ⊕286 5245 for more details.

Sports

Dublin offers a wide range of participation **sports** activities for visitors to enjoy, but its real forte is spectator sports (and betting on the outcome): **rugby**, **soccer**, **hurling**, **Gaelic football** and **horse racing** are all avidly followed.

The following guide doesn't pretend to be exhaustive, but should give an idea of what's on offer and point you in the right direction for more detailed information.

EQUESTRIAN SPORTS

Equestrian sports are extremely popular in Ireland, with less of the snobbery that's attached in Britain. **Horse racing** is an Irish passion, as you'll find out if you visit Dublin's nearest large racecourse, **Leopardstown** (Map 2, G7; ☏ 289 3607, ⓦ www.leopardstown.com), in the southern suburb of Foxrock (bus #114 from Blackrock DART station, plus special buses on race days from Eden Quay). Races are held at weekends throughout the year and on Wednesday evenings in summer, the main events being the four-day Christmas Festival starting on St Stephen's Day (Dec 26), and the Hennessy Cognac Gold Cup in February. The Irish Grand National is held on Easter Monday at **Fairyhouse** (☏ 825 6167, ⓦ www.fairyhouseracecourse.ie), 15 miles northwest of Dublin, followed in April by the four-day Irish National Hunt Festival at **Punchestown** (☏045/897704), 25 miles southwest of Dublin near Naas. Flat-racing classics are held at **The Curragh**, 31 miles southwest of the capital (☏045/441205): the Irish 1000 Guineas and 2000 Guineas in May, the Irish Derby in June, the Irish Oaks in July and the Irish St Leger in September. Bus Éireann and Iarnród Éireann (see p.14) lay on race-day transport to Fairyhouse, Punchestown and the Curragh.

Show jumping has more of an elitist image, and the **Dublin Horse Show** at the Royal Dublin Society (RDS) pavilion in Ballsbridge (just off map 3, J8) in August was once the highlight of Anglo-Irish social life. While no longer the focus of diplomatic receptions, it's still a prestigious international event, with top riders competing in the Nations Cup, and prizes in ninety different classes of jumping and dressage. More than 1500 horses compete, before an aggregate audience of 100,000. Though day-tickets might be available, you'd be wise to book ahead (☏240 7213, ⓦwww.rds.ie). The RDS pavilion is accessible by DART to Sandymount or by bus #5, #7 or #45.

If you'd like to go **riding**, there are plenty of opportunities in the rolling countryside to the south of Dublin. One of the best places is Brennanstown Riding School (☏286 3778), two miles south of Bray off the Dublin–Wexford road, which offers all levels of tuition and cross-country rides in the glorious Wicklow Hills.

FISHING

Ireland is renowned for its **fishing**, as you can read for yourself in several leaflets published by the tourist board. The River Liffey has **trout** fishing between Celbridge and Millicent Bridge, 12.5 miles west of the centre, and there are **salmon** in other stretches of the river. There's a rainbow trout fishery at Rathbeggan Lakes, Dunshaughlin, 18.5 miles northwest of Dublin in County Meath (☎824 0197), and **sea fishing** is popular off Dublin Bay. Dublin's tackle shops, such as Rory's Fishing Tackle, 17A Temple Bar (☎677 2351), can supply permits, rods, bait and advice.

GAELIC FOOTBALL AND HURLING

Gaelic football and hurling occupy a special place in Ireland, as ancient sports whose renaissance was entwined with the Celtic revival movement and the struggle for independence. The Gaelic Athletic Association (GAA) fostered a network of local clubs that are still the heart and soul of many communities, with political clout in the provinces.

Although Dubliners are generally less keen on either sport, especially hurling, the national stadium for Gaelic games (hurling, Gaelic football, handball and camogie, a version of hurling for women) is at **Croke Park** (☎836 3222, ⓦwww.gaa.ie), near the Royal Canal. Named after Archbishop Croke, an advocate of athletics and teetotalism, it is hallowed by sporting triumphs and the "Bloody Sunday" massacre of 1920 (see p.156). While the stadium may not be used for any sport not played by the ancient Gaels, the GAA have permitted U2 and Live Aid concerts to be held there.

Croke Park is home to the excellent GAA museum – see p.155.

Hurling is said to have descended from a game played by the legendary warrior Cúchulainn. The ball (*slíothar*) is belted prodigious distances, caught and carried on the flattened end of the player's hurley stick. It's a game of constant movement and aggression that doesn't permit a defensive, reactive style of play. Dublin has a poor record at hurling – the big boys are Cork, Kilkenny and Tipperary, with Tipp the victor in 2001 – so the crowd at the **All-Ireland Final** on the first or second Sunday in September mainly consists of out-of-towners.

To the uninitiated, **Gaelic football** resembles a cross between soccer and rugby. Whereas hurling's strongholds are in the southern counties of the island, footballing prowess is more widely spread – Cork, Kerry, Galway, Meath, Dublin and one of the northern counties are usually likely to make a challenge. The **All-Ireland Final** occurs on the third or fourth Sunday in September and has been won by Dubliners on 22 occasions (a record beaten only by Kerry); more people watch the game than any other event in Ireland. Like hurling, Gaelic football is played throughout the year.

GOLF

Golf is Ireland's fastest-growing sport and a major tourist activity. There are more than twenty private courses in and around Dublin, and as many public ones, the majority of them affiliated to the Golfing Union of Ireland, Glencar House, 81 Eglinton Rd, Donnybrook (℡269 4111, ⓦwww.gui.ie), who can provide a list of contact details. The Royal Dublin on North Bull Island (℡833 6346) and Portmarnock (℡846 2794) are Dublin's top clubs, but you're rather more likely to get a round at Hollystown (℡820 7444, ⓦwww.hollystown.com), the Open Golf Centre in St Margarets (℡864 0324), the Deer Park at Howth (℡832 2624) or Dún Laoghaire Golf Club in Eglinton Park (℡280 3916). In addition, there are many short pitch-and-putt courses – for information, contact the Pitch & Putt Union of Ireland, House of Sport, Long Mile Rd, Dublin 12 (℡450 9299).

Tournaments occur all over Ireland for much of the year;

the biggest are the **Irish Open** in late June/early July and the **Smurfit European Open** in July.

GREYHOUND RACING

If you fancy a flutter or just a fun evening out, **greyhound racing** requires little experience of betting and draws a lively crowd of Dubliners from all walks of life. There are races most nights of the week throughout the year (admission €6–8). The **Shelbourne Park Greyhound Stadium** on South Lotts Road, Ringsend (Map 3, J6), is just fifteen minutes' walk east of the city centre and has a comfortable enclosure for watching the races (Wed, Thurs & Sat 8pm; ☎668 3502, or ☎1850/646566). The other venue, **Harold's Cross Stadium**, off Harold's Cross Road, can be reached by bus #16 or #49 (Mon, Tues & Fri 8pm; ☎497 1081).

RUGBY

Lansdowne Road (☎647 3800, ⓦwww.irfu.ie) in Ballsbridge is Irish rugby union's holy of holies, where national and international championships take place in the spring. The **All-Ireland Finals** is the climax of the club season, while the **Six Nations Championship** is the showcase for international rugby. The latter matches are nearly always sell-outs, but you're quite likely to be able to get tickets for Leinster's **inter-provincial** and **European** games at Donnybrook (☎668 9599).

SOCCER

Although the fortunes of Ireland's national football team are a matter of keen concern for almost everyone, with home games at Lansdowne Road, Dublin **soccer** fans are less enthusiastic about local teams. Ireland's national league (Ⓦwww.fai.ie) can hardly compete with the money, allure and success of English football, where Dublin-born players like Liam Brady and Robbie Keane have achieved international stardom. This explains why the most popular teams among Dubliners are Liverpool and Manchester United (both from cities with a large Irish community), a state of affairs acknowledged by RTÉ, which relays coverage of top English matches far more often than Irish ones. The city currently has five teams in the League of Ireland's premier division – Bohemians, Shamrock Rovers, St Patrick's Athletic, Shelbourne and UCD.

SWIMMING AND WATERSPORTS

The coastline north and south of Dublin offers ample opportunities for watersports. Though the water seldom rises above chilly even on hot days, Dubliners enjoy **swimming** in the sea in summertime, when sunbathers pack the shingle **beaches** to the south of the city at Killiney and Bray, and the sandy ones to the north at Sutton, Malahide and Donabate (all accessible by DART or suburban train). Though the beach at Sandycove is small, it's only three miles from the centre, and near the famous Forty Foot Pool (see p.163). Among **swimming pools**, the recently renovated Markevicz Leisure Centre, right in the centre on Townsend Street (Ⓣ672 9121, Ⓦwww.dublincorp.ie), is your best bet.

The other great activity along the coast is **sailing**, with long-established yacht clubs in Dún Laoghaire, Howth, Malahide and Clontarf. Unfortunately, many are members-only, so you won't be able to use the facilities unless you belong to a club with reciprocal membership. Contact the Irish Sailing Association, 3 Park Rd, Dún Laoghaire (Ⓣ280 0239, Ⓦwww.sailing.ie), for details. The Irish National

Sailing School (☎284 4195, ⓦwww.inss.ie) by Dún Laoghaire's West Pier offers courses at all levels.

Though the west coast is more rewarding, there are some fine spots for **diving** around Dublin, like Dalkey Island and Lambay Island. Oceantec, 10 Marine Terrace, Dún Laoghaire (☎280 1083; ⓦwww.oceantecadventures.com) is a PADI Five-Star Instructor Development Centre which runs courses, rents gear and organizes trips to local sites, as well as further afield.

Windsurfing is equally popular around Dalkey and Dún Laoghaire, where Wind & Wave, at 16A The Crescent in Monkstown (☎284 4177, ⓦwww.windandwave.ie), rents gear and offers tuition. If you're less bothered about the setting, you can go windsurfing in the Grand Canal Dock basin at Ringsend, where Surf Dock (☎668 3945) runs courses and rents sailboards by the hour.

Directory

Airlines Aer Lingus, reservations ℡ 886 8888, flight enquiries ℡ 886 6705, ⓦ www.aerlingus.com; BMI British Midland reservations ℡ 407 3036, flight enquiries ℡ 814 4259, ⓦ www.flybmi.com; British Airways ℡ 1800/626747, ⓦ www.british-airways.com; Ryanair ℡ 609 7800, ⓦ www.ryanair.com.

Dentist In the case of dental emergencies, contact the Eastern Health Board, Dr Steeven's Hospital, Dublin 8 ℡ 679 0700 or ℡ 1800/520520.

Disabled travellers The government agency Comhairle, Hume House, Dublin 4 (℡ 605 9000, ⓦ www.comhairle.ie), and Dublin Tourism (see p.6) both offer advice and information to people with disabilities visiting

Ireland. Dublin Tourism's yearly accommodation guide (available from all offices) identifies the wheelchair-accessible establishments in the city. Wheelchairs can be hired for €30 per week from the Irish Wheelchair Association, Blackheath Drive, Clontarf, Dublin 3 (℡ 833 8241, ⓦ www.iwa.ie), who can also provide advice on accessible accommodation and other amenities in Ireland. Dublin Bus (see p.12 – the relevant page of their website is ⓦ www.dublinbus.ie /about_us/accessibility.asp) now operates low-floor fully accessible buses on around twenty routes, with more planned. If you let them know in advance, Iarnród Éireann (see p.14 – the relevant page of their website is

Ⓦ www.irishrail.ie/about_us /accessibility.asp) will arrange for staff to meet and help you on your DART or train journey. For information on wheelchair-accessible taxis, see p.14. Other useful contacts include the National Council for the Blind of Ireland, Whitworth Rd, Dublin 9 (Ⓣ 830 7033, Ⓦ www.ncbi.ie); and the National Association for Deaf People, 35 North Frederick St, Dublin 1 (Ⓣ 872 3800, Ⓦ www.iol.ie/~nad).

Electricity 220–240 volts, 50Hz AC is standard, with three square-pin plugs the norm. All British devices should function normally, though North American ones will require both a transformer and a plug adapter. Australian and New Zealand appliances will only need an adapter.

Embassies Australia, Fitzwilton House, Wilton Terrace Ⓣ 676 1517; Canada, 65 St Stephen's Green Ⓣ 478 1988; New Zealand (Honorary Consul), 37 Leeson Park Ⓣ 660 4233; UK, 31 Merrion Rd Ⓣ 205 3700; US, 42 Elgin Rd Ⓣ 668 8777.

Emergencies Ring Ⓣ 999 or Ⓣ 112 for emergency medical aid, fire services or police.

Ferry companies Irish Ferries Ⓣ 1890/313131, Ⓦ www .irishferries.com; Isle of Man Steam Packet Co (Seacat) Ⓣ 1800/551743, Ⓦ www .seacat.co.uk; Norse Merchant Ferries Ⓣ 819 2999, Ⓦ www.norsemerchant.com; P&O Ⓣ 1800/409049, Ⓦ www .poirishsea.com; Stena Line Ⓣ 204 7777, Ⓦ www.stenaline.ie.

Health Residents of European Union countries are entitled to free medical treatment under the EU Reciprocal Medical Treatment arrangement, provided that a completed E111 form is held (available from post offices in Britain). Citizens of most non-EU countries are charged for all medical services including those provided by hospital accident and emergency departments. Reciprocal medical agreements may apply between other countries – Medicare in Australia, for example, has such an agreement with Ireland and Britain – but check the precise terms before departure. In all cases, it's advisable to take out travel insurance.

Helplines Rape Crisis Centre ☎661 4911 or ☎1800/778888; Samaritans ☎1850/609090; Victim Support ☎878 0870.

Hospitals Beaumont Hospital, Beaumont Rd ☎837 7755; Mater Misericordiae, Eccles St ☎830 1122; St James's, James St ☎453 7941; and St Vincent's, Merrion Rd ☎269 4533. All have accident and emergency departments. In emergencies dial ☎999 or ☎112 for an ambulance.

Internet cafés Central Cybercafé, 6 Grafton St ☎677 8298, ⊛www.centralcafe.ie; Global Internet Café, 8 O'Connell St Lower ☎878 0295, ⊛www.global.cafe.ie; Planet Cyber, 13 St Andrews St ☎670 5183.

Laundries Most self-service laundrettes are open Mon–Fri 8am–8pm, with earlier closing on Saturday. Central ones include All American, Wicklow Court, South Great George's St ☎677 2779; and Wash to Iron, 45 Francis St ☎473 1876. For

dry-cleaning, a central option is Craft Cleaners, 12 Baggot St Upper ☎668 8198.

Left Luggage There are left luggage offices and/or lockers at the airport (☎814 4633), Busáras (☎703 2434), Heuston Station and Connolly Station (both ☎836 6222).

Lost property For items lost on Dublin Bus ring ☎703 1312; at the airport ☎814 4483; for those left on trains, Connolly Station (☎703 2363) or Heuston Station (☎703 2102).

Pharmacies Dame St Pharmacy, 16 Dame St ☎670 4523; O'Connell's, 55 O'Connell St Lower ☎873 0427. Both open until 10pm daily.

Photography Most types of film are readily available from pharmacies and specialist camera shops. For rapid developing try One Hour Photo, 110 Grafton St ☎677 4472; 6 St Stephen's Green ☎671 8578; and the ILAC Centre, Henry St ☎872 8824.

Police The main Garda station for the Dublin region is in Harcourt Square ☎666 6666. In emergencies dial ☎999 or 112.

Post offices The General Post Office is on O'Connell St Lower (Mon–Sat 8am–8pm, Sun 10am–6pm; ☎705 8833 or ☎872 8084). Another handy post office is situated in St Andrew's St, near the Suffolk Street Tourism Centre (☎705 8256). Stamps may also be purchased at many newsagents.

Public holidays New Year's Day; St Patrick's Day (March 17); Good Friday; Easter Monday; First Monday in May; First Monday in June; First Monday in August; Last Monday in October; Christmas Day; St Stephen's Day (December 26).

Public toilets Public toilets are few and far between and often require a coin for entry. Key locations include St Stephen's Green West, most large shopping centres, and railway and bus stations.

Tax Value Added Tax rates vary, but visitors from outside the EU can claim a VAT refund on all goods bought in Ireland. Ask for a special VAT receipt when you purchase an item – you should then get this stamped at cus-toms in the airport and a cash refund will be given.

Telephones Local calls from a phone box cost a minimum of 30c. Many phones also accept prepaid cards obtainable from newsagents and post offices. For operator assistance, including reverse-charge calls, for Ireland and Britain dial ☎10, for the rest of the world ☎114; directory enquiries is ☎11811 for numbers in Ireland, ☎11818 international. Phone numbers with the prefix ☎1800 or 1850 are free. The area code for Dublin is ☎01, and the country code for Ireland is ☎353 – so if dialling from the UK, for example, prefix ☎00 353 1 to Dublin numbers. The international access code for calls from Ireland is ☎00, followed by the relevant country code: 44 for Britain, 1 for the US and Canada, 61 for Australia, 64 for New Zealand. For calls to Northern Ireland, dial ☎048, followed by the user number. For cheap-rate international calls, go to Talkshop, 20 Temple Lane South, Temple Bar ☎672 7212.

Time Ireland is in the same time zone as Britain. Clocks are moved forward one hour in March and back again at the end of October for daylight saving.

Travel agents USIT (youth/student travel), 19–21 Aston Quay ⑦602 1600 for Europe and the US, ⑦602 1700 for the rest of the world; Thomas Cook, 118 Grafton St ⑦677 1721; CIE Tours (Irish tour organizer), 35 Abbey St Lower ⑦703 1888; Trailfinders (long-haul flights), 4-5 Dawson St ⑦677 7888.

CONTEXTS

History

The Vikings

When Dublin Bay was first settled can never be determined, though it may have been as long as five thousand years ago. The Egyptian astrologer Ptolemy marked a place called Eblana in his map of 140 AD, but major habitation of the area only began when **Viking** raiders arrived from Norway in the first half of the ninth century.

Before the Vikings arrived there were two small settlements: Áth Cliath ("the ford of the hurdles"), a fortified enclosure used for trading purposes since the sixth century, which gave rise to the city's Gaelic name **Báile Átha Cliath** ("the town of the ford of the hurdles"); and a monastic site located at the point of convergence of the rivers Liffey and Poddle, an area known as **Dubh Linn** ("dark pool"), from which the city's current English name is derived. It was this latter area that the Norse raiders attacked in 837 and transformed into a port. The Dubh Linn settlement became an important trading post for the Vikings; large amounts of amber and silver, as well as artefacts such as a set of weighing scales, recovered from the Wood Quay area and the Viking graveyard near Kilmainham, testify to its importance. Once the Norsemen were established here, Dubh Linn became the focus for attacks not only from the Irish, but also from Danish Vikings who had arrived from England in 851. The internal feuding weakened the Viking position, and, when the Norsemen split to follow two different leaders, it ultimately led to their defeat by the King of Leinster in 902, forcing them to withdraw. However in 917 they returned and laid the foundations for a permanent settlement by building wooden houses in the **Wood Quay** and **Christ Church** areas, with the result that, over the next decade, a flourishing town life developed and Dublin's role as a centre of commerce intensified.

The first half of the tenth century saw the Norsemen gradually become Gaelicized, as they intermarried with the Irish and started converting to **Christianity** (the first Viking king to convert was Olaf Cuarán, who was baptized in 943). This, plus the need to defend their settlement, resulted in the Vikings' heightened involvement in internal battles. As well as allying themselves with various factions vying for power, the Norsemen made contact with another Viking settlement in York, who then sent large fleets from England to plunder Ireland anew and precipitated a series of conflicts with the Irish kings that would continue for the rest of the century. The Vikings lost their impetus when the kingdom of York collapsed in 954. In an attempt to counter the threat posed by **Brian Ború**, the Irish High King, they became part of an alliance centred around their former adversary, the King of Leinster. However, their combined forces failed to prevent decisive defeat by Ború at the **Battle of Clontarf** in 1014, after which Dublin became a Christian vassal state. The Norsemen were then completely assimilated into the Gaelic world, and with the ensuing **Hiberno-Norse** culture came a great deal of Christian development, particularly under the kingship of Sitric "Silkbeard" IV.

THE VIKINGS

The Normans

The eleventh and twelfth centuries saw the Hiberno-Norse of Dublin become further embroiled in Gaelic struggles for supremacy, which, at the end of the twelfth century, led to **Dermot MacMurrough**, the Ard-rí (high king) of Leinster, fleeing to the court of the **Norman** king Henry II to request assistance in regaining power. In return for his fealty, Henry dispatched a band of mainly Welsh knights under the leadership of Richard FitzGilbert de Clare, more usually known as **Strongbow**. Dublin was rapidly conquered in 1170, and the following year Henry granted the town a charter and established a court there, thus opening the way for further migration, mainly from Bristol. The new invaders circumscribed the town with walls, erected Dublin Castle and the cathedrals of Christ Church and St Patrick, along with other churches such as St Audoen's. Dublin's status as a Christian centre developed rapidly, and during the thirteenth century it became a focal point for pilgrimages, particularly as the reputed *bacall Íosa* ("staff of Jesus") resided in the city.

The Irish rose against subjugation in the early fourteenth century, and Dublin suffered during **Edward II**'s abortive attempt to reconstitute English control. Although the town was seen as the capital of the English colony in Ireland, in reality only a small tract of land was under English jurisdiction and even this area, known as **the Pale** (from which the expression "beyond the Pale" arises), was vulnerable to attack. Dublin was under constant threat, with major restrictions placed on the movement and entry of Gaels, and the people crammed within the city's walls facing the medieval scourges of plague and fire.

The Tudors and the Stuarts

During the late 1400s, the English attempted to exercise further control over areas outside the Pale by supporting the stronger Irish lords, most notably the Fitzgeralds of Kildare and the Butlers, Earls of Ormonde. However **Henry VIII** reversed this policy after he came to power in 1509, preferring to extend royal control regardless of the Irish families. In 1534 the Fitzgeralds protested by staging a symbolic rebellion against Dublin Castle, led by **Silken Thomas**. It didn't last long; the young Fitzgerald could not have anticipated the ferocity of the king's response when he sent over a large army to confiscate all the Fitzgerald lands – he was captured and executed the following year.

Dublin thus became the focus for recolonization, and the town grew once again as a new wave of migrants swarmed in. Henry's **reformation of the Church** resulted in Dublin being declared an Anglican city; in 1537 the monasteries were dissolved (All Saints became Trinity College), the *bacall Íosa* was burnt and many relics and images destroyed. However this period also saw some of Ireland's strongest acts of **rebellion**, with the Irish kings resisting the impingement on their powers. **Elizabeth I**, on taking over the throne, believed that the struggle for supremacy in Ireland was vital to England's security (her fear being that the Spanish would use it as a base to attack England) so she devoted large resources to defeating the rebellion, which was finally quelled at the **Battle of Kinsale** in 1601. The resulting Treaty of Mellifont, which included the confiscation of half a million acres of land from the native Irish, established power firmly in London, and led to the mass departure of Irish chiefs to continental Europe in 1607, known as the **Flight of the Earls**.

In 1633 the reformer Thomas Wentworth was appointed to the position of Lord Deputy and began implementing plans to develop Dublin. Much of his work was undone, however, when Ireland became a pawn in the **English Civil War**, and the capital was half-destroyed as various factions attempted to assert their control (on top of this, the plague once again swept through the city). Oliver Cromwell's ruthless campaign in Ireland and his subsequent **Act of Settlement** (1652), which provided for further massive confiscation of land from the native Irish, took a heavy toll, but the restoration of the monarchy in 1660 led to the appointment of the **duke of Ormonde** as Lord Deputy of Ireland and to the resurgence of Dublin. A rapid building programme began, which included the salvaging of Dublin Castle and the start of work on the Royal Hospital at Kilmainham, and the town again became a self-sustaining and prosperous trading entity. The arts flourished and the theatre, first established before the war, was revived.

The Williamite Wars and the eighteenth century

However, another reversal came with the **Williamite Wars**. The Catholic King **James II** took the English throne in 1685, replaced Ormonde with the Catholic Earl of Tyrconnell and repealed the Act of Settlement. In reply, the horrified English establishment invited the Protestant Dutch prince, **William of Orange**, to take over the English throne, precipitating a series of confrontations between the two sides. The decisive clash, the **Battle of the Boyne** in 1690, saw James and his Irish Catholic supporters defeated by William, who then imposed the **penal laws** barring Catholics from holding any office of state, voting or buying land, among other measures. With three-quarters of Irish soil now belonging to Anglo-Irish Protestants or absentee English landlords, a rural migration followed, ensuring that Dublin had a **Catholic majority** by the middle of the eighteenth century. Sectarian violence became commonplace in the city, with regular gang wars taking place.

Dublin prospered during the eighteenth century while the rest of Ireland, with few exceptions, sank into extreme poverty. The capital enjoyed its architectural heyday: the **Wide Streets Commission** of the 1750s undertook the gentrification of the city, with a view to transforming it into a European-style capital with boulevards and tree-lined squares (those which so characterize Dublin today); the **Royal Exchange**, the **Four Courts**, the **Custom House** and the west front of **Trinity** were all built around this time; and plutocrats commissioned their own extravagant townhouses, like **Leinster House** and **Powerscourt House**. While Dublin's Protestant upper-middle classes patronized craftsmen and virtuosi in the written and musical arts (Handel's *Messiah* was premiered by the composer himself in Dublin in 1742), the aspirations of a rising Catholic middle class were denied.

The Act of Union

Henry Grattan's Declaration of Rights during the parliament of 1782 came close to declaring Irish (or, at least, Protestant Anglo-Irish) independence. The following years saw the establishment of the **United Irishmen**, a movement inspired by a combination of the ideas of the patriot **Wolfe Tone** and the success of the French Revolution (see p.116). Seeking social reform and justice, they were driven underground by the government's declaration of their illegality in 1794. The subsequent revolt of 1798 was suppressed, leading to the 1801 **Act of Union**, which abolished the Irish Parliament and instigated direct rule from London. The cause of the United Irishmen was briefly taken up by **Robert Emmet**, the brother of one of its leaders, when he staged his own attempted rebellion in Dublin in 1803, but this too was crushed (see p.120).

The impact on Dublin of the transferral of power to London was enormous. Although the social whirl continued to revolve around the new vice-regent's lodge in Phoenix Park, it was with the participation of a rapidly diminishing upper class. With Dublin's economic decline, and its population now over seventy percent Catholic, the town became the stage for political ferment and agitation for **Catholic emancipation**. It came in 1829, when "The Liberator", **Daniel O'Connell**, became the first Catholic MP of modern times, and, after the Municipal Corporation Act of 1840 had declared that city officials could only be elected by ratepayers, he also became Dublin's first Catholic Lord Mayor. However his attempts at securing the repeal of the Union resulted in his eventual trial and imprisonment for sedition.

The Famine, Parnell and Home Rule

The **Great Famine** of 1845–49 had a disastrous effect on Ireland. Almost 1.5 million out of a population of 8.5 million starved to death and nearly another 1.5 million emigrated, mainly to North America. Dublin's slums were already bulging at the seams when the Irish potato crop first failed in 1845 and thousands of refugees fleeing starvation began to arrive, increasing the city's population to 247,000 by 1851. The workhouses closed their doors, and diseases of deprivation reaped further havoc among those left on the streets. Resentment focused on the failure of the British government to intervene and on the absentee landlords who had continued to profit while remaining indifferent to the suffering of their tenants (ironically a visit by Queen Victoria to Dublin in 1849 passed without incident and was generally seen as a success).

The result of this deprivation was a growing hostility, advocated in particular by the most prominent group of rebels at this time, the **Fenians**, formed by James Stephens and James O'Mahony around 1858. Although the rebellion they staged in 1867 was a failure, many members went on to join the Irish Republican Brotherhood, the organization whose primary focus was on securing **Home Rule** for Ireland: the establishment of its own independent government. The driving force behind this movement was **Charles Stewart Parnell** (see p.142), MP for Meath and president of the Irish Land League, whose objective, as part of the agitation for Home Rule, was "Irish land for Irish people". A breakthrough appeared to be imminent until two officials of the British government were killed in 1882 in **Phoenix Park** by an obscure organization called "The Invincibles" (see p.175). Attempts to implicate Parnell in the crime failed, but when his own long-standing affair with a married woman, Kitty O'Shea, became public knowledge, the Home Rule Party split bitterly and Parnell died not long afterwards in 1891. A year later yet another Irish Home Rule Bill was voted down by the British Parliament, stimulating pressure for reform from all quarters of Ireland.

In 1893, **Douglas Hyde** co-founded the **Gaelic League** in Dublin, using as his model the Gaelic Athletic Association, established eight years previously. Its aim was the preservation of Irish as a spoken language and its success prefigured the Celtic literary revival pioneered by **W.B. Yeats** and **Lady Gregory** and the establishment of the **Abbey Theatre** in 1903. Simultaneously, there was an expansion in the impact of political groups such as **Sinn Féin** (meaning "We, Ourselves") and a revival of the IRB (Irish Republican Brotherhood). The focus for political struggle this time, however, became the establishment of trade unionism in Ireland, which was brought to a head by the **great lock-out** of 1913, during which Dublin's first "Bloody Sunday" took place, leaving over 200 people injured. The resultant heightening of political activity led to the formation in Dublin of the **Irish Citizens' Army** as a worker's defence force by socialists **James Larkin** and **James Connolly**.

The 1916 Easter Rising and the War of Independence

The British parliament eventually passed the Home Rule Bill of 1912, despite threats from Ulster Unionists that they would forcibly resist any move towards an Irish parliament. However, the outbreak of **World War I** halted proceedings, with the implementation of the Bill suspended for the duration. Around 180,000 Irish volunteers fought for Britain in the war, many of whom were committed nationalists hoping to return home to Irish self-government.

However, alternative plans were already being made by a small group of dedicated revolutionaries. In 1916, with the Irish nationalist sentiment "England's difficulty is Ireland's opportunity" rapidly gaining currency in this circle, the move to rebellion increased, and former members of the IRB (which evolved into the Irish Republican Army or IRA), younger Republicans such as **Pádraig Pearse**, and socialists led by James Connolly joined forces to participate in what would become the **Easter Rising** (see p.136). Initial plans for the rising were made for Easter Sunday, but when the leader of the Irish Volunteers cancelled their involvement (due to a confusion), it was postponed until the next day. On Monday, April 24, 1916, only one thousand men showed up, with Pádraig Pearse reading his **Proclamation of the Republic** at the GPO before seizing the building, along with others in the city, including Jacobs' Biscuit Factory and Liberty Hall. After six days of fighting, with 300 civilians, 130 British and 60 Republicans dead, the rebels surrendered.

The initial reaction to the uprising amongst Dubliners was hostile – they resented the rebels for the damage they had caused – but attitudes changed when the leaders of the rebellion were executed. This, combined with a widespread fear that conscription would be extended to Ireland, resulted in a revival of Sinn Féin and overwhelming success in the election of 1918. Instead of taking their seats at Westminster however, the newly elected MPs met as the **Dáil Éireann** in Dublin and declared independence under the leadership of **Éamon de Valera**. One member of the cabinet was **Michael Collins**, who, though he held the nominal position of Minister of Finance, began mobilizing the IRA for further military action.

In January 1919 the first killings in what became known as the **War of Independence** took place when two members of the Royal Irish Constabulary were murdered in County Tipperary. Two years of fighting ensued against the British, who employed a ruthless paramilitary army known as the **Black and Tans** (because of the colour of their uniform) to oppose the rebels. In Dublin, Collins established his own unit of men ("the Apostles") to track and murder G-men, detectives of the Dublin Metropolitan Police who had detailed knowledge of the actions of the city's Republicans (this unit proved so successful that, in December 1919, they almost succeeded in murdering the viceroy, Lord French, in the outskirts of the city). An increasingly ugly cycle of reprisals between the two sides culminated in the city's second "**Bloody Sunday**" on November 11, 1920 when, as an act of vengeance for the murder of fourteen undercover spies by Collins and his team, the Black and Tans opened fire at a Gaelic football match at Croke Park, killing eleven spectators and the captain of the Tipperary hurling team, Michael Hogan.

The Irish Free State and Civil War

Despite the IRA's greatest show of strength in May 1921, when they took over the Custom House and set it alight, the war with the British had taken a severe toll on their resources; on July 9, 1921, de Valera met with representatives of the British government and a truce was signed. Negotiations then ensued to formulate a treaty, and an Irish team headed by Michael Collins and Arthur Griffith was sent to London – Éamon de Valera was conspicuous by his absence. Collins and his team signed the **Anglo-Irish Treaty** on December 6, 1921, and the **Irish Free State** was brought into being. However, it did so at the expense of many of the fundamental tenets of Republican ideology; not only did it partition Ireland, but members of the new parliament were obliged to swear allegiance to George V. De Valera rejected the document and, when it was passed by a small majority in the Dáil, he and his supporters stormed out, precipitating the **Irish Civil War**.

The first major military action taken in the Civil War was on June 28, 1922, when Collins' Free State forces shelled the Four Courts buildings being held by Republicans (known as the "**Irregulars**"), so destroying the public records office, which had titles and deeds dating back to Henry II. Republican forces followed almost identical tactics to those in 1916, occupying prominent buildings in the city centre, particularly around O'Connell Street, only to be bombarded by the heavy artillery of the Free State forces. Outside Dublin, conventional resistance from the anti-treaty Irregulars ended on August 12, when a seaborne force captured Cork city, forcing units to flee to hills in the southwest of the country and enter into a guerrilla campaign (the most notable success of which was the killing of Collins on August 22). Like the War of Independence before it the Civil War descended into a series of bloody recriminations, often involving erstwhile comrades. Acts of violence committed by the anti-treaty side were countered with the execution of Republican prisoners – in all, 77 prisoners were shot in this way by the Free State forces and up to 12,000 Republicans imprisoned before a truce was eventually called on May 24, 1923.

Recent history

With the ending of the Civil War the Free State became virtually a one-party monopoly until 1926, when de Valera split from the defeated Republicans to form a new parliamentary party called **Fianna Fáil** ("Soldiers of Destiny"). Fianna Fáil contested the 1927 elections, achieved a majority in 1932 and proceeded to dominate Irish political life over the next seventy years – though ironically it was the political descendants of the Free State forces, **Fine Gael** ("Tribes of Gaels"), who introduced the **Republic of Ireland Bill** in November 1948. Fianna Fáil started with the political isolationism of de Valera's economic policy, and then moved to a more expansionist one, introduced by **Séan Lemass** in 1959. The trend towards participation on the international stage was further reflected by Ireland's joining of the United Nations and then the **European Community** in 1972.

The last real celebration of Republicanism came in 1966, on the fiftieth anniversary of the Easter Rising, when the event was officially commemorated in Dublin by the building of the Garden of Remembrance on Parnell Square, and unofficially by the blowing up of Nelson's Pillar on O'Connell Street. Increasing **sectarian violence** in Northern Ireland had little impact on the people of Dublin, though there were violent street protests in the aftermath of Derry's "Bloody Sunday" in 1972, with rioters attacking and burning the British Embassy, and, in

1974, 25 people were killed by three car bombs, planted by loyalist paramilitaries. Despite this, many Dubliners see themselves as post-nationalist in their politics, reflected in the overwhelming endorsement in 1998 of removing the articles in the Republic's constitution which claimed sovereignty over Northern Ireland.

Architecturally the city stagnated during the post-independence period, and a good deal of its Georgian heritage was destroyed in a glut of **development** in the 1960s, which one commentator referred to as "post-colonial vandalism". This period also saw the clearance of many of the inner-city slums, with former inhabitants being moved to huge estates in the suburbs, which, with very high levels of crime, unemployment and, latterly, drug addiction, quickly degenerated. The city's **drug problem** became an epidemic in the 1980s, and was finally brought to a head in 1996, when a campaigning journalist was shot at the behest of one of the drug barons. This acted as a catalyst for the police, who subsequently took on those controlling the drugs trade in the city with considerable success, though high levels of addiction still remain.

In the 1990s Dublin was transformed with the birth of the much celebrated "Celtic Tiger" – an epithet used to describe the similarity of the Irish economy, the fastest growing in Europe, to the tiger economies of Southeast Asia. One of the results of this economic boom was a cultural renaissance in Dublin, and in 1991 it was named the European City of Culture. **Regeneration** was the keynote, spearheaded by the Temple Bar development, whose architects sought to express the city's new-found confidence in a modern Irish style. Urban renewal reversed the trend for people to move out of the centre, and the city's wealth became apparent from a vibrancy and cosmopolitanism not known to Dublin since its Georgian heyday.

Over the last few years, however, the tiger's roar has

become rather hoarse, as the side-effects of rapid economic development have presented themselves. The new apartments in formerly run-down areas of the quays have been gobbled up by the rich, while the less affluent are priced out of the market in the city centre. Ireland, and Dublin in particular, has attracted thousands of refugees, temporary workers and students from as far afield as Nigeria, China and Romania, and despite a long history of emigration, but with little experience of **immigration**, Dubliners have struggled to assimilate these newcomers. **Transport**, too, has become a headache, as more and more people own cars and use them to clog up Dublin's streets for large parts of every day; the Luas light-rail system, due to open in 2003, should help to free up the gridlock in some parts of the city, but substantial improvement will probably not come for over a decade, with the planned completion of the metro system in 2016. In late 2001, the director of Ireland's Central Bank announced rather dramatically that the Celtic Tiger era was over, but Fianna Fáil were emphatically returned to government in the May 2002 general election – with Fine Gael all but obliterated in the Dublin constituencies – suggesting the country is largely happy with its lot. With continuing, albeit slower, economic growth and the apparently seamless changeover to the new European single currency, the euro, it seems clear that there will be no return to the dark decades of economic stagnation, unemployment and emigration.

Music

Traditional Irish music

Traditional Irish music is alive and well in Dublin, and on any night of the week you'll find a session in full swing (see p.300 for recommended listings). Yet fifty years ago, many feared that the music itself was in terminal decline, a process exacerbated by emigration. Thousands left Dublin to work overseas while new arrivals from rural areas were eager to become city slickers and shed any vestige of their bucolic roots. Collectors such as Séamus Ennis and Breandán Breathnach ensured that tunes and songs were not lost to posterity, but many of these might never have been played nor sung again, but for two key developments.

The first of these was inspired by the Cork-born musician, composer and scholar **Seán Ó Riada**, who, while working as musical director at the Abbey Theatre from 1957 to 1962 (see p.133), adapted classical and jazz ensemble formats to traditional Irish music. Previously, the predominant group format in traditional music had been the **céilí band**, whose purpose was entirely geared towards providing accompaniment for dancing. Ó Riada, however, took his group Ceoltóirí first to the Abbey, and then on to concert stages, film soundtracks and radio programmes.

TRADITIONAL INSTRUMENTS

The instruments you'll most likely encounter at a traditional music session are the fiddle, flute, button accordion and tin whistle, while accompaniment is usually provided by a guitar or bouzouki (an Irish adaptation of the Greek eight-stringed instrument) and a bodhrán (a goatskin-hide frame drum). You might be lucky enough to see the uilleann pipes (an Irish form of bagpipes powered via an airbag pumped by the elbow), but, despite being the national symbol and Guinness logo, the harp is not considered a traditional instrument by most musicians.

While he played bodhrán and harpsichord (the latter in an attempt to replicate the sound of the old brass-strung harp), the band's multi-instrumental format allowed instruments and harmonic permutations to be highlighted during performance, setting a template for others to follow. The earliest band to do so were **The Chieftains**, formed in 1963 as an offshoot of this experimentation and still going strong after forty years and umpteen albums. They were followed by equally seminal **Planxty** and the **Bothy Band** in the 1970s.

The second development was inspired by the **folk revival** in the USA, inspired by the singer Woody Guthrie, which began in the late 1950s and produced such figures as Joan Baez, Pete Seeger and Bob Dylan. However, it was the American success of three brothers from Co. Tipperary (Tom, Pat and Liam Clancy) combined with the Armagh singer Tommy Makem which had a more lasting impact on Ireland. The trademark Aran sweaters and exuberant style of **The Clancy Brothers and Tommy Makem** inspired a ballad boom in Ireland, and Irish publicans opened their doors to a host of sweater-clad imitators who followed in the foursome's wake. While a knock-on effect was the first real appearance of the pub session in Ireland (brought back to the country from the UK by returning migrants), the boom also produced another Dublin success story, **The Dubliners**, still treading the boards four decades later. Other Dublin-born musicians to achieve success included **The Fureys** (featuring the lightning-quick uilleann piper, Finbar Furey) and **Sweeney's Men**, who introduced the current session mainstay, the bouzouki, to Irish music.

Subsequent developments largely focused on attempts to fuse elements of rock and traditional music. The first band to concoct such a blend in the 1970s was **Horslips**, but it was the success of **Moving Hearts** in the early 1980s (led by the charismatic singer Christy Moore) that had a more lasting impact. Their gigs at the now defunct *Baggot Inn* on Baggot Street Lower became the stuff of folklore, and several of the band's members remain leading lights in the musical scene, including the multi-instrumentalist and producer **Dónal Lunny** – like Moore, from Co. Kildare – and the uilleann piper, **Davy Spillane**. Since then, a number of singers have spanned the divide between rock and traditional music, including some (such as Dublin-born **Mary Black** and her sister Frances) whose careers were either rejuvenated or kick-started by 1992's phenomenally popular *A Woman's Heart* compilation album; the title track's composer, **Eleanor McEvoy**, has developed her own significant rock following. Contemporary bands exploring the frontiers include the effervescent **Kíla**, fronted by the powerful singer Rossa Ó Snodaigh, who has concocted his own bodhrán-backed form of Gaelic rap; and the jazz-inspired **Galldubh**.

Then, of course, there was a certain **Bill Whelan**, a respected composer, producer and session musician who found major notoriety in 1993, when he was invited to compose an intermission showpiece for the Eurovision Song Contest, held in Ireland the following year. The subsequent "seven minutes which shook the world" featured a musical fusion of traditional and modern elements and a host of electrifying hard-shoe step dancers. The impact was astounding; the subsequent single remained at number one in the Irish chart for eighteen weeks and, by the time it finally slipped, plans were fully in place for the full-length show version of **Riverdance**. This debuted at Dublin's Point Theatre in 1995 to massive acclaim, launching the solo careers of step dancers Michael Flatley and Jean Butler and, eventually, three full companies taking *Riverdance* around the world, while simultaneously breathing new life into dancing in Ireland itself (and into the sales of dance shoes).

While resisting similar cross-border explorations, the capital continues to produce a plethora of sublimely skilled musicians and there's still plenty of undiluted traditional music to be heard in Dublin. Dublin's long tradition of uilleann piping is well represented by musicians such as Neillidh Mulligan, Mick O'Brien, Ronan Browne, Kevin Rowsome and the hugely influential, now USA-based, **Paddy Keenan** (once of the Bothy Band). Fiddlers are well represented too, including The Chieftains' **Seán Keane**, whose brother James (again, American based) is a consummate button accordionist, and **Paddy Glackin** and **Paul O'Shaugnessy**, both inspired by the traditional music of Donegal. If the flute takes your fancy, look out for Paul McGrattan or Conor Byrne (Christy Moore's nephew), while Dublin has produced two of Ireland's best whistlers in **Mary Bergin** and Cormac Breathnach. Singers of note include the honey-voiced **Niamh Parsons** and the notable song-collector **Frank Harte**, who has a huge repertoire of Dublin street songs.

Rock to dance

Dublin has had greatest success as a **rock** city. While show-bands clad in shiny suits roamed the rest of Ireland in the 1960s, pounding out cover versions with variable accuracy, Dublin experienced its own beat boom. Maybe it was the proximity to Liverpool, or perhaps it was all down to Ian Whitcomb, an American studying at Trinity College whose band Bluesville had a top-ten USA hit in 1965 with *You Turn Me On*. Or maybe it was envy at the success of **Van Morrison**'s Belfast band Them. Whatever the reason, Dublin's music scene began to follow in Britain's tracks from the mid-1960s onwards. While bands like The Greenbeats and Purple Pussycat are long – and perhaps best – forgotten, there's no doubt that these beat groups formed a fecund spawning-ground for Ireland's later successes, fuelled by increasing access to pirate radio and the UK's Radio One.

Though Donegal-born **Rory Gallagher** was blasting out the blues with Taste, the first Irish rock band to have a real impact outside Ireland were Dublin's own **Skid Row**. The original band featured Brush Shiels on bass (still a luminary of the contemporary scene) and an incredibly young Gary Moore on guitar, later to be replaced by Eric Bell. One of the lead singers was **Phil Lynott** and, while acts like Dr Strangely Strange and Granny's Intentions were twiddling with psychedelia and others like Horslips and Spud were beginning the experiment of amalgamating traditional music with rock, it was the black Dubliner who led the first Irish band to dominate the rock world. **Thin Lizzy**'s first major success was a proto-metal version of *Whiskey in the Jar* (1973), but for many their finest hour was *Jailbreak* (1976), featuring *The Boys are Back in Town*, an album dominated by the band's trademark twin lead guitar sound. In complete contrast, Leo O'Kelly and Sonny

Condell's acoustic duo **Tír na nÓg** also achieved success in Britain and Europe during the 1970s, with Condell going on to form the soft-rock-meets-traditional band Scullion and recording his own solo albums, though occasionally hooking up again with O'Kelly.

Punk hit Dublin in the mid-1970s via visiting British bands who played *Moran's Hotel* and other local venues. One local R&B act took special notice and transformed both its image and its music. "We were the first neighbourhood rock heroes to happen in ten years", the singer **Bob Geldof** noted, with typical modesty. His band, the **Boomtown Rats**, had considerable success with singles such as *Rat Trap* and *I Don't Like Mondays*, before Geldof achieved worldwide fame through his co-organization of Live Aid. Dublin's punk scene also produced a horde of bands like Radiators from Space (with Phil Chevron, later of The Pogues), The Virgin Prunes (with Gavin Friday), The Blades and The Vipers, all of whose influence would be long-lasting, while a certain Larry Mullen stuck a note on his school notice board looking for co-pupils with whom to form a punk band.

That band, **U2**, released its first album, *Boy*, in 1980. Listen to it now, more than twenty years later, and it's possible to discern how this then young group might later become the biggest thing since sliced soda bread. For despite the recent critical backlash, some of it geared towards Bono's assumption of statesmanlike gravitas, U2 remain one of the biggest rock bands in the world. Their 1987 album *The Joshua Tree* broke them worldwide and also begat one-time popular Dublin parodists, The Joshua Trio. Since then, a series of albums (most notably *Rattle and Hum*, *Achtung Baby*, *Pop* and the recent *All That You Can't Leave Behind*) have cemented the band's success, which they've fed back into the city through such initiatives as their own (now defunct) Mother label for new Irish acts.

ROCK TO DANCE

A number of other Dublin bands (In Tua Nua, Aslan, Light a Big Fire) were signed to major labels in the wake of U2's success, but though producing stimulating and often innovative music, none achieved lasting success –though Aslan have recently reformed after a long absence from the scene. One which failed even to get signed up was Ton Ton Macoute, amongst whose ranks was a certain **Sinéad O'Connor**. Her Prince-composed solo single *Nothing Compares 2 U* was a massive international hit in 1989, bringing a degree of fame which did not always sit pretty on her shoulders.

Hailing from Limerick, **The Cranberries** were Ireland's most successful export after U2 during the 1990s, but Dublin bands which made an impact during that decade include **Hothouse Flowers**, fronted by Liam O'Maonlai who, since the band's split, has recorded with Tim Finn (Split Enz/Crowded House) and Belfast singer Andy White. **Something Happens**, probably the best buskers ever to appear on Grafton Street, produced some wonderful pop but eventually faded, while the quirky **A House**, fronted by singer Dave Couse, struggled with the perversity of record labels. Both the mellifluous Stars of Heaven and the soulful, if unfortunately named, Fat Lady Sings are no more, but the latter's singer/guitarist Nick Kelly has released an acclaimed solo album. Gavin Friday continues to appear in a variety of incarnations, and Lesley Dowdall of **In Tua Nua** revamped her solo career during the late 1990s. For a while, the success of Alan Parker's 1991 film *The Commitments* seemed likely to spawn a whole new era of Irish **soul** bands, including one fronted by the movie's young singer, Andrew Strong, who enjoyed a brief spell in the spotlight, as well another bearing the film's name, which was comprised of a few members of the cast. The film-band's bass player Glen Hansard has also continued to produce startlingly powerful music with his band **The Frames**.

ROCK TO DANCE

Of current singer/songwriters, Damien Dempsey and Mark Dignam have a loyal local following, though Damien Rice, formerly of the band Juniper, looks the likeliest to achieve international success. The Jacques Brel-influenced **Jack L** has also garnered acclaim for his riveting stage show and emotion-packed albums. Of the bands, the greatest hope is attached to the full-on (if increasingly mellow) **Cyclefly**, led by the pink-haired Declan O'Shea, though Romolos Pop, Horizon and Crayonz are also currently catching critical attention.

Yet, contrastingly, the greatest recent successes have been the result of entrepreneurial marketing. Despite an outrageously gauche 1993 debut appearance on *The Late Late Show*, **Boyzone** became a huge international success, setting the template for future boy bands such as **Westlife** (formed by Boyzone's Ronan Keating) and the girl band **B★witched** to mirror their saccharin pop achievements. Other than the commercial dance diva **Samantha Mumba**, who came to prominence at the beginning of 2000, solo successes have been relatively limited.

Today, you'll still find plenty of young hopefuls plying their trade in places such as **Eamonn Doran's** (see Live Music and Clubs, p.298), but the dominant music in Dublin is **dance**. The city has a thriving underground scene, with several dance labels promoting and producing their own artists; most notable among these are **Influx**, who feature Dublin's most celebrated DJ Johnny Moy and showcase each Saturday at the Tivoli (see p.308).

ROCK TO DANCE

Books

M̲ost of the **books** listed below are in print and in paperback – those that are out of print (o/p) should be easy to track down in libraries, second-hand bookshops or through book-finding services of the kind offered by Waterstones. **Publishers** follow each title; first the UK or Irish publisher, then the US. Only one publisher is listed if the UK/Irish and US publishers are the same. Where books are published in only one of these countries, UK, IRE or US follows the publisher's name.

Prose fiction

Peter Ackroyd, *The Last Will and Testament of Oscar Wilde* (o/p). Hilarious parody of the tragic artist in exile, and a must for devotees of Wilde's epigrammatic wit.

John Banville, *Eclipse, The Book of Evidence, Ghosts, Athena* and *The Untouchable* (all Picador; Vintage). A selection of novels from the most important Irish novelist since McGahern. His 1989 Booker Prize nomination, *The Book of Evidence*, tells a sleazy tale of a weird Dublin murder.

Samuel Beckett, *More Pricks Than Kicks* and *Molly/Malone Dies/The Unnamable* (all Calder; Grove Press). The former, Beckett's earliest publication, consists of ten tales describing the grotesque existence, marriages and accidental death of his Dublin eccentric, Belacqua Shuah. The latter is a wonderful trilogy of breakdown and glum humour.

Brendan Behan, *The Scarperer* (Arena, o/p; Queens House, o/p). Originally serialized in the *Irish Times* in 1953 under the pseudonym Emmet Street, this slight crime tale roams the bars and police stations of north Dublin.

Maeve Binchy, *Dublin Four* (Arrow, UK). Ireland's (and often Britain's) most popular author's four tales of Dublin life feature flat-hunting in Ringsend and disastrous dinner parties in Donnybrook.

Dermot Bolger, *The Journey Home* (Penguin, UK, o/p). One of the most powerful of contemporary Irish writers, Bolger set his third novel around the bleak lives of young people in his own native Finglas. *A Second Life* (Penguin, o/p; Viking, o/p) is an assured novel about a man who, miraculously given a second chance at life, sets out to find the truth about his adoption; and *Father's Music* (Flamingo; HarperCollins) is a psychological thriller set in Dublin. Bolger's latest, *The Valparaiso Voyage* (Flamingo, UK), deals with themes of political corruption and social alienation in Ireland in a tale of a violent homecoming.

Christy Brown, *Down All the Days* (Minerva; Stein & Day). The author of *My Left Foot* (see p.388) later wrote this flamboyantly styled but hugely enjoyable tale of working-class life in Crumlin in the 1940s and 1950s.

Philip Casey, *The Fabulists* (Serif, US). A deftly-woven love story and depiction of the lean side of contemporary Dublin in a debut novel which illuminates the inner lives of the powerless.

J.P. Donleavy, *The Ginger Man* (Abacus; Atlantic Monthly Press). A raucous, rambunctious romp of a book tracing the exploits of Donleavy's semi-autobiographical and dangerously cynical law student, Sebastian Dangerfield, in post-war Dublin; banned for some years in Ireland.

Emma Donoghue, *Stir Fry* (Penguin, UK). A finely crafted lesbian love story from a young Dubliner, conjuring up a delightful image of the city.

Roddy Doyle, *The Commitments* (Vintage); *The Snapper*, *The Van*, *Paddy Clarke Ha Ha Ha*, *The Woman Who Walked into Doors* and *A Star Called Henry* (all Vintage; Penguin). Doyle drew upon his experiences as a teacher in his native Kilbarrack to pen the first three works, known also as *The Barrytown Trilogy*, centred around the hilarious exploits of the north Dublin Rabbitte family and written in a vernacular style. The fourth and fifth novels are respectively, an amusing and moving account of working-class family life which won the Booker Prize in 1993, and a sensitive tale of a woman trying to escape a life of domestic violence. Doyle's latest novel centres on hero Henry Smart, interweaving the violence of early twentieth-century Irish history with his own irreverent humour.

Hugo Hamilton, *Dublin Where the Palm Trees Grow* (Faber &

Faber, UK, o/p). A fine collection of stories set with equal assurance in Berlin and middle-class Dublin.

Neil Jordan, *The Past* (Vintage, o/p; Braziller, o/p). Film-maker Jordan's first full-length work is an ambitious account of the troubled first years of the Irish Free State.

James Joyce, *Dubliners*, *A Portrait of the Artist As a Young Man*, *Ulysses* and *Finnegans Wake* (all Penguin). *Ulysses* is Joyce's masterwork, a sublimely evocative account of 24 hours in the intertwining lives of Dublin, Stephen Dedalus and Leopold and Molly Bloom. The story and its characters are loosely drawn from Homer's *Odyssey*, but the style is a breathtaking melange of parody, fantasy, realism and (Joyce's major innovation) stream-of-consciousness. Following its completion, Joyce strove for sixteen years to construct *Finnegans Wake*, a cyclical concoction, following the Vicoesque concept of history as inevitable repetition. Often profoundly obscure, there are pas-

BOKS: PROSE FICTION

sages of great lyricism and humour in its account of the Earwicker family: Humphrey Chimpden Earwicker, his wife Anna Livia Plurabelle, and their two sons and pub in Chapelizod.

Ferdia Mac Anna, *The Last of the High Kings* (Penguin, o/p; Talk Miramax, o/p). A funny and perceptive look at Irish family life, centred on seventeen-year-old Frankie Griffin, who dreams of escape from the eccentric and chaotic world created by his relatives.

John McGahern, *The Leavetaking* and *That They May Face the Rising Sun* (both Faber & Faber, UK). The former is a spare and stark tale of a teacher in a Clontarf national school reviewing his life on the day he expects to be sacked for marrying an American divorcée. The latter, McGahern's latest novel, is a dark and elegiac narrative set in rural Co. Leitrim (published as *By the Lake* by Knopf in the US).

Seán Moncrieff, *Dublin* (Doubleday, UK). Stark but gritty

thriller focused on Dublin's darker side.

Iris Murdoch, *The Red and the Green* (Penguin; Viking). Dubliner Murdoch rarely wrote about Ireland – this fictional account of an Anglo-Irish family during the time leading up to the Easter Rising is something of an exception.

Flann O'Brien, *At Swim-Two-Birds* (Penguin; Dalkey Archive Press), *The Dalkey Archive*, *The Third Policeman* and *The Best of Myles* (all Flamingo; Dalkey Archive Press). The first is a surreal and fantastically funny concoction of books within books, where characters rebel against their author, Gaelic folk heroes roam and Dublin bars are visited where "A pint of plain is your only man"; the later works (in order) feature St Augustine and Joyce working behind a bar, a man turning into a bicycle as a consequence of molecular transference, and side-splitting extracts from Flann O'Brien's *Irish Times* column, which is an excellent introduction to his off-the-wall humour.

Joseph O'Connor, *Cowboys and Indians* (Flamingo, UK). "Dublin at Christmas was a dangerous town. Too many familiar people, all waiting to jump out of the shadows and wave their latest attitude in your face." Life on the peripheries of Dublin and London with Eddie Virago. *Desperadoes* (Flamingo, UK) is a love story ranging from 1950s Dublin to modern-day Nicaragua, while *The Salesman* (Vintage, UK) is O'Connor's most trenchant novel to date, a darkly humorous tale of suffering and schematic revenge.

Julia O'Faolain, *No Country for Young Men* (Carroll & Graf, US). Republican politics and its repercussions seen through the eyes of four generations of the O'Malley family.

Liam O'Flaherty, *The Informer* (Wolfhound Press; Harcourt Brace). O'Flaherty's best-known work is a racy tale of Gypo Nolan, a former Republican, who betrays a colleague to the Garda and is hunted down amongst the slums around the Custom House by his erstwhile associates.

James Plunkett, *Strumpet City* (Arrow, UK). Hefty and well-written novel set in Dublin in the years leading up to World War II, this was extremely popular when it was first published in 1969.

James Stephens, *The Charwoman's Daughter* (North Books, US). Stephens is one of Ireland's comic geniuses; here he delivers a whimsical fairy tale, real rags-to-riches stuff, in turn-of-the-century Dublin.

Bram Stoker, *Dracula* (Penguin; Signet). Stoker woke up after a nightmare brought on by a hefty lobster supper, and proceeded to write his way into the nightmares of the twentieth century.

Francis Stuart, *Black List: Section H* (Penguin). Although mainly focusing on Stuart's experiences in wartime Germany, the early chapters are set amongst the literary salons of 1920s Dublin.

Jonathan Swift, *Gulliver's Travels* (Penguin; New American Library Classics); *The Tale of a Tub and Other Stories* (Oxford University Press). Acerbic satire

CONTEXTS

from the only writer in the English language with as sharp a pen as Voltaire.

Colm Tóibín, *The South*, *The Heather Blazing*, *The Blackwater Lightship* and *The Story of the Night* (all Picador; Penguin). Four powerful novels from one of Ireland's finest writers. The story of a Dublin judge reflecting upon his life while on holiday with his family, *The Heather Blazing* is particularly good.

William Trevor, *Mrs Eckdorf in O'Neill's Hotel* (Penguin). A barmy American photographer flies to Dublin to undertake a study of the said hotel and encounters a bunch of bizarre characters staying there.

Poetry and drama

Sebastian Barry, *Our Lady of Sligo* and *Plays 1* (both Methuen). Characters from Barry's family history are central to his plays, all characterized by a rich use of language. Of the latters *The Steward of Christendom*, relating the story of the Catholic head of the Dublin Metropolitan Police before the change in regime in 1922, is particularly compelling. His latest play, *Hinterland* (Faber & Faber, UK), a melodramatic portrayal of disgraced former Taoiseach Charles Haughey, met with such harsh reviews that Barry threatened to leave Ireland.

Samuel Beckett, *Complete Dramatic Works* (Faber & Faber, UK). Bleak hilarity from the laureate of the void, including his seminal masterpiece *Waiting For Godot*, and other absurdist treats such as *Endgame*. Recently out in pricey hardback is *Poems 1930–1989* (Calder, UK), the most complete collection of his poetry, in both English and French (with his own translations), and including translations of major twentieth-century French poets such as Rimbaud and Eluard.

Brendan Behan, *The Complete Plays* (Methuen; Grove Press). Of Behan's dramatic works, *The*

BOOKS: POETRY AND DRAMA

Quare Fellow remains the most important: with events revolving around a prison execution, Behan draws attention to society's complicity in the act.

Patrick Crotty (ed), *Modern Irish Poetry: An Anthology* (Blackstaff; Dufour). Covers a broad range of poetry from 1922 onwards, includes English and Irish translations of a number of poems, and provides highly accessible introductions to both the period and the individual poets represented.

Brian Friel, *Plays: Two* (Faber & Faber). A selection of the Derry playwright's work, including *Dancing at Lughnasa*, a family drama which examines the tensions between Catholicism and paganism in Irish society.

Seamus Heaney, *Opened Ground: Poems 1966–96* (Faber & Faber; Farrar Straus & Giroux). An extensive selection of works from the most important Irish poet since Yeats. His poems are immediate and passionate, even when dealing with intellectual problems and radical social divisions.

Patrick Kavanagh, *The Complete Poems* (Goldsmith Press; Peter Hand Kavanagh Press). One of Ireland's best-loved poets of the rural scene, Kavanagh is perhaps most famous for *The Great Hunger*, in which he attacked sexual repression in 1940s Ireland.

Derek Mahon, *The Yellow Book* (The Gallery Press; Wake-Forest). Highly allusive, sensuous verse belying Mahon's *fin-de-siècle* disenchantment with the "sado-monetarism" of Ireland.

Martin McDonagh, *Plays Volume 1* (Methuen, UK), *The Beauty Queen of Leenane and Other Plays* (Random House, US), *The Cripple of Inishmaan* (Methuen; Vintage) and *The Lieutenant of Inishmore* (Methuen). Festering familial hatred, murder and isolation on the west coast of Ireland, dished up with aplomb by this wickedly funny, abrasive young dramatist.

Frank McGuinness, *Plays* (Faber & Faber) and *Plays 2* (Faber & Faber, UK).

Collections of the major works from one of Ireland's most important playwrights. The former includes *Observe the Sons of Ulster Marching towards the Somme*, an examination of the Ulster Protestant experience of World War I, and the latter *Someone To Watch Over Me*, an exploration of the cultural resources that sustain three hostages – one English, one Irish and one American – in the Middle East.

Conor McPherson, *McPherson: Four Plays* (Nick Hern Books, UK), *The Weir and Other Plays* (Consortium, US). A collection including *This Lime Tree Bower*, a very funny play in which the lives of three men change in the course of a weekend; and *The Weir*, an eerie, compelling drama set in an isolated village in the west of Ireland.

Sean O'Casey, *Three Plays* (Papermac; St Martin's). Contains the socialist playwright's famous Dublin trilogy *Juno and the Paycock*, *Shadow of a Gunman* and *The Plough*

and the Stars, which challenged the revolutionary rhetoric and political orthodoxies of the day.

John Millington Synge, *The Complete Plays* (Methuen; Vintage). Plenty of "begorras" and "mavourneens" in Synge's invented dialogue of the Irish peasantry; his humorous masterpiece *The Playboy of the Western World*, depicting the rebellion of a peasant youth, incited audiences to riot.

Oscar Wilde, *The Complete Works of Oscar Wilde* (Collins; HarperCollins). The full emotional range, from the glittering satire of *Lady Windermere's Fan* and *The Importance of Being Earnest*, to the moving verse of *The Ballad of Reading Gaol*, written during his imprisonment.

William Butler Yeats, *The Poems* (Everyman UK) and *The Collected Poems* (Scribner US). They're all here, poems of rhapsody, love, revolution and eventual rage at a disconnected and failed Ireland "fumbling in the greasy till".

Books on Dublin

Douglas Bennett, *An Encyclopaedia of Dublin* (Gill & Macmillan, IRE). An assiduously compiled reference book detailing everything you might ever wish to know about Dublin – and then some.

John Bradley (ed), *Viking Dublin Exposed: The Wood Quay Saga* (O'Brien, IRE, o/p). Absorbing account of the archeological discoveries made at Wood Quay, covering the political battle for adequate excavation and demonstrating the international significance of the material found.

Joseph Brady and Anngret Simms (eds), *Dublin Through Space and Time* (Four Courts Press). Authoritative and thought-provoking study, mapping the city's development from around 900 to 1900 from both geographical and historical perspectives.

W.J. Brennan-Whitmore, *Dublin Burning* (Gill & Macmillan, IRE). A vivid and engaging memoir of the 1916 uprising by the Irish Volunteers officer commanding Earl Street North.

Peter Costello, *Dublin Churches* (Gill & Macmillan, IRE). More than 150 churches are described and photographed in this detailed study.

John Cowell, *Dublin's Famous People: Where They Lived* (O'Brien Press; Irish American Book Co). Brief biographies of literati and glitterati.

Maurice Craig, *Dublin 1660–1860* (Penguin, UK, o/p). Revised since its original publication in 1952, this is a classic account of the Dublin of Ormonde, Swift and Grattan and the three great eras of the city's development.

Mary E. Daly, *Dublin: The Deposed Capital* (Cork University Press). A comprehensive social and economic anatomy of Dublin's development and decay between 1860 and 1914.

Desmond Guinness, *Georgian Dublin* (Batsford, o/p). A photographic celebration of Dublin's

BOOKS ON DUBLIN

Georgian heritage, from grand public edifices to domestic interiors and decorative plasterwork.

Kevin C. Kearns, *Dublin Tenement Life: An Oral History* (Gill & Macmillan; Penguin) and *Dublin Voices* (Gill & Macmillan, IRE). Two in a series of vibrant and stimulating accounts by Kearns based on the reminiscences of Dubliners.

Pat Liddy, *Dublin: A Celebration* (Dublin Corporation, IRE); *Secret Dublin* and *Walking Dublin* (both New Holland; McGraw Hill). The former is an impressive tome, providing a detailed photographic history right up to the present day. The latter two are essential guides to the city, providing detailed routes around some of Dublin's best-kept secrets, each written with wit and insight.

Joss Lynam, *Easy Walks Near Dublin* (Gill & Macmillan, IRE). An excellent guide to forty walks, including several in the Wicklow Mountains.

Frank McDonald, *The Construction of Dublin* (Gandon, IRE). Weighty and authoritative hardback by the *Irish Times'* noted environment correspondent, examining issues of transport, housing and administration and putting the spotlight on the planners, politicians and other often controversial figures.

Irish history, politics and society

John Ardagh, *Ireland and the Irish: Portrait of a Changing Society* (Penguin). A comprehensive and lively anatomy of contemporary Irish society and its attempts to come to terms with a changing world.

J.C. Beckett, *The Making of Modern Ireland 1603–1923* (Faber & Faber, UK, o/p). A classic account of the complexities of Irish history.

Terence Brown, *Ireland: A Social and Cultural History 1922–1985* (Cornell University Press, US). A brilliantly perceptive survey of writers' responses to the state of post-revolutionary Ireland.

Max Caulfield, *The Easter Rebellion* (Gill & Macmillan; Roberts Rinehart, o/p). This essential account of the events of 1916, originally published in 1963, has recently been revised and reissued.

Michael Collins, *In His Own Words* (Gill & Macmillan, IRE). Extracts from the Irish revolutionary's writings and speeches.

Tim Pat Coogan, *Wherever Green is Worn: The Story of the Irish Diaspora* (Arrow; Macmillan). Stunning, groundbreaking account of Irish emigration and the impact of the émigrés on culture throughout the world.

Liam Fay, *Beyond Belief* (Hot Press, IRE). An irreverent and often hysterically funny investigation into the state of religion in modern Ireland, written by a *Hot Press* regular.

Roy Foster, *Modern Ireland 1600–1972* (Penguin). Superb and provocative book, generally reckoned to be unrivalled in its scholarship and acuity, although it has been criticized for what some feel to be an excessive sympathy towards the Anglo-Irish. Not recommended for beginners.

Roy Foster (ed), *The Oxford History of Ireland* (OUP). Succinct, yet never wavering summation of Ireland's development from pre-history to modern times. Declan Kibberd's chapter on the relationship between Irish literature and history is characteristically incisive.

Robert Kee, *The Green Flag* (Penguin). Awesomely assiduous history and masterful analysis of Ireland from the first plantations to the creation of the Free State. Three volumes.

George Morrison, *The Irish Civil War* (Seven Dials). A powerful collection of photographic images of the Irish Civil War, accompanied by commentary by Tim Pat Coogan.

Fintan O'Toole, *The Ex-Isle of Erin: Images of Global Ireland* (New Island Books, IRE). *Irish Times* journalist O'Toole examines the impact of globalism upon Irish society.

Colm Tóibín, *The Irish Famine* (Profile; Thomas Dunne). Tóibín's highly readable and thought-provoking analysis of the 1845–49 famine, which takes an incisive look both at the issues surrounding the failure of the potato crop, and the inadequacy of previous historical accounts of the crisis.

John Waters, *An Intelligent Person's Guide to Modern Ireland* (Duckworth, UK). Controversial examination of Ireland's self-styled progression, by the *Irish Times'* gadfly columnist, arguing that the Irish have lost their cohesiveness in the drive for a "perverse and lonely" prosperity.

Biography and autobiography

Brendan Behan, *Borstal Boy* (Arrow; David R. Godine). Behan's at times romanticized account of his involvement in the Republican movement and his early years in jail.

Christy Brown, *My Left Foot* (Minerva; Heinemann). Born with cerebral palsy, Brown painstakingly typed out this unsentimental autobiography, published in 1954 when he was twenty-two, focusing on his upbringing in a huge southside family, dominated by the remarkable endurance and character of his mother.

Noel Browne, *Against the Tide* (Gill & Macmillan; Irish Books and Media). Fine autobiography of one of Ireland's most radical

ministers, and particularly illuminating on the role of Catholicism in Irish politics.

Anthony Cronin, *Dead as Doornails: A Chronicle of Life* (Liliput), *No Laughing Matter: The Life and Times of Flann O'Brien* (Paladin, o/p; Grafton, o/p), *Samuel Beckett: The Last Modernist* (Flamingo; Da Capo). Cronin's work ranges from his sparkling account of literary bohemia in the 1950s and 1960s via an illuminating biography of Brian O'Nolan (alias Flann O'Brien) to his 1997 analysis of Beckett's life and work.

Ruth Dudley Edwards, *James Connolly* (Gill & Macmillan, IRE). A short, direct biography of the socialist leader, which gathers pace around the time of his relations with Larkin, the 1913 lockout and the 1916 uprising.

Richard Ellmann, *James Joyce* (Oxford University Press), *Oscar Wilde* (Penguin; Vintage). Ellmann's wonderful biography of Joyce is a literary masterpiece in its own right. His work on Wilde was, unfortunately, unfinished when he died, but is still an excellent insight into the work of this often misunderstood writer.

Christopher Fitz-Simon, *The Boys* (New Island, IRE). Frank and conscientious biography of the founders of the Gate Theatre, Micheál MacLíammóir and his equally mysterious lifelong lover, Hilton Edwards.

Oliver St John Gogarty, *As I Was Going Down Sackville Street* (O'Brien Press; Irish American Book Co) and *Intimations* (Sphere, o/p). Two of the poet and surgeon's accounts, once considered racy, of Dublin in the 1920s and 1930s; the author, much to his own disgust, was the model for Joyce's Buck Mulligan.

Michael Holroyd, *Bernard Shaw* (Vintage; Chatto & Windus). Outstanding biography of GBS, made more accessible to the general reader in this abridged, one-volume edition.

James Knowlson, *Damned to Fame: The Life of Samuel Beckett* (Bloomsbury; Touchstone, o/p). This biography, by one of the world's pre-eminent Beckett scholars, makes a good complement to the more anecdotal and gossipy style of Cronin's book (see opposite), which came out at the same time.

Hugh Leonard, *Home before Night; Out after Dark* (Methuen, UK). Beautifully written evocations by the noted playwright of, respectively, his childhood and his adolescence in south Dublin around the 1940s. At times moving, often hilarious.

Brenda Maddox, *Nora: A Biography of Nora* (Penguin, UK, o/p), *Nora: The Real Life of Molly Bloom* (Houghton Mifflin, US). This is a hugely enjoyable account of the life of Nora Barnacle, wife of James Joyce and an absolute treasure in her own right.

Christy Moore, *One Voice: My Life in Song* (Hodder & Stoughton, UK). A Dubliner by inclination rather than birth, Moore's biography collates the lyrics of many of his favourite songs while simultaneously offering insights into both his own and Ireland's musical development and idiosyncrasies.

Ulick O'Connor, *Brendan Behan* (Abacus; Grove Press). An absorbing and sometimes pathetically touching account of the life of probably Dublin's most provocative dramatist and drinker.

Nuala O'Faolain, *Are You Somebody?* (New Island; Owl Books). The best-selling memoirs of *Irish Times* journalist O'Faolain offer a unique perspective on attitudes to women in Irish society.

Antoinette Quinn, *Paddy Kavanagh: A Biography* (Gill & MacMillan, IRE). Astute and often gently paced account of the life and poetry of Co. Monaghan's favourite son, who became a Dublin legend in his own lunchtime.

Peter Sheridan, *44: A Dublin Memoir* (Macmillan). From an author known more for his plays and films, this is a colourful and moving account of an inner-city childhood in the 1960s. Followed up by *47 Roses* (Macmillan), a witty, moving memoir of his parents' relationship.

INDEX

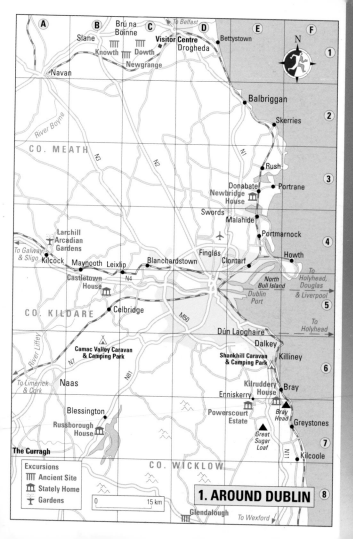

1. AROUND DUBLIN

Excursions
- ⅏ Ancient Site
- 🏛 Stately Home
- ⚓ Gardens

0 ____ 15 km

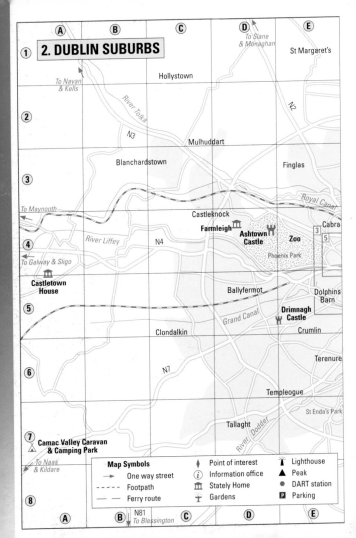

2. DUBLIN SUBURBS

St Margaret's

To Slane & Monaghan

To Navan & Kells

Hollystown

River Tolka

N3

Mulhuddart

N2

Blanchardstown

Finglas

Royal Canal

To Maynooth

Castleknock

Cabra

Farmleigh

Ashtown Castle

Zoo

3

River Liffey

N4

Phoenix Park

5

To Galway & Sligo

Castletown House

Ballyfermot

Dolphins Barn

Grand Canal

Drimnagh Castle

Clondalkin

Crumlin

N7

Terenure

Templeogue

St Enda's Park

Tallaght

River Dodder

Camac Valley Caravan & Camping Park

To Naas & Kildare

Map Symbols

→ One way street
----- Footpath
— — Ferry route

♦ Point of interest
ⓘ Information office
🏛 Stately Home
🍴 Gardens

🗼 Lighthouse
▲ Peak
● DART station
🅿 Parking

N81
To Blessington

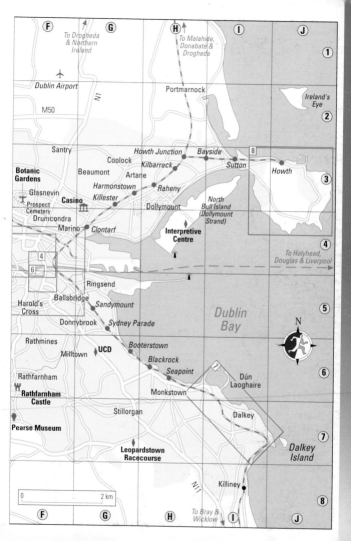

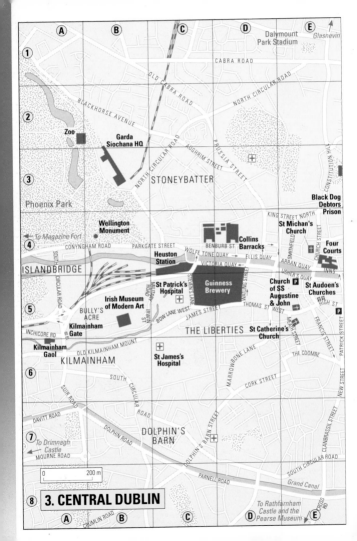

3. CENTRAL DUBLIN

Dalymount Park Stadium
Glasnevin
CABRA ROAD
OLD CABRA ROAD
BLACKHORSE AVENUE
NORTH CIRCULAR ROAD
Zoo
Garda Siochana HQ
PRUSSIA STREET
AUGHRIM STREET
STONEYBATTER
CONSTITUTION HILL
Phoenix Park
Black Dog Debtors Prison
KING STREET NORTH
St Michan's Church
Wellington Monument
SMITHFIELD
CHURCH STREET
Four Courts
To Magazine Fort
CONYNGHAM ROAD
PARKGATE STREET
BENBURB ST
Collins Barracks
ELLIS QUAY
ARRAN QUAY
ISLANDBRIDGE
Heuston Station
WOLFE TONE QUAY
VICTORIA QUAY
USHER'S QUAY
INNS
SOUTH CIRCULAR ROAD
St Patrick's Hospital
Guinness Brewery
WELLINGTON QUAY
St Audoen's Churches
Irish Museum of Modern Art
STEVEN'S LANE
MILITARY RD
IRWIN ST
BOW LANE WEST
JAMES STREET
THOMAS ST WEST
Church of SS Augustine & John
HIGH ST
Bully's Acre
Kilmainham Gate
St Catherine's Church
FRANCIS STREET
PATRICK STREET
INCHICORE RD
THE LIBERTIES
Kilmainham Gaol
OLD KILMAINHAM MOUNT
St James's Hospital
MARROWBONE LANE
THE COOMBE
NEW STREET
KILMAINHAM
SOUTH CIRCULAR ROAD
CORK STREET
SUIR ROAD
DAVITT ROAD
DOLPHIN ROAD
DOLPHIN'S BARN
DOLPHIN'S BARN STREET
CLANBRASSIL STREET
To Drimnagh Castle
MOURNE ROAD
PARNELL ROAD
SOUTH CIRCULAR ROAD
Grand Canal
CRUMLIN ROAD
To Rathfarnham Castle and the Pearse Museum
CROSS RD

0   200 m

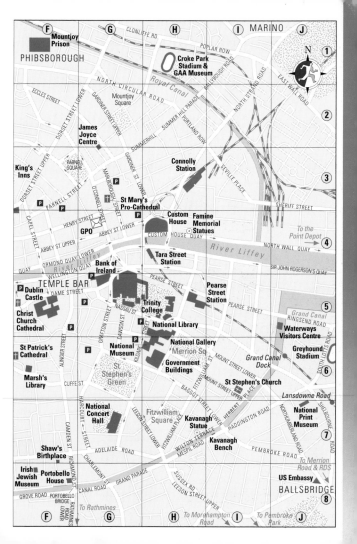

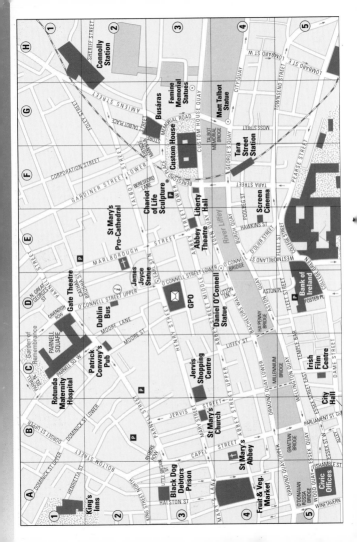

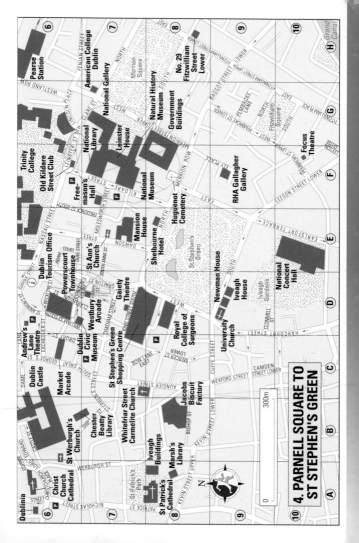

4. PARNELL SQUARE TO ST STEPHEN'S GREEN

Grand Canal

Pearse Station

American College Dublin

National Gallery

National Library

Leinster House

Natural History Museum

No. 29 Fitzwilliam Street Lower

Government Buildings

Trinity College

Old Kildare Street Club

Free-mason's Hall

National Museum

Huguenot Cemetery

RHA Gallagher Gallery

Focus Theatre

Fitzwilliam Square

Dublin Tourism Office

Powerscourt Townhouse

St Ann's Church

Mansion House

Shelbourne Hotel

St Stephen's Green

Andrew's Lane Theatre

Dublin Civic Museum

Gaiety Theatre

Westbury Arcade

Dublin Castle

Market Arcade

Royal College of Surgeons

St Stephen's Green Shopping Centre

University Church

Newman House

Iveagh House

Iveagh Gardens

National Concert Hall

Chester Beatty Library

St Werburgh's Church

Whitefriar Street Carmelite Church

Jacobs Biscuit Factory

Christ Church Cathedral

Dublinia

Iveagh Buildings

Marsh's Library

St Patrick's Cathedral

St Patrick's Park

N

300m

0

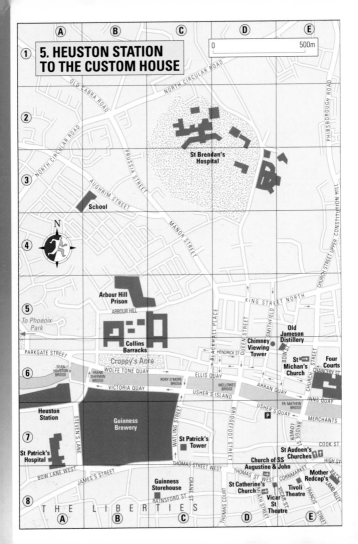

5. HEUSTON STATION TO THE CUSTOM HOUSE

0   500m

OLD CABRA ROAD

NORTH CIRCULAR ROAD

NORTH CIRCULAR ROAD

PHIBSBOROUGH ROAD

PRUSSIA STREET

St Brendan's
Hospital

AUGHRIM STREET

School

MANOR STREET

CHURCH STREET UPPER CONSTITUTION HILL

N

Arbour Hill
Prison

ARBOUR HILL

KING STREET NORTH

BLACKHALL PLACE

QUEEN STREET

HENDRICK ST

SMITHFIELD

Chimney
Viewing
Tower

Old
Jameson
Distillery

Collins
Barracks

To Phoenix
Park

PARKGATE STREET

Croppy's Acre

Wolfe Tone Quay

SEAN
HEUSTON
BRIDGE

FRANK
SHERWIN
BRIDGE

RORY O'MORE
BRIDGE

Victoria Quay

Ellis Quay

MELLOWES
BRIDGE

Usher's Island

BOW

St Michan's
Church

CHURCH STREET

CHANCERY ST

Four
Courts

ARRAN QUAY

INNS QUAY

FR. MATHEW
BRIDGE

USHER'S QUAY

MERCHANTS

P

BRIDGE ST LOWER

BRIDGEFOOT STREET

Heuston
Station

STEVEN'S LANE

Guinness
Brewery

WATLING STREET

St Patrick's
Tower

COOK ST

St Audoen's
Churches

St Patrick's
Hospital

BOW LANE WEST

JAMES'S STREET

THOMAS STREET WEST

CRANE STREET

THOMAS COURT

Church of SS
Augustine & John

THOMAS ST WEST

HIGH ST

Mother
Redcap's

Guinness
Storehouse

RAINSFORD ST

St Catherine's
Church

Vicar
St
Theatre

THOMAS ST

VICAR STREET

Tivoli
Theatre

FRANCIS STREET

CORNMARKET

BACK LANE

LAMB ALLEY

THE   LIBERTIES

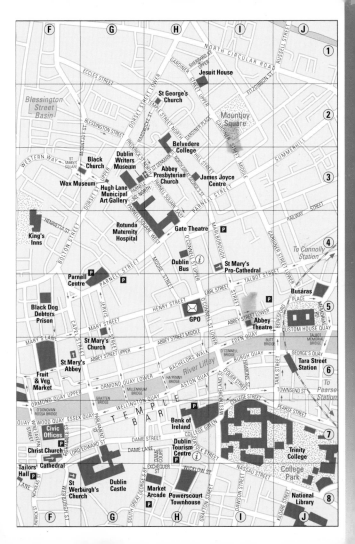

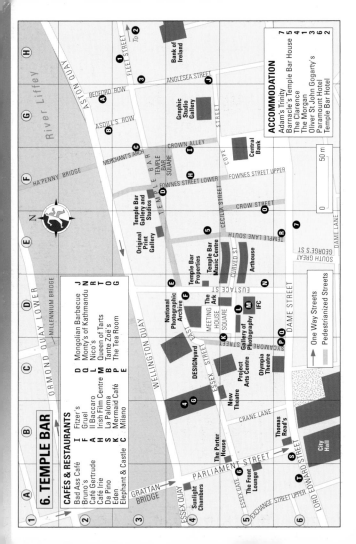

6. TEMPLE BAR

CAFÉS & RESTAURANTS

Bad Ass Café	I	Fitzer's	J
Bruno's	F	Gruel	A
Café Gertrude	A	Il Baccaro	Q
Café Irie	H	Irish Film Centre	L
Da Pino	S	La Paloma	B
Eden	K	Mermaid Café	C
Elephant & Castle		Milano	
		Mongolian Barbecue	D
		Monty's of Kathmandu	N
		Nico's	R
		Queen of Tarts	T
		Tante Zoé's	O
		The Tea Room	G

River Liffey

0   50 m

One Way Streets
Pedestrianized Streets

To 2

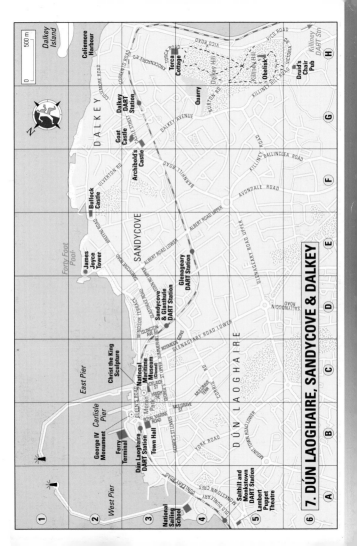

7. DÚN LAOGHAIRE, SANDYCOVE & DALKEY

0 — 500 m

Dalkey Island

Coliemore Harbour

D A L K E Y

Coliemore Road

Sorrento Road

Knocknacree Rd

Torca Road
Torca Cottage

Torca

Vico Road

Killiney DART Stn

Dalkey Hill

Killiney Hill

Obelisk

Victoria Rd

Druid's Chair Pub

Dalkey DART Station

Goat Castle

Castle Street

Archibold's Castle

Ulverton Rd

Dalkey Avenue

Burton Rd

Quarry

Killiney Hill Road

Bullock Castle

SANDYCOVE

Breffni Road

Barnhill Road

Killiney Ballinclea Road

James Joyce Tower

Sandycove Road

Glasthule Road

Albert Road Lower

Albert Road Upper

Avondale Road

Glenageary Road Upper

Glenageary DART Station

Glenageary Road Lower

Salrynoggin Road

Sandycove & Glasthule DART Station

Windsor Terrace

Islington Ave

Summerhill Rd

St George's St Upper

Rosmeen Gdns

Tivoli Rd

Mounttown Road Lower

Forty Foot Pool

Christ the King Sculpture

National Maritime Museum (Closed)

Adelaide St

Marine Rd

Haigh Terr

George's St Upper

Mellifont Ave

Cross Av

Crosthwaite Terr

Corrig Rd

D Ú N   L A O G H A I R E

East Pier

George IV Monument

Ferry Terminal

Dún Laoghaire DART Station

Town Hall

Queen's Road

Royal Marine Road

Mulgrave St

York Road

George's St Lower

Mount Town Road Lower

West Pier

National Sailing School

Dunleary Road

Old Dunleary Road

Sallhill and Monkstown DART Station

Monkstown Cres

Lambert Puppet Theatre

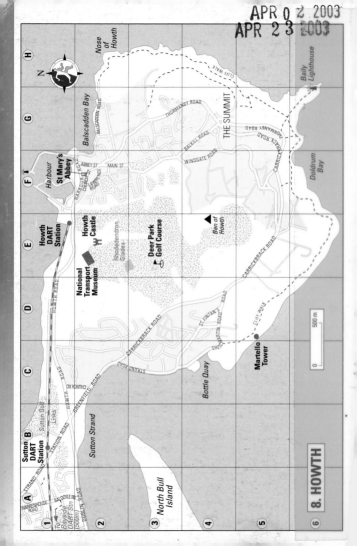

N

Nose of Howth

Balscadden Bay

BALSCADDEN ROAD

THORMANBY ROAD

BALKILL ROAD

THE SUMMIT

THORMANBY ROAD

CARRICKBRACK ROAD

Baily Lighthouse

CLIFF WALK

Harbour

St Mary's Abbey

ABBEY ST

MAIN ST

HARBOUR ROAD

CHURCH ST

GRACE ROAD

WINDGATE ROAD

Doldrum Bay

Howth DART Station

Howth Castle

National Transport Museum

Rhododendron Glades

Deer Park Golf Course

Ben of Howth

CARRICKBRACK ROAD

HOWTH ROAD

ST FINTAN'S ROAD

SHIELMARTIN ROAD

CLIFF WALK

Sutton DART Station

STRAND ROAD

Sutton Golf Links

STATION ROAD

GREENFIELD ROAD

CHURCH RD

HOWTH RD

CARRICKBRACK ROAD

STRAND ROAD

Martello Tower

Sutton Strand

Bottle Quay

WAREHOUSE ROAD

BALSCALE RD

DUBLIN ROAD

To Bayside DART Stn

North Bull Island

500 m

0

8. HOWTH

A   B   C   D   E   F   G   H

1   2   3   4   5   6